About the Author

Christopher LaMonica received his B.A. in Economics and French at the University of Massachusetts in Amherst, a *Certificat de Scolarité* from the University of Paris-I/Panthéon-Sorbonne, a Masters in Public Policy (M.P.P.) from Harvard University, and an M.A. and Ph.D. from Boston University. Since 1998, he has taught political science and history at the University of Rhode Island and is a part-time faculty member of the Department of Political Science at Boston University. Prior to teaching, Dr. LaMonica worked in ocean freight shipping in London, England, for the Organization for Economic Cooperation and Development (OECD) in Paris, France, for the Harvard Institute for International Development (HIID) in Cambridge, Massachusetts, and for the U.S. Agency for International Development (USAID) in Lusaka, Zambia.

International Politics:
The Classic Texts

Christopher LaMonica

KENDALL/HUNT PUBLISHING COMPANY
4050 Westmark Drive   Dubuque, Iowa 52002

Contents

Bibliography   **283**

Preface

The determination as to what is considered "classic" is ultimately a subjective matter. Nevertheless, I have endeavored to provide a balanced survey of what might be considered the classics as they are presented in introductory courses on international politics. A trend in Western education is to consider only secondary interpretations of these ideas, ignoring the original texts. This book has been prepared with the firm belief that the study of such classic texts, in their original form, should be an essential part of a liberal arts education.[1] This is not to say that Western sources are the only ones worth consideration. In fact, this selection of texts is clearly biased in favor of Western contributions to the field.

With the understanding that the ideas that underlie international theory and practice are becoming increasingly global, the present volume is intended to be the first part of a two-part selection of original texts. This volume, Part One, includes the classics of international politics as they are taught in Western academia, to Western and non-Western students alike; Part Two (forthcoming) surveys non-Western contributions to the field, using the same four paradigms used here: **Realism, Idealism, Liberalism,** and **Structuralism.** Although the interest in non-Western texts is clearly on the rise—as it should be—there can be little doubt that Western sources still dominate the field of political science. With each passing day, as the dialogue of international politics does become increasingly global, the need for a truly global survey of contributions to the field becomes more urgent. As many non-Western observers of the social sciences have already commented, power not only impacts the direction of politics, it also impacts the realm of ideas that underlies international practice.[2]

In truth, it was only after reading many other contributions to the subject of international politics that I began to appreciate why texts included in the present volume are considered classics at all. Always more of an autodidact, my circuitous quest for learning generally involved reading anything I could get my hands on. My passion for books (or, more specifically, the realm of ideas on politics and history within them) led me, as a young man, to reading on bookstore floors—and elsewhere when I could afford the books—and to a variety of biblio-sites in Massachusetts, London, then to Paris, a brief stint in the streets of

---

[1] Albeit often translated from the original language. Writers, such as Michel Foucault, have written extensively on this inherent dilemma arguing further that political discourse must be understood within defined institutional and historical contexts. Although undoubtedly true, few scholars bother to contemplate the inherent problems of "intertextual" dialogue as it further complicates the already challenging questions posed in international politics. See: James Der Derian and Michael J. Shapiro, *International/Intertextual Relations: Postmodern Readings of World Politics* (Lexington, MA: Lexington Books, 1989).

[2] Perhaps the clearest statement on this point is offered by the late Claude Ake in *Social Science as Imperialism: A Theory of Political Development* (Ibadan: University Press, 1979). Better known is the work of Edward W. Said, *Culture and Imperialism* (New York: Vintage, 1993). Another concise text, from Western observers of this issue, is: Bill Ashcroft, et al., *The Empire Writes Back: Theory and Practice in Post-Colonial Literatures* (London: Routledge, 1989).

Lusaka, and finally to my home in North Kingstown, Rhode Island. In many ways, finding books and new ideas are what have led the way for me to the graduate school classroom and, ultimately, to university teaching. Reading texts from Mark Twain to Cicero, and from Joseph Campbell to Hans Morgenthau, and from Thomas Mann to W.E.B. DuBois, and back again, made the decidedly more structured approach to the study of international relations, used by Professor Michael Corgan at Boston University, all the more valuable. To him, I am especially grateful as he helped me organize the many debates of political philosophy in a way that made a great deal of sense. A version of Corgan's table of IR paradigms is provided in the present volume.

This selection of classic texts on international politics, therefore, did not simply "drop out of the sky"; these texts are considered classics by a countless many who have struggled to find answers to the big questions of international politics. One of my goals here is to structure others' quests for answers in a way that clearly demonstrates patterns of theoretical differences that have, ultimately, led to different patterns of political practice. The reader should note that, in an effort to elucidate the historical significance of certain selections, reactions of scholars (not necessarily considered "classic" contributions per se) are sometimes provided; this is explained prior to each relevant text.

It should also be noted at the outset that the term "international politics" is being used here over the seemingly more popular term "international relations." The latter is generally used in an effort to include more—not traditionally political—international actors. The assumption that most authors make is that the term international relations is more comprehensive, taking us beyond the traditional activities of professional diplomats or of international politics per se, to issues such as the global environment, international refugees, and NGOs. The inclusion of these additional international issues, it is argued, necessitates the more comprehensive title of "international relations." James N. Rosenau, for example, suggests that *international relations* is "a generic concept for a vast array of activities, ideas, and goods that do or can cross national boundaries [and] embraces social, cultural, economic, and political exchanges that occur in ad hoc as well as institutional contexts."[3] The assumption being made in the present text is that these international issues are, and always have been, political; hence the term used for the title of this book: *international politics*.

This understanding of *international politics* is different from, say, Hans J. Morgenthau, who argues that the subject of politics should not be intermingled with other disciplines, notably economics. In his words: "Intellectually, the political realist maintains the autonomy of the political sphere, as the economist, the lawyer, the moralist maintain theirs."[4] At the time that Morgenthau was writing, however, *economic* interpretations of politics were especially suspect as they were viewed as not only leftist but also Marxist.[5] Over time there has been less ideological resistance to the idea that other issues, including the economic struggle for resources, are indeed essential to a proper understanding of politics and, ulti-

---

[3] James N. Rosenau in Krieger, et al., eds., *The Oxford Companion to Politics of the World* (New York and Oxford: Oxford University Press, 1993), p. 455. Similar assumptions abound. Cf. Joshua S. Goldstein, *International Relations,* 3rd ed. (New York: Longman, 1999); Karen Mingst, *Essentials of International Relations* (New York: W. W. Norton & Co., 1999); and E. F. Penrose, *The Revolution in International Relations* (London: Frank Cass & Co., Ltd. 1965).

[4] Morgenthau's Sixth Principle of Political Realism, *Politics Among Nations,* 4th ed. (New York: Alfred A. Knopf, 1973, originally published in 1948), p. 12.

[5] One need not look further than the early twentieth-century works of Charles A. Beard, and how they were received in Western academic circles, to understand this point. Beard's book, *An Economic Interpretation of the Constitution of the United States* (New York: Macmillan, 1913), altered the "climate of opinion" (Beard himself suggests this in his Introduction to the 1935 edition, p. v) in a way that struck fear in the hearts of many Americans.

mately, differences of political power. For example, U.S. National Security Advisor Condoleezza Rice recently stated unequivocally: "Economics and security are inextricably linked."[6] Assuredly, comments of the kind are not limited to Rice (and we can be sure she is not a Marxist!) but one has to listen for them. To the pragmatic, nonideological thinker of the post-cold war world, this can only be interpreted as fact.

Another way of thinking of the difference in terminology between international politics and international relations is in terms of *high politics* and *low politics.* Usage of the term *international relations* is an attempt to move beyond discussions of high politics to be more comprehensive. The problem with the use of international relations, over international politics, is that it may well lead one to believe that these additional "relations" are nonpolitical. Used in this way, international *politics* would be limited to matters of high politics addressed by state leaders and diplomats. High politics, therefore, might include diplomatic relations, dialogue concerning international organization and law, decisions regarding the use of force, and the like, whereas low politics might include matters such as civil society, community development, local governance, and refugees. The point that I am making here is that although the impact may not be immediately apparent, matters of low politics impact relations between states and should therefore, by definition, be considered part of international politics. Only together can they offer a comprehensive survey of the subject, international politics.

I would like to thank Professor Maureen Moakley, Chair of the Political Science Department at the University of Rhode Island, for her continued support, as well as Professor Michael Honhart, Chair of the History Department at URI, and Professor David Mayers, Chair of the Department of Political Science at Boston University. Thanks to Professor Al Killilea of URI, who reacted very graciously as I repeatedly asked the same question: "But what did the Romans *really* offer in the way of political thought?" To Professor Marc Genest, I thank you for your discussions on the subject and your office space! To Professor Art Stein, I thank you for pointing me in the direction of substantive ideas for a Part Two to the present volume, to include some of the non-Western texts—a project that is now well underway, in collaboration with Boston University colleague and friend, Racha Aribarg. Finally thanks to my wife, Nikki, for providing continued support for these "intellectual pursuits" when I need it and for taking me birdwatching when I needed that.

---

[6] CNN quotes Rice as saying: "Economics and security are inextricably linked. You only have to look at what happened in a place like Bali when you had the terrorist attack there." "Bush in Japan on Six Nation Asia Tour," CNN.com, October 17, 2003. See also, Rice's comments regarding President Bush's recent tour of Asian states: "Bush Departs for Asian Tour," Cox News Service, October 14, 2003.

Chapter One

Introduction

This book surveys the "classics" of international politics that are generally found in introductory courses on the subject. Whereas many textbooks make only brief references to the authors of the classic texts, and to their principle ideas, the aim of the present volume is to offer a more in-depth view of what Mortimer Adler termed the "Great Ideas."[7] To gain more insight into how the arguments are originally presented, excerpts from the authors' primary texts are provided—rather than a secondary interpretation of them—as well as a brief biographical sketch of each author and a brief overview of the relevant historical context. As I like to remind students, these classic texts did not simply "drop out of the sky." In many cases, they were written in an effort to correct the errors of those who, in the view of each author, simply "did not understand" the subject. That is, many of these ideas are perhaps best understood within the context of a heated theoretical debate, a debate that has often led to changes in international political practice.

Domestic State Politics and International Politics

The study of politics is concerned with how one guides or influences government policy.[8] This can be looked at in terms of domestic state policy and/or policy that guides or influences relations between states. In political science, inquiries on the subject of politics are

---

[7] Mortimer J. Adler, *How to Think About the Great Ideas: From the Great Books of Western Civilization* (Chicago: Open Court Publishing, 2000). Adler is perhaps best known for having compiled the *Great Books of the Western World* series, which includes a total of fifty-four volumes. Another well-known proponent of the "classic" texts is Leo Strauss of the University of Chicago. For a broad survey of political philosophy that is clearly written, well organized, and recommended, cf. Leo Strauss and Joseph Cropsey, *History of Political Philosophy,* 3rd ed. (Chicago: University of Chicago Press, 1987).

[8] Of course, definitions on what "politics" entails abound. Similarly, statements made by state leaders on what appropriate political practice entails abound. Rather than contemplate a range of comments here, suffice it to say that this is what this book is really over but from an international perspective (i.e. different theories as to what 'international politics' entails and/or should entail).

generally addressed within one of five subfields: American Politics, Comparative Politics, International Politics, Political Theory, and Public Policy. In all political science subfields, the ability to express an opinion—one's will—within a political system and, ultimately, to impact the direction of government policy can be thought of in terms of *power.* Put simply, the acquisition, maintenance, and application of *power* (sometimes referred to as the ability to *coerce*) is important to political outcomes.[9]

In international politics power is sometimes defined as "the ability to make someone do something they otherwise would not do."[10] Accordingly, the measure of power is crucial to the field, although theorists (herein **Realists, Idealists, Liberals,** and **Structuralists**) disagree as to how this should be accomplished. Political realists, for example, might emphasize military might; the idealist or the political liberal might emphasize the free exchange and/or power of "ideas" or culture; whereas the structuralist might emphasize the historic bases for differences of material wealth. In truth, all of these do offer some insight into what *power* entails.

The most fundamental rift in politics, however, is between those who emphasize conservatism ("what is") and those who emphasize change ("what ought to be"). And this rift is found in both domestic and international politics. Joshua Goldstein suggests that "a conservative world view generally values maintenance of the status quo" while other perspectives on politics range from revolutionary (overthrow of status quo) to liberal (gradual change of status quo).[11] This too is a pattern that one finds in both domestic and international politics.

Given the varying needs, perspectives, and propensities—the political will—of political actors, an age-old concern among democratic theorists is how to manage all of this. Aristotle, for example, argued that one of the primary objectives of political theorists was to help organize secular life, which, of course, includes how people organize to govern. Today, among the 192 or so states of the world, there are various methods employed to organize differences of political will. The democratic states of the world, of which there are now 119 (62 percent of all sovereign states), have distinct institutional arrangements that, using a variety of methods, should allow for the expression of political will.[12] How effective individual states are at doing so is an important question of political science, and scholars disagree as to how freedom of political expression can be achieved.[13] What is

---

[9] One text on the subject suggests: "To put it another way, when one speaks of the *politics* part of world politics, one is faced with the issue of power." W. Raymond Duncan, et al., *World Politics in the 21st Century,* 2nd ed. (New York: Pearson Longman, 2004), p. 87. Others emphasize the importance of "winning over" an adversary, describing power as "a psychological relationship in which one actor influences another to behave differently than it would have if left alone." See: Richard W. Mansbach, *The Global Puzzle: Issues and Actors in World Politics,* 2nd ed. (Boston: Houghton Mifflin, 1997), p. 66.

[10] Mansbach (1997) suggests this. Others IR texts offer similar definitions. See: Donald M. Snow and Eugene Brown, *International Relations: Contours of Power* (New York: Pearson, 1999).

[11] Goldstein, op cit., p. 5.

[12] According to the World Resources Institute, the number of sovereign states holding elections has grown from 22 of 154 (14.3%) in 1950 to 119 of 192 (62%) in 2002. See: www.wri.org. In his much-discussed article, now book, Fareed Zakaria warns us that the process of elections has made a great many states formal "democracies," but they lack political freedoms that have become an essential part of Western democracy. See: Fareed Zakaria, *The Future of Freedom: Illiberal Democracy at Home and Abroad* (New York: W. W. Norton & Co., 2003), originally argued by Zakaria in "The Rise of Illiberal Democracy," *Foreign Affairs* (1995).

[13] Stated briefly here, the debate is largely over how much weight should be placed on *external* versus *internal* factors that help or hinder the prospects for democratic liberalization. Is it appropriate, for example, to place the blame for illiberal circumstances in certain states on *external* influences such as the history of colonialism, the legacy of capitalist priorities, or *internal* influences, such as the inability or unwillingness of citizens to make political demands? See, e.g., Christopher LaMonica, "The Politics of Strengthening Local Government Institutions in Zambia," Doctoral dissertation (Boston University, 2000). As will be seen in Chapter 5, the structuralist paradigm emphasizes external influences, whereas others that focus on internal impediments to political liberalization include "culture" theorists from the 1950s to present.

clear is that, since the fall of the Berlin Wall, the number of formally democratic states has clearly risen, yet in many states political freedom remains elusive. As some writers have emphasized in recent years, it is true that a small majority of states have governing institutions that are democratic in form, yet they are influenced by a host of unique historical circumstances, cultures, geographies, etc. that help or hinder the prospects for democratic liberalization.[14]

In political science, rightly or wrongly, how today's governing institutions came to be is generally a matter of domestic state politics inquiry. For example, within the subfield of American politics, we start with a consideration of the logic of the founding fathers; we learn that in the United States political power is shared between the federal and state governments (termed *federalism*); that the federal government is organized as a frustrated system of powers "checked" among the executive, judicial, and legislative branches; that the legislative branch has an upper (Senate) and lower house (State Representatives), and so on. The subfield of American politics can be viewed, inter alia, as one state's method of organizing differences of political will.

In comparative politics, classifications of individual state's political systems—including those of the United States—are made by political scientists, and arguments are made as to which political systems function best. For example, within the subfield of comparative politics one might ask: Is "political will" best managed by a presidential or parliamentary system? What criteria will be used in making the decision as to what form of government functions best? Which form of government is best for "development"? What criteria will be used in making the decision as to what "development" entails? The subfields of American politics and comparative politics, therefore, compare and contrast "explanatory variables" (such as the unique intellectual roots, histories, cultures, and geographies) that have led to present-day differences of political practice and the varying structures of governing institutions.[15]

The subfield of international politics begins with the assumption that all states are sovereign entities (i.e., that matters of domestic political authority, law, and government or-

---

[14] The literature on this point is growing. See, e.g., Zakaria (2003) and the reemphasis on culture by such writers as Samuel P. Huntington and Lawrence E. Harrison, eds., *Culture Matters* (New York: Basic Books, 2000). For a discussion on the "culture" literature of the 1950s and 1960s, see Irene L. Gendzier, *Development Against Democracy: Manipulating Political Change in the Third World,* (Hampton, CT and Washington, DC: Tyrone Press, 1995), p. 119 et seq. The "unique" historical circumstances of the United States are famously emphasized by Louis Hartz, *The Liberal Tradition in America* (New York: Harcourt, Brace, 1955). The historical influence of variables such as geography, environment, and climate on "development" is emphasized by Jared Diamond, in his best-seller, *Guns, Germs and Steel: The Fates of Human Societies* (New York: W. W. Norton & Co., 1999). The impact of Diamond's thesis on the field of comparative politics, in particular, is noted by Thomas M. Magstadt, *Nations and Governments: Comparative Politics in Regional Perspective* (Belmont, CA: Wadsworth, 2001), Ch. 1.

[15] It is worth noting that this is why we refer to political science as a science and not an art. That is, political scientists have competing theories that emphasize different sets of explanatory variables in response to political questions such as: Why did the Cold War end? or Why do certain states have federal or unitary governing systems, a bicameral or unicameral legislature, etc.? Some political scientists structure their theoretical analysis using regression analysis, which is an extension of the algebraic $y = mx + b$ format (where $y =$ the dependent variable or that which is being explained; $m =$ the slope or *impact* of the explanatory variable, x on y, and $b =$ the y-intercept, i.e. the starting point for measuring the impact of an explanatory variable on the dependent variable). Regression analysis can be viewed as a way of including more explanatory variables (x's) into the traditional $y = mx + b$ format, traditionally written as: $Y = \alpha + \beta x_1 + \beta x_2 + \beta x_3 \ldots \beta x_n + \varepsilon$. Not all political scientists structure their theories in this way, but there are those who believe that it could prove helpful if more did. The argument is that identifying variables would help others to clearly understand the theories being proposed within the field. See, e.g., Gary King, Robert O. Keohane, and Sidney Verba, *Designing Social Inquiry* (Princeton, NJ: Princeton University Press, 1994). Increasingly, to the dismay of many, contributions to the *American Political Science Review (APSR)* will use regression analysis.

ganization are resolved *within* the established borders of sovereign states). In effect, this means that no one outside a sovereign state can legitimately demand political change within the borders of any one sovereign state. Although political conflicts among political entities (e.g., cities, kingdoms, empires, states) have assuredly existed since these entities were first formed, state-to-state ergo "international" politics is said to have started with the Westphalian system of political organization.

Before the Treaty of Westphalia (1648), before the principle of state sovereignty existed, claims were made by individuals that they were given the legitimate right to rule directly from a divine authority. Throughout human history, political theories have been offered to support this idea of the divine right to political authority. One of the still dominant "divine right" political theories of seventeenth-century England, for example, was that of Sir Robert Filmer. In his written work, *Patriarcha,* Filmer argued that the best political system was that which represented the will of God: Monarchy.[16] According to this system, the monarch's political authority was beyond challenge or question. To demonstrate the right of the Stuart line of kings to rule in England, he described an "indisputable genealogical line from Adam."[17] Clearly an absurd idea, it nevertheless was the assumption of other influential political theorists of the time—notably Thomas Hobbes—who supported the notion of absolute monarchy.[18] The modern state system, therefore, began with the notion of absolute sovereignty, an intersovereign state system that accepted the divine rule of kings, a notion to which we shall now turn.

▮▪▣▪▣▪▣▪▣▪▣▪▮▣▪▣▪▣▪▣▪▣▪▮▣▪▣▪▣▪▣▪▣▪▮▣▪▣▪▣▪▣▪▣▪▮

Sovereignty

The establishment of the notion **Absolute Sovereignty** (i.e., the absolute right of the monarch to rule within a sovereign territory) is often credited to French theorist Jean Bodin. Writing in 1576, Bodin defined sovereignty as "supreme power over citizens and subjects, unrestrained by law."[19] Although the system of a God-given right to rule was not yet questioned by political theorists, differences existed among West European monarchs as to which religious sect was to be followed: Protestant or Catholic. This, of course, was one of the primary political conflicts of the Middle Ages in Europe.[20] The **Thirty Years War** (1618–1648) was largely a battle over religion, within and among West European

---

[16] Sir Robert Filmer's *Patriarcha* was written some time prior to his death in 1653 and formally published in 1680. It is Filmer's work, and not that of Hobbes (1651), that John Locke (1690) chose to attack as being wrong-headed in his seminal *Two Treatises on Government,* op cit.

[17] See: Thomas I. Cook's discussion in Preface, *Two Treatises of Government by John Locke with a supplement Patriarcha by Robert Filmer* (New York: Hafner Press, 1947), pp. x–xi.

[18] Thomas Hobbes, *The Leviathan* (1651) is cited and discussed in Chapter 2.

[19] Jean Bodin, cited in Sabine, op cit., p. 405. Bodin's voluminous work, *Six Books of a Commonwealth* (1576), focused on the internal dimensions of sovereignty (i.e., he viewed the doctrine of sovereignty as a way of locating the center of political authority in relation to domestic conflict). The notion of sovereignty was later applied to interstate relations, notably in the Treaty of Westphalia (1648).

[20] Political theories of the Middle Ages were largely concerned with balancing the claims to political authority of a local monarch with those of religious authorities, notably the Roman Catholic Church. A national best-seller, and thoroughly pleasant read on this subject, is William Manchester's *A World Lit Only By Fire: The Medieval Mind and the Renaissance* (Boston: Little, Brown, 1993).

states, that culminated in the **Treaty of Westphalia** (1648).[21] Bodin's theories of political legitimacy help to resolve the conflict by suggesting that it should ultimately be up to the local absolute monarch as to what religion was to be followed within his/her state. The modern state system, which emphasizes the importance of state sovereignty, is sometimes referred to as the Westphalian state system.

The notion of sovereignty was further developed during the Enlightenment (seventeenth to eighteenth centuries) by such writers as Voltaire, Locke, Montesquieu, and Rousseau. It is during this period in history that the "inalienable rights" of the individual were publicly debated and entertained. Consider, for example, the comments of John Locke: ". . . no one ought to harm another in his Life, Health, Liberty, or Possessions."[22] Of course, it is widely acknowledged that Thomas Jefferson used this argument as the basis for his consideration of "inalienable rights" in the *U.S. Declaration of Independence* (1776): "Life, Liberty, and the Pursuit of Happiness." Like other Enlightenment thinkers, Locke also wrote that government was created by consent of the governed in order to protect these natural "inalienable" rights. If the government did not protect these rights, people had the right to rebel and dissolve the government. This was the philosophical justification for the French and American Revolutions and, ultimately, the notion of **Popular Sovereignty** (i.e., the idea that political legitimacy requires the support of the governed).[23]

Of course, today, this modern form of sovereignty is not universally practiced among individual sovereign states. For a variety of reasons, the arguments made by classic liberal thinkers regarding *individualism* and Lockian understandings of *political freedom* are not universally accepted. It is therefore important to keep in mind that many of today's assumptions underlying political legitimacy and "inalienable" individual rights come from the Enlightenment thinkers and form a fundamental part of the Western tradition, a tradition that, at this moment, remains questioned by many. Today, perhaps more than ever, the student of international politics must contemplate Western/Enlightenment ideas, such as individualism, to make sense of some of the existing rifts of ideas in the modern world.[24] One need not venture far into the pages of Enlightenment texts to see that, today, these ideas are far from being universally accepted. Consider, for example, Voltaire's classic statement, whose writings became the basis for the First Amendment to the U.S. Constitu-

---

[21] The Thirty Years' War (1618–1648) is sometimes considered to be the German phase of a longer battle, the Eighty Years' War, between Spain and Holland. The peace of Westphalia was negotiated in the Westphalian towns of Muenster and Osnabrueck, in modern Germany. Whereas the Spanish-Dutch treaty was signed on January 30, 1648, the treaty of October 24, 1648, included several German princes and many other representatives of European royalty. Only England, Poland, Muscovy, and Turkey were not represented at the two assemblies of 1648.

[22] John Locke, *Two Treatises on Government,* cited in Nelson (1996), p. 199. In Locke's case his writings were, at least initially, considered to be radical and largely kept underground.

[23] The notion of popular sovereignty is traditionally attributed to the writings of Jean-Jacques Rousseau, who argued that sovereignty resided in civil society or in the people. See: J. J. Rousseau, *The Social Contract,* Ch. 12, in Nigel Warburton, *Philosophy: The Classics,* 2nd ed. (London: Routledge, 2001). Popular sovereignty, of course, is the underlying logic of the democratic state. U.S. President Abraham Lincoln had a similar understanding of sovereignty when he spoke of a government "of the people, by the people, for the people [that] shall not perish from the earth." See Abraham Lincoln, "Gettysburg Address" (1863) in Diane Ravitch, et al., eds., *The Democracy Reader: Classic and Modern Speeches, Essays, Poems, Declarations and Documents on Freedom and Human Rights Worldwide* (New York: Harper Collins, 1992). G. H. Sabine makes the argument that *prior* medieval political thought, although feudal, had similar arrangements (i.e., at least in some cases, rule of a monarchy necessitated the consent of the governed). This is demonstrated, most famously, by the coerced signing of the Magna Charta (1215) but carries through much of the medieval period. See: Sabine (1937, 1966), op. cit., pp. 203–4, p. 209: "Medieval theory . . . assumes a continuous cooperation between the king and his subjects . . ." and p. 219 (regarding *legalized constraint* upon the king), etc.

[24] See: Richard Tarnas, *The Passion of the Western Mind: Understanding the Ideas That Have Shaped Our World View* (New York: Ballantine Books, 1993).

tion and, more generally, for freedom of speech: "I may disagree with what you say, but I will defend 'til death your right to say it."[25] The Western model, therefore, not only emphasizes individualism; it also assumes that the conflict of ideas is desirable. And, at least in some parts of the world, these fundamental Enlightenment ideas remain highly controversial. The free expression of ideas and other goals of "classic" liberalism are considered in more detail in Chapter 4.

Realism versus Idealism

Throughout history, realists have argued that matters of most concern to idealists (morality, ethics, justice, change) are secondary to the acquisition and maintenance of political power. Realists remind us that the primary concern of any state leader is *survival* for, to put it bluntly, "What good is state policy to someone who is dead?" To the realist, survival is paramount and independent decision making is considered crucial to the rational pursuit of state interests. Realists tend to resist those who attempt to complicate matters, particularly those who attempt to bring in other, not traditionally "political" concerns.

Contributions to both realist and idealist thought often stem from a frustration with the direction of the debate over international policy. For example, when realist Hans J. Morgenthau published his seminal text, *Politics Among Nations,* in 1948, he was concerned—as all political realists were—with the institutional and other gains being made by political idealists (whom he termed moralists). Leading into the Second World War, political realists had been successful at halting the activities of the League of Nations, established at the Paris Peace Conference in 1919.[26] In the 1940s realists like Morgenthau were well aware, and weary, of the new institutional arrangements being made in the name of "international cooperation," as outlined in the United Nations Charter in 1945. The rapid establishment of U.N. resolutions, such as the Universal Declaration of Human Rights (adopted by the U.N. General Assembly in 1948) were viewed by realists as being of little practical use. In fact, to this day, these efforts are viewed by realists as not only wrongheaded; they are, in their view, potentially dangerous to the true prospects for world peace.[27] It is only when one understands this historic struggle that one begins to truly understand the arguments being made by Morgenthau. His definitive list of the six principles of realism have been a classic of international politics ever since.[28]

By contrast, idealists contend that such cooperative international arrangements are indeed the best path to world peace. If anything, in their view, the establishment of new networks of communication, possible through transnational endeavors (such as the League of

---

[25] Writers such as Voltaire and Rousseau had a tremendous impact on the thinking of prerevolutionary French elites that emphasized liberal ideals such as: "civil equality, religious toleration, and liberation of the human personality from all institutions which kept it immature." Georges Lefebvre, *The Coming of the French Revolution* (Princeton, NJ: Princeton University Press, 1979), p. 49.

[26] The League continued to function during World War II, although its security operations were halted in 1941. It was formally disbanded in 1946.

[27] This was certainly true of critics of the League, including Massachusetts Senator Henry Cabot Lodge, cited infra. A more recent realist position on this point is to be found in Henry Kissinger, *Diplomacy* (New York: Touchstone, 1995) or Patrick Buchanan, *A Republic, Not An Empire* (Washington, DC: Regnery Publishing, 2002).

[28] Morgenthau, op cit., His "Six Principles of Realism" are provided in Chapter 2.

Nations or the U.N.) is one of the best guarantees of avoiding future conflict. Certainly this was the thought of our idealist U.S. President Woodrow Wilson who, in his effort to convince others of the need for a League of Nations, stated:

> There is only one power to put behind the liberation of mankind, and that is the power of mankind. *It is the power of the united moral forces of the world, and in the Covenant of the League of Nations the moral forces of the world are mobilized.* For what purpose? Reflect, my fellow citizens, that the membership of this great League is going to include all the great fighting nations of the world, as well as the weak ones.[29]

We then read the reactions of political realists of the time, who with the same enthusiasm and sense of urgency, argued the exact opposite. Consider the words of U.S. Senator, Henry Cabot Lodge, one of Wilson's fiercest opponents to the League of Nations.

> No doubt many excellent and patriotic people see a coming fulfillment of noble ideals in the words "league for peace." We all respect and share these aspirations and desires, but some of us see no hope, but rather defeat, for them in this murky covenant. For we, too, have our ideals, even if we differ from those who have tried to establish a monopoly of idealism. Our first ideal is our country, and we see her in the future, as in the past, giving service to all her people and to the world. Our ideal of the future is that she should continue to render that service of her own free will. She has great problems of her own to solve, very grim and perilous problems, and a right solution, if we can attain to it, would largely benefit mankind. We would have our country strong to resist a peril from the West, as she has flung back the German menace from the East. We would not have our politics distracted and embittered by the dissensions of other lands. *We would not have our country's vigor exhausted or her moral force abated, by everlasting meddling and muddling in every quarrel, great and small, which afflicts the world. Our ideal is to make her ever stronger and better and finer, because in that way alone, as we believe, can she be of the greatest service to the world's peace and to the welfare of mankind.*[30]

The debate over the virtue of such transnational organizations continues to this day. The conservative American politician and columnist Pat Buchanan recently went as far as to suggest that the United States should kick the United Nations headquarters out of the country, adding, "If you have trouble leaving we'll send up 10,000 U.S. Marines to help you pack."[31]

By contrast, in the 1970s, Princeton University professor Richard Falk considered transnational networks of communication to be so important to the prospects for world peace he helped to establish what he termed the World Order Model Project (WOMP), through which he and others published a great many articles and books.[32] Like Morgenthau before him, Falk argues that the other group—in his case the political realists—is wrongheaded and their focus on *power* potentially dangerous. Not only does Falk believe that realists "do not understand," he goes further by arguing that it might well take someone from the southern hemisphere to lead the way. In his view we in the West are simply too entrenched in our discussions of power to consider alternatives. Falk argues that the consideration of alternatives to power politics takes place in a kind of "shadowland" of academic marginalization and that, for those of us in the industrialized West, it can be "dan-

[29] President Woodrow Wilson, September 25, 1919. Emphasis mine.

[30] U.S. Senator Henry Cabot Lodge, "Against the League of Nations," Washington, DC, August 12, 1919. Emphasis mine.

[31] "UN Dismisses Pat Buchanan's Call for US to Kick Them Out," *Associated Press*, September 20, 2000.

[32] Richard Falk's book, *A Study of Future Worlds* (New York: Free Press, 1975) is excerpted and discussed in Chapter 3.

gerous intellectual work that often engenders rejection . . ."[33] Some would argue that certain Western scholars, notably Noam Chomsky, have built their entire careers on critiquing power politics.[34] Nevertheless, in his admiration of Hugo Grotius' forward-looking vision of the seventeenth century, Falk argues

> Grotius came from an independent state in the Protestant north of Europe that was the setting for revolt against the holistic domination of all Europe by the Catholic south. One would similarly expect that *our Grotius, if he or she emerges, will come from the Third World rather than from the advanced industrial countries.* The shadowland is more accessible to those who are victims of the old order, apostles of the new order, but who yet see that the hopes for a benign transition depend on the success of an ideological synthesis.[35]

In one way or another, the political idealist is generally concerned with wrongs associated with the existing order and looking for answers. In the case of Falk, the perspective needed for answers will likely come from a citizen of the oppressed Third World.[36] In the case of Plato, the perspective needed for finding solutions to societal woes will come from a "philosopher king."[37] And, in all cases, answers generally necessitate change. More ideas from political idealists are considered in Chapter 3.

▮▪▮▮

Conflict versus Cooperation

In political philosophy the aforementioned debate—between realism and idealism—is often placed within the framework of a dichotomy: Conflict versus Cooperation.[38] On the one hand, realists make certain assumptions about self-interested human behavior and the absolute need for *power.* By looking at history, realists argue that, although we might like

---

[33] Richard Falk, "The Grotian Quest," *International Law: A Contemporary Perspective* (R. Falk, F. Kratchowil, and S. Mendlovitz, eds. 1985), pp. 36–42, cited in Burns H. Weston, Richard Falk, and Anthony D'Amato, *International Law and World Order* (St. Paul: West Publishing Company, 1990), p. 1087.

[34] See, e.g., Noam Chomsky, *The Umbrella of U.S. Power: The Universal Declaration of Human Rights and the Contradictions of U.S. Policy* (New York: Seven Stories Press, 2002); focusing largely on the Vietnam era, see: *For Reasons of the State* (New York: New Press, 2003); *Rogue States: The Rule of Force in World Affairs* (Cambridge, MA: South End Press, 2000), and Chomsky's ever popular *Deterring Democracy* (New York: Hill and Wang, 1992).

[35] Falk (1985) in Weston, et al. (1990), p. 1091. Emphasis mine.

[36] Since the end of the Cold War, the term *Third World* has become somewhat dated (although, at the start of the twenty-first-century, one will still find it being used by some). During the Cold War, the term *First World* did refer to the politically free world (U.S. and its allies); the *Second World* to the communist bloc states of the world (USSR and its allies); and the *Third World* to the remainder—generally underdeveloped states.

[37] This famous argument is made in Plato's *Republic.* Some have argued that this aspect of Plato's work can therefore be interpreted as the intellectual basis for the formation of a vanguard and/or communism. George H. Sabine, for example, contemplates this question in: *A History of Political Theory,* 3rd ed. (New York: Henry Holt and Co., 1937, 1966), p. 56 et seq. Certainly, this is not the general conclusion drawn by Western readers of Plato's work. His quest for an "ideal state" can also be viewed as an idealist pursuit. See, e.g., the discussion of Plato, Ch. 2, in Brian R. Nelson, *Western Political Thought: From Socrates to the Age of Ideology* (Englewood Cliffs, New Jersey: Prentice Hall, 1996).

[38] See, e.g., Mark R. Amstutz, *International Conflict and Cooperation: An Introduction to World Politics* (New York: McGraw-Hill, 1998) and Marc Genest, *Conflict and Cooperation: Evolving Theories of International Relations* (New York: Harcourt Brace, 1998).

individuals to behave altruistically, they are looking at *what really happens* in politics (i.e., practical reality). On the other hand, idealists argue that we should not limit our options to what has occurred in the past and contemplate *what ought to be*—what, in their view, generally entails more political cooperation. Although idealists argue that politics ought to be more cooperative and just, the realist reminds us that conflict, due to individuals' will to power (which can be viewed as individual expressions for justice), is a recurring phenomenon.[39] Because people will always disagree as to what "justice" entails, conflict is an inevitable part of politics. For the political realist, then, politics is *conflict*. Conflict is not only inevitable, it is also a constant of history and, if one is to establish a "free society," allowing for it is even desirable (i.e., different expressions of free will inevitably lead to conflict). On this point Samuel Huntington favorably describes American politics as the "promise of disharmony."[40] Indeed, in the United States, the viewer of Sunday morning political talk shows or the listener of talk radio programs is bombarded with all kinds of heated arguments over political issues. These open conflicts of political opinion can be understood as an essential part of the Western tradition. That is, we welcome free and open debate on all public issues as we believe that this method offers the best path to better ideas and ultimately, through our political institutions, better government policies.[41] Although it might be shocking to a non-Westerner to see people fighting over issues so freely, it is an important part of what the Western political culture is all about. Realists would argue that, through history, people have disagreed as to what is "right" or what "justice" entails and that, if anything, people have always tended to act in their self-interest.

The self-interested nature of people, and the resulting conflicts of individual will, are the fundamental assumptions behind the realist method of political organization. For Hobbes and, later, Hegel, the need for the state, therefore, "emerges from violence; the first relationship among men is one of conflict, which puts into play two fundamental passions, vanity (or the desire for recognition) and the fear of violent death."[42] For the realist, the assumptions behind the self-interested nature of man in a domestic state are carried over into interstate relations. Accordingly, in international politics the primary and most appropriate aim is to act in one's **national interest**—the "vital" interest of the state. A key to effective realist diplomacy, therefore, is to determine the national interests of other states, while staying focused on the crucial goals defined by one's own national interest.[43] National in-

---

[39] The innate psychological need to dominate, to control, to have *power* has been argued by a great many psychologists, including Sigmund Freud, who argued that the aggression behind the will to power was activated by such phenomena as "organ inferiority" and sexual libido. According to Freud: "It is clearly not easy for men to give up the satisfaction of this inclination to aggression. They do not feel comfortable without it." Sigmund Freud, "Civilization and Its Discontents," in Neil J. Kressel, ed., *Political Psychology: Classic and Contemporary Readings* (New York: Paragon, 1993), p. 65; See also: Freud's essay, "The Sexual Aberrations," in A. A. Brill, ed., *The Basic Writings of Sigmund Freud* (New York: Modern Library, 1938), p. 553 et seq. Austrian psychologist Alfred Adler argued in even simpler terms that all human beings simply had a "general lust to dominate." See: Frank McLynn, *Carl Gustav Jung: A Biography* (New York: St. Martin's Griffin, 1996), p. 260. In Adler's words: "The general goal of man. . . [man's] psyche has as its objective the *goal of superiority*," Alfred Adler, "Individual Pyschology, Its Assumptions and Its Results," in Clara Thompson, et al., eds., *An Outline of Pycho-Analysis* (New York: Modern Library, 1955), p. 289.

[40] Samuel P. Huntington, *American Politics: The Promise of Disharmony* (Cambridge, MA: Harvard University Press, 1983).

[41] This interpretation of the forward movement of ideas through open debate was advocated most notably by the early nineteenth-century German philosopher, Georg W. F. Hegel. See: Hegel, *Lectures on the Philosophy of History*, discussed in Leo Strauss and Joseph Cropsey, eds., *History of Political Philosophy*, 3rd ed. (Chicago: University of Chicago Press, 1987), p. 732 et seq.

[42] Strauss, et al., op. cit., p. 735.

[43] This view is clearly expressed by Morgenthau (1973); a survey that emphasizes the "successes" of realist practice is provided by Henry Kissinger in *Diplomacy* (1995). See also: Michael J. Smith, *Realist Thought From Weber to Kissinger* (Baton Rouge: Louisiana State University Press, 1986).

terest can also be viewed as the pursuit of state priorities in international politics and is sometimes considered the justification for the use of force. Certainly, integrity and security of a state's territory is of crucial importance to all states' national interests, as are economic strength and political independence.

A fundamental challenge to individual states pursuing their own national interests, in the name of self-defense, is described as the **security dilemma.** One way of describing this phenomenon in international politics is through the classic example of the clash between the Spartans and Athenians. Initially, around 500 BC, Athens and Sparta were allies in a war against Persia. Athens, however, was an expansionist sea-based power, whereas Sparta focused more on its development of land-based defenses. By 465 BC, it was already clear that Athens was more interested in defending its own interests and thought it had the ability to do so, as Athens received revenue from other "allied" states paying tribute for protection from Persia. To protect what they considered to be their more sophisticated culture and way of life, the Athenians built long walls to ward off a land-based attack.[44] The Spartans by this time perceived the wall as threatening and, with the help of tribute-paying states, attacked the Athenians. Many of the battles that followed are most famously described by the Athenian general Thucydides, and the Athenian Empire did eventually fall. The lesson from this episode is that actions undertaken in the name of defense, such as the building of a wall, can be perceived as an act of aggression by other states.

Yet, as will be seen in the writings of realist thinkers, such as Machiavelli, the primary aim of the state rightly ought to be *survival.* The priority of survival is considered universal practice, and what follows, for the realist, are assumptions regarding the **rational behavior** of state leaders. The starting point, in attempting to determine state behavior, is to assume that the primary aim behind state action is state survival.

Using this logic, the **rational actor model** is used by some political scientists to determine future behavior or to help explain past events. Perhaps one of the best-known applications of the model is that used by Graham Allison to help explain events surrounding the Cuban missile crisis of October 1962, wherein Allison uses the rational actor model to help explain the actions of state leaders. [45] In the case of the Cuban missile crisis, the conundrum is that state leaders—from President John F. Kennedy to Soviet Premier Nikita Kruschev—while acting in their own "rational" self-interest led us to the brink of a U.S.–Soviet nuclear confrontation. Accordingly, idealists will often criticize the rational actor assumption as, they argue, it will not always lead to the most effective solution. Perfect information is virtually impossible to obtain, and all state leaders are under time constraints that rarely allow a full cost-benefit analysis of all possible policy alternatives. Further, in many cases, state leaders have little control over actual outcomes. That is, in some cases, things "just happen." Recently Chalmers Johnson has argued that even when foreign policies appear to go well in the short term, some time later unintended consequences— what he terms **"blowback"**—can occur.[46]

In an attempt to demonstrate the problem of accurately predicting political outcomes, rational actor assumptions are employed in a modeling game referred to as the **Prisoner's Dilemma.** The scenario is as follows. Two individuals have committed a crime (perhaps a theft) and they are both captured, after the crime has been committed, and placed in sepa-

---

[44] J. B. Bury, *A History of Greece* (New York: Modern Library, 1913), p. 360.

[45] Graham Allison and Phillip Zelikow, *Essence of Decision: Explaining the Cuban Missile Crisis,* 2nd ed. (New York: Pearson Longman, 1999). Other models were used by Allison, including the Organizational Process Model and the Bureaucratic Process Model.

[46] Chalmers Johnson, *Blowback: The Costs and Consequences of American Empire* (New York: Owl Books, 2003).

rate prison cells. Since their capture the two prisoners have not had the opportunity to communicate and no one but the prisoners is sure of exactly who did what. Each prisoner is left with two options, which leave each of them with different outcomes, or "payoffs" (measured in terms of total numeric utility to each prisoner): (1) To tell, i.e. to *defect* and admit to the crime, with the hope that there will be a lighter sentence as a result; or (2) To not tell, i.e. to *cooperate* with the other prisoner, with the hope that the other prisoner will do the same. The scenario is summarized in a payoff matrix:

Table 1.1
Prisoner's Dilemma
Payoff Matrix

		Prisoner #2	
		Don't Tell (Cooperate)	*Tell (Defect)*
Prisoner #1	*Don't Tell (Cooperate)*	(3,3)	(1,4)
	Tell (Defect)	(4,1)	(2,2)

The first number is Prisoner #1's payoff (benefit); the second number is Prisoner #2's payoff (benefit) that would result from a given decision, either to cooperate (don't tell) or to defect (tell). If both prisoners do not tell on each other (i.e., do not admit to the crime), they have a net benefit of 3 each (top left-hand corner)—a total benefit, for the two of them, of 6. This would be the optimal outcome. But remember, these prisoners cannot speak with one another. There is an incentive (i.e., it is most "rational" to defect, as there is a potential benefit of 4 for either prisoner in the case where the other does not tell). Both, however, fearful of what the other might do, would likely tell, leaving the two prisoners with the least potential net benefit of 2 each (bottom right-hand corner). The prisoner's dilemma model is used to explain why it is that individuals acting in their own rational self-interested behavior, and not knowing what the other will do, will tend to pick the lesser outcome. That is, there is a disincentive for cooperative behavior, where greater net benefits could be had.

Again, the logic of individual behavior is carried over to state behavior where the prisoners are replaced by states, such as the United States and the former Soviet Union, or India and Pakistan, in a nuclear arms race.[47] In this way, the "rationality" of a nuclear arms race can be demonstrated. That is, each state acting in its own rational self-interest will lead to less desirable outcomes than cooperation, as neither side knows what the other will do in advance. It is worth noting that, through repeated cycles of the prisoner's dilemma problem, "game theorists" have demonstrated that "the possibility of reciprocity makes it [more] rational to cooperate."[48]

---

[47] See, e.g., Joshua Goldstein, *International Relations,* 2nd ed. (New York: Longman, 1999), pp. 74–76.

[48] Ibid, p. 76.

Why War?

The most pressing questions of international politics have to do with security and, in particular, the recurring phenomenon of war. Certainly, political outcomes are not always due to the actions of one individual as the Rational Actor Model might lead us to conclude. In an effort to categorize theories of politics that attempt to explain political outcomes and, in particular, war, Kenneth Waltz wrote the seminal *Man, the State, and War.*[49] Brilliant for its organizational clarity, Waltz argues that the reasons for political outcomes can be broken down into **levels of analysis.** His "first image," or level for organizing political theories, focuses on individual *human behavior.* In this first level of analysis Waltz suggests that some theories attribute "political ills to a fixed nature of man, defined in terms of an inherent potentiality for evil as well as for good . . . a theme that constantly recurs in the thought of Augustine, Spinoza, Niebuhr, and Morgenthau."[50] The second image investigates the *internal structure of states,* and the third image the problem of *international anarchy* and the challenge of international organization. In response to the question: Why do we have *cooperative* or *conflictual* political outcomes? Waltz's levels of analysis can be summarized as follows.

Table 1.2
Levels of Analysis

Waltz	Political Science Theories	Emphasis on
Level 1. "Individual Image"	Thomas Hobbes; Hans J. Morgenthau; St. Augustine; Mahatma Gandhi.	State leaders: Napoleon; Hitler; Kruschev; Kennedy; Churchill; DeGaulle; Castro, etc.
Level 2. "Internal Structure of States"	Max Weber's "bureaucracy" theories (and all that have followed suit); today's advocates of Structural Reform.	The internal functioning of states: Standard Operating Procedures (SOPs); bureaucratic "turf" battles; interorganizational behavior/politics.
Level 3. "International Anarchy"	Hedley Bull; NeoRealists; Kenneth Waltz (1979).[51]	The challenge of international organization; international bargaining among sovereign states.

---

[49] Kenneth N. Waltz, *Man, the State and War: A Theoretical Analysis* (New York: Columbia University Press, 1959). Written as his doctoral dissertation at Columbia University, Waltz aimed at getting a clearer picture of what the already existing great body of political theory had to say about the causes of war.

[50] Ibid, p. 27.

[51] Kenneth Waltz, *Theory of International Politics* (New York: McGraw-Hill, 1979), pp. 88 et seq.

It is important to note that Waltz makes the case, as all realists do, that international politics is characterized by the absence of a central government (i.e., **anarchy**). To those who argue that there is an "international society" of this kind or other, realists such as Hedley Bull remind us that there exists only an "anarchical society."[52]

The challenge to world peace, according to this view, is to promote a **balance of power** and, certainly, not to replace power politics with something else. Writing in 1977, near the end of his life, Morgenthau warned ". . . the candidate of the Democratic Party for the Presidency can declare: 'We must replace balance of power politics with world order politics' . . ."[53] This was the mistake, according to Morgenthau, that idealists had made throughout the twentieth century, arguing that such a view was only "echoing Woodrow Wilson's message to the Senate of January 22, 1917: 'There must not be a balance of power but a community of power.'"[54] The argument that idealists such as Wilson have made is that national interests can be defended in a community of states through what is termed **collective security.** Efforts of this kind, such as the North Atlantic Treaty Organization (NATO), do require a certain level of international effort and cooperation. The classic realist vision, as expressed at the Congress of Vienna (1815), is to balance existing powers. In 1815 this was attempted in what was termed the "Concert of Europe." History has shown that a balance of power can take place in three main forms, or systems: (1) unipolar, (2) bipolar, and (3) multipolar. The latter case is perhaps best demonstrated by nineteenth-century efforts behind the Concert of Europe; bipolarism by the Cold War rivalry between the United Sates and the Soviet Union; and unipolarism by the examples of *pax romana, pax britanica,* and today's *pax americana.*

In 1977 Morgenthau saw that although East–West relations were still crucial to U.S. national interest, the American public was becoming increasingly aware of and concerned with poverty and strife in the developing world. Again, he warned Americans that they should not lose sight of what was most important in international politics: power. As far as he was concerned, "the foreign and domestic policies [of Third World states] are but of minimal or no interest at all for the foreign policies of the United States."[55] "Most nations of the Third World," he argued, "prefer to be miserable in their own way to being happy in the American, Soviet, or Chinese way."[56]

Although seemingly blunt, the argument that Morgenthau is making is that individuals should be given the choice to organize their governments in the way they deem fit. Yet he is also clear on the point that, as a realist, he does not believe that morality should be a guiding principle of politics. In his view, realists are *aware* of the moral significance of political action. This is most clearly expressed in his earlier work, *Politics Among Nations.* Again, power is what matters most to conduct in international politics; economics and ethics are, at best, secondary. We will see similar arguments, by other realists, in Chapter 2.

Another way of looking at political conflict leading to war is to distinguish between *tangible* and *nontangible* variables. **Nontangible** reasons for war have included differences of ideology, ethnicity, and religion.[57] As Francis Fukuyama reminds us, many of the twentieth-century conflicts were over ideology: fascism, communism, and democratic lib-

---

[52] Hedley Bull, *The Anarchical Society,* 3rd ed. (New York: Columbia University Press, 1977, 2002).

[53] *New York Times,* August 1, 1976, Section IV, page 2, cited in Hans J. Morgenthau, "The Pathology of American Power," *International Security,* Vol. 1, Issue 3 (Winter 1977): 3–20.

[54] Ibid.

[55] Ibid., p. 16.

[56] Ibid.

[57] Goldstein, op. cit., makes the distinction between *nontangible* and *tangible* reasons for war.

eralism.[58] Although Fukuyama suggests that democratic liberalism has prevailed in the post-Cold War world, a recent group of theorists has argued that democratic liberalism has brought on unexpected challenges to peace. Amy Chua, for example, has suggested that the end of the Cold War has indeed brought on an increase in the debates of ideas and of free mobility but it has also brought on an increase in nontangible reasons for conflict.[59] Perhaps the clearest examples of this can be seen by the breakup of existing sovereign states into smaller groups of sovereign states (e.g., notably former Yugoslavia), a post-Cold War phenomenon referred to as **Balkanization.** If one considers recent developments on the African continent, it seems clear that similar secessionist movements are likely to continue for some time.[60] Secessionist movements are not always the result of nontangibles like religious or ethnic differences; they can also be motivated by material, or tangible, aims.

Tangible reasons for engaging in war include struggles over natural resources, disparities of wealth, and disputes over territory. The emphasis on tangibles as a basis for political conflict really depends on who you ask. For example, is it fair to say that the Russia–Chechnya conflict or the 1991 Gulf War were largely over oil? Or should these conflicts be characterized as battles over protecting the principle of state sovereignty? It is interesting to compare the statements that are made by government leaders that generally defend national interest in terms of defense of ideals versus theories that are more critical and tend to focus on the tangible benefits of foreign policy action. If one is to consider the arguments made by Noam Chomsky regarding U.S. government leaders' justifications for the use of force against other states, or those of other critics against U.S. foreign policy, the reasons provided often focus on the tangible—especially oil.[61] In the aftermath of both the 1991 Gulf War and following the recent invasion of Iraq, U.S. policy makers were quick to respond that oil was not the principle reason for the use of force. To use the aforementioned examples: (1) The 1991 Gulf War was primarily justified as the protection of Kuwait's state sovereignty, which had been violated by Iraq, in violation of international law; and (2) the war with Iraq was justified due to threats to U.S. national security (i.e., as discussed earlier, we had the right to protect our vital national interest).[62] The point, simply, is that although there may well be both tangible and intangible reasons for going to war, it is not always clear which of these was most important in making the decision.

---

[58] Francis Fukuyama, *The End of History and the Last Man* (New York: Avon, 1993).

[59] See, e.g., Amy Chua, *World on Fire: How Exporting Free-Market Democracy Breeds Ethnic Hatred and Global Instability* (New York: Doubleday, 2002). For the record, similar ideas regarding the inherent dangers of political and economic liberalization—at least in the shorter term—were argued by Samuel P. Huntington, *Political Order in Changing Societies* (New Haven, CT: Yale University Press, 1968) and Richard Sandbrook, *The Politics of Africa's Economic Stagnation* (New York: Cambridge University Press, 1985), who focuses on the rise of ethnic conflicts, which he links to rapid capitalist change on the African continent.

[60] Greg Barrow, BBC News, "Africa: More Shooting in Rebellious Region," August 3, 1999, (http://news.bbc.co.uk). Barrow asks: "Is secession the answer to Africa's minority troubles?" Africanist Jeffrey Herbst has argued that African state boundaries are problematic as they were arbitrarily drawn during the Berlin Conference of 1884–85, unlike those of continental Europe that are largely the result of wars through history. Jeffrey Herbst, *States and Power in Africa: Comparative Lessons in Authority and Control* (Princeton, NJ: Princeton University Press, 2000). Similar conclusions can be drawn regarding other formerly colonized regions of the world.

[61] Consider Stephen Pelletiere, *Iraq and the International Oil System* (New York: Praeger, 2001) or Milan Rai, Noam Chomsky, *War Plan Iraq: Against War With Iraq* (New York: Verso Books, 2002). The now seminal text that focuses on the issue of oil is that of Daniel Yergen, *The Prize: The Epic Quest for Oil, Money, and Power* (New York: Free Press, 1991).

[62] Much has been written in the media on these points, and I need not list the many hundreds of articles and other scholarly sources. The 1991 Gulf War did ultimately safeguard Kuwait's sovereign state status whereas the outcome of the conflict with Iraq remains unclear.

In Chapter 5 we will see that the primary emphasis of structuralists is the tangible, material basis for political conflict. The structuralists' focus, therefore, is on the historic control over natural resources that, in their view, has led to great disparities of wealth. Again, for other political scientists, differences of material wealth, in particular, are wholly rejected in their analysis. A clear example of this is offered by Hans J. Morgenthau. To those (like structuralists) who see a causal relationship between Northern wealth and Southern poverty, Morgenthau states

> The moral obligation on the part of the industrialized, rich nations to raise the standard of living of the non-industrialized poor ones throughout the world is specifically grounded in the causal relationship which is presumed to exist between the policies and the high standard of living of the former and the low standard of living of the latter. However, the assumption of a simple causal relationship of this kind is a myth.[63]

In Morgenthau's view, international politics inevitably involves conflict and the goal therefore, for each state, is to protect and promote its own national interest. Indeed, that is, as Robert Jackson has pointed out, the responsibility of sovereign state leaders.[64] This view has also been expressed in what is now termed the **Bush Doctrine.** Since the new doctrine was first declared by Condoleezza Rice in December 2001, it has been interpreted in a variety of ways. On the one hand, there are those who fear that the reasons for preemptive action, as defined by the Bush Doctrine, are overly broad; on the other, there are those who hail the courage of the Bush administration to "act aggressively, with others or alone, to promote a balance of power that favors freedom."[65] Still others have interpreted the Bush Doctrine as the logical extension of logic that prevailed in the early 1990s, such as ending "welfare as we know it"; the idea being that both individuals and states should take full responsibility for their own affairs.[66] According to Goldstein, the Bush Doctrine "emphasizes that states are responsible for what goes on inside their state borders [therefore] those harboring terrorists would be targeted themselves."[67]

Paradigms of International Politics

The chapters that follow survey some of the classic contributions to four paradigms of international politics, as they are presented in Table 1.3. The goal for each of these chapters (Chapter 2: **Realism;** Chapter 3: **Idealism;** Chapter 4: **Liberalism,** and Chapter 5: **Structuralism**) is to consider the "intellectual roots" of each paradigm, with a brief synopsis of the historical context. Chapter 6, the concluding chapter, considers some of the current debates within the field of international politics.

---

[63] Morgenthau (1977), p. 19.

[64] Robert H. Jackson, *The Global Covenant: Human Conduct in a World of States* (New York: Oxford University Press, 2000).

[65] Peter Beaumont, "Now for the Bush Doctrine," *The Observer,* September 22, 2002; Jackson Diehl, "Bush's Foreign Policy First," *Washington Post,* September 30, 2003, p. A19.

[66] This interpretation of the Bush Doctrine is offered by Joshua Goldstein, *International Relations—Brief Edition* (New York: Pearson Longman, 2002). Of course, the statement "end welfare as we know it" was made by President Clinton, in his 1992 reelection campaign and thereafter.

[67] Goldstein (2004), p. 61.

Table 1.3
Paradigms of International Politics

	Realism	**Idealism**	**Liberalism**	**Structuralism**
Focus	"What is"; history; status quo	"What ought to be"; alter status quo	Freedom (political and economic); gradual evolution of status quo	Exploitation
Assumptions	Belief in *universals*: self-interest; power; order is desirable	An objective understanding of morality is possible and worth striving for (international law); unless the existing order is just, change is warranted	Comparative advantage (we all have something to offer); principle of self-determination; positive-sum logic	Limited global wealth; individual workers *(proletariat)* and LDCs are poor due to the exploitative behavior of elites *(bourgeois)*
Key Terms	Power; order	Justice; change	Laissez-faire; individualism	Historical materialism; determinism; imperialism; class struggle; core-periphery analysis
Solutions	Balance of power; state sovereignty	Philospher kings (Plato); international cooperation; international law; transnational solutions	Free market; Bretton Woods Institutions: IMF, WB, WTO	Revolution; UNCTAD and other UN General Assembly aims; NIEO demands
Critique	Does might make right? In a world where weapons of mass destruction (i.e. "power") can be hidden in a vial in someone's top pocket, is this still a good organizing principle?	Proposed solutions are too far removed from actual political practice (i.e. 'impracticality;') Fundamentalism; Religious fanatics; Utopian goals	Distributional flaws	Zero-sum logic
Contributors	Thucydides Hobbes Machiavelli Bismark Morgenthau Kissinger	Ancient Greeks Hugo Grotius Gandhi Wilson Falk	Locke Jefferson Rawls Smith Ricardo Friedman	Marx Lenin Prebisch Dos Santos Wallerstein

Chapter Two

Realism

"I shall be satisfied if my own words are judged useful by those who desire a clear understanding of the events which occurred in the past and which will occur again, in much the same way, in the future, human nature being what it is."

". . the contest not being an equal one, with honour as the prize and shame as the penalty, but a question of self-preservation and of not resisting those who are far stronger than you are."

Thucydides, *History of the Pelponnesian War*, 431–404 BCE.

The Athenian general Thucydides is often referred to as the earliest realist thinker and is regularly cited as someone who has offered us some of the more compelling ideas of realist political thought. Although Thucydides recounts a war that began in 431 BC, his book, *History of the Peloponnesian War,* is in fact deceptively modern. Many of his arguments regarding politics among states are now commonplace. Specifically, Thucydides emphasized national interest, the amorality of political matters, individuals as isolated state actors, and even the primacy of the state in international relations.

The background, in brief, is as follows. Athens and Sparta had fought as allies in an ongoing battle against Persia. Gradually, however, Athens took the lead in the anti-Persian alliance, which was formalized as the Delian League. As a direct result of this, the two Greek city-states became fierce rivals.[68] It is important to note that, culturally and otherwise, they

---

[68] Details regarding the sources of conflict between the Athenians and the Spartans are provided in a great many texts on classical history. See, e.g., Michael Grant, *The Founders of the Western World: A History of Greece and Rome* (New York: Charles Scribner's Sons, 1991); John Boardman, et al., eds., *The Oxford History of the Classical World* (Oxford: Oxford University Press, 1986), pp. 124–125; and Donald Kagan, Ch. 1, *On the Origins of War and the Preservation of Peace* (New York: Doubleday, 1995). Indeed, perhaps the best source is Thucydides himself. See: *The Complete Writings of Thucydides* (New York: The Modern Library, 1934), "Chapter II: The Causes of the War," pp. 16–37.

were also remarkably different. Athens was a much more open and democratic society that, due to its strong naval fleet, had acquired substantial wealth from contact with allies and colonies. By contrast, Sparta was a closed and highly disciplined agrarian society, and her economy relied heavily on state-owned slave labor. The Spartans were better prepared to fight a land war. In terms of population, they outnumbered the Athenians two to one. And it is often said that their entire culture was centered around preparing men for battle.[69]

At the start of the conflict, it was the Spartans who invaded Attica and began burning crops in order to starve the Athenians into submission. But the Athenians had strengths of their own that would allow them to hold out against the Spartans for years. The Athenians had a functioning harbor, a powerful navy and a very capable Athenian general and political leader, Pericles.[70] With his powerful navy, Pericles also knew that he could bring large numbers of Athenian troops right to Sparta, far from Athenian lines, to engage in battle. Pericles, however, died in the second year of the war in a plague that devastated Athens. Nevertheless, the Athenians continued to pursue the Periclean strategy in the years that followed.

It was a good strategy for the Athenians. After ten years of battle, there was no clear victor. A fifty-year truce was signed, dubbed the Peace of Nicias. Nicias, another Athenian general and politician, had rivals in government, notably a student of Socrates named Alcibiades. In 415 BC, Alcibiades was able to convince the Athenians of the need to attach the Greek city-states on the island of Sicily so that they could be controlled by Athens. Primary responsibility of the expedition, however, fell squarely on the shoulders of Nicias, who took responsibility for what followed. In short order, by 413 BC, the entire Athenian army that had been dispatched on the island was defeated, and a large part of the Athenian fleet was destroyed in the harbor of Syracuse. This posed grave problems for Nicias as the Athenian fleet was the basis of Athenian military power.

Taking note of the failed expedition to Sicily, the Spartans soon attacked Athens and, to make matters worse, the Persians joined in the battle against Athens. Despite the courageous efforts of the Athenians and several brief victories in battle, Athens was forced to surrender completely to Sparta in 404 BC. The Spartans responded by tearing down the walls of the city and establishing their own nondemocratic government. At this point, the Age of Athens, the Age of Pericles, the Athenian Empire all came to an end.

It was during this tumultuous period that Thucydides documented this historic dilemma with the people residing on the island of Melos. Both the Spartans and the Athenians were keen to have as many allied peoples of the region on their own side as possible. But, as we shall see, the Melians resisted Athenian demands. In this Athenian–Melian dialogue, the Athenians asserted in clear terms the "law of nature" that the strong should rule over the weak. This is a doctrine that the Ancient Greeks, before and after the Melian dialogue, were to follow; what is perhaps unusual is the frank terms in which it is enunciated by Thucydides.[71]

---

[69] J. P. Mahaffy, *Social Life in Greece* (London: MacMillan, 1894), pp. 23–24; "The Spartan Code," in Will Durant, *The Life of Greece* (New York: Simon and Schuster, 1939), pp. 81–89.

[70] A "classic" discussion—indeed—of Pericles is offered by no less than Plutarch, in *The Lives of the Noble Grecians and Romans* (New York: Modern Library), pp. 182–212. For a more modern interpretation of Pericles' significance to Ancient Greek history, see: Donald Kagan, *Pericles of Athens and the Birth of Democracy* (New York: Free Press, 1991).

[71] Historian J. B. Bury suggests that the conquest of Melos "is remarkable, not for the rigorous treatment of the Melians, which is merely another example of the inhumanity which [was already witnessed] in the cases of Plataea, Mytilene, Scione, but for the unprovoked aggressions of Athens, without any tolerable pretext," Bury (1913), p. 446.

▮▮▮

READING 1: THUCYDIDES

THUCYDIDES

A HISTORY OF THE PELOPONNESIAN WAR, 431–404 BCE

SIXTEENTH YEAR OF THE WAR—THE MELIAN CONFERENCE—FATE OF MELOS

B.C. 416: ATHENIAN EXPEDITION TO MELOS—DISCUSSION OF ENVOYS—MELIANS REFUSE TO SUBMIT— SIEGE OF MELOS—MELIANS MASSACRED AND MADE SLAVES.

The next summer Alcibiades sailed with twenty ships to Argos and seized the suspected persons still left of the Lacedæmonian faction to the number of three hundred, whom the Athenians forthwith lodged in the neighbouring islands of their empire. The Athenians also made an expedition against the isle of Melos with thirty ships of their own, six Chian, and two Lesbian vessels, sixteen hundred heavy infantry, three hundred archers, and twenty mounted archers from Athens, and about fifteen hundred heavy infantry from the allies and the islanders. The Melians are a colony of Lacedæmon that would not submit to the Athenians like the other islanders, and at first remained neutral and took no part in the struggle, but afterwards upon the Athenians using violence and plundering their territory, assumed an attitude of open hostility. Cleomedes, son of Lycomedes, and Tisias, son of Tisimachus, the generals, encamping in their territory with the above armament, before doing any harm to their land, sent envoys to negotiate. These the Melians did not bring before the people, but bade them state the object of their mission to the magistrates and the few; upon which the Athenian envoys spoke as follows:—

Athenians.—'Since the negotiations are not to go on before the people, in order that we may not be able to speak straight on without interruption, and deceive the ears of the multitude by seductive arguments which would pass without refutation (for we know that this is the meaning of our being brought before the few), what if you who sit there were to pursue a method more cautious still! Make no set speech yourselves, but take us up at whatever you do not like, and settle that before going any farther. And first tell us if this proposition of ours suits you.'

The Melian commissioners answered:—

Melians.—'To the fairness of quietly instructing each other as you propose there is nothing to object; but your military preparations are too far advanced to agree with what you say, as we see you are come to be judges in your own cause, and that all we can reasonably expect from this negotiation is war, if we prove to have right on our side and refuse to submit, and in the contrary case, slavery.'

Athenians.—'If you have met to reason about presentiments of the future, or for anything else than to consult for the safety of your state upon the facts that you see before you, we will give over; otherwise we will go on.'

Melians.—'It is natural and excusable for men in our position to turn more ways than one both in thought and utterance. However, the question in this conference is, as you say, the safety of our country; and the discussion, if you please, can proceed in the way which you propose.'

Athenians.—'For ourselves, we shall not trouble you with specious pretences—either of how we have a right to our empire because we overthrew the Mede, or are now attacking you because of wrong that you have done us—and make a long speech which would not be believed; and in return we hope that you, instead of thinking to influence us by saying that you did not join

---

The Complete Writings of Thucydides: The Peloponnesian War, (Modern Library, 1934).

the Lacedæmonians, although their colonists, or that you have done us no wrong, will aim at what is feasible, holding in view the real sentiments of us both; since you know as well as we do that right, as the world goes, is only in question between equals in power, while the strong do what they can and the weak suffer what they must.'

Melians.—'As we think, at any rate, it is expedient—we speak as we are obliged, since you enjoin us to let right alone and talk only of interest—that you should not destroy what is our common protection, the privilege of being allowed in danger to invoke what is fair and right, and even to profit by arguments not strictly valid if they can be got to pass current. And you are as much interested in this as any, as your fall would be a signal for the heaviest vengeance and an example for the world to meditate upon.'

Athenians.—'The end of our empire, if end it should, does not frighten us: a rival empire like Lacedæmon, even if Lacedæmon was our real antagonist, is not so terrible to the vanquished as subjects who by themselves attack and overpower their rulers. This, however, is a risk that we are content to take. We will now proceed to show you that we are come here in the interest of our empire, and that we shall say what we are now going to say, for the preservation of your country; as we would fain exercise that empire over you without trouble, and see you preserved for the good of us both.'

Melians.—'And how, pray, could it turn out as good for us to serve as for you to rule?'

Athenians.—'Because you would have the advantage of submitting before suffering the worst, and we should gain by not destroying you.'

Melians.—'So that you would not consent to our being neutral, friends instead of enemies, but allies of neither side.'

Athenians.—'No; for your hostility cannot so much hurt us as your friendship will be an argument to our subjects of our weakness, and your enmity of our power.'

Melians.—'Is that your subjects' idea of equity, to put those who have nothing to do with you in the same category with peoples that are most of them your own colonists, and some conquered rebels?'

Athenians.—'As far as right goes they think one has as much of it as the other, and that if any maintain their independence it is because they are strong, and that if we do not molest them it is because we are afraid; so that besides extending our empire we should gain in security by your subjection; the fact that you are islanders and weaker than others rendering it all the more important that you should not succeed in baffling the masters of the sea.'

Melians.—'But do you consider that there is no security in the policy which we indicate? For here again if you debar us from talking about justice and invite us to obey your interest, we also must explain ours, and try to persuade you, if the two happen to coincide. How can you avoid making enemies of all existing neutrals who shall look at our case and conclude from it that one day or another you will attack them? And what is this but to make greater the enemies that you have already, and to force others to become so who would otherwise have never thought of it?'

Athenians.—'Why, the fact is that continentals generally give us but little alarm; the liberty which they enjoy will long prevent their taking precautions against us; it is rather islanders like yourselves, outside our empire, and subjects smarting under the yoke, who would be the most likely to take a rash step and lead themselves and us into obvious danger.'

Melians.—'Well then, if you risk so much to retain your empire, and your subjects to get rid of it, it were surely great baseness and cowardice in us who are still free not to try everything that can be tried, before submitting to your yoke.'

Athenians.—'Not if you are well advised, the contest not being an equal one, with honour as the prize and shame as the penalty, but a question of self-preservation and of not resisting those who are far stronger than you are.'

Melians.—'But we know that the fortune of war is sometimes more impartial than the disproportion of numbers might lead one to suppose; to submit is to give ourselves over to despair, while action still preserves for us a hope that we may stand erect.'

Athenians.—'Hope, danger's comforter, may be indulged in by those who have abundant re-sources, if not without loss at all events without ruin; but its nature is to be extravagant, and those who go so far as to put their all upon the venture see it in its true colours only when they are ruined; but so long as the discovery would enable them to guard against it, it is never found wanting. Let not this be the case with you, who are weak and hang on a single turn of the scale; nor be like the vulgar, who, abandoning such security as human means may still afford, when visible hopes fail them in extremity, turn to invisible, to prophecies and oracles, and other such inventions that delude men with hopes to their destruction.'

Melians.—'You may be sure that we are as well aware as you of the difficulty of contending against your power and fortune, unless the terms be equal. But we trust that the gods may grant us fortune as good as yours, since we are just men fighting against unjust, and that what we want in power will be made up by the alliance of the Lacedæmonians, who are bound, if only for very shame, to come to the aid of their kindred. Our confidence, therefore, after all is not so utterly irrational.'

Athenians.—'When you speak of the favour of the gods, we may as fairly hope for that as yourselves; neither our pretensions nor our conduct being in any way contrary to what men believe of the gods, or practice among themselves. Of the gods we believe, and of men we know, that by a necessary law of their nature they rule wherever they can. And it is not as if we were the first to make this law, or to act upon it when made: we found it existing before us, and shall leave it to exist for ever after us; all we do is to make use of it, knowing that you and everybody else, having the same power as we have, would do the same as we do. Thus, as far as the gods are concerned, we have no fear and no reason to fear that we shall be at a disadvantage. But when we come to your notion about the Lacedæmonians, which leads you to believe that shame will make them help you, here we bless your simplicity but do not envy your folly. The Lacedæmonians, when their own interests or their country's laws are in question, are the worthiest men alive; of their conduct towards others much might be said, but no clearer idea of it could be given than by shortly saying that of all the men we know they are most conspicuous in considering what is agreeable honourable, and what is expedient just. Such a way of thinking does not promise much for the safety which you now unreasonably count upon.'

Melians.—'But it is for this very reason that we now trust to their respect for expediency to prevent them from betraying the Melians, their colonists, and thereby losing the confidence of their friends in Hellas and helping their enemies.'

Athenians.—'Then you do not adopt the view that expediency goes with security, while justice and honour cannot be followed without danger; and danger the Lacedæmonians generally court as little as possible.'

Melians.—'But we believe that they would be more likely to face even danger for our sake, and with more confidence than for others, as our nearness to Peloponnese makes it easier for them to act, and our common blood insures our fidelity.'

Athenians.—'Yes, but what an intending ally trusts to, is not the goodwill of those who ask his aid, but a decided superiority of power for action; and the Lacedæmonians look to this even more than others. At least, such is their distrust of their home resources that it is only with numerous allies that they attack a neighbour; now is it likely that while we are masters of the sea they will cross over to an island?'

Melians.—'But they would have others to send. The Cretan sea is a wide one, and it is more difficult for those who command it to intercept others, than for those who wish to elude them to do so safely. And should the Lacedæmonians miscarry in this, they would fall upon your land, and upon those left of your allies whom Brasidas did not reach; and instead of places which are not yours, you will have to fight for your own country and your own confederacy.'

Athenians.—'Some diversion of the kind you speak of you may one day experience, only to learn, as others have done, that the Athenians never once yet withdrew from a siege for fear of any. But we are struck by the fact, that after saying you would consult for the safety of your country, in all this discussion you have mentioned nothing which men might trust in and think to be saved by. Your strongest arguments depend upon hope and the future, and your actual resources are too scanty, as compared with those arrayed against you, for you to come out victorious. You will therefore show great blindness of judgment, unless, after allowing us to retire, you can find some counsel more prudent than this. You will surely not be caught by that idea of disgrace, which in dangers that are disgraceful, and at the same time too plain to be mistaken, proves so fatal to mankind; since in too many cases the very men that have their eyes perfectly open to what they are rushing into, let the thing called disgrace, by the mere influence of a seductive name, lead them on to a point at which they become so enslaved by the phrase as in fact to fall will fully into hopeless disaster, and incur disgrace more disgraceful as the companion of error, than when it comes as the result of misfortune. This, if you are well advised, you will guard against; and you will not think it dishonourable to submit to the greatest city in Hellas, when it makes you the moderate offer of becoming its tributary ally, without ceasing to enjoy the country that belongs to you; nor when you have the choice given you between war and security, will you be so blinded as to choose the worse. And it is certain that those who do not yield to their equals, who keep terms with their superiors, and are moderate towards their inferiors, on the whole succeed best. Think over the matter, therefore, after our withdrawal, and reflect once and again that it is for your country that you are consulting, that you have not more than one, and that upon this one deliberation depends its prosperity or ruin.'

The Athenians now withdrew from the conference; and the Melians, left to themselves, came to a decision corresponding with what they had maintained in the discussion, and answered, 'Our resolution, Athenians, is the same as it was at first. We will not in a moment deprive of freedom a city that has been inhabited these seven hundred years; but we put our trust in the fortune by which the gods have preserved it until now, and in the help of men, that is, of the Lacedæmonians; and so we will try and save ourselves. Meanwhile we invite you to allow us to be friends to you and foes to neither party, and to retire from our country after making such a treaty as shall seem fit to us both.'

Such was the answer of the Melians. The Athenians now departing from the conference said, 'Well, you alone, as it seems to us, judging from these resolutions, regard what is future as more certain than what is before your eyes, and what is out of sight, in your eagerness, as already coming to pass; and as you have staked most on, and trusted most in, the Lacedæmonians, your fortune, and your hopes, so will you be most completely deceived.'

The Athenian envoys now returned to the army; and the Melians showing no signs of yielding, the generals at once betook themselves to hostilities, and drew a line of circumvallation round the Melians, dividing the work among the different states. Subsequently the Athenians returned with most of their army, leaving behind them a certain number of their own citizens and of the allies to keep guard by land and sea. The force thus left stayed on and besieged the place.

About the same time the Argives invaded the territory of Phlius and lost eighty men cut off in an ambush by the Phliasians and Argive exiles. Meanwhile the Athenians at Pylos took so much plunder from the Lacedæmonians that the latter, although they still refrained from breaking off the treaty and going to war with Athens, yet proclaimed that any of their people that chose might plunder the Athenians. The Corinthians also commenced hostilities with the Athenians for private quarrels of their own; but the rest of the Peloponnesians stayed quiet. Meanwhile the Melians attacked by night and took the part of the Athenian lines over against the market, and killed some of the men, and brought in corn and all else that they could find useful to them, and so returned and kept quiet, while the Athenians took measures to keep better guard in future.

Summer was now over. The next winter the Lacedæmonians intended to invade the Argive territory, but arriving at the frontier found the sacrifices for crossing unfavourable, and went back again. This intention of theirs gave the Argives suspicions of certain of their fellow-citizens, some of whom they arrested; others, however, escaped them. About the same time the Melians again took another part of the Athenian lines which were but feebly garrisoned. Reinforcements afterwards arriving from Athens in consequence, under the command of Philocrates, son of Demeas, the siege was now pressed vigorously; and some treachery taking place inside, the Melians surrendered at discretion to the Athenians, who put to death all the grown men whom they took, and sold the women and children for slaves, and subsequently sent out five hundred colonists and inhabited the place themselves.

"Veni, vici, vici."
Julius Caesar, 47 BCE

"We have become too humane not to be repelled by Caesar's triumphs."
J. W. von Goethe

"Reflect, I pray you, and be wise in time; remember your ancestors and not your associates." *Cicero, 43 BCE*

"We are the servants of the law in order that we may be free." *Cicero, ca. 44 BCE*

Roman Contributions to Political Realism

Given the nature and methods of Roman conquest, there can be no doubt that realist ideas were a crucial part of Ancient Roman thinking. Yet, there are few texts on international politics that dare to cite a Roman thinker for having what might be termed "realist" views on politics. This is due, in part, to the fact that the period of *Pax Romana* was largely atheoretical. Great Roman orators, such as Cicero, were known for taking many points of view into account, rather than advocating any one political theory. Perhaps the better way to think of Roman contributions to realist thinking is by bringing Greek terms and ideas into the language and by providing snippits of realist thought in the oratories and dialogues that have been passed down through the ages. Certainly, the importance of ideas from Polybius, Caesar, and Cicero to political thinkers like Thomas Jefferson is well documented.[72] What, then, were the Romans thinking? Why the continued interest in Roman ideas?

In the earliest years of the Roman Empire, educated Romans were first impressed by the ideas of the Stoic School, considered to be the last of the great Athenian schools.[73] Sabine comments: "No other Greek system was so well qualified as Stoicism to appeal to

---

[72] References to the Romans can be seen in *The Life and Selected Writings of Thomas Jefferson* (New York: Modern Library, 1944). More generally, when writers of American political history speak of the influences on the framers of the U.S. Constitution, they will often include Cicero and others. Consider the following comment: "Late eighteenth-century men were deeply in love with the classical societies and their statesmen, generals, historians. College students did not read English literature. They read instead Caesar's *Commentaries*, the *Orations* of Cicero, the *Politics* of Aristotle; and they constantly referred to what Polybius or Plato thought on a given subject." Christopher Collier, et al., *Decision in Philadelphia: The Constitutional Convention of 1787* (New York: Ballantine Books, 1986), pp. 53–54.

[73] The end of the Athenian schools coincides with the start of a new Hellenistic School.

the native virtues of self-control, devotion to duty, and public spirit to which the Roman took especial pride . . ."[74] But the first inclination of the Stoic School, in Rome, was to turn it "into a kind of philosophy of humanism."[75] The older ideals of the Romans were to be replaced by a more enlightened, cultivated manner that emphasized goodwill toward others and gentleness. It was this early group of Roman aristocrats that used the term *humanitas,* considered to be "a corrective for the crudeness of the society drunk with power and enlightened by taste or ideas . ."[76] And yet one of the best-known chroniclers of Roman history, Polybius, explains that this period, the early history of Rome, quickly turned the region from Spain to Asia Minor under Roman domination in "less than fifty-three years."[77] One might ask: How can this be, if the dominant philosophy of gentleness and goodwill toward others, just described, prevailed?

One needs to consider the logic of the Stoic School in more depth to answer this question. The roots of Stoic thought are to be found in Plato, who was, at least to some extent, a rationalist.[78] This is said because Plato maintained what is referred to as *dualism* in much of his thought, "whether between universals and particulars of logic, between ideas and things, or between the Divine realm, in which is found both God and the ideas, and this created world in which we live."[79] As I see it, there are two main controversies that stem from Plato's emphasis on dualism: first, it may lead one to believe that Plato was pointing in the direction of atheism; and second, this can lead to a philosophical approach, normally attributed to the Persian thinker, Manes (or Manichaeus), that divides the world into "good" versus "evil"—termed **Manichaean** thinking. Whether or not Plato actually *believed* in dualism (juxtaposing terms such as "positive–negative," "body(mind)-soul," "mortal–immortal," "changing–unchanging," and so on), is irrelevant to us here. What is important to us is that this led to, in the years following his death, a philosophy of rationalism.[80]

The philosophy of Epicurus, who was born in 341 BC, about five years after the death of Plato, was influenced by these trends of thought. Epicurus sought primarily to rid men of the fears that "tainted their lives, namely the fear of gods which led to superstitious enormities, and fear of death."[81] He believed that the aim of philosophy was to help us live well,

---

[74] George H. Sabine, *A History of Political Theory,* 3rd ed. (London: Harrap, 1966), p. 153.

[75] Ibid.

[76] Ibid., p. 156.

[77] Polybius, cited in ibid., p. 154. Polybius, in fact, describes this region as "the world." Indeed, it was the world as far as the Romans were concerned, with the exception of a few remaining "fringe" areas (later to be explored by, and sometimes conquered by, people like Julius Caesar.) Sabine points out that, for Polybius, Roman domination was an unquestioned fact. This perspective, of course, does change over time, the evidence of which can be seen in later Roman writings.

[78] Whitney J. Oates, in Introduction to *The Stoic and Epicurean Philosophers: The Complete Writings of Epicurus, Epictetus, Lucretius, and Marcus Aurelius* (New York: Modern Library, 1940), p. xvi. Zeno of Citium is usually credited as being the formal "founder" of Stoicism, ca. 334 BC.

[79] Ibid. Similar discussions regarding Plato's dualism can be found in Sabine, op. cit., and Brian R. Nelson, Ch. 2, *Western Political Thought: From Socrates to the Age of Ideology,* 2nd ed. (Englewood Cliffs, NJ: Prentice Hall, 1982). Many have argued that Plato's critique of dualism is ignored and that, therefore, one cannot—as many do—say that Plato believed in dualism per se. An example of Plato's influence on dualistic thinking in the West can be seen in the writings of Joseph Campbell. That is, in describing the differences between Eastern and Western philosophies (or "realities"), Joseph Campbell would regularly refer to dualism. For Campbell, the West preaches a division between humans and God and between their bodies and their souls; the East, by contrast, preaches the identity of the body with the soul. See: Robert A. Segal, *Joseph Campbell: An Introduction* (New York: Penguin, 1990), pp. 116–117, as well as Campbell's *Masks of God* series. Classic examples of "radical dualism," explains Segal, are Plato's *Phaedo* and Apuleius' *Golden Ass.* The debate is ongoing among scholars of classical philosophy and need not concern us here.

[80] Oates (1940), p. xvi. Of course, the controversies with Plato do not end there. Many of his ideas are considered to be akin to communism. See: Sabine (1966), op. cit.

[81] Ibid., p. xvii and p. xix.

not hedonistically, but *well*—to attain a "pleasant life"—through practical wisdom. Titus Lucretius Carus (ca. 96–55 BC) was Rome's chief exponent of Epicurean ideas. Of him, we know little other than one book (a poem), *De Rerum Natura,* literally "on the nature of things." Like Epicurus, Lucretius, as he is known, argued that all that could not be rationally understood, including gods, mythology, rituals, cult behavior, all religion, were suggestions of ignorance. In other words, Lucretius insisted in a *realistic* outlook.[82]

What prevailed in the "Golden Age" of Rome (83 BCE–17 AD), then, was the notion that the ideal life was one of rational restraint, duty to the state, and certainly not of passions or desires. By this time, it was clear that the Romans had filled the political power vacuum throughout the Mediterranean that was left by the Ancient Greeks; the ongoing civil war in Greece, aggravated by the goals of the Persians, and the overextension of Alexander the Great left the Romans in political control in the region and beyond for hundreds of years.[83] The Roman Empire, at its height of power, extended well into northern Europe, southward into northern Africa, and eastward into Asia Minor.

One of the most remarkable Roman warriors, later emperor of Rome, was Julius Caesar (100–44 BCE). The renowned Roman biographer Seutonius described Caesar as "an imposing, energetic figure with a magnetic personality and remarkably alert mind."[84] Yet Caesar's fascination with *power,* although clear, is notably less theoretical than other contributors to the subject of realism. In his writings, he is descriptive and sometimes entertaining but his overarching purpose is to document his military strategies, regularly employing ideas such as *blitzkrieg* and "divide and conquer" in his military exploits.

Julius Caesar's life was nothing short of remarkable. He first saw military service in Asia (81 BCE), where he served as aide-de-camp to Marcus Thermus.[85] Moving rapidly up the military ranks, the Assembly of Rome soon voted him to the rank of colonel, then quaestor, and he was sent to Spain. There, it is said, Caesar saw a statue of Alexander the Great. And there, the biographer Suetonius tells us, Caesar was "overheard to sigh impatiently: vexed . . . that an age when Alexander had already conquered the world, he himself had done nothing in the least epoch making."[86] According to Suetonius, Caesar was so eager for political power that he even contemplated revolution in Rome itself, wherein Caesar would give an "agreed signal . . . letting his gown fall and expose the shoulder."[87] However, due to the death of a Gnaeus Piso, Governor of Spain, who was to lead a revolt in Spain simultaneous to Caesar's revolt in Rome, the plan was cancelled. In the years that followed, Caesar did all that he could to win popular favor, such as sponsoring gladiatorial shows. Eventually he tried to gain control of Egypt by popular vote. Weary of Caesar's growing popularity, members of the Senate in Rome opposed the measure, and so "Caesar took vengeance by replacing the public monuments" that had commemorated Roman victories in the region.[88] Obliged to abandon his ambition of governing Egypt, Caesar continued his quest for political power through connection, bribes, and alliances. Caesar was ultimately elected to the position of Consul, along with Marcus Bibulus, who was ultimately

---

[82] Sabine interprets the ethics of the Epicurians and the Skeptics of the early Roman period as being more "negative" in that it linked the functioning of "nature with individual self-interest." See: Sabine (1966), p. 159.

[83] The history of Rome can be broken down into the Roman Republic (240–84 BC), the Golden Age (83 BC–17 AD), the Silver Age (14–117 AD), and the Late Empire (117–395 AD).

[84] Gaius Suetonius Tranqillus, *The Twelve Caesars,* trans. Robert Graves (London: Penguin Books, 1957, 1979).

[85] Suetonius, pp. 1–2.

[86] Ibid., p. 3.

[87] Ibid., p. 4.

[88] Ibid., p. 5.

made politically insignificant. Suetonius tells us that, in the end, Caesar was thus able to govern alone and do as he pleased.

> It became a joke to sign and seal bogus documents: "Executed during the Consulship of Julius and Caesar," rather than: ". . . during the Consulship of Bibulus and Caesar."[89]

Caesar's exploits were far from over. In fact, fearful of his seemingly unending thirst for power, the Senate determined that he should ultimately govern a province "of the smallest possible importance, designated as 'woods and mountain-pastures.'"[90] This only further strengthened Caesar's resolve. After conducting a survey of "the many provinces open to him he chose Gaul (modern France) as being the most likely to supply him with wealth and triumphs."[91] This campaign Caesar famously documented in *De Bello Gallico,* wherein he tells us everything from the observed practices of druids, the racial divisions of Gaul, to military strategies behind the eventual conquest of Gaul (58–51 BCE).[92] His military commentaries range from brilliant tactics of "divide and conquer" to the outside influences of, notably, German invasion of Gaul, to panic in the Roman Army.

As if his victory in Gaul was not remarkable enough, the story continues as Caesar successfully invaded northward. Along the way, he describes the names and physical descriptions of the various tribes that he encounters. Writing in 55 BC, he commented, for example,

> During winter two German tribes, the Usipetes and Tencteri, crossed the Rhine not far from its mouth. Long provocation by the Suebi had developed into open hostilities, farming had been brought to a standstill, and wholesale migration was the result. The Suebi are by far the largest of the German peoples . . . providing an annual quota of soldiers for foreign service. The remaining civilian population supports the army as well as itself, and next year relieves the troops who carried on without interruption side by side with military instruction and field-training. There is, however, no private property in land . . . . The Suebi eat little cereal food: they subsist mainly on milk and meat, and spend a good deal of their time hunting. From childhood they enjoy perfect freedom of action without any kind of restraint or discipline; and that, together with their diet and constant physical exercise, makes them strong and of enormous bodily stature. Despite a bitterly cold climate they are used to bathing in the rivers and to wearing only skins, which are so scanty as to leave a large part of the body naked . . . .
>
> It is particularly remarkable that, unlike the Gauls who are extremely fond of horses and pay high prices for them, the Germans import none: their home breed, though small and ugly, is capable of the hardest work as a result of constant exercise. In cavalry actions these natives often dismount and fight on foot; but their horses are trained to stand quite still . . . .[93]

There can be no doubt that Caesar's narrative was useful to the successful administration of a growing Roman Empire. While descriptive, as stated earlier, Caesar also paid close attention to the issue of *power* and the influences on its maintenance:

---

[89] Ibid., p. 9.

[90] Ibid., p. 8.

[91] Ibid., p. 10.

[92] Julius Caesar, *The Conquest of Gaul,* trans. J. A. Hanford (London: Penguin Books, 1983). See also: Meier (1982), Ch. 11 "Achievement in Gaul," pp. 224–348.

[93] Excerpted from Book IV (55 BC) of *De Bello Gallico,* John Warrington, ed., *Caesar's War Commentaries, De Bello Gallico and De Bello Civili* (London: Everyman's Library, 1915, 1953).

Imports of wine are absolutely forbidden on the grounds that it makes men soft and unequal to hard work.

The Ubii were, at one time, a large and prosperous people . . . slightly more civilized
than other German tribes because they live on the Rhine . . They [have] nevertheless been
reduced to the state of tributaries with considerable loss of power and prestige.[94]

Caesar had as his next goal the crossing of the English channel. As the British had provided
military assistance to the Gauls, he now deemed Britain an enemy of Rome. He tells of his
preparation.

Summer was drawing to a close, and winter sets in rather early in these parts, as Gual lies
wholly in northern latitudes. Nevertheless I hurried on preparations for an expedition to
Britain, knowing that Britain had rendered assistance to the enemy in nearly all my Gallic
campaigns. Although it was too late in the year for military operations I thought it would
be a great advantage merely to have visited the island, to have seen what kind of people the
inhabitants were, and to have learned something about the country with its harbours and
landing-places. Of all this the Gauls knew virtually nothing . . . .

Interviews with numerous merchants elicited nothing as to the size of the island, the
names and strength of the native tribes, their military and civil organization, or the harbours which might accommodate a large fleet.[95]

While planning an invasion of Britain, gathering his troops in Artois, his naval fleet from
neighboring regions and new vessels built for a Venetian campaign, some traders revealed
his plans to the Britons. Roman protection of the British was eventually offered. Reports
back from Britain were that they asked to be excused for their recent hostile involvement in
supporting the Gauls "on the grounds that they were uncivilized folk, ignorant of Roman
institutions, buy they promised obedience in the future."[96] Caesar saw only the goal of
British conquest in mind, stating: ". . . the British expedition was clearly more important
than conquest of these petty states [on the European continent]."[97] A fleet of about eighty
Roman ships was eventually commissioned and assembled. Further north, some eighty
miles up the coast, an additional eighteen transports were available and allotted to the cavalry. Caesar continues,

Arrangements were now complete, the weather was favorable, and we cast off just before
midnight. The cavalry had been ordered to make for the northern port, embark there, and
follow on; but they were rather slow about carrying out these instructions, and started, as
we shall see, too late. I reach Britain with the leading vessels at about 9 a.m. and saw the
enemy forces standing under arms all along the heights. At this point of the coast the precipitous cliffs tower over the water, making it possible to fire from above directly on to the
beaches. It was clearly no place to attempt a landing . . . .

The Britons were scared by the strange forms of warships, by the motion of the oars,
and by the artillery which they had never seen before: they halted, then fell back a little; but
our men hesitated, mainly because of the deep water . . . .[98]

---

[94] Excerpted from Book IV (55 BC) of *De Bello Gallico,* in Warrington, op. cit., p. 56 et seq.

[95] Ibid. See also, Meier (1982), pp. 280–282.

[96] Ibid., pp. 64–65.

[97] Ibid., p. 65.

[98] Ibid., p. 66.

A commander of the Tenth Legion, after calling on the gods to bless the legion through his act, shouted,

> "Come on men! Jump, unless you want to betray your standard to the enemy! I, at any rate, shall do my duty to my country and my commander . . ." The Britons, of course, knew all the shallows: standing on dry land, they watched the men disembark in small parties, galloped down, attacked them as they struggled through the surf, and surrounded them with superior numbers . . .[99]

Chieftans of the "natives" nevertheless began to arrive from the surrounding districts, not to fight, but to ask for protection. "Peace," according to Caesar, "was thus concluded." But the battle was far from over. On the fourth day after the initial landing in Britain, the eighteen transports with cavalry on board, who had initially experienced a "gentle breeze" encountered a violent storm. The transports were driven back to the continent, or drifted westward, down channel. Several ships were lost. At this point, the inevitable happened.

> The British chieftans at my headquarters sized up the situation and put their heads together. They knew we had no cavalry and were short of grain and shipping; they judged the weakness of our forces from the inconsiderable area of our camp . . . and decided to renew the offensive.[100]

The Romans, at one point, were forced to form a circle and defend themselves. But thousands more "natives" were to arrive on the scene. Caesar ordered his cavalry to their assistance and "in the meantime they stood their ground, putting up a magnificent fight for almost four hours and inflicting heavy casualties at the cost of only a few wounded."[101] Winter was now at hand and "the natives had concealed themselves in the thick forest" leaving Caesar with no option but to return "all the legions to winter in Belgic territory."[102]

Preparations for a second British expedition were immediately underway. Caesar wasted no time assigning tasks and noted his standing alliances as well as those who might cause him trouble. In the northern reaches of France, for example, Caesar had to contend with two local authorities: Indutiomarus and Cingetorix. Of them he observes

> Directly Cingetorix learned of our approach he paid me a visit, emphasized that he and his followers intended to support the Roman alliance, and gave me an account of the state of affairs in his country. Intutiomarus, on the other hand, began preparing for war: he assembled forces of cavalry and infantry, and concealed all those above or below military age in the great forest of Ardennes, which stretches from the Rhine . . . to the eastern borders of Champagne.[103]

Suetonius sums up the remainder of Caesar's campaign in the region as follows: "He invaded Britain, a hitherto unknown country, and defeated the natives, from whom he exacted a large sum of money as well as hostages for future good behavior."[104]

---

[99] Ibid., p. 67.

[100] Ibid.

[101] Ibid., p. 70.

[102] Ibid., p. 71.

[103] Ibid., p. 73.

[104] Suetonius, p. 14. It is worth noting that this Roman expedition was, in fact, short-lived. Almost 100 years later, in 43 AD, Claudius would return to Britain with the Roman army to establish Londinium along the Thames River. Evidence of the Roman walls surrounding the modern city of London exists to this day as do coins, armor, and the like, in London's British Museum.

In 48–47 BCE Caesar supported the young Egyptian queen, Cleopatra, in a battle against Ptolemy.[105] After emerging victorious and keeping other uprising in Asia Minor at bay, Caesar returned to Rome to declare, simply: "Veni, vidi, vici." ("I came, I saw, I conquered.") Suetonius suggests that the "constant exercise of power gave Caesar a love of it; and that, after weighing his enemies' strength against his own, he took a chance of fulfilling his youthful dreams by making a bid for the monarchy."[106]

Once in Rome, Caesar made several tragic errors in judgment due, most say, to his own arrogance.[107] Apparently, Caesar offended members of the Senate, sixty of whom conspired to kill him. It is said that Caesar was warned of the conspirator's plot, that "someone handed him a note containing details of the plot against his life, but he merely added it to the bundle of petitions in his left hand, which he intended to read later."[108] When Tillius Cimber, who took the lead, came up close pretending to ask a question and put his hands on Caesar's shoulders, Caesar exclaimed: "This is violence!" Within moments Caesar had twenty-three dagger thrusts as he stood there. It is said that, when Caesar saw his friend Marcus Brutus about to deliver the second blow, he said to him in Greek, although it is normally translated into the Latin: "Et tu Brute?"[109] ("You too, Brutus?")

Interpretations as to what Caesar *really* stood for began almost immediately. Plutarch tells us that the Senate "ordered that Caesar should be worshipped as a divinity, and nothing, even of the slightest consequence, should be revoked which he had enacted during his government."[110] Suetonius tells us that, for some time afterward, the settlement of disputes would be made by "oaths taken in Caesar's name."[111] Yet the works of Cicero are often considered to be the earliest interpretations of Caesar's significance, in terms of political theory. Cicero, however, cannot be considered an unbiased observer of Caesar's politics. When he heard of Caesar's death Cicero applauded the deed as, in his view, Caesar harbored "such a desire for wrong-doing that he delighted in doing wrong even when he had no cause to."[112] In fact, in the civil war between Pompey and Caesar (49–48 BCE), Cicero had joined Pompey (i.e., Cicero might even be considered an enemy of Caesar). As we shall see, Cicero argued that public virtue and "justice" were linked. The fact that he consistently opposed Caesar has led some to believe that Caesar was nothing more than a self-serving warmonger. As a result many scholars have since come to Caesar's defense, in-

---

[105] Suetonius tells us that among Caesar's mistresses were several queens. "The most famous of these queens was Cleopatra." Seutonius, p. 25. More descriptions of what is known and hypotheses are provided in Meier (1982), pp. 408–412.

[106] Suetonius, p. 15.

[107] Suetonius, pp. 35 et seq.

[108] Suetonius, p. 40.

[109] "Et tu Brute," "You, too, Brutus," or "And also you, Brutus," is the famous line in Shakespeare's play *Julius Caesar.* It is sometimes said that Shakespeare's play uses Plutarch's translation of the story, which used the Latin phrase, whereas Caesar's last words were actually in Greek—"kai su teknon" (και σθ τεκνον)— which means, "And also you, child." Although this is often said, the fact is that Plutarch says nothing of kind. Rather, he tells us that Caesar fought back in vain, asking "Vile Casca, what does this mean?" and crying out "Brother, help!" Drawn swords were "leveled at his face and eyes" and he "was encompassed like a wild beast in the toils on every side." "Brutus also gave him one stab in the groin . . . and when he saw Brutus's sword drawn, he covered his face with his robe and submitted." *Plutarch: The Lives of the Noble Grecians and Romans* (New York: The Modern Library, n.d.), pp. 892–893.

[110] Plutarch, p. 893.

[111] Suetonius, p. 43. Tacitus is another important source for the history of Rome but his work is said to be less objective than that of Suetonius. See, *Introduction to Suetonius* (2003), p. x. In any case, *The Complete Works of Tacitus* (New York: The Modern Library, 1942), starts much later (i.e., at the death of Augustus in 14 AD), making only scant references to the past and therefore does not provide the reader with new insights regarding Caesar's last days in power.

[112] Cicero, cited in Christian Meier, *Caesar: A Biography* (New York: MJF Books, 1982), p. 483.

cluding a modern biographer, Christian Meier, who comments "Caesar's immorality is not as unequivocal as it appeared to his opponents."[113]

Marcus Tullius Cicero, whose life span (106–43 BCE) roughly coincides with that of Julius Caesar (100–44 BCE), is considered to be one of the greatest of all Latin writers and perhaps Rome's greatest orator. In a sense, he was a throwback to an earlier time in Rome, when Hellenistic, Epicurian, and Stoic philosophies had prevailed—today his Greco-Roman thinking would be referred to as *classical*.[114] His ideas included the cooperation of "all good men" who, in his view, were those of the *equestrian order*—those who "wished to share in the prerogatives of the virtual oligarchy."[115] As had been the case for Caesar, Cicero regarded statesmanship a higher calling than philosophy.[116] Cicero's goal, which greatly influenced Western thinkers later, was the preservation of a *Republic*. But it was not a democratic republic that Cicero had in mind; rather, it was an aristocratic order that he wished to maintain. In support of a ruling banking class and of a Senate, Cicero's plan was to create a *concordia ordinum,* literally a "harmony among the classes." Cicero, therefore, was never interested in radical change. His concern was the preservation of *order,* which helps us to understand this kind of advice: "Consider the wisdom of our ancestors in this matter."[117]

In seeking answers to virtuous conduct, therefore, whether it was in politics, business, or law, Cicero would regularly refer back to his forefathers. This he felt was one of his greatest tasks as an orator and an obligation that was incumbent on him as a learned Roman citizen. The fact that he would also be optimistic about the future of Rome has made many interpret him as not only *republican* but also as an *idealist*. It is true that, in referring back to the ways of the ancients, he would speak of morality and virtuous behavior. But this is probably best understood as part of the political culture of the time and of his role in it. In fact, when speaking of conflict, Cicero adamantly defended the Republic, even if this meant violation of the law. The phrase *inter arma silent leges* (in time of war, laws fall silent) is attributed to Cicero.[118]

Many have remarked that Cicero, more than other political theorists, had many contradictions in his work yet certain themes do come through (e.g., the importance of *duty*).[119] In doing so, Cicero would often tread into realist logic. This can be seen in the way Hugo Grotius cites Cicero. "In the third book of his offices," Grotius states, "Cicero said that there is nothing repugnant in the law of nature in spoiling the effects of the enemy, who by the same law we are authorized to kill."[120] As we will see in the next chapter, the main concern of Grotius is the establishment of a functioning international law, and Cicero's acknowledgment that "on certain occasions, some acts of dissimulation, that is, of conceal-

---

[113] Christian Meier (1982), p. 483.

[114] According to Moses Hadas, ed., *The Basic Works of Cicero* (New York: The Modern Library, 1951): "He preferred the Stoic to the Epicurian, and the Academic to both . . . ," p. xi. The claim that Cicero's views can be considered "classical" is made by Brian R. Nelson, *Western Political Thought: From Socrates to the Age of Ideology,* 2nd ed. (Englewood Cliffs, NJ: Prentice Hall, 1996) in Ch. 4, p. 69. After summing up all the Greek contributions that may have influenced the thinking of Cicero, Nelson, p. 77, simply states: "Cicero was an eclectic who drew upon a variety of Greek schools in developing his own political philosophy."

[115] Habas (1951), p. xii.

[116] As argued in Nelson (1996), p. 77.

[117] Cicero, *The Laws,* cited in Nelson, p. 93.

[118] As Cicero claimed that his wisdom came from those before him, it is sometimes difficult to know if he actually came up with these ideas himself!

[119] Sabine comments: "His idea of morality in public life was tied to the Roman virtue of public service but Cicero would contradict himself, which makes reading his works for a distinct political theory difficult." Seemingly out of frustration, Sabine concludes: "Cicero lacked the originality to strike out a new theory for himself . . ." Sabine (1966), p. 163.

[120] Hugo Grotius, *De Jure Belli ac Pacis,* 1648, Chapter 5, Part I. Grotius, whose work is excerpted in Chapter 3, was influenced by the readings of, notably, Cicero, Polybius, and Livy. See also: Sabine, op. cit., pp. 422 et seq.

ment, may be lawful" is fully acknowledged by Grotius as fact. In striving to break new ground by surveying the norms, customs, and rules of international behavior, Grotius has no choice but to acknowledge the wisdom of Cicero's realist arguments. Like it or not, Cicero seems to remind us, lies are sometimes told and people are sometimes killed in the name of the Republic. These are talents, which Cicero, "in many parts of his writings, acknowledges are absolutely necessary for a statesman to possess."[121]

Nearing the end of his life, Cicero's concern was that the Romans would lose their way, forget their duty to the state, and thereby suffer the fate of political disorder. Yet, as Meier reminds us, in retrospect: "When Cicero declared that the republic was lost it was still in existence. When Augustus said it was restored it had come to an end."[122] Ultimately, in the streets of Formiae, outside Rome, he was stalked and murdered.[123] Perhaps the best lesson that the Romans have left us with can be summed up as *historia magistra vitae* (i.e., history is the best teacher of life).

---

[121] Grotius, op. cit.

[122] Meier (1982), p. 496. Cicero notably impacted the thinking of Emperor Justinian. In Sabine's view: "The significance of Cicero on Justinian cannot be understated. Justinian's Institutes impacted the direction of Roman legal thinking and Roman law became one of the greatest intellectual forces in the history of European civilization." Sabine (1966), p. 168.

[123] The details are even grimmer; Cicero was beheaded. His head and right hand were then put on public display.

READING 2: NICCOLÒ MACHIAVELLI

At twenty-six, Machiavelli met the cruel, belligerent Cesare Borgia while working in the Florentine diplomatic service. With the fall of the republic in 1512, the young Machiavelli was suddenly unemployed. Now exiled from Florence, he wrote *The Prince* in haste, dedicating it to Lorenzo de Medici. His hope was that he might find employment with the powerful de Medici family. Tragically for Machiavelli the "letter" was never read by Lorenzo.[124]

Machiavelli's writing coincides with the development of powerful city–states in northern Italy, many of which were making fortunes through trade.[125] Starting at about the same time in Europe, in a period that lasted from roughly 1500–1750, the practice of mercantilism also thrived. The logic of mercantilists was that there was only so much wealth in the world and to gain state power one had to acquire it. Their primary aim was to place as much *gold* in their own state coffers as possible and by any means necessary, including theft and plunder. The issue that Machiavelli is fascinated with—as all European leaders were—is the issue of *power:* how to acquire it and how to maintain it. In practice, however, mercantilism was not the only path to power. Also throughout Europe, modern capitalism was now taking hold, and merchant bankers were making fortunes financing seagoing

---

[124] In fact, Machiavelli's work was plagiarized for years afterward. This has been researched by Jean Félix Nourrison in *Machiavel* (Paris 1875), who argues that *The Prince* was plagiarized by Augustino Nifo in 1523, nine years before the *Prince* text, that we now know, appeared. For this, and other details regarding this period, see J. Bronowski and Bruce Mazlish, *The Western Intellectual Tradition: From Leonardo to Hegel* (New York: Harper & Row, 1960), Ch. 3. Details regarding plagiarism in note 1, p. 29.

[125] Starting at about the same time, in a period that lasted from roughly 1500–1750, the practice of Mercantilism also thrived. The logic of Mercantilists was that there was only so much wealth in the world and to gain state power one had to acquire it. Their primary aim was to place as much *gold* in their own state coffers as possible and by any means necessary, including theft and plunder.

traders. Although formal theories on free trade were not yet developed, all of these sudden changes in power challenged the hierarchy of European society that had dominated during the feudal era.[126] Individuals of all kinds were now making fortunes in new ways including artists, like Leonardo DaVinci, who were supported by both the old order and the *nouveau riche* alike. This was the height of the Italian Renaissance wherein advances in the arts, literature, and modern science seemed to offer limitless possibilities. Alongside these great advances, another art was developing: the art of diplomacy.[127]

---

[126] The era is brilliantly described in Bronowski and Mazlish (1960), Chapter 2.

[127] Ibid., p. 21.

Niccolò Machiavelli

The Prince, ca. 1513

Of the Things for which Men, and Especially Princes, are Praised or Blamed

It now remains to be seen what are the methods and rules for a prince as regards his subjects and friends. And as I know that many have written of this, I fear that my writing about it may be deemed presumptuous, differing as I do, especially in this matter, from the opinions of others. *But my intention being to write something of use to those who understand, it appears to me more proper to go to the real truth of the matter than to its imagination; and many have imagined republics and principalities which have never been seen or known to exist in reality; for how we live is so far removed from how we ought to live, that he who abandons what is done for what ought to be done, will rather learn to bring about his own ruin than his preservation. A man who wishes to make a profession of goodness in everything must necessarily come to grief among so many who are not good. Therefore it is necessary for a prince, who wishes to maintain himself, to learn how not to be good, and to use this knowledge and not use it, according to the necessity of the case.*

Leaving on one side, then, those things which concern only an imaginary prince, and speaking of those that are real, I state that all men, and especially princes, who are placed at a greater height, are reputed for certain qualities which bring them either praise or blame. Thus one is considered liberal, another *misero* or miserly (using a Tuscan term, seeing that *avaro* with us still means one who is rapaciously acquisitive and *misero* one who makes grudging use of his own); one a free giver, another rapacious; one cruel, another merciful; one a breaker of his word, another trustworthy; one effeminate and pusillanimous, another fierce and high-spirited; one humane, another haughty; one lascivious, another chaste; one frank, another astute; one hard, another easy; one serious, another frivolous; one religious, another an unbeliever, and so on. I know that every one will admit that it would be highly praiseworthy in a prince to possess all the above-named qualities that are reputed good, but as they cannot all be possessed or observed, human conditions not permitting of it, it is necessary that he should be prudent enough to avoid the scandal of those vices which would lose him the state, and guard himself if possible against those which will not lose it him, but if not able to, he can indulge them with less scruple. And yet he must not mind incurring the scandal of those vices, without which it would be difficult to save the state, for if one considers well, it will be found that some things which seem virtues would, if followed, lead to one's ruin, and some others which appear vices result in one's greater security and wellbeing.

▣▮▣▮

Niccolò Machiavelli, *The Prince and the Discourses*, (Modern Library College Editions, 1950).

OF CRUELTY AND CLEMENCY, AND WHETHER IT IS BETTER TO BE LOVED OR FEARED

Proceeding to the other qualities before named, I say that every prince must desire to be considered merciful and not cruel. He must, however, take care not to misuse this mercifulness. Cesare Borgia was considered cruel, but his cruelty had brought order to the Romagna, united it, and reduced it to peace and fealty. If this is considered well, it will be seen that he was really much more merciful than the Florentine people, who, to avoid the name of cruelty, allowed Pistoia to be destroyed. A prince, therefore, must not mind incurring the charge of cruelty for the purpose of keeping his subjects united and faithful; for, with a very few examples, he will be more merciful than those who, from excess of tenderness, allow disorders to arise, from whence spring bloodshed and rapine; for these as a rule injure the whole community, while the executions carried out by the prince injure only individuals. And of all princes, it is impossible for a new prince to escape the reputation of cruelty, new states being always full of dangers. Wherefore Virgil though the mouth of Dido says:

Res dura, et regni novitas me talia cogunt Moliri, et late fines custode tueri.

Nevertheless, he must be cautious in believing and acting, and must not be afraid of his own shadow, and must proceed in a temperate manner with prudence and humanity, so that too much confidence does not render him incautious, and too much diffidence does not render him intolerant. From this arises the question whether it is better to be loved more than feared, or feared more than loved. The reply is, that one ought to be both feared and loved, but as it is difficult for the two to go together, it is much safer to be feared than loved, if one of the two has to be wanting. For it may be said of men in general that they are ungrateful, voluble, dissemblers, anxious to avoid danger, and covetous of gain; as long as you benefit them, they are entirely yours; they offer you their blood, their goods, their life, and their children, as I have before said, when the necessity is remote; but when it approaches, they revolt. And the prince who has relied solely on their words, without making other preparations, is ruined; for the friendship which is gained by purchase and not through grandeur and nobility of spirit is bought but not secured, and at a pinch is not to be expended in your service. And men have less scruple in offending one who makes himself loved than one who makes himself feared; for love is held by a chain of obligation which, men being selfish, is broken whenever it serves their purpose; but fear is maintained by a dread of punishment which never fails.

Still, a prince should make himself feared in such a way that if he does not gain love, he at any rate avoids hatred; for fear and the absence of hatred may well go together, and will be always attained by one who abstains from interfering with the property of his citizens and subjects or with their women. And when he is obliged to take the life of any one, let him do so when there is a proper justification and manifest reason for it; but above all he must abstain from taking the property of others, for men forget more easily the death of their father than the loss of their patrimony. Then also pretexts for seizing property are never wanting, and one who begins to live by rapine will always find some reason for taking the goods of others, whereas causes for taking life are rarer and more fleeting.

But when the prince is with his army and has a large number of soldiers under his control, then it is extremely necessary that he should not mind being thought cruel; for without this reputation he could not keep an army united or disposed to any duty. Among the noteworthy actions of Hannibal is numbered this, that although he had an enormous army, composed of men of all nations and fighting in foreign countries, there never arose any dissension either among them or against the prince, either in good fortune or in bad. This could not be due to anything but his inhuman cruelty, which together with his infinite other virtues, made him always venerated and terrible in the sight of his soldiers, and without it his other virtues would not have sufficed to produce that effect. Thoughtless writers admire on the one hand his actions, and on the other blame the principal cause of them.

And that it is true that his other virtues would not have sufficed may be seen from the case of Scipio (famous not only in regard to his own times, but all times of which memory remains), whose armies rebelled against him in Spain, which arose from nothing but his excessive kindness, which allowed more licence to the soldiers than was consonant with military discipline. He was reproached with this in the senate by Fabius Maximus, who called him a corrupter of the Roman militia. Locri having been destroyed by one of Scipio's officers was not revenged by him, nor was the insolence of that officer punished, simply by reason of his easy nature; so much so, that some one wishing to excuse him in the senate, said that there were many men who knew rather how not to err, than how to correct the errors of others. This disposition would in time have tarnished the fame and glory of Scipio had he persevered in it under the empire, but living under the rule of the senate this harmful quality was not only concealed but became a glory to him.

I conclude, therefore, with regard to being feared and loved, that men love at their own free will, but fear at the will of the prince, and that a wise prince must rely on what is in his power and not on what is in the power of others, and he must only contrive to avoid incurring hatred, as has been explained.

◼◻◼◻

To Found a New Republic, or to Reform Entirely the Old Institutions of an Existing One, Must be the Work of One Man Only

It may perhaps appear to some that I have gone too far into the details of Roman history before having made any mention of the founders of that republic, or of her institutions, her religion, and her military establishment. Not wishing, therefore, to keep any longer in suspense the desires of those who wish to understand these matters, I say that many will perhaps consider it an evil example that the founder of a civil society, as Romulus was, should first have killed his brother, and then have consented to the death of Titus Tatius, who had been elected to share the royal authority with him; from which it might be concluded that the citizens, according to the example of their prince, might, from ambition and the desire to rule, destroy those who attempt to oppose their authority. This opinion would be correct, if we do not take into consideration the object which Romulus had in view in committing that homicide. *But we must assume, as a general rule, that it never or rarely happens that a republic or monarchy is well constituted, or its old institutions entirely reformed, unless it is done by only one individual; it is even necessary that he whose mind has conceived such a constitution should be alone in carrying it into effect.* A sagacious legislator of a republic, therefore, whose object is to promote the public good, and not his private interests, and who prefers his country to his own successors, should concentrate all authority in himself; and a wise mind will never censure any one for having employed any extraordinary means for the purpose of establishing a kingdom or constituting a republic. It is well that, when the act accuses him, the result should excuse him; and when the result is good, as in the case of Romulus, it will always absolve him from blame. *For he is to be reprehended who commits violence for the purpose of destroying, and not he who employs it for beneficent purposes.* The lawgiver should, however, be sufficiently wise and virtuous not to leave this authority which he has assumed either to his heirs or to any one else; for mankind, being more prone to evil than to good, his successor might employ for evil purposes the power which he had used only for good ends. Besides, although one man alone should organize a government, yet it will not endure long if the administration of it remains on the shoulders of a single individual; it is well, then, to confide this to the charge of many, for thus it will be sustained by the many. Therefore, as the organization of anything cannot be made by many, because the divergence of their opinions hinders them from agreeing as to what is best, yet, when once they do understand it, they will not readily agree to abandon it. That Romulus deserves to be excused for the death of his brother and that of his associate, and that what he had done was for the general good, and not for the gratification of his own ambition, is proved by the fact that he immediately instituted a Senate with which to consult, and according to the opinions of which he might form his resolutions. And on carefully considering the authority which Romulus reserved for himself, we see that all he kept was the command of the army in case of war, and the power of convoking the Senate. This was seen when Rome became free, after the expulsion of the Tarquins, when there was no other innovation made upon the existing order of things than the substitution of two Consuls, appointed annually, in place of an hereditary king; which proves clearly that all the original institutions of that city were more in conformity with the requirements of a free and civil society than with an absolute and tyrannical government.

The above views might be corroborated by any number of examples, such as those of Moses, Lycurgus, Solon, and other founders of monarchies and republics, who were enabled to establish laws suitable for the general good only by keeping for themselves an exclusive authority; but all these are so well known that I will not further refer to them. I will adduce only one instance, not so celebrated, but which merits the consideration of those who aim to become good legislators: it is this. Agis, king of Sparta, desired to bring back the Spartans to the strict observance of the laws of Lycurgus, being convinced that, by deviating from them, their city had lost much of her ancient virtue, and consequently her power and dominion; but the Spartan Ephores had him promptly killed, as one who attempted to make himself a tyrant. His successor, Cleomenes, had conceived the same desire, from studying the records and writings of Agis, which he had found, and which explained his aims and intentions. Cleomenes was convinced that he would be unable to render this service to his country unless he possessed sole authority; for he judged that, owing to the ambitious nature of men, he could not promote the interests of the many against the will of the few; and therefore he availed of a convenient opportunity to have all the Ephores slain, as well as all such others as might oppose his project, after which he restored the laws of Lycurgus entirely. This course was calculated to resuscitate the greatness of Sparta, and to give Cleomenes a reputation equal to that of Lycurgus, had it not been for the power of the Macedonians and the weakness of the other Greek republics. For being soon after attacked by the Macedonians, and Sparta by herself being inferior in strength, and there being no one whom he could call to his aid, he was defeated; and thus his project, so just and laudable, was never put into execution. Considering, then, all these things, I conclude that, to found a republic, one must be alone; and that Romulus deserves to be absolved from, and not blamed for, the death of Remus and of Tatius.

READING 3: THOMAS HOBBES

Thomas Hobbes studied the classics at Oxford, a college in which Puritanism was then a dominant force. While at Oxford, Hobbes developed the skills necessary to work on a complete translation of Thucydides' *History of the Peloponnesian War*—an endeavor that took him many years to complete. There can be little doubt that this endeavor gave Hobbes some concrete ideas about realist practice in history. Like his contemporary on the European continent, René Descartes, Hobbes was anxious to turn his back on the Jesuit approaches to learning and to look in the direction of science, toward learned men such as Galileo.[128]

---

[128] During his lifetime, Hobbes was able to meet with both Descartes and Galileo. See: Bronowski and Mazlish (1960), p. 195.

Religion was the primary issue with which Hobbes had to struggle when presenting his political ideas. He circulated among friends an essay entitled *Elements of Law* (1640) that espoused a theory of "undivided sovereignty without divine right."[129] Nevertheless, after his publication of *De Cive* (1642), Hobbes became known on the continent as a staunch supporter of Protestantism. Hobbes was also a supporter of absolute monarchy, and he was known, during his lifetime, as a "royalist." For this reason he was forced to leave for France during the civil war that engulfed seventeenth-century England. After six years of exile in Paris (1640–1646) Hobbes was able to return safely to England under Cromwell.[130] Later, following the death of Cromwell in 1658, Hobbes would be disappointed as the divine right monarchy of the Stuarts required that political changes be made to the Latin version of *The Leviathan* (1688).

---

[129] Herbert W. Schneider, ed., *Thomas Hobbes: The Leviathan, Parts I and II* (New York: Bobbs-Merrill, 1958), p. viii.

[130] Ibid., pp. viii–ix.

THOMAS HOBBES

THE LEVIATHAN, 1661

OF THE NATURAL CONDITION OF MANKIND AS CONCERNING THEIR FELICITY AND MISERY

Nature has made men so equal in the faculties of the body and mind as that, though there be found one man sometimes manifestly stronger in body or of quicker mind than another, yet, when all is reckoned together, the difference between man and man is not so considerable as that one man can thereupon claim to himself any benefit to which another may not pretend as well as he. For as to the strength of body, the weakest has strength enough to kill the strongest, either by secret machination or by confederacy with others that are in the same danger with himself.

And as to the faculties of the mind, setting aside the arts grounded upon words, and especially that skill of proceeding upon general and infallible rules called science—which very few have and but in few things, as being not a native faculty born with us, nor attained, as prudence, while we look after somewhat else—I find yet a greater equality among men than that of strength. For prudence is but experience, which equal time equally bestows on all men in those things they equally apply themselves unto. That which may perhaps make such equality incredible is but a vain conceit of one's own wisdom, which almost all men think they have in a greater degree than the vulgar—that is, than all men but themselves and a few others whom, by fame or for concurring with themselves, they approve. For such is the nature of men that howsoever they may acknowledge many others to be more witty or more eloquent or more learned, yet they will hardly believe there be many so wise as themselves, for they see their own wit at hand and other men's at a distance. But this proves rather that men are in that point equal than unequal. For there is not ordinarily a greater sign of the equal distribution of anything than that every man is contented with his share.

From this equality of ability arises equality of hope in the attaining of our ends. And therefore if any two men desire the same thing, which nevertheless they cannot both enjoy, they be-

---

Thomas Hobbes, *Leviathan, Parts One and Two,* (Library of Liberal Arts, 1958) (Lib. Arts Press).

come enemies; and in the way to their end, which is principally their own conservation, and sometimes their delectation only, endeavor to destroy or subdue one another. And from hence it comes to pass that where an invader has no more to fear than another man's single power, if one plant, sow, build, or posses a convenient seat, others may probably be expected to come prepared with forces united to dispossess and deprive him, not only of the fruit of his labor, but also of his life or liberty. And the invader again is in the like danger of another.

And from this diffidence of one another there is no way for any man to secure himself so reasonable as anticipation—that is, by force or wiles to master the persons of all men he can, so long till he see no other power great enough to endanger him; and this is no more than his own conservation requires, and is generally allowed. Also, because there be some that take pleasure in contemplating their own power in the acts of conquest, which they pursue farther than their security requires, if others that otherwise would be glad to be at ease within modest bounds should not by invasion increase their power, they would not be able, long time, by standing only on their defense, to subsist. And by consequence, such augmentation of dominion over men being necessary to a man's conservation, it ought to be allowed him.

Again, men have no pleasure, but on the contrary a great deal of grief, in keeping company where there is no power able to overawe them all. For every man looks that his companion should value him at the same rate he sets upon himself; and upon all signs of contempt or undervaluing naturally endeavors, as far as he dares (which among them that have no common power to keep them in quiet is far enough to make them destroy each other), to extort a greater value from his contemners by damage and from others by the example.

So that in the nature of man we find three principal causes of quarrel: first, competition; secondly, diffidence; thirdly, glory.

The first makes men invade for gain, the second for safety, and the third for reputation. The first use violence to make themselves masters of other men's persons, wives, children, and cattle; the second, to defend them; the third, for trifles, as a word, a smile, a different opinion, and any other sign of undervalue, either direct in their persons or by reflection in their kindred, their friends, their nation, their profession, or their name.

Hereby it is manifest that, during the time men live without a common power to keep them all in awe, they are in that condition which is called war, and such a war as is of every man against every man. For WAR consists not in battle only, or the act of fighting, but in a tract of time wherein the will to contend by battle is sufficiently known; and therefore the notion of *time* is to be considered in the nature of war as it is in the nature of weather. For as the nature of foul weather lies not in a shower or two of rain but in an inclination thereto of many days together, so the nature of war consists not in actual fighting but in the known disposition thereto during all the time there is no assurance to the contrary. All other time is PEACE.

Whatsoever, therefore, is consequent to a time of war where every man is enemy to every man, the same is consequent to the time wherein men live without other security than what their own strength and their own invention shall furnish them withal. In such condition there is no place for industry, because the fruit thereof is uncertain: and consequently no culture of the earth; no navigation nor use of the commodities that may be imported by sea; no commodious building; no instruments of moving and removing such things as require much force; no knowledge of the face of the earth; no account of time; no arts; no letters; no society; and, which is worst of all, continual fear and danger of violent death; and the life of man solitary, poor, nasty, brutish, and short.

It may seem strange to some man that has not well weighed these things that nature should thus dissociate and render men apt to invade and destroy one another; and he may therefore, not trusting to this inference made from the passions, desire perhaps to have the same confirmed by experience. Let him therefore consider with himself—when taking a journey he arms himself and seeks to go well accompanied, when going to sleep he locks his doors, when even in his house he locks his chests, and this when he knows there be laws and public officers, armed, to revenge all injuries shall be done him—what opinion he has of his fellow subjects when he rides armed, of his fellow citizens when he locks his doors, and of his children and servants when he locks his chests. Does he not there as much accuse mankind by his actions as I do by my words? But neither of us accuse man's nature in it. The desires and other passions of man are in themselves no sin. No more are the actions that proceed from those passions till they know a law that forbids them, which, till laws be made, they cannot know, nor can any law be made till they have agreed upon the person that shall make it.

It may peradventure be thought there was never such a time nor condition of war as this, and I believe it was never generally so over all the world; but there are many places where they live so now. For the savage people in many places of America, except the government of small families, the concord whereof depends on natural lust, have no government at all and live at this day in that brutish manner as I said before. Howsoever, it may be perceived what manner of life there would be where there were no common power to fear by the manner of life which men that have formerly lived under a peaceful government use to degenerate into in a civil war.

But though there had never been any time wherein particular men were in a condition of war one against another, yet in all times kings and persons of sovereign authority, because of their independency, are in continual jealousies and in the state and posture of gladiators, having their weapons pointing and their eyes fixed on one another—that is, their forts, garrisons, and guns upon the frontiers of their kingdoms, and continual spies upon their neighbors—which is a posture of war. But because they uphold thereby the industry of their subjects, there does not follow from it that misery which accompanies the liberty of particular men.

To this war of every man against every man, this also is consequent: that nothing can be unjust. The notions of right and wrong, justice and injustice, have there no place. Where there is no common power, there is no law; where no law, no injustice. Force and fraud are in war the two cardinal virtues. Justice and injustice are none of the faculties neither of the body nor mind. If they were, they might be in a man that were alone in the world, as well as his senses and passions. They are qualities that relate to men in society, not in solitude. It is consequent also to the same condition that there be no propriety, no dominion, no *mine* and *thine* distinct; but only that to be every man's that he can get, and for so long as he can keep it. And thus much for the ill condition which man by mere nature is actually placed in, though with a possibility to come out of it consisting partly in the passions, partly in his reason.

The passions that incline men to peace are fear of death, desire of such things as are necessary to commodious living, and a hope by their industry to obtain them.

■■■■

OF THE OFFICE OF THE SOVEREIGN REPRESENTATIVE

The office of the sovereign, be it a monarch or an assembly, consists in the end for which he was trusted with the sovereign power, namely, the procuration of *the safety of the people*; to which he is obliged by the law of nature, and to render an account thereof to God, the author of that law, and to none but him. But by safety here is not meant a bare preservation but also all other contentments of life which every man by lawful industry, without danger or hurt to the commonwealth, shall acquire to himself.

And this is intended should be done, not by care applied to individuals further than their protection from injuries when they shall complain, but by a general providence contained in public instruction, both of doctrine and example, and in the making and executing of good laws, to which individual persons may apply their own cases.

And because, if the essential rights of sovereignty, specified before in the eighteenth chapter, be taken away, the commonwealth is thereby dissolved and every man returns into the condition and calamity of a war with every other man, which is the greatest evil that can happen in this life, it is the office of the sovereign to maintain those rights entire, and consequently against his duty, first, to transfer to another or to lay from himself any of them. For he that deserts the means deserts the ends; and he deserts the means that, being the sovereign, acknowledges himself subject to the civil laws and renounces the power of supreme judicature, or of making war or peace by his own authority, or of judging of the necessities of the commonwealth, or of levying money and soldiers when and as much as in his own conscience he shall judge necessary, or of making officers and ministers both of war and peace, or of appointing teachers and examining what doctrines are conformable or contrary to the defense, peace, and good of the people. Secondly, it is against his duty to let the people be ignorant or misinformed of the grounds and reasons of those his essential rights, because thereby men are easy to be seduced and drawn to resist him when the commonwealth shall require their use and exercise.

And the grounds of these rights have the rather need to be diligently and truly taught, because they cannot be maintained by any civil law or terror of legal punishment. For a civil law that shall forbid rebellion (and such is all resistance to the essential rights of the sovereignty) is not, as a civil law, any obligation, but by virtue only of the law of nature that forbids the violation of faith; which natural obligation if men know not, they cannot know the right of any law the sovereign makes. And for the punishment, they take it but for an act of hostility which, when they think they have strength enough, they will endeavor by acts of hostility to avoid.

But they say again that though the principles be right, yet common people are not of capacity enough to be made to understand them. I should be glad that the rich and potent subjects of a kingdom or those that are accounted the most learned were no less incapable than they. But all men know that the obstructions to this kind of doctrine proceed not so much from the difficulty of the matter as from the interest of them that are to learn. Potent men digest hardly anything that sets up a power to bridle their affections, and learned men anything that discovers their errors and thereby lessens their authority; whereas the common people's minds, unless they be tainted with dependence on the potent or scribbled over with the opinions of their doctors, are like clean paper, fit to receive whatsoever by public authority shall be imprinted in them. Shall whole nations be brought to *acquiesce* in the great mysteries of the Christian religion which are above reason, and millions of men be made believe that the same body may be in innumerable places at one and the same time, which is against reason; and shall not men be able, by their teaching and preaching, protected by the law, to make that received which is so consonant to reason that any unprejudicated man needs no more to learn it than to hear it? I conclude, therefore, that in the instruction of the people in the essential rights which are the natural and fundamental laws of sovereignty there is no difficulty, while a sovereign has his power entire, but what proceeds from his own fault or the fault of those whom he trusts in the administration of the commonwealth; and consequently, it is his duty to cause them so to be instructed, and not only his duty but his benefit also, and security against the danger that may arrive to himself in his natural person from rebellion.

And, to descend to particulars, the people are to be taught, first, that they ought not to be in love with any form of government they see in their neighbor nations more than with their own, nor, whatsoever present prosperity they behold in nations that are otherwise governed than they, to desire change. For the prosperity of a people ruled by an aristocratical or democratical assembly comes not from aristocracy nor from democracy but from the obedience and concord of the subjects; nor do the people flourish in a monarchy because one man has the right to rule them but because they obey him. Take away in any kind of state the obedience and consequently the concord of the people, and they shall not only not flourish but in short time be dissolved. And they that go about by disobedience to do no more than reform the commonwealth shall find they do thereby destroy it; like the foolish daughters of Pelius in the fable, which, desiring to renew the youth of their decrepit father, did by the counsel of Medea cut him in pieces and boil him together with strange herbs, but made not of him a new man. This desire of change is like the breach of the first of God's commandments, for there God says *Non habebis Deos alienos*—Thou shalt not have the Gods of other nations[1] and in another place concerning *kings* that they are *Gods*.[2]

Secondly, they are to be taught that they ought not to be led with admiration of the virtue of any of their fellow subjects, how high soever he stand or how conspicuously soever he shine in the commonwealth; nor of any assembly, except the sovereign assembly, so as to defer to them any obedience or honor appropriate to the sovereign only, whom, in their particular stations, they represent; nor to receive any influence from them but such as is conveyed by them from the sovereign authority. For that sovereign cannot be imagined to love his people as he ought that is not jealous of them but suffers them by the flattery of popular men to be seduced from their loyalty, as they have often been, not only secretly, but openly, so as to proclaim marriage with them in *facie ecclesiae*[3] by preachers and by publishing the same in the open streets—which may fitly be compared to the violation of the second of the ten commandments.[4]

Thirdly, in consequence to this, they ought to be informed how great a fault it is to speak evil of the sovereign representative, whether one man or an assembly of men; or to argue and dispute his power; or any way to use his name irreverently, whereby he may be brought into contempt with his people, and their obedience, in which the safety of the commonwealth consists, slackened. Which doctrine the third commandment by resemblance points to.[5]

Fourthly, seeing people cannot be taught this, nor when it is taught remember it, nor after one generation past so much as know in whom the sovereign power is placed, without setting apart from their ordinary labor some certain times in which they may attend those that are appointed to instruct them, it is necessary that some such times be determined wherein they may assemble together and, after prayers and praises given to God, the sovereign of sovereigns, hear those their duties told them, and the positive laws, such as generally concern them all, read and expounded, and be put in mind of the authority that makes them laws. To this end had the Jews every seventh day a Sabbath, in which the law was read and expounded, and in the solemnity whereof they were put in mind: that their king was God; that having created the world in six days, he rested the seventh day; and by their resting on it from their labor, that that God was their king which redeemed them from their servile and painful labor in Egypt and gave them a time, after they had rejoiced in God, to take joy also in themselves by lawful recreation.[6] So that the first table of the commandments is spent all in setting down the sum of God's absolute power—not only as God but as king by pact, in peculiar, of the Jews; and may therefore give light to those that have sovereign power conferred on them by the consent of men to see what doctrine they ought to teach their subjects.

And because the first instruction of children depends on the care of their parents, it is necessary that they should be obedient to them while they are under their tuition; and not only so, but that also afterwards, as gratitude requires, they acknowledge the benefit of their education by external signs of honor. To which end they are to be taught that originally the father of every man was also his sovereign lord, with power over him of life and death; and that the fathers of families, when by instituting a commonwealth they resigned that absolute power, yet it was never intended they should lose the honor due unto them for their education. For to relinquish

---

[1] [Exod. 20:3; Deut. 5:7.]

[2] [The reference is to the ancient origins of the belief in the divine right of kings.]

[3] [This refers to the Church's doctrine that a marriage, to be valid, must be solemnized by ecclesiastical rites.]

[4] [Exod. 20:4–5; Deut. 5:8–10.]

[5] [Exod. 20:7; Deut. 5:11.]

[6] [Exod. 20:8–11; Deut. 5:13–15.]

such right was not necessary to the institution of sovereign power, nor would there be any reason why any man should desire to have children or take the care to nourish and instruct them if they were afterwards to have no other benefit from them than from other men. And this accords with the fifth commandment.[7]

Again, every sovereign ought to cause justice to be taught, which, consisting in taking from no man what is his, is as much as to say, to cause men to be taught not to deprive their neighbors, by violence or fraud, of anything which by the sovereign authority is theirs. Of things held in propriety, those that are dearest to a man are his own life and limbs; and in the next degree, in most men, those that concern conjugal affection; and after them, riches and means of living. Therefore the people are to be taught to abstain from violence of one another's person by private revenges; from violation of conjugal honor; and from forcible rapine and fraudulent surreption of one another's goods. For which purpose also it is necessary they be showed the evil consequences of false judgment, by corruption either of judges or witnesses, whereby the distinction of propriety is taken away and justice becomes of no effect—all which things are intimated in the sixth, seventh, eighth, and ninth commandments.[8]

Lastly, they are to be taught that not only the unjust facts but the designs and intentions to do them, though by accident hindered, are injustice, which consists in the pravity of the will as well as in the irregularity of the act. And this is the intention of the tenth commandment[9] and the sum of the second table, which is reduced all to this one commandment of mutual charity, *thou shalt love thy neighbor as thyself,*[10] as the sum of the first table is reduced to *the love of God,* whom they had then newly received as their king.

■■■■

To the care of the sovereign belongs the making of good laws. But what is a good law? By a good law I mean not a just law, for no law can be unjust. The law is made by the sovereign power, and all that is done by such power is warranted and owned by every one of the people; and that which every man will have so, no man can say is unjust. It is in the laws of a commonwealth as in the laws of gaming: whatsoever the gamesters all agree on is injustice to none of them. A good law is that which is *needful* for the *good of the people,* and withal *perspicuous.*

For the use of laws, which are but rules authorized, is not to bind the people from all voluntary actions but to direct and keep them in such a motion as not to hurt themselves by their own impetuous desires, rashness, or indiscretion—as hedges are set, not to stop travelers, but to keep them in their way. And therefore a law that is not needful, having not the true end of a law, is not good. A law may be conceived to be good when it is for the benefit of the sovereign though it be not necessary for the people; but it is not so. For the good of the sovereign and people cannot be separated. It is a weak sovereign that has weak subjects, and a weak people whose sovereign wants power to rule them at his will. Unnecessary laws are not good laws but traps for money, which, where the right of sovereign power is acknowledged, are superfluous, and where it is not acknowledged, insufficient to defend the people.

■■■■

A commander of any army in chief, if he be not popular, shall not be beloved nor feared as he ought to be by his army and consequently cannot perform that office with good success. He

---

[7] [Exod. 20:12; Deut. 5:16.]

[8] [Exod. 20:13–16; Deut. 5:17–20.]

[9] [Exod. 20:17; Deut. 5:21.]

[10] [Lev. 19:18.]

must therefore be industrious, valiant, affable, liberal, and fortunate that he may gain an opinion both of sufficiency and of loving his soldiers. This is popularity, and breeds in the soldiers both desire and courage to recommend themselves to his favor; and protects the severity of the general in punishing, when need is, the mutinous or negligent soldiers. But this love of soldiers, if caution be not given of the commander's fidelity, is a dangerous thing to sovereign power, especially when it is in the hands of an assembly not popular. It belongs therefore to the safety of the people both that they be good conductors and faithful subjects to whom the sovereign commits his armies.

But when the sovereign himself is popular—that is, reverenced and beloved of his people— there is no danger at all from the popularity of a subject. For soldiers are never so generally unjust as to side with their captain, though they love him, against their sovereign, when they love not only his person but also his cause. And therefore those who by violence have at any time suppressed the power of their lawful sovereign, before they could settle themselves in his place have been always put to the trouble of contriving their titles to save the people from the shame of receiving them. To have a known right to sovereign power is so popular a quality as he that has it needs no more, for his own part, to turn the hearts of his subjects to him but that they see him able absolutely to govern his own family; nor, on the part of his enemies, but a disbanding of their armies. For the greatest and most active part of mankind has never hitherto been well contented with the present.

Concerning the offices of one sovereign to another, which are comprehended in that law which is commonly called the *law of nations,* I need not say anything in this place because the law of nations and the law of nature is the same thing. And every sovereign has the same right in procuring the safety of his people that any particular man can have in procuring the safety of his own body. And the same law that dictates to men that have no civil government what they ought to do and what to avoid in regard of one another dictates the same to commonwealths— that is, to the consciences of sovereign princes and sovereign assemblies, there being no court of natural justice but in the conscience only, where not man but God reigns, whose laws, such of them as oblige all mankind, in respect of God as he is the author of nature are *natural,* and in respect of the same God as he is King of kings are *laws.* But of the kingdom of God as King of kings and as King also of a peculiar people, I shall speak in the rest of this discourse.

READING 4: HANS J. MORGENTHAU

Hans Joachim Morgenthau's intellectual development took place in Germany during the Weimar Republic. What he witnessed there was the eventual victory of fascism over democracy. As a German and a Jew Morgenthau was forced to flee to America, where he was able to eventually write his greatly influential text, *Politics Among Nations.* Following its publication and the growing tensions between East and West, Morgenthau was regularly sought out as a key contributor to the ongoing Cold War debates over foreign policy.[131]

---

[131] We now have the first "intellectual biography" on Hans J. Morgenthau, written by Swiss political science professor, Christoph Frei (translated from the original German text): *Hans J. Morgenthau: An Intellectual Biography* (Baton Rouge: Louisiana State University Press, 2001). As an undergraduate student from 1980–84 (i.e., the last years of the Cold War), Morgenthau's text was still considered by many professors to be the most authoritative statement on the subject of international politics.

A) HANS J. MORGENTHAU,

POLITICS AMONG NATIONS, 1948

A REALIST THEORY OF INTERNATIONAL POLITICS

This book purports to present a theory of international politics. The test by which such a theory must be judged is not *a priori* and abstract but empirical and pragmatic. The theory, in other words, must be judged not by some preconceived abstract principle or concept unrelated to reality, but by its purpose: to bring order and meaning to a mass of phenomena which without it would remain disconnected and unintelligible. It must meet a dual test, an empirical and a logical one: Do the facts as they actually are lend themselves to the interpretation the theory has put upon them, and do the conclusions at which the theory arrives follow with logical necessity from its premises? In short, is the theory consistent with the facts and within itself?

The issue this theory raises concerns the nature of all politics. The history of modern political thought is the story of a contest between two schools that differ fundamentally in their conceptions and the nature of man, society, and politics. One believes that a rational and moral political order, derived from universally valid abstract principles, can be achieved here and now. It assumes the essential goodness and infinite malleability of human nature, and blames the failure of the social order to measure up to the rational standards on lack of knowledge and understanding, obsolescent social institutions, or the depravity of certain isolated individuals or groups. It trusts in education, reform, and the sporadic use of force to remedy these defects.

The other school believes that the world, imperfect as it is from the rational point of view, is the result of forces inherent in human nature. To improve the world one must work with those forces, not against them. This being inherently a world of opposing interests and of conflict among them, moral principles can never be fully realized, but must at best be approximated through the ever temporary balancing of interests and the ever precarious settlement of conflicts. This school, then, sees in a system of checks and balances a universal principle for all pluralist societies. It appeals to historic precedent rather than to abstract principles, and aims at the realization of the lesser evil rather than of the absolute good.

This theoretical concern with human nature as it actually is, and with the historic processes as they actually take place, has earned for the theory presented here the name of realism. What are the tenets of political realism? No systematic exposition of the philosophy of political realism can be attempted here; it will suffice to single out six fundamental principles, which have frequently been misunderstood.

SIX PRINCIPLES OF POLITICAL REALISM

1. Political realism believes that politics, like society in general, is governed by objective laws that have their roots in human nature. In order to improve society it is first necessary to understand the laws by which society lives. The operation of these laws being impervious to our preferences, men will challenge them only at the risk of failure.

Realism, believing as it does in the objectivity of the laws of politics, must also believe in the possibility of developing a rational theory that reflects, however imperfectly and one-sidedly, these objective laws. It believes also, then, in the possibility of distinguishing in politics between truth and opinion—between what is true objectively and rationally, supported by evidence and illuminated by reason, and what is only a subjective judgment, divorced from the facts as they are and informed by prejudice and wishful thinking.

Human nature, in which the laws of politics have their roots, has not changed since the classical philosophies of China, India, and Greece endeavored to discover these laws. Hence, novelty is not necessarily a virtue in political theory, nor is old age a defect. The fact that a theory of politics, if there be such a theory, has never been heard of before tends to create a presumption against, rather than in favor of, its soundness. Conversely, the fact that a theory of politics was developed hundreds or even thousands of years ago—as was the theory of the balance of power—does not create a presumption that it must be outmoded and obsolete. A theory of politics must be subjected to the dual test of reason and experience. To dismiss such a theory because it had its flowering in centuries past is to present not a rational argument but a modernistic prejudice that takes for granted the superiority of the present over the past. To dispose of the revival of such a theory as a "fashion" or "fad" is tantamount to assuming that in matters political we can have opinions but no truths.

For realism, theory consists in ascertaining facts and giving them meaning through reason. It assumes that the character of a foreign policy can be ascertained only through the examination of the political acts performed and of the foreseeable consequences of these acts. Thus we can find out what statesmen have actually done, and from the foreseeable consequences of their acts we can surmise what their objectives might have been.

Yet examination of the facts is not enough. To give meaning to the factual raw material of foreign policy, we must approach political reality with a kind of rational outline, a map that suggests to us the possible meanings of foreign policy. In other words, we put ourselves in the position of a statesman who must meet a certain problem of foreign policy under certain circumstances, and we ask ourselves what the rational alternatives are from which a statesman may choose who must meet this problem under these circumstances (presuming always that he acts in a rational manner), and which of these rational alternatives is particular statesman, acting under these circumstances, is likely to choose. It is the testing of this rational hypothesis against the actual facts and their consequences that gives theoretical meaning to the facts of international politics.

2. The main signpost that helps political realism to find its way through the landscape of international politics is the concept of interest defined in terms of power. This concept provides the link between reason trying to understand international politics and the facts to be understood. It sets politics as an autonomous sphere of action and understanding apart from other spheres, such as economics (understood in terms of interest defined as wealth), ethics, aesthetics, or religion. Without such a concept a theory of politics, international or domestic, would be altogether impossible, for without it we could not distinguish between political and nonpolitical facts, nor could we bring at least a measure of systematic order to the political sphere.

We assume that statesmen think and act in terms of interest defined as power, and the evidence of history bears that assumption out. That assumption allows us to retrace and anticipate, as it were, the steps a statesman—past, present, or future—has taken or will take on the political scene. We look over his shoulder when he writes his dispatches; we listen in on his conversation with other statesmen; we read and anticipate his very thoughts. Thinking in terms of interest defined as power, we think as he does, and as disinterested observers we understand his thoughts and actions perhaps better than he, the actor on the political scene, does himself.

The concept of interest defined as power imposes intellectual discipline upon the observer, infuses rational order into the subject matter of politics, and thus makes the theoretical understanding of politics possible. On the side of the actor, it provides for rational discipline in action and creates that astounding continuity in foreign policy which makes American, British, or Russian foreign policy appear as an intelligible, rational continuum, by and large consistent within itself, regardless of the different motives, preferences, and intellectual and moral qualities of successive statesmen. A realist theory of international politics, then, will guard against two popular fallacies: the concern with motives and the concern with ideological preferences.

To search for the clue to foreign policy exclusively in the motives of statesmen is both futile and deceptive. It is futile because motives are the most illusive of psychological data, distorted as they are, frequently beyond recognition, by the interests and emotions of actor and observer alike. Do we really know what our own motives are? And what do we know of the motives of others?

Yet even if we had access to the real motives of statesmen, that knowledge would help us little in understanding foreign policies, and might well lead us astray. It is true that the knowledge of the statesman's motives may give us one among many clues as to what the direction of his foreign policy might be. It cannot give us, however, the one clue by which to predict his foreign policies. History shows no exact and necessary correlation between the quality of motives and the quality of foreign policy. This is true in both moral and political terms.

We cannot conclude from the good intentions of a statesman that his foreign policies will be either morally praiseworthy or politically successful. Judging his motives, we can say that he will not intentionally pursue policies that are morally wrong, but we can say nothing about the probability of their success. If we want to know the moral and political qualities of his actions, we must know them, not his motives. How often have statesmen been motivated by the desire to improve the world, and ended by making it worse? And how often have they sought one goal, and ended by achieving something they neither expected nor desired?

Neville Chamberlain's politics of appeasement were, as far as we can judge, inspired by good motives; he was probably less motivated by considerations of personal power than were many other British prime ministers, and he sought to preserve peace and to assure the happiness of all concerned. Yet his policies helped to make the Second World War inevitable, and to bring untold miseries to millions of men. Sir Winston Churchill's motives, on the other hand, were much less universal in scope and much more narrowly directed toward personal and national power, yet the foreign policies that sprang from these inferior motives were certainly superior in moral and political quality to those pursued by his predecessor. Judged by his motives, Robespierre was one of the most virtuous men who ever lived. Yet it was the utopian radicalism of that very virtue that made him kill those less virtuous than himself, brought him to the scaffold, and destroyed the revolution of which he was a leader.

Good motives give assurance against deliberately bad policies; they do not guarantee the moral goodness and political success of the policies they inspire. What is important to know, if one wants to understand foreign policy, is not primarily the motives of a statesman, but his intellectual ability to comprehend the essentials of foreign policy, as well as his political ability to translate what he has comprehended into successful political action. It follows that while ethics in the abstract judges the moral qualities of motives, political theory must judge the political qualities of intellect, will, and action.

A realist theory of international politics will also avoid the other popular fallacy of equating the foreign policies of a statesman with his philosophic or political sympathies, and of deducing the former from the latter. Statesmen, especially under contemporary conditions, may well make a habit of presenting their foreign policies in terms of their philosophic and political sympathies in order to gain popular support for them. Yet they will distinguish with Lincoln between their *"official* duty," which is to think and act in terms of the national interest, and their *"personal* wish," which is to see their own moral values and political principles realized throughout the world. Political realism does not require, nor does it condone, indifference to political ideals and moral principles, but it requires indeed a sharp distinction between the desirable and the possible—between what is desirable everywhere and at all times and what is possible under the concrete circumstances of time and place.

It stands to reason that not all foreign policies have always followed so rational, objective, and unemotional a course. The contingent elements of personality, prejudice, and subjective preference, and of all the weaknesses of intellect and will which flesh is heir to, are bound to deflect foreign policies from their rational course. Especially where foreign policy is conducted under the conditions of democratic control, the need to marshal popular emotions to the support of foreign policy cannot fail to impair the rationality of foreign policy itself. Yet a theory of foreign policy which aims at rationality must for the time being, as it were, abstract from these irrational elements and seek to paint a picture of foreign policy which presents the rational essence to be found in experience, without the contingent deviations from rationality which are also found in experience.

Deviations from rationality which are not the result of the personal whim or the personal psychopathology of the policy maker may appear contingent only from the vantage point of rationality, but may themselves be elements in a coherent system of irrationality. The conduct of the Indochina War by the United States suggests that possibility. It is a question worth looking into whether modern psychology and psychiatry have provided us with the conceptual tools which would enable us to construct, as it were, a counter-theory of irrational politics, a kind of pathology of international politics.

The experience of the Indochina War suggests five factors such a theory might encompass: the imposition upon the empirical world of a simplistic and *a priori* picture of the world derived from folklore and ideological assumption, that is, the replacement of experience with superstition; the refusal to correct this picture of the world in the light of experience; the persistence in a foreign policy derived from the misperception of reality and the use of intelligence for the purpose not of adapting policy to reality but of reinterpreting reality to fit policy; the egotism of the policy makers widening the gap between perception and policy, on the one hand, and reality, on the other; finally, the urge to close the gap at least subjectively by action, any kind of action, that creates the illusion of mastery over a recalcitrant reality. According to the *Wall Street Journal* of April 3, 1970, "the desire to 'do something' pervades top levels of Government and may overpower other 'common sense' advice that insists the U.S. ability to shape events is negligible. The yen for action could lead to bold policy as therapy."

The difference between international politics as it actually is and a rational theory derived from it is like the difference between a photograph and a painted portrait. The photograph shows everything that can be seen by the naked eye; the painted portrait does not show everything that can be seen by the naked eye, but it shows, or at least seeks to show, one thing that the naked eye cannot see: the human essence of the person portrayed.

Political realism contains not only a theoretical but also a normative element. It knows that political reality is replete with contingencies and systemic irrationalities and points to the typical influences they exert upon foreign policy. Yet it shares with all social theory the need, for the sake of theoretical understanding, to stress the rational elements of political reality; for it is these rational elements that make reality intelligible for theory. Political realism presents the theoretical construct of a rational foreign policy which experience can never completely achieve.

At the same time political realism considers a rational foreign policy to be good foreign policy; for only a rational foreign policy minimizes risks and maximizes benefits and, hence, complies both with the moral precept of prudence and the political requirement of success. Political realism wants the photographic picture of the political world to resemble as much as possible its painted portrait. Aware of the inevitable gap between good—that is, rational—foreign policy and foreign policy as it actually is, political realism maintains not only that theory must focus upon the rational elements of political reality, but also that foreign policy ought to be rational in view of its own moral and practical purposes.

Hence, it is no argument against the theory here presented that actual foreign policy does not or cannot live up to it. That argument misunderstands the intention of this book, which is to present not an indiscriminate description of political reality, but a rational theory of international politics. Far from being invalidated by the fact that, for instance, a perfect balance of power policy will scarcely be found in reality, it assumes that reality, being deficient in this respect, must be understood and evaluated as an approximation to an ideal system of balance of power.

3. Realism assumes that its key concept of interest defined as power is an objective category which is universally valid, but it does not endow that concept with a meaning that is fixed

once and for all. The idea of interest is indeed of the essence of politics and is unaffected by the circumstances of time and place. Thucydides' statement, born of the experiences of ancient Greece, that "identity of interests is the surest of bonds whether between states or individuals" was taken up in the nineteenth century by Lord Salisbury's remark that "the only bond of union that endures" among nations is "the absence of all clashing interests." It was erected into a general principle of government by George Washington:

> A small knowledge of human nature will convince us, that, with far the greatest part of mankind, interest is the governing principle; and that almost every man is more or less, under its influence. Motives of public virtue may for a time, or in particular instances, actuate men to the observance of a conduct purely disinterested; but they are not of themselves sufficient to produce persevering conformity to the refined dictates and obligations of social duty. Few men are capable of making a continual sacrifice of all views of private interest, or advantage, to the common good. It is vain to exclaim against the depravity of human nature on this account; the fact is so, the experience of every age and nation has proved it and we must in a great measure, change the constitution of man, before we can make it otherwise. No institution, not built on the presumptive truth of these maxims can succeed.[1]

It was echoed and enlarged upon in our century by Max Weber's observation:

> Interests (material and ideal), not ideas, dominate directly the actions of men. Yet the "images of the world" created by these ideas have very often served as switches determining the tracks on which the dynamism of interests kept actions moving.[2]

Yet the kind of interest determining political action in a particular period of history depends upon the political and cultural context within which foreign policy is formulated. The goals that might be pursued by nations in their foreign policy can run the whole gamut of objectives any nation has ever pursued or might possibly pursue.

The same observations apply to the concept of power. Its content and the manner of its use are determined by the political and cultural environment. Power may comprise anything that establishes and maintains the control of man over man. Thus power covers all social relationships which serve that end, from physical violence to the most subtle psychological ties by which one mind controls another. Power covers the domination of man by man, both when it is disciplined by moral ends and controlled by constitutional safeguards, as in Western democracies, and when it is that untamed and barbaric force which finds its laws in nothing but its own strength and its sole justification in its aggrandizement.

Political realism does not assume that the contemporary conditions under which foreign policy operates, with their extreme instability and the ever present threat of large-scale violence, cannot be changed. The balance of power, for instance, is indeed a perennial element of all pluralistic societies, as the authors of *The Federalist* papers well knew; yet it is capable of operating, as it does in the United States, under the conditions of relative stability and peaceful conflict. If the factors that have given rise to these conditions can be duplicated on the international scene, similar conditions of stability and peace will then prevail there, as they have over long stretches of history among certain nations.

---

[1] *The Writings of George Washington,* edited by John C. Fitzpatrick (Washington: United States Printing Office, 1931–44), Vol. X, p. 363.

[2] Marianne Weber, *Max Weber* (Tuebingen: J. C. B. Mohr, 1926), pp. 347–8. See also Max Weber, *Gesammelte Aufsätze zur Religionssociology* (Tuebingen: J. C. B. Mohr, 1920), p. 252.

What is true of the general character of international relations is also true of the nation state as the ultimate point of reference of contemporary foreign policy. While the realist indeed believes that interest is the perennial standard by which political action must be judged and directed, the contemporary connection between interest and the nation state is a product of history, and is therefore bound to disappear in the course of history. Nothing in the realist position militates against the assumption that the present division of the political world into nation states will be replaced by larger units of a quite different character, more in keeping with the technical potentialities and the moral requirements of the contemporary world.

The realist parts company with other schools of thought before the all-important question of how the contemporary world is to be transformed. The realist is persuaded that this transformation can be achieved only through the workmanlike manipulation of the perennial forces that have shaped the past as they will the future. The realist cannot be persuaded that we can bring about that transformation by confronting a political reality that has its own laws with an abstract ideal that refuses to take those laws into account.

4. Political realism is aware of *the moral significance of political action.* It is also aware of the ineluctable tension between the moral command and the requirements of successful political action. And it is unwilling to gloss over and obliterate that tension and thus to obfuscate both the moral and the political issue by making it appear as though the stark facts of politics were morally more satisfying than they actually are, and the moral law less exacting than it actually is.

Realism maintains that universal moral principles cannot be applied to the actions of states in their abstract universal formulation, but that they must be filtered through the concrete circumstances of time and place. The individual may say for himself: "*Fiat justitia, pereat mundus* (Let justice be done, even if the world perish)," but the state has no right to say so in the name of those who are in its care. Both individual and state must judge political action by universal moral principles, such as that of liberty. Yet while the individual has a moral right to sacrifice himself in defense of such a moral principle, the state has no right to let its moral disapprobation of the infringement of liberty get in the way of successful political action, itself inspired by the moral principle of national survival. There can be no political morality without prudence; that is, without consideration of the political consequences of seemingly moral action. Realism, then, considers prudence—the weighing of the consequences of alternative political actions—to be the supreme virtue in politics. Ethics in the abstract judges action by its conformity with the moral law; political ethics judges action by its political consequences. Classical and medieval philosophy knew this, and so did Lincoln when he said:

> I do the very best I know how, the very best I can, and I mean to keep doing so until the end. If the end brings me out all right, what is said against me won't amount to anything. If the end brings me out wrong, ten angels swearing I was right would make no difference.

5. Political realism refuses to identify the moral aspirations of a particular nation with the moral laws that govern the universe. As it distinguishes between truth and opinion, so it distinguishes between truth and idolatry. All nations are tempted—and few have been able to resist the temptation for long—to clothe their own particular aspirations and actions in the moral purposes of the universe. To know that nations are subject to the moral law is one thing, while to pretend to know with certainty what is good and evil in the relations among nations is quite another. There is a world of difference between the belief that all nations stand under the judgment of God, inscrutable to the human mind, and the blasphemous conviction that God is always on one's side and that what one wills oneself cannot fail to be willed by God also.

The lighthearted equation between a particular nationalism and the counsels of Providence is morally indefensible, for it is that very sin of pride against which the Greek tragedians and the Biblical prophets have warned rulers and ruled. That equation is also politically pernicious, for it is liable to engender the distortion in judgment which, in the blindness of crusading frenzy, destroys nations and civilizations—in the name of moral principle, ideal, or God himself.

On the other hand, it is exactly the concept of interest defined in terms of power that saves us from both that moral excess and that political folly. For if we look at all nations, our own included, as political entities pursuing their respective interests defined in terms of power, we are able to do justice to all of them. And we are able to do justice to all of them in a dual sense: We are able to judge other nations as we judge our own and, having judged them in this fashion, we are then capable of pursing policies that respect the interests of other nations, while protecting and promoting those of our own. Moderation in policy cannot fail to reflect the moderation of moral judgment.

6. The difference, then, between political realism and other schools of thought is real, and it is profound. However much the theory of political realism may have been misunderstood and misinterpreted, there is no gainsaying its distinctive intellectual and moral attitude to matters political.

Intellectually, the political realist maintains the autonomy of the political sphere, as the economist, the lawyer, the moralist maintain theirs. He thinks in terms of interest defined as power, as the economist thinks in terms of interest defined as wealth; the lawyer, of the conformity of action with legal rules; the moralist, of the conformity of action with moral principles. The economist asks: "How does this policy affect the wealth of society, or a segment of it?" The lawyer asks: "Is this policy in accord with the rules of law?" The moralist asks: "Is this policy in accord with moral principles?" And the political realist asks: "How does this policy affect the power of the nation?" (Or of the federal government, of Congress, of the party, of agriculture, as the case may be.)

The political realist is not unaware of the existence and relevance of standards of thought other than political ones. As political realist, he cannot but subordinate these other standards to those of politics. And he parts company with other schools when they impose standards of thought appropriate to other spheres upon the political sphere. It is here that political realism takes issue with the "legalistic-moralistic approach" to international politics. That this issue is not, as has been contended, a mere figment of the imagination, but goes to the very core of the controversy, can be shown from many historical examples. Three will suffice to make the point.[3]

In 1939 the Soviet Union attacked Finland. This action confronted France and Great Britain with two issues, one legal, the other political. Did that action violate the Covenant of the League of Nations and, if it did, what countermeasures should France and Great Britain take? The legal question could easily be answered in the affirmative, for obviously the Soviet Union had done what was prohibited by the Covenant. The answer to the political question depends, first, upon the manner in which the Russian action affected the interests of France and Great Britain; second, upon the existing distribution of power between France and Great Britain, on the one hand, and the Soviet Union and other potentially hostile nations, especially Germany, on the other; and, third, upon the influence that the countermeasures were likely to have upon the interests of France and Great Britain and the future distribution of power. France and Great Britain, as the leading members of the League of Nations, saw to it that the Soviet Union was expelled from the League, and they were prevented from joining Finland in the war against the Soviet Union only by Sweden's refusal to allow their troops to pass though Swedish territory on their way to Finland. If this refusal by Sweden had not saved them, France and Great Britain would shortly have found themselves at war with the Soviet Union and Germany at the same time.

---

[3] See the other examples discussed in Hans J. Morgenthau, "Another 'Great Debate': The National Interest of the United States," *The American Political Science Review,* Vol. XLVI (December 1952), pp. 979 ff. See also Hans J. Morgenthau, *Politics in the 20th Century,* Vol. I, *The Decline of Democratic Politics* (Chicago: University of Chicago Press, 1962), pp. 79 ff; and abridged edition (Chicago: University of Chicago Press, 1971), pp. 204 ff.

The policy of France and Great Britain was a classic example of legalism in that they allowed the answer to the legal question, legitimate within its sphere, to determine their political actions. Instead of asking both questions, that of law and that of power, they asked only the question of law; and the answer they received could have no bearing on the issue that their very existence might have depended upon.

The second example illustrates the "moralistic approach" to international politics. It concerns the international status of the Communist government of China. The rise of that government confronted the Western world with two issues, one moral, the other political. Were the nature and policies of that government in accord with the moral principles of the Western world? Should the Western world deal with such a government? The answer to the first question could not fail to be in the negative. Yet it did not follow with necessity that the answer to the second question should also be in the negative. The standard of thought applied to the first—the moral—question was simply to test the nature and the policies of the Communist government of China by the principles of Western morality. On the other hand, the second—the political—question had to be subjected to the complicated test of the interests involved and the power available on either side, and of the bearing of one or the other course of action upon these interests and power. The application of this test could well have led to the conclusion that it would be wiser not to deal with the Communist government of China. To arrive at this conclusion by neglecting this test altogether and answering the political question in terms of the moral issue was indeed a classic example of the "moralistic approach" to international politics.

The third case illustrates strikingly the contrast between realism and the legalistic-moralistic approach to foreign policy. Great Britain, as one of the guarantors of the neutrality of Belgium, went to war with Germany in August 1914 because Germany had violated the neutrality of Belgium. The British action could be justified either in realistic or legalistic-moralistic terms. That is to say, one could argue realistically that for centuries it had been axiomatic for British foreign policy to prevent the control of the Low Countries by a hostile power. It was then not so much the violation of Belgium's neutrality per se as the hostile intentions of the violator which provided the rationale for British intervention. If the violator had been another nation but Germany, Great Britain might well have refrained from intervening. This is the position taken by Sir Edward Grey, British Foreign Secretary during that period. Under Secretary for Foreign Affairs Hardinge remarked to him in 1908: "If France violated Belgian neutrality in a war against Germany, it is doubtful whether England or Russia would move a finger to maintain Belgian neutrality, while if the neutrality of Belgium was violated by Germany, it is probable that the converse would be the case." Whereupon Sir Edward Grey replied: "This is to the point." Yet one could also take the legalistic and moralistic position that the violation of Belgium's neutrality per se, because of its legal and moral defects and regardless of the interests at stake and of the identity of the violator, justified British and, for that matter, American intervention. This was the position which Theodore Roosevelt took in his letter to Sir Edward Grey of January 22, 1915:

> To me the crux of the situation has been Belgium. If England or France had acted toward Belgium as Germany has acted I should have opposed them, exactly as I now oppose Germany. I have emphatically approved your action as a model for what should be done by those who believe that treaties should be observed in good faith and that there is such a thing as international morality. I take this position as an American who is no more an Englishman than he is a German, who endeavors loyally to serve the interests of his own country, but who also endeavors to do what he can for justice and decency as regards mankind at large, and who therefore feels obliged to judge all other nations by their conduct on any given occasion.

This realist defense of the autonomy of the political sphere against its subversion by other modes of thought does not imply disregard for the existence and importance of these other modes of thought. It rather implies that each should be assigned its proper sphere and function. Political realism is based upon a pluralistic conception of human nature. Real man is a composite of "economic man," "political man," "moral man," "religious man," etc. A man who was nothing but "political man" would be a beast, for he would be completely lacking in moral restraints. A man who was nothing but "moral man" would be a fool, for he would be completely lacking in prudence. A man who was nothing but "religious man" would be a saint, for he would be completely lacking in worldly desires.

Recognizing that these different facets of human nature exist, political realism also recognizes that in order to understand one of them one has to deal with it on its own terms. That is to say, if I want to understand "religious man," I must for the time being abstract from the other aspects of human nature and deal with its religious aspect as if it were the only one. Furthermore, I must apply to the religious sphere the standards of thought appropriate to it, always remaining aware of the existence of other standards and their actual influence upon the religious qualities of man. What is true of this facet of human nature is true of all the others. No modern economist, for instance, would conceive of his science and its relations to other sciences of man in any other way. It is exactly through such a process of emancipation from other standards of thought, and the development of one appropriate to its subject matter, that economics has developed as an autonomous therapy of the economic activities of man. To contribute to a similar development in the field of politics is indeed the purpose of political realism.

It is in the nature of things that a theory of politics which is based upon such principles will not meet with unanimous approval—nor does, for that matter, such a foreign policy. For theory and policy alike run counter to two trends in our culture which are not able to reconcile themselves to the assumptions and results of a rational, objective theory of politics. One of these trends disparages the role of power in society on grounds that stem from the experience and philosophy of the nineteenth century; we shall address ourselves to this tendency later in greater detail. The other trend, opposed to the realist theory and practice of politics, stems from the very relationship that exists, and must exist, between the human mind and the political sphere. For reasons that we shall discuss later the human mind in its day-by-day operations cannot bear to look the truth of politics straight in the face. It must disguise, distort, belittle, and embellish the truth—the more so, the more the individual is actively involved in the processes of politics, and particularly in those of international politics. For only by deceiving himself about the nature of politics and the role he plays on the political scene is man able to live contentedly as a political animal with himself and his fellow men.

Thus it is inevitable that a theory which tries to understand international politics as it actually is and as it ought to be in view of its intrinsic nature, rather than as people would like to see it, must overcome a psychological resistance that most other branches of learning need not face. A book devoted to the theoretical understanding of international politics therefore requires a special explanation and justification.

■ ■

B) HANS J. MORGENTHAU

"THE MAINSPRINGS OF AMERICAN FOREIGN POLICY: THE NATIONAL INTEREST VS. MORAL ABSTRACTIONS," THE AMERICAN POLITICAL SCIENCE REVIEW, 1950

THE MAINSPRINGS OF AMERICAN FOREIGN POLICY: THE NATIONAL INTEREST VS. MORAL ABSTRACTIONS

It is often said that the foreign policy of the United States is in need of maturing and that the American people and their government must grow up if they want to emerge victorious from the trials of our age. It would be truer to say that this generation of Americans must shed the illusions of their fathers and grandfathers and relearn the great principles of statecraft which guided the path of the republic in the first decade and—in moralistic disguise—in the first century of its existence. The United States offers the singular spectacle of a commonwealth whose political wisdom did not grow slowly through the accumulation and articulation of experiences. Quite to the contrary, the full flowering of its political wisdom was coeval with its birth as an independent nation—nay, it owed its existence and survival as an independent nation to those extraordinary qualities of political insight, historic perspective, and common sense which the first generation of Americans applied to the affairs of state.

This classic age of American statecraft comes to an end with the physical disappearance of that generation of American statesmen. The rich and varied landscape in which they had planted all that is worthwhile in the tradition of Western political thought was allowed to go to waste. It became a faint and baffling remembrance, a symbol to be worshipped rather than a source of inspiration and a guide for action. Until very recently the American people seemed to be content to live in a political desert whose intellectual barrenness and aridity were relieved only by some sparse and neglected oases of insight and wisdom. What in that period, stretching over more than a century, went under the name of foreign policy was either improvisation in the face of an urgent problem which had to be dealt with somehow, or—and especially in our century—the invocation of some abstract moral principle in the image of which the world was to be made over. Improvisation as a substitute for foreign policy was largely successful, for in the past the margin of American and allied power to spare generally exceeded the degree to which American improvidence fell short of the demands of the hour. The invocation of abstract moral principles was in part hardly more than an innocuous pastime; for embracing everything it came to grips with nothing. In part, however, it was a magnificent instrument for marshalling public opinion in support of war and warlike policies—and for losing the peace to follow. The intoxication with moral abstractions which as a mass phenomenon started with the Spanish-American War, and which in our time has become the prevailing substitute for political thought, is indeed one of the great sources of weakness and failure in American foreign policy.

It is, however, worthy of note that underneath this political dilettantism, nourished by improvidence and a sense of moral mission, there has remained alive an almost instinctive awareness of the perennial interests of the United States. This has especially been true with regard to Europe and the Western Hemisphere; for in these regions the national interest of the United States has from the beginning been obvious and clearly defined.

I

In the Western Hemisphere we have always endeavored to preserve the unique position of the United States as a predominant power without rival. We have not been slow in recognizing that this predominance was not likely to be effectively threatened by any one American nation or combination of them, acting without support from outside the Western Hemisphere. It was, then, imperative for the United States to isolate the Western Hemisphere from the political and military policies of non-American nations. The interference of non-American nations in the affairs of the Western Hemisphere, especially through the acquisition of territory, was the only way in which the predominance of the United States could have been challenged from within the Western Hemisphere itself. The Monroe Doctrine and the policies implementing it express that permanent national interest of the United States in the Western Hemisphere.

Since a threat to the national interest of the United States in the Western Hemisphere can come only from outside it, that is, historically from Europe, the United States has always striven to prevent the development of conditions in Europe which would be conducive to a European nation's interference in the affairs of the Western Hemisphere or to a direct attack upon the United States. Such conditions would be most likely to arise if a European nation had gained such predominance that it could afford to look across the sea for conquest without fear of being menaced at the center of its power, that is, Europe itself. It is for this reason that the United States has consistently—the War of 1812 is the sole major exception—pursued policies aiming at the maintenance of the balance of power in Europe. It has opposed whatever European nation—be it Great Britain, France, Germany, or Russia—seemed to be likely to gain that ascendancy over its European competitors which would have jeopardized the hemispheric predominance and eventually the very independence of the United States. Conversely, it has supported whatever European nation seemed to be most likely to restore the balance of power by offering successful resistance to the would-be conqueror. While it is hard to imagine a greater contrast in the way of thinking about matters political than that which separates Alexander Hamilton from Woodrow Wilson, in this concern for the maintenance of the balance of power in Europe—for whatever different reasons—they are one. It is by virtue of this concern that the United States has intervened in both World Wars on the side of the initially weaker coalition and that its European policies have so largely paralleled those of Great Britain; for from Henry VIII to this day Great Britain has invariably pursued one single objective in Europe: the maintenance of the balance of power.

With Asia the United States has been vitally concerned only since the turn of the century, and the relation of Asia to the national interest of the United States has never been obvious or clearly defined. In consequence, the Asiatic policies of the United States have never as unequivocally expressed the permanent national interest as have the hemispheric and European ones; nor have they for that reason commanded the bipartisan support which the latter have largely enjoyed. As a further consequence, they have been subjected to moralistic influences in a measure from which the European and hemispheric policies of the United States have been largely immune. Yet beneath the confusions, reversals of policy, and moralistic generalities, which have made up the surface of our Asiatic policy since McKinley, one can detect an underlying consistency which, however vaguely, reflects the permanent interest of the United States in Asia. And this interest is again the maintenance of the balance of power. The principle that expresses it is the "open door" in China. Originally its meaning was purely commercial. However, in the measure in which other nations, especially Japan, threatened to close the door to China not only commercially, but also militarily and politically, the principle of the "open door" was interpreted to cover the territorial integrity and political independence of China not for commercial but political reasons. However unsure of itself the Asiatic policy of the United States has been, it has always assumed that the domination of China by another nation would create so great an accumulation of power as to threaten the security of the United States.

II

Not only with regard to Asia, however, but wherever American foreign policy has operated, political thought has been divorced from political action. Even where our long-range policies reflect faithfully, as they do in the Americans and in Europe, the true interests of the United States, we think about them in terms which have at best but a tenuous connection with the actual character of the policies pursued. We have acted on the international scene, as all nations must, in power-political terms; we have tended to conceive of our actions in non-political, moralistic terms. This aversion to seeing problems of international politics as they are and the inclination to viewing them instead in non-political, moralistic terms can be attributed both to certain misunderstood peculiarities of the American experience in foreign affairs and to the general climate of opinion prevailing in the Western world during the better part of the nineteenth and the first decade of the twentieth centuries. Of these peculiarities of the American experience three stand out: the uniqueness of the American experiment, the actual isolation during the nineteenth century of the United States from the centers of world conflict, and the humanitarian pacifism and anti-imperialism of American ideology.

The uniqueness of the American experiment in foreign policy contains two elements: the negative one of distinctiveness from the traditional power-political quarrels of Europe and the positive one of a continental expansion which created the freest and richest nation on earth without conquest or subjugation of others.

That the severance of constitutional ties with the British crown was meant to signify the initiation of an American foreign policy distinct from what went under the name of foreign policy in Europe was a conviction common to the founders of the republic. As Washington's Farewell Address put it: "Europe has a set of primary interests, which to us have none, or a very remote relation. Hence she must be engaged in frequent controversies, the causes of which are essentially foreign to our concerns. Hence, therefore, it must be unwise in us to implicate ourselves, by artificial ties, in the ordinary vicissitudes of her politics, or the ordinary combinations and collisions of her friendships or enmities." In 1796, European politics and power politics were identical; there was no other power politics but the one engaged in by the princes of Europe. "The toils of European ambition, rivalship, interest, humor or caprice" were the only manifestations, on the international scene, of the struggle for power before the American eye. The retreat from European politics, as proclaimed by Washington, could, therefore, be taken to mean retreat from power politics as such.

The expansion of the United States up to the Spanish-American War seemed to provide conclusive proof both for the distinctiveness and moral superiority of American foreign policy. The settlement of the better part of a continent by the thirteen original states seemed to be an act of civilization rather than of conquest and as such essentially different from, and morally superior to, the imperialistic ventures, wars of conquest, and colonial acquisitions with which the history of other nations is replete. Yet it was not so much political virtue as the contiguity of the sparsely settled object of conquest with the original territory of departure, which put the mark of uniqueness upon American expansion. As was the case with Russia's simultaneous eastward expansion toward the Pacific, the United States, in order to expand, did not need to cross the oceans and fight wars of conquest in strange lands, as did the other great colonizing nations. Furthermore, the utter political, military, and numerical inferiority of the Indian opponent tended to obscure the element of power, which was less obtrusive in, but no more absent from, the continental expansion of the United States than the expansionist movements of other nations. Thus it came about that what was in actuality the fortuitous concatenation of two potent historic accidents could take on, in the popular imagination, the aspects of an ineluctable natural development, a "manifest destiny," thus confirming the uniqueness of American foreign policy in its freedom from those power-political blemishes which degrade the foreign policies of other nations.

Yet American isolation from the European tradition of power politics was more than a political program or a moralistic illusion. As concerns involvement in the political conflicts of which Europe was the center, and the commitments and risks which such involvement of necessity implies, American isolation was an established political fact until the end of the nineteenth century. The actuality of this fact was a result of deliberate choice as well as of the objective conditions of geography. Popular writers might see in the uniqueness of America's geographic position the hand of God which had unalterably prescribed the course of American expansion as well as isolation. But more responsible observers, from Washington on, have been careful to emphasize the conjunction of geographic conditions and of a foreign policy which chooses its ends in the light of geography and which uses geographic conditions to attain those ends. Washington referred to "our detached and distant situation" and asked, "Why forego the advantages of so peculiar a situation?"

From the shores of the North American continent, the citizens of the new world watched the strange spectacle of the struggle for power unfolding on the distant scenes of Europe, Africa, and Asia. Since for the better part of the nineteenth century their foreign policy enabled them to retain the role of spectators, what was actually the result of a passing historic constellation appeared to Americans as a permanent condition, self-chosen as well as naturally ordained. At worst they would continue to watch the game of power politics played by others. At best the time was close at hand when, with democracy established everywhere, the final curtain would fall and the game of power politics would no longer be played.

To aid in the achievement of this goal was conceived to be part of America's mission. Throughout the nation's history, the national destiny of the United States has been understood in anti-militaristic, libertarian terms. Where that national mission finds a nonaggressive, abstentionist formulation, as in the political philosophy of John C. Calhoun, it is conceived as the promotion of domestic liberty. Thus we may "do more to extend liberty by our example over this continent and the world generally, than would be done by a thousand victories." When the United States, in the wake of the Spanish-American War, seemed to desert this anti-imperialist and democratic ideal , William Graham Sumner restated its essence: "Expansion and imperialism are a grand onslaught on democracy . . . expansion and imperialism are at war with the best traditions, principles, and interests of the American people." Comparing the tendencies of European power politics with the ideals of the American tradition, Sumner thought with Washington that they were incompatible. Yet, as a prophet of things to come, he saw that with the conclusion of the Spanish-American War America was irrevocably committed to the same course which was engulfing Europe in revolution and war.

To understand the American mission in such selfless, humanitarian terms was the easier as the United States—in contrast to the other great powers—was generally not interested, at least outside the Western Hemisphere, in a particular advantage to be defined in terms of power or of territorial gain. Its national interest was exhausted by the preservation of its predominance in the Western Hemisphere and of the balance of power in Europe and Asia. And even this interest in general stability rather than special advantage was, as we know, not always recognized for what it was.

Yet while the foreign policy of the United States was forced, by circumstance if not by choice, to employ the methods, to shoulder the commitments, to seek the objectives, and to run the risks, from which it had thought to be permanently exempt, American political thought continued to uphold that exemption at least as an ideal—an ideal which was but temporarily beyond the reach of the American people, because of the wickedness and stupidity either of American or, preferably, of foreign statesmen. In one sense, this ideal of a free, peaceful, and prosperous world, from which popular government had banished power politics forever, was a natural outgrowth of the American experience. In another sense, this ideal expressed in a particularly eloquent and consistent fashion the general philosophy which during the better part of the nineteenth century dominated the Western world. This philosophy contains two basic propositions: that the struggle for power on the international scene is a mere accident of history, naturally associated with non-democratic government and, hence, destined to disappear with the triumph of democracy throughout the world; and that, in consequence, conflicts between democratic and non-democratic nations must be conceived not as struggles for mutual advantage in terms of power but primarily as a contest between good and evil, which can only end with the complete triumph of good and with evil being wiped off the face of the earth.

The nineteenth century developed this philosophy of international relations from its experience of domestic politics. The distinctive characteristic of this experience was the domination of the middle classes by the aristocracy. By identifying this domination with political domination of any kind, the political philosophy of the nineteenth century came to identify the opposition to aristocratic politics with hostility to any kind of politics. After the defeat of aristocratic government, the middle classes developed a system of indirect domination. They replaced the traditional division into the governing and governed classes and the military method of open violence, characteristic of aristocratic rule, with the invisible chains of economic dependence. This economic system operated through a network of seemingly equalitarian legal rules which concealed the very existence of power relations. The nineteenth century was unable to see the political nature of these legalized relations. They seemed to be essentially different from what had gone, so far, under the name of politics. Therefore, politics in its aristocratic, that is, open and violent form, was identified with politics as such. The struggle, then, for political power—in domestic as well as in international affairs—appeared to be only an historic accident, coincident with autocratic government and bound to disappear with the disappearance of autocratic government.

It is easy to see how this general climate of opinion, prevailing in the Western world, nourished similar tendencies in the American mind, grown from the specific experiences of American history. Thus it is not an accident that nowhere in the Western world was there such depth of conviction and tenacity in support of the belief that involvement in power politics is not inevitable but only a historic accident, and that nations have a choice between power politics and another kind of foreign policy conforming to moral principles and not tainted by the desire for power. Nor is it by accident that this philosophy of foreign policy found its most dedicated and eloquent spokesman in an American President, Woodrow Wilson.

III

The illusion that a nation can escape, if it only wants to, from power politics into a realm where action is guided by moral principles rather than by considerations of power, not only is deeply rooted in the American mind; it also took more than a century for this illusion to crowd out the older notion that international politics is an unending struggle for power in which the interests of individual nations must necessarily be defined in terms of power. Out of the struggle between these two opposing conceptions three types of American statesmen emerge: the realist, thinking in terms of power and represented by Alexander Hamilton; the ideological, acting in terms of power, thinking in terms of moral principles, and represented by Thomas Jefferson and John Quincy Adams; the moralist, thinking and acting in terms of moral principles and represented by Woodrow Wilson. To these three types, three periods of American foreign policy roughly correspond: the first covering the first decade of the history of the United States as an independent nation, the second covering the nineteenth century to the Spanish-American War, the third covering the half century after that war. That this division of the history of American foreign policy refers only to prevailing tendencies and does by no means preclude the operation side by side of different tendencies in the same period, will become obvious in the discussion.

It illustrates both the depth of the moralist illusion and the original strength of the opposition to it that the issue between these two opposing conceptions of foreign policy was joined at the very beginning of the history of the United States, decided in favor of the realist position, and formulated with unsurpassed simplicity and penetration by Alexander Hamilton. The memorable occasion was Washington's proclamation of neutrality in the War of the First Coalition against revolutionary France.

In 1792, the War of the First Coalition had ranged Austria, Prussia, Sardinia, Great Britain, and the United Netherlands against revolutionary France, which was tied to the United States by a treaty of alliance. On April 22, 1793, Washington issued a proclamation of neutrality, and it was in defense of that proclamation that Hamilton wrote the "Pacificus" and "Americanus" articles. Among the arguments directed against the proclamation were three derived from moral principles. Faithfulness to treaty obligations, gratitude toward a country which had lent its assistance to the colonies in their struggle for independence, and the affinity of republican institutions were cited to prove that the United States must side with France. Against these moral principles, Hamilton invoked the national interest of the United States:

There would be no proportion between the mischiefs and perils to which the United States would expose themselves, by embarking in the war, and the benefit which the nature of their stipulation aims at securing to France, or that which it would be in their power actually to render her by becoming a party.

This disproportion would be a valid reason for not executing the guaranty. All contracts are to receive a reasonable construction. Self-preservation is the first duty of a nation; and though in the performance of stipulations relating to war, good faith requires that its ordinary hazards should be fairly met, because they are directly contemplated by such stipulations, yet it does not require that extraordinary and extreme hazards should be run. . . .

The basis of gratitude is a benefit received or intended, which there was no right to claim, originating in a regard to the interest or advantage of the party on whom the benefit is, or is meant to be, conferred. If a service is rendered from views relative to the immediate interest of the party who performs it, and is productive of reciprocal advantages, there seems scarcely, in such a case, to be an adequate basis for a sentiment like that of gratitude. . . . It may be affirmed as a general principle, that the predominant motive of good offices from one nation to another, is the interest or advantage of the nation which performs them.

Indeed, the rule of morality in this respect is not precisely the same between nations as between individuals. The duty of making its own welfare the guide of its actions, is much stronger upon the former than upon the latter; in proportion to the greater magnitude and importance of national compared with individual happiness, and to the greater permanency of the effects of national than of individual conduct. Existing millions, and for the most part future generations, are concerned in the present measures of a government; while the consequences of the private actions of an individual ordinarily terminate with himself, or are circumscribed within a narrow compass.

Whence it follows that an individual may, on numerous occasions, meritoriously indulge the emotions of generosity and benevolence, not only without an eye to, but even at the expense of, his own interest. But a government can rarely, if at all, be justifiable in pursuing a similar course; and, if it does so, ought to confine itself within much stricter bounds. . . . Good offices which are indifferent to the interest of a nation performing them, or which are compensated by the existence or expectation of some reasonable equivalent, or which produce an essential good to the nation to which they are rendered, without real detriment to the affairs of the benefactors, prescribe perhaps the limits of national generosity or benevolence. . . .

But we are sometimes told, by way of answer, that the cause of France is the cause of liberty; and that we are bound to assist the nation on the score of their being engaged in the defence of that cause. . . .

The obligation to assist the cause of liberty must be deduced from the merits of that cause and from the interest we have in its support.

■█▌█▌

An examination into the question how far *regard to the cause of Liberty* ought to induce the United States to take part with France in the present war, is rendered necessary by the efforts which are making [*sic*] to establish an opinion that it ought to have that effect. In order to a right judgment on the point, it is requisite to consider the question under two aspects.

I. Whether the cause of France be truly the cause of Liberty, pursued with justice and humanity, and in a manner likely to crown it with honorable success.

II. Whether the degree of service we could render, by participating in the conflict, was likely to compensate, by its utility to the cause, the evils which would probably flow from it to ourselves.

If either of these questions can be answered in the negative, it will result, that the consideration which has been stated ought not to embark us in the war. . . .

The certain evils of our joining France in the war, are sufficient dissuasives from so intemperate a measure. The possible ones are of a nature to call for all our caution, all our prudence.

To defend its own rights, to vindicate its own honor, there are occasions when a nation ought to hazard even its existence. Should such an occasion occur, I trust those who are most averse to commit the peace of the country, will not be the last to face the danger, nor the first to turn their backs upon it.

But let us at least have the consolation of not having rashly courted misfortune. Let us have to act under the animating reflection of being engaged in repelling wrongs, which we neither sought nor merited; in vindicating our rights invaded without provocation; in defending our honor, violated without cause. Let us not have to reproach ourselves with having voluntarily bartered blessings for calamities.

But we are told that our own liberty is at stake upon the event of the war against France—that if she falls, we shall be the next victim. The combined powers, it is said, will never forgive in us the origination of those principles which were the germs of the French Revolution. They will endeavor to eradicate them from the world.

If this suggestion were ever so well founded, it would perhaps be a sufficient answer to it to say, that our interference is not likely to alter the case; that it would only serve prematurely to exhaust our strength.

But other answers more conclusive present themselves.

The war against France requires, on the part of her enemies, efforts unusually violent. They are obliged to strain every nerve, to exert every resource. However it may terminate, they must find themselves spent in an extreme degree; a situation not very favorable to the undertaking anew, and even to Europe combined, an immense enterprise.

To subvert by force republican liberty in this country, nothing short of entire conquest would suffice. This conquest, with our present increased population, greatly distant as we are from Europe, would either be impracticable, or would demand such exertions, as following immediately upon those which will have been requisite to the subversion of the French Revolution, would be absolutely ruinous to the undertakers. . . .

There are two great errors in our reasoning upon this subject. One, that the combined powers will certainly attribute to us the same principles, which they deem so exceptionable in France; the other, that our principles are in fact the same.

If left to themselves, they will all, except one, naturally see in us a people who originally resorted to a revolution in government, as a refuge from encroachments on rights and privileges *antecedently* enjoyed, not as a people who from choice sought a radical and entire change in the established government, in pursuit of new privileges and rights carried to an extreme, irreconcilable perhaps with any form of regular government. They will see in us a people who have a due respect for property and personal security; who, in the midst of our revolution, abstained with exemplary moderation from every thing violent or sanguinary, instituting governments adequate to the protection of persons and property; who, since Completion of our revolution, have in a very short period, from mere reasoning and reflection, without tumult or bloodshed, adopted a form of general government calculated, as well as the nature of things would permit, to remedy antecedent defects, to give strength and security to the nation, to rest the foundations of liberty on the basis of justice, order and law; who have at all times been content to govern themselves without intermeddling with the affairs or governments of other nations; in fine, they will see in us sincere republicans, but decided enemies to licentiousness and anarchy; sincere republicans, but decided friends to the freedom of opinion, to the order and tranquility of all mankind. They will not see in us a people whose best passions have been misled, and whose best qualities have been perverted from their true direction by headlong, fanatical, or designing leaders, to the perpetration of acts from which humanity shrinks, to the commission of outrages over which the eye of reason weeps, to the profession and practice of principles which tend to shake the foundations of morality, to dissolve the social bands, to disturb the peace of mankind, to substitute confusion to order, anarchy to government. . . .

It is therefore matter of real regret, that there should be an effort on our part to level the distinctions which discriminate our case from that of France, to confound the two cases in the view of foreign powers, and to pervert or hazard our own principles by persuading ourselves of a similitude which does not exist. . . .

But let us not corrupt ourselves by false comparisons or glosses, nor shut our eyes to the true nature of transactions which ought to grieve and warn us, nor rashly mingle our destiny in the consequences of the errors and extravagances of another nation.

Must a nation subordinate its security, its happiness, nay, its very existence to the respect for treaty obligations, to the sentiment of gratitude, to sympathy with a kindred political system? This was the question which Hamilton proposed to answer, and his answer was an unequivocal "no."

Hamilton unswervingly applied one standard to the issues raised by the opposition to Washington's proclamation of neutrality: the national interest of the United States. He put the legalistic and moralistic arguments of the opposition, represented by Madison under the pseudonym "Helvidius," into the context of the concrete power situation in which the United States found itself on the international scene and asked: If the United States were to join France against virtually all of Europe, what risks would the United States run, what advantages could it expect, what good could it do for its ally?

IV

Considerations such as these, recognized for what they are, have guided American foreign policy but for a short period, that is, as long as the Federalists were in power. *The Federalist* and Washington's Farewell Address are their classic expression. Yet these considerations, not recognized for what they are, sometimes even rejected, have determined the great objectives of American foreign policy to this day. During the century following their brief flowering, they have by and large continued to influence policies as well, under the cover, as it were, of those moral principles with which from Jefferson onward American statesmen have liked to justify their moves on the international scene. Thus this second period witnessed a discrepancy between political thought and political action, yet a coincidence in the intended results of both. What was said of Gladstone could also have been said of Jefferson, John Quincy Adams, Theodore Roosevelt, the war policies of Wilson and Franklin D. Roosevelt: what the moral law demanded was by felicitous coincidence always identical with what the national interest seemed to require. Political thought and political action moved on different planes, which, however, were so inclined as to merge in the end.

John Quincy Adams is the classic example of the political moralist in thought and word who cannot help being a political realist in action. Yet even in Jefferson, whose dedication to abstract morality was much stronger and whose realist touch in foreign affairs was much less sure, the moral pretense yielded often, especially in private utterance, to the impact of the national interest upon native good sense.

Thus during the concluding decade of the Napoleonic Wars Jefferson's thought on international affairs was a reflection of the ever-changing distribution of power in the world rather than of immutable moral principles. In 1806, he favored "an English ascendancy on the ocean" as being "safer for us than that of France." In 1807, he was by the logic of events forced to admit:

I never expected to be under the necessity of wishing success to Buonaparte. But the English being equally tyrannical at sea as he is on land, & that tyranny bearing on us in every point of either honor or interest, I say, "down with England" and as for what Buonaparte is then to do to us, let us trust to the chapter of accidents, I cannot, with the Anglomen, prefer a certain present evil to a future hypothetical one.

However, in 1812, when Napoleon was at the pinnacle of his power, Jefferson hoped for the restoration of the balance of power. Speaking of England, he said that

it is for the general interest that she should be a sensible and independent weight in the scale of nations, and be able to contribute, when a favorable moment presents itself, to reduce under the same order, her great rival in flagitiousness. We especially ought to pray that the powers of Europe may be so poised and counterpoised among themselves, that their own security may require the presence of all their forces at home, leaving the other quarters of the globe in undisturbed tranquility.

In 1814, again compelled by the logic of events, he came clearly out against Napoleon and in favor of a balance of power which would leave the power of Napoleon and of England limited, but intact:

Surely none of us wish to see Bonaparte conquer Russia, and lay thus at his feet the whole continent of Europe. This done, England would be but a breakfast; and, although I am free from the visionary fears which the votaries of England have effected to entertain, because I believe he cannot effect the conquest of Europe; yet put all Europe into his hands, and he might spare such a force to be sent in British ships, as I would as leave not have to en-counter, when I see how much trouble a handful of British soldiers in Canada has given us. No. It cannot be to our interest that all Europe should be reduced to a single monarchy. The true line of interest for us, is, that Bonaparte should be able to effect the complete exclusion of England from the whole continent of Europe, in order, as the same letter said, "by this peaceable engine of constraint, to make her renounce her views of dominion over the ocean, of permitting no other nation to navigate it but with her license, and on tribute to her, and her aggressions on the persons of our citizens who may choose to exercise their right of passing over that element." And this would be effected by Bonaparte's succeeding so far as to close the Baltic against her. This success I wished him the last year, this I wish him this year; but were he again advanced to Moscow, I should again wish him such disasters as would prevent his reaching Petersburg. And were the consequences even to be the longer continuance of our war, I would rather meet them than see the whole force of Europe wielded by a single hand.

Similarly, in 1815, Jefferson wrote:

For my part, I wish that all nations may recover and retain their independence; that those which are overgrown may not advance beyond safe measures of power, that a salutary balance may be ever maintained among nations, and that our peace, commerce, and friendship, may be sought and cultivated by all.

It was only when, after 1815, the danger to the balance of power seemed to have passed that Jefferson allowed himself again to indulge in the cultivation of moral principles divorced from the political exigencies of the hour.

From this tendency to which Jefferson only too readily yielded, John Quincy Adams was well-nigh immune. We are here in the presence of a statesman who had been reared in the re-alist tradition of the first period of American foreign policy, who had done the better part of his work of statecraft in an atmosphere saturated with Jeffersonian principles, and who had achieved the merger of these two elements of his experience into an harmonious whole. Be-tween John Quincy Adams' moral principles and the traditional interest of the United States there was hardly ever a conflict. The moral principles were nothing but the political interests for-mulated in moral terms, and vice versa. They fit the interests as a glove fits the hand. Adam's great contributions to the tradition of American foreign policy, freedom of the seas, the Monroe Doctrine, and Manifest Destiny, are witness to this achievement.

The legal and moral principle of the freedom of the seas was in the hands of Adams a weapon, as it had been two centuries earlier in the hands of Grotius wielded on behalf of the Low Countries, through which an inferior naval power endeavored to safeguard its indepen-dence against Great Britain, the mistress of the seas. The Monroe Doctrine's moral postulates of anti-imperialism and mutual non-intervention were the negative conditions for the safety and enduring greatness of the United States. Their fulfillment vouchsafed the isolation of the United States from the power struggles of Europe and, through it, the continuing predomi-nance of the United States in the Western Hemisphere. Manifest Destiny was the moral justi-fication as well as the moral incentive for the westward expansion of the United States, the pe-culiar American way—foreordained by the objective conditions of American existence—of founding an empire, the "American Empire," as one of the contemporary opponents of Adams' policies put it.

V

Jefferson and John Quincy Adams stand at the beginning of the second period of American thought on foreign policy, both its most eminent representatives and the heirs of a realist tradition which continued to mould political action, while it had largely ceased to influence political thought. At the beginning of the third period, McKinley leads the United States, as a great world power, beyond the confines of the Western Hemisphere, ignorant of the bearing of this step upon the national interest and guided by moral principles which are completely divorced from the national interest. When at the end of the Spanish-American War the status of the Philippines had to be determined, McKinley expected and found no guidance in the traditional national interests of the United States. According to his own testimony, he knelt beside his bed in prayer, and in the wee hours of the morning he heard the voice of God telling him—as was to be expected—to annex the Philippines.

This period initiated by McKinley, in which moral principles no longer justify the enduring national interest as in the second, but replace it as a guide for action, finds its fulfillment in the political thought of Woodrow Wilson. Wilson's thought not only disregards the national interest, but is explicitly opposed to it on moral grounds. "It is a very perilous thing," he said in his address at Mobile on October 27, 1913,

> to determine the foreign policy of a nation in the terms of material interest. It not only is unfair to those with whom you are dealing, but it is degrading as regards your own actions. . . . We dare not turn from the principle that morality and not expediency is the thing that must guide us, and that we will never condone iniquity because it is most convenient to do so.

Wilson's war-time speeches are but an elaboration of this philosophy. An excerpt from his address of September 27, 1918, opening the campaign for the Fourth Liberty Loan, will suffice to show the continuity of that philosophy:

> It is of capital importance that we should also be explicitly agreed that no peace shall be obtained by any kind of compromise or abatement of the principles we have avowed as the principles for which we are fighting. . . .
>
> First, the impartial justice meted out must involve no discrimination between those to whom we wish to be just and those to whom we do not wish to be just. It must be a justice that plays no favorites and knows no standard but the equal rights of the several peoples concerned;
>
> Second, no special or separate interest of any single nation or any group of nations can be made the basis of any part of the settlement which is not consistent with the common interest of all;
>
> Third, there can be no leagues or alliances or special covenants and understandings within the general and common family of the League of Nations.
>
> Fourth, and more specifically, there can be no special, selfish economic combinations within the League and no employment of any form of economic boycott or exclusion except as the power of economic penalty by exclusion from the markets of the world may be vested in the League of Nations itself as a means of discipline and control.
>
> Fifth, all international agreements and treaties of every kind must be made known in their entirety to the rest of the world.
>
> Special alliances and economic rivalries and hostilities have been the prolific source in the modern world of the plans and passions that produce war. It would be an insincere as well as insecure peace that did not exclude them in definite and binding terms. . . .
>
> National purposes have fallen more and more into the background and the common purpose of enlightened mankind has taken their place. The counsels of plain men have become on all hands more simple and straightforward and more unified than the counsels of sophisticated

men of affairs, who still retain the impression that they are playing a game of power and playing for high stakes. That is why I have said that this is a people's war, not a statesmen's. Statesmen must follow the clarified common thought or be broken.

Yet in his political actions, especially under the pressure of the First World War, Wilson could no more than Jefferson before him discount completely the national interest of the United States. Wilson's case, however, was different from Jefferson's in two respects. For one, Wilson was never able, even when the national interest of the United States was directly menaced, to conceive of the danger in other than moral terms. It was only the objective force of the national interest, which no rational man could escape, that imposed upon him as the object of his moral indignation the source of America's mortal danger. Thus in 1917 Wilson led the United States into war against Germany for the same reasons, only half-known to himself, for which Jefferson had wished and worked alternately for the victory of England and of France. Germany threatened the balance of power in Europe, and it was in order to remove that threat—and not to make the world safe for democracy—that the United States put its weight into the Allies' scale. Wilson pursued the right policy, but he pursued it for the wrong reasons.

Not only did the crusading fervor of moral reformation obliterate the awareness of the United States' traditional interest in the maintenance of the European balance of power, to be accomplished through the defeat of Germany. Wilson's moral fervor also had politically disastrous effects, for which there is no precedent in the history of the United States. Wilson's moral objective required the destruction of the Kaiser's autocracy, and this happened also to be required by the political interests of the United States. The political interests of the United States required, beyond this immediate objective of total victory, the restoration of the European balance of power, traditional guarantor of American security. Yet it was in indignation at the moral deficiencies of that very balance of power, "forever discredited," as he thought, that Wilson had asked the American people to take up arms against the Central Powers! Once military victory had put an end to the immediate threat to American security, the very logic of his moral position—let us remember that consistency is the moralist's supreme virtue—drove him toward substituting for the concrete national interest of the United States the general postulate of a brave new world where the national interest of the United States, as that of all other nations, would disappear in a community of interests comprising mankind.

Consequently, Wilson considered it to be the purpose of victory not to restore a new, viable balance of power, but to make an end to it once and forever. "You know," he told the English people at Manchester on December 30, 1918,

> that the United States has always felt from the very beginning of her history that she must keep herself separate from any kind of connection with European politics, and I want to say very frankly to you that she is not now interested in European politics. But she is interested in the partnership of right between America and Europe. If the future had nothing for us but a new attempt to keep the world at a right poise by a balance of power, the United States would take no interest, because she will join no combination of power which is not the combination of all of us. She is not interested merely in the peace of Europe, but in the peace of the world.

Faced with the national interests of the great allied powers, Wilson had nothing to oppose or support them with but his moral principles, with the result that the neglect of the American national interest was not compensated for by the triumph of political morality. In the end Wilson had to consent to a series of uneasy compromises which were a betrayal of his moral principles—for principles can, by their very nature, not be made the object of compromise—and which satisfied nobody's national aspirations. These compromises had no relation at all to the traditional American national interest in a viable European balance of power. Thus Wilson returned from Versailles a compromised idealist, an empty-handed statesman, a discredited ally. In that triple failure lies the tragedy not only of Wilson, a great yet misguided man, but of Wilsonianism as a political doctrine as well.

Yet Wilson returned to the United States, unaware of his failure. He offered the American people what he had offered the allied nations at Paris: moral principles divorced from political reality. "The day we have left behind us," he proclaimed at Los Angeles on September 20, 1919,

> was a day of balances of power. It was a day of "every nation take care of itself or make a part-nership with some other nation or group of nations to hold the peace of the world steady or to dominate the weaker portions of the world." Those were the days of alliances. This project of the League of Nations is a great process of disentanglement.

VI

While before Paris and Versailles these moral principles rang true with the promise of a new and better world, they now must have sounded to many rather hollow and platitudinous. Yet what is significant for the course which American foreign policy was to take in the interwar years is not so much that the American people rejected Wilsonianism, but that they rejected it by ratifying the denial of the American tradition of foreign policy which was implicit in the political thought of Wilson. We are here indeed dealing with a tragedy not of one man, but of a political doctrine and, as far as the United States is concerned, of a political tradition. The isolationism of the interwar period could delude itself into believing that it was but the restorer of the early realist tradition of American foreign policy. Did it not, like that tradition, proclaim the self-sufficiency of the United States within the Western Hemisphere? Did it not, like that tradition, refuse to become involved in the rivalries of European nations? The isolationists of the twenties and thirties did not see what was the very essence of the policies of the Founding Fathers—that both the isolated and the preponderant position of the United States in the Western Hemisphere was not a fact of nature, and that the freedom from entanglements in European conflicts was not the result of mere abstention on the part of the United States. Both benefits were the result of political conditions outside the Western Hemisphere and of policies carefully contrived and purposefully executed in their support. For the realists of the first period, isolation was an objective of policy, which had to be striven for to be attained. For the isolationists of the interwar period, isolation was, as it were, a natural state, which only needed to be left undisturbed in order to continue forever. Conceived in such terms, it was the very negation of foreign policy.

Isolationism, then, is in its way as oblivious to political reality as is Wilsonianism—the internationalist challenge, to which it had thought to have found the American answer. In consequence, they are both strangers not only to the first, realist phase of American foreign policy, but to its whole tradition. Both refused to face political reality either in realistic or ideological terms. They refused to face it at all. Thus isolationism and Wilsonianism have more in common than their historic enmity would lead one to suspect. In a profound sense they are brothers under the skin. Both are one in maintaining that the United States has no interest in any particular political and military constellation outside the Western Hemisphere. While isolationism stops here, Wilsonianism asserts that the American national interest is nowhere in particular but everywhere, being identical with the interests of mankind itself. The political awareness of both refuses to concern itself with the concrete issues with regard to which the national interest must be asserted. Isolationism stops short of them, Wilsonianism soars beyond them. Both have but a negative relation to the national interest of the United States outside the Western Hemisphere. They are unaware of its very existence. This being so, both substitute abstract moral principles for the guidance of the national interest, derived from the actual conditions of American existence. Wilsonianism applies the illusory expectations of liberal reform to the whole world, isolationism empties the realist political principle of isolationism of all concrete political content and transforms it into the unattainable parochial ideal of automatic separation.

In view of this inner affinity between isolationism and Wilsonianism, it is not surprising that the great debate of the twenties and thirties between internationalism and isolationism was carried on primarily in moral terms. Was there a moral obligation for the United States to make its contribution to world peace by joining the League of Nations and the World Court? Was it morally incumbent upon the United States, as a democracy, to oppose Fascism in Europe and to uphold international law in Asia? Such were the questions which were raised in that debate and the answers depended upon the moral position taken. The question which was central to the national interest of the United States, that of the balance of power in Europe and Asia, was hardly ever faced squarely, and when it was, it was dismissed on moral grounds. Mr. Cordell Hull, Secretary of State of the United States from 1933–1944 and one of the most respected spokesmen of internationalism, summarizes in his *Memoirs* his attitude toward this central problem of American foreign policy in these terms:

> I was not, and am not, a believer in the idea of balance of power or spheres of influence as a means of keeping the peace. During the First World War I had made an intensive study of the system of spheres of influence and balance of power, and I was grounded to the taproots in their iniquitous consequences. The conclusions I then formed in total opposition to this system stayed with me.

When internationalism triumphed in the late thirties, it did so in the moral terms of Wilsonianism. That in this instance the moral postulates which inspired the administration of Franklin D. Roosevelt happened to coincide with the exigencies of the American national interest was again, as in the case of Jefferson and of the Wilson of 1917, due to the impact of a national emergency upon innate common sense and to the strength of a national tradition which holds in its spell the actions even of those who deny its validity in words. However, as soon as the minds of the American leaders were freed from the inescapable pressures of a primarily military nature and turned toward the political problems of the war and its aftermath, they thought and acted again as Wilson had acted under similar circumstances. That is to say, they thought and acted in moral terms, divorced from the political conditions of America's existence.

The practical results of this philosophy of international affairs, as applied to the political war and post-war problems, were, then, bound to be quite similar to those which had made the allied victory in the First World War politically meaningless. Conceived as it was as a "crusade"—to borrow from the title of General Eisenhower's book—against the evil incarnate in the Axis Powers, the purpose of the Second World War could only be the destruction of that evil, transacted through the instrumentality of "unconditional surrender." Since the threat to the Western world emanating from the Axis was conceived primarily in moral terms, it was easy to imagine that all conceivable danger was concentrated in that historic constellation of hostile powers and that with its destruction political evil itself would disappear from the world. Beyond "unconditional surrender" there was, then, a brave new world after the model of Wilson's, which would liquidate the heritage of the defeated evil, not "peace-loving" nations and would establish an order of things where war, aggressiveness, and the struggle for power itself were to be no more. Thus Mr. Cordell Hull could declare on his return in 1943 from the Moscow Conference that the new international organization would mean the end of power politics and usher in a new era of international collaboration. Three years later, Mr. Philip Noel-Baker, then British Minister of State, echoed Mr. Hull by stating in the House of Commons that the British Government was "determined to use the institutions of the United Nations to kill power politics, in order that by the methods of democracy, the will of the people shall prevail."

With this philosophy dominant in the West—Mr. Churchill provides almost the sole, however ineffective, exception—the strategy of the war and of the peace to follow could not help being oblivious to those considerations of the national interest which the great statesmen of the West, from Hamilton through Castelreagh, Canning and John Quincy Adams to Disraeli and Salisbury, had brought to bear upon the international problems of their day. War was no longer regarded as a means to a political end. The only end the war was to serve was total victory, which is another way of saying that the war became an end in itself. Hence, it became irrelevant how the war was won politically, as long as it was won speedily, cheaply, and totally. The thought that the war might be waged in view of a new balance of power to be established after the war, occurred in the West only to Winston Churchill—and, of course, to Joseph Stalin. The national interest of the Western nations was, then, satisfied insofar as it required the destruction of the threat to the balance of power emanating from Germany and Japan; for insofar, the moral purposes of the war happened to coincide with the national interest. However, the national interest of the Western nations was jeopardized insofar as their security required the creation of a new viable balance of power after the war.

How could statesmen who boasted that they were not "believers in the idea of balance of power"—like a scientist not believing in the law of gravity—and who were out "to kill power politics," understand the very idea of the national interest which demanded above all protection from the power of others? Thus it was with deeply and sincerely felt moral indignation that the Western world, expecting a brace new world without power politics, found itself confronted with a new and more formidable threat to its security as soon as the old one had been subdued. There was good reason for moral indignation, however misdirected this one was. That a new balance of power will rise out of the ruins of an old one and that nations with political sense will avail themselves of the opportunity to improve their position within it, is a law of politics for whose validity nobody is to blame. Yet blameworthy are those who in their moralistic disdain for the laws of politics endanger the interests of the nations which are in their care.

The history of American foreign policy since the end of the Second World War is the story of the encounter of the American mind with a new political world. That mind was weakened in its understanding of foreign policy by half a century of ever more complete intoxication with moral abstractions. Even a mind less weakened would have found it hard to face with adequate understanding and successful action and unprecedented novelty and magnitude of the new political world. American foreign policy in that period presents itself as a slow, painful, and incomplete process of emancipation from deeply ingrained error and of rediscovery of long-forgotten truths.

The fundamental error which has thwarted American foreign policy in thought and action is the antithesis of national interest and moral principles. The equation of political moralism with morality and of political realism with immorality is itself untenable. The choice is not between moral principles and the national interest, devoid of moral dignity, but between one set of moral principles, divorced from political reality, and another set of moral principles, derived from political reality. The basic fact of international politics is the absence of a society able to protect the existence, and to promote the interests, of the individual nations. For the individual nations to take care of their own national interests is, then, a political necessity. There can be no moral duty to neglect them; for as the international society is at present constituted, the consistent neglect of the national interest can only lead to national suicide. Yet it can be shown that there exists even a positive moral duty for the individual nation to take care of its national interests.

Self-preservation for the individual as well as for societies is not only a biological and psychological necessity, but in the absence of an overriding moral obligation a moral duty as well. In the absence of an integrated international society, in particular, the attainment of a modicum of order and the realization of a minimum of moral values are predicated upon the existence of national communities capable of preserving order and realizing moral values within the limits of their power. It is obvious that such a state of affairs falls far short of that order and realized morality to which we are accustomed in national societies. The only relevant question is, however, what the practical alternative is to these imperfections of an international society based upon the national interests of its component parts. The attainable alternative is not a higher morality realized through the application of universal moral principles, but moral deterioration through either political failure or the fanaticism of political crusades. The juxtaposition of the morality of political moralism and the immorality of the national interest is mistaken. It operates with a false concept of morality, developed by national societies but unsuited to the conditions of international society. In the process of its realization, it is bound to destroy the very moral values which it is its purpose to promote. Hence, the antithesis between moral principles and the national interest is not only intellectually mistaken but also morally pernicious. A foreign policy derived from the national interest is in fact morally superior to a foreign policy inspired by universal moral principles. Albert Sorel, the Anglophobe historian of the French Revolution, well summarized the real antithesis when he said in grudging admiration of Castelreagh:

> He piqued himself on principles to which he held with an unshakable constancy, which in actual affairs could not be distinguished from obstinacy; but these principals were in no degree abstract or speculative, but were all embraced in one alone, the supremacy of English interests; they all proceeded from this high reason of state.

May as much be said by a future historian of the American foreign policy of our time!

READING 5: HEDLEY BULL

British scholar Hedley Bull is one of the most influential contributors to the study of international politics. His concern was that many young idealists of the sixties and seventies were forgetting the most fundamental principle of conduct in international affairs: state sovereignty. The title of his book, *The Anarchical Society,* is a reminder to those who make references to an "international society." His argument is that there is only anarchy (i.e., no central governing authority in international politics). Bull's approach is simple yet powerful: sovereign states form among themselves a society, and this society must be understood on its own terms.

HEDLEY BULL,

THE ANARCHICAL SOCIETY, 1977

INTERNATIONAL ORDER

By international order I mean a pattern of activity that sustains the elementary or primary goals of the society of states, or international society. Before spelling out in more detail what is involved in the concept of international order I shall first set the stage by indicating what I mean by states, by a system of states, and by a society of states, or international society.

The starting point of international relations is the existence of *states,* or independent political communities, each of which possesses a government and asserts sovereignty in relation to a particular portion of the earth's surface and a particular segment of the human population. On the one hand, states assert, in relation to this territory and population, what may be called internal sovereignty, which means supremacy over all other authorities within that territory and population. On the other hand, they assert what may be called external sovereignty, by which is meant not supremacy but independence of outside authorities. The sovereignty of states, both internal and external, may be said to exist both at a normative level and at a factual level. On the one hand, states assert the right to supremacy over authorities within their territory and population and independence of authorities outside it; but, on the other hand, they also actually exercise, in varying degrees, such supremacy and independence in practice. An independent political community which merely claims a right to sovereignty (or is judged by others to have such a right), but cannot assert this right in practice, is not a state properly so-called.

The independent political communities that are states in this sense include city-states, such as those of ancient Greece or renaissance Italy, as well as modern nation-states. They include states in which government is based on dynastic principles of legitimacy, such as predominated in modern Europe up to the time of the French Revolution, as well as states in which government is based upon popular or national principles of legitimacy, such as have predominated in Europe since that time. They include multinational states, such as the European empires of the nineteenth century, as well as states of a single nationality. They include states whose territory is scattered in parts, such as the oceanic imperial states of Western Europe, as well as states whose territory is a single geographical entity.

There are, however, a great variety of independent political communities that have existed in history and yet are not states in this sense. The Germanic peoples of the Dark Ages, for example, were independent political communities, but while their rulers asserted supremacy over a population, they did not assert it over a distinct territory. The kingdoms and principalities of Western Christendom in the Middle Ages were not states: they did not possess internal sovereignty because they were not supreme over authorities within their territory and population; and at the same time they did not possess external sovereignty since they were not independent of the Pope or, in some cases, the Holy Roman Emperor. In parts of Africa, Australia and Oceania, before the European intrusion, there were independent political communities held together by ties of lineage of kinship, in which there was no such institution as government. Entities such as these fall outside the purview of 'international relations', if by this we mean (as we generally do) not the relations of nations but the relations of states in the strict sense. The relations of these independent political communities might be encompassed in a wider theory of the relations of *powers,* in which the relations of states would figure as a special case, but lie outside the domain of 'international relations' in the strict sense.

A *system of states* (or international system) is formed when two or more states have sufficient contact between them, and have sufficient impact on one another's decisions, to cause them to behave—at least in some measure—as parts of a whole. Two or more states can of course exist without forming an international system in this sense: for example, the independent political communities that existed in the Americas before the voyage of Columbus did not form an international system with those that existed in Europe; the independent political communities that existed in China during the Period of Warring States (*circa* 481–221 B.C.) did not form an international system with those that existed in Greece and the Mediterranean at the same time.

But where states are in regular contact with one another, and where in addition there is interaction between them sufficient to make the behaviour of each a necessary element in the calculations of the other, then we may speak of their forming a system. The interactions among states may be direct—as when two states are neighbours, or competitors for the same object, or partners in the same enterprise. Or their interactions may be indirect—the consequence of the dealings each of them has with a third party, or merely of the impact each of them makes on the system as a whole. Nepal and Bolivia are neither neighbours, nor competitors, nor partners in a common enterprise (except, perhaps, as members of the United Nations). But they affect each other through the chain of links among states in which both participate. The interactions among states by which an international system is defined may take the form of co-operation, but also of conflict, or even of neutrality or indifference with regard to one another's objectives. The interactions may be present over a whole range of activities—political, strategic, economic, social—as they are today, or only in one or two; it may be enough, as Raymond Aron's definition of an international system implies, that the independent political communities in question 'maintain regular relations with each other' and 'are all capable of being implicated in a generalised war'.

Martin Wight, in classifying different kinds of states system, has distinguished what he calls an 'international states system' from a 'suzerain-state system'. The former is a system composed of states that are sovereign, in the sense in which the term has been defined here. The latter is a system in which one state asserts and maintains paramountcy or supremacy over the rest. The relations of the Roman Empire to its barbarian neighbours illustrate the concept of a suzerain-state system; so do the relations of Byzantium to its lesser neighbours, of the Abbasid Caliphate to surrounding lesser powers, or of Imperial China to its tributary states. In some of what Martin Wight would call 'international states systems', it has been assumed that at any one time there is bound to be a dominant or hegemonial power: the classical Greek city-state system, for example, and the later system of Hellenistic kingdoms, witnessed a perpetual contest as to which state was to be *hegemon*. What distinguishes a 'suzerain-state system' such as China-and-its-vassals from an 'international states system', in which one or another state at any one time exerts hegemonial power, is that in the former one power exerts a hegemony that is permanent and for practical purposes unchallengeable, whereas in the latter, hegemony passes from one power to another and is constantly subject to dispute.

In terms of the approach being developed here, only what Wight calls an 'international states system' is a states system at all. Among the independent political entities constituting a 'suzerain-state system' such as China-and-its-vassals, only one state—the suzerain state itself—possesses sovereignty, and therefore one of the basic conditions of the existence of a states system, that there should be two or more sovereign states, is absent.

A second distinction made by Martin Wight is between 'primary states systems' and 'secondary states systems'. The former are composed of states, but the latter are composed of systems of states—often of suzerain-state systems. He gives as examples of a 'secondary states system' the relationship between Eastern Christendom, Western Christendom and the Abbasid Caliphate in the Middle Ages and the relationship of Egypt, the Hittites and Babylon in the Armana Age. This is a distinction which may prove a helpful one if a general historical analysis of the political structure of the world as a whole—today almost completely uncharted territory—is ever attempted. The distinction does not help us very much if, as here, we confine our attention to what are strictly systems of states. If the systems of which 'secondary states systems' are composed, each contains a multiplicity of states, then if there is contact and interaction sufficient between these states and other states, the states as a whole form a 'primary states system'. If, on the other hand, the systems concerned do *not* contain states—as Western Christendom did not, for example—then the interactions between such systems are of interest to a theory of world politics, but are not systems of states at all. In terms of our present approach we need take account only of 'primary states systems'.

The term 'international system' has been a fashionable one among recent students of international relations, principally as a consequence of the writings of Morton A. Kaplan. Kaplan's use of the term is not unlike that employed here, but what distinguishes Kaplan's work is the attempt to use the concept of a system to explain and predict international behaviour, especially by treating international systems as a particular kind of 'system of action'. Here nothing of this sort is intended, and the term is employed simply to identify a particular kind of international constellation.

It should be recognized; however, that the term 'system of states' had a long history, and embodied some rather different meanings, before it came to have its present one. It appears to have begun with Pufendorf, whose tract *De systematibus civitatum* was published in 1675. Pufendorf, however, was referring not to the European states system as a whole, but to particular groups of states within that system, which were sovereign yet at the same time connected so as to form one body—like the German states after the peace of Westphalia. While the term 'system' was applied to European states as a whole by eighteenth-century writers such as Rousseau and Nettelbladt, it was writers of the Napoleonic period, such as Gentz, Ancillon and Heeren, who were chiefly responsible for giving the term currency. At a time when the growth of French power threatened to destroy the states system and transform it into a universal empire, these writers sought to draw attention to the existence of the system, and also to show why it was worth preserving; they were not merely the analysts of the states system, but were also its apologists or protagonists. Of their works, the most important was A. H. L. Heeren's *Handbuch der Geschichte des Europaischen Staatensystems und seiner Kolonien,* first published in 1809. The term 'states system' first appeared in English in the translation of this work that was published in 1834, the translator noting that it was 'not strictly English'.

For Heeren the states system was not simply a constellation of states having a certain degree of contact and interaction, as it is defined here. It involved much more than simply the causal connection of certain sets of variables to each other, which Kaplan takes to define a 'system of action'. A states system for Heeren was 'the union of several contiguous states, resembling each other in their manners, religion and degree of social improvement, and cemented together by a reciprocity of interests'. He saw a states system, in other words, as involving common interests and common values and as resting upon a common culture or civilisation. Moreover, Heeren had a sense of the fragility of the states system, the freedom of its members to act so as to maintain the system or allow it to be destroyed, as the Greek city-state system had been destroyed by Macedon, and as later the system of Hellenistic states that succeeded Alexander's empire had in turn been destroyed by Rome. Indeed, Heeren in the 'Preface' to his first and second editions thought that Napoleon had in fact destroyed the European states system, and that he was writing its epitaph. Such a conception of the states system differs basically from what is called an international system in the present study, and is closer to what I call here an international society.

A *society of states* (or international society) exists when a group of states, conscious of certain common interests and common values, form a society in the sense that they conceive themselves to be bound by a common set of rules in their relations with one another, and share in the working of common institutions. If states today form an international society (to what extent they do is the subject of the next chapter), this is because, recognising certain common interests and perhaps some common values, they regard themselves as bound by certain rules in their dealings with one another, such as that they should respect one another's claims to independence, that they should honour agreements into which they enter, and that they should be subject to certain limitations in exercising force against one another. At the same time they co-operate in the working of institutions such as the forms of procedures of international law, the machinery of diplomacy and general international organisation, and the customs and conventions of war.

An international society in this sense presupposes an international system, but an international system may exist that is not an international society. Two or more states, in other words, may be in contact with each other and interact in such a way as to be necessary factors in each other's calculations without their being conscious of common interests or values, conceiving themselves to be bound by a common set of rules, or co-operating in the working of common institutions. Turkey, China, Japan, Korea, and Siam, for example, were part of the European-dominated international system before they were part of the European-dominated international society. That is to say, they were in contact with European powers, and interacted significantly with them in war and commerce, before they and the European powers came to recognise common interests or values, to regard each other as subject to the same set of rules and as co-operating in the working of common institutions. Turkey formed part of the European-dominated international system from the time of its emergence in the sixteenth century, taking part in wars and alliances as a member of the system. Yet in the first three centuries of this relationship it was specifically denied on both sides that the European powers and Turkey possessed any common interests or values; it was held on both sides that agreements entered into with each other were not binding, and there were no common institutions, such as united the European powers, in whose working they co-operated. Turkey was not accepted by the European states as a member of international society until the Treaty of Paris of 1856, terminating the Crimean War, and perhaps did not achieve full equality of rights within international society until the Treaty of Lausanne in 1923.

In the same way Persia and Carthage formed part of a single international system with the classical Greek city-states, but were not part of the Greek international society. That is to say, Persia (and to a lesser extent Carthage) interacted with the Greek city-states, and was always an essential factor in the strategic equation, either as an outside threat against which the Greek city-states were ready to combine, or as a power able to intervene in the conflicts among them. But Persia was perceived by the Greeks as a barbarian power; it did not share the common values of the Greeks, expressed in the Greek language, the pan-Hellenic games or consultation of the Delphic oracle; it was not subject to the rules which required Greek city-states to limit their conflicts with one another; and it was not a participant in the *amphictyonae* in which institutional co-operation among the Greek states took place, or in the diplomatic institution of *proxenoi*.

When, as in the case of encounters between European and non-European states from the sixteenth century until the late nineteenth century, states are participants in a single international system, but not members of a single international society, there may be communication, exchanges of envoys or messengers and agreements—not only about trade but also about war, peace and alliances. But these forms of interaction do not in themselves demonstrate that there is an international society. Communication may take place, envoys may be exchanged and agreements entered into without there being a sense of common interests or values that gives such exchange substance and a prospect of permanence, without any sense that there are rules which lay down how the interaction should proceed, and without the attempt of the parties concerned to co-operate in institutions in whose survival they have a stake. When Cortes and Pizarro parleyed with the Aztec and Inca kings, when George III sent Lord Macartney to Peking, or when Queen Victoria's representatives entered into agreements with the Maori chieftains, the Sultan of Sokoto or the Kabaka of Buganda, this was outside the framework of any shared conception of an international society of which the parties on both sides were members with like rights and duties.

Whether or not these distinguishing features of an international society are present in an international system, it is not always easy to determine: as between an international system that is clearly also an international society, and a system that is clearly not a society, there lie cases where a sense of common interests is tentative and inchoate; where the common rules perceived are vague and ill-formed, and there is doubt as to whether they are worthy of the name of rules; or where common institutions—relating to diplomatic machinery or to limitations in war—are implicit or embryonic. If we ask of modern international society the questions 'when did it begin?' or 'what were its geographical limits?' we are at once involved in difficult problems of the tracing of boundaries.

But certain international systems have quite clearly been international societies also. The chief examples are the classical Greek city-state system; the international system formed by the Hellenistic kingdoms in the period between the disintegration of Alexander's empire and the Roman conquest; the international system of China during the Period of Warring States; the states system of ancient India; and the modern states system, which arose in Europe and is now worldwide.

A common feature of these historical international societies is that they were all founded upon a common culture or civilisation, or at least on some of the elements of such a civilisation: a common language, a common epistemology and understanding of the universe, a common religion, a common ethical code, a common aesthetic or artistic tradition. It is reasonable to suppose that where such elements of a common civilisation underlie an international society, they facilitate its working in two ways. On the one hand, they may make for easier communication and closer awareness and understanding between one state and another, and thus facilitate the definition of common rules and the evolution of common institutions. On the other hand, they may reinforce the sense of common interests that impels states to accept common rules and institutions with a sense of common values.

■■■■

International society has in fact treated preservation of the independence of particular states as a goal that is subordinate to preservation of the society of states itself; this reflects that predominant role played in shaping international society by the great powers, which view themselves as its custodians. Thus international society has often allowed the independence of individual states to be extinguished, as in the great process of partition and absorption of small powers by greater ones, in the name of principles such as 'compensation' and the 'balance of power' that produced a steady decline in the number of states in Europe from the Peace of Westphalia in 1648 until the Congress of Vienna in 1815. In the same way, international society, at least in the perspective of the great powers which see themselves as its guardians, treats the independence of particular states as subordinate to the preservation of the system as a whole when it tolerates or encourages limitation of the sovereignty or independence of small states through such devices as spheres-of-influence agreements, or agreements to create buffer or neutralised states.

There is the goal of peace. By this is meant not the goal of establishing universal and permanent peace, such as has been the dream of irenists or theorists of peace, and stands in contrast to actual historical experience: this is not a goal which the society of states can be said to have pursued in any serious way. Rather what is meant is the maintenance of peace in the sense of the absence of war among member states of international society as the normal condition of their relationship, to be breached only in special circumstances and according to principles that are generally accepted.

Peace in this sense has been viewed by international society as a goal subordinate to that of the preservation of the states system itself, for which it has been widely held that it can be right to wage war; and as subordinate also to preservation of the sovereignty or independence of individual states, which have insisted on the right to wage war in self-defence, and to protect other rights also. The subordinate status of peace in relation to these other goals is reflected in the phrase 'peace and security', which occurs in the United Nations Charter. Security in international politics means no more than safety: either objective safety, safety which actually exists, or subjective safety, that which is felt or experienced. What states seek to make secure or safe is not merely peace, but their independence and the continued existence of the society of states itself which that independence requires; and for these objectives, as we have noted, they are ready to resort to war and the threat of war. The coupling of the two terms together in the Charter reflects the judgment that the requirements of security may conflict with those of peace, and that in this event the latter will not necessarily take priority.

■■■■

THE IDEA OF INTERNATIONAL SOCIETY

Throughout the history of the modern states system there have been three competing traditions of thought: the Hobbesian or realist tradition, which views international politics as a state of war; the Kantian or universalist tradition, which views international politics as a state of war; the Kantian or universalist tradition, which sees at work in international politics a potential community of mankind; and the Grotian or internationalist tradition, which views international politics as taking place within an international society. Here I shall state what is essential to the Grotian or internationalist idea of international society, and what divides it from the Hobbesian or realist tradition on the one hand, and from the Kantian or universalist tradition on the other. Each of these traditional patterns of thought embodies a description of the nature of international politics and a set of prescriptions about international conduct.

The Hobbesian tradition describes international relations as a state of war of all against all, an arena of struggle in which each state is pitted against every other. International relations, on the Hobbesian view, represent pure conflict between states and resemble a game that is wholly distributive or zero-sum: the interests of each state exclude the interests of any other. The particular international activity that, on the Hobbesian view, is most typical of international activity as a whole, or best provides the clue to it, is war itself. Thus peace, on the Hobbesian view, is a period of recuperation from the last war and preparation for the next.

The Hobbesian prescription for international conduct is that the state is free to pursue its goals in relation to other states without moral or legal restrictions of any kind. Ideas of morality and law, on this view, are valid only in the context of a society, but international life is beyond the bounds of any society. If any moral or legal goals are to be pursued in international politics, these can only be the moral or legal goals of the state itself. Either it is held (as by Machiavelli) that the state conducts foreign policy in a kind of moral and legal vacuum, or it is held (as by Hegel and his successors) that moral behaviour for the state in foreign policy lies in its own self-assertion. The only rules or principles which, for those in the Hobbesian tradition, may be said to limit or circumscribe the behaviour of states in their elations with one another are rules of prudence or expediency. Thus agreements may be kept if it is expedient to keep them, but may be broken if it is not.

The Kantian or universalist tradition, at the other extreme, takes the essential nature of international politics to lie not in conflict among states, as on the Hobbesian view, but in the transnational social bonds that link the individual human beings who are the subjects or citizens of states. The dominant theme of international relations, on the Kantian view, is only apparently the relationship among states, and is really the relationship among all men in the community of mankind—which exists potentially, even if it does not exist actually, and which when it comes into being will sweep the system of states into limbo.

Within the community of all mankind, on the universalist view, the interests of all men are one and the same; international politics, considered from this perspective, is not a purely distributive or zero-sum game, as the Hobbesians maintain, but a purely cooperative or non-zero-sum game. Conflicts of interest exist among the ruling cliques of states, but this is only at the superficial or transient level of the existing system of states; properly understood, the interests of all peoples are the same. The particular international activity which, on the Kantian view, most typifies international activity as a whole is the horizontal conflict of ideology that cuts across the boundaries of states and divides human society into two camps—the trustees of the immanent community of mankind and those who stand in its way, those who are of the true faith and the heretics, the liberators and the oppressed.

The kantian or universalist view of international morality is that, in contrast to the Hobbesian conception, there are moral imperatives in the field of international relations limiting the action of states, but that these imperatives enjoin not coexistence and co-operation among states but rather the overthrow of the system of states and its replacement by a cosmopolitan society. The community of mankind, on the Kantian view, is not only the central reality in international politics, in the sense that the forces able to bring it into being are present; it is also the end or object of the highest moral endeavour. The rules that sustain coexistence and social intercourse among states should be ignored if the imperatives of this higher morality require it. Good faith with heretics has no meaning, except in terms of tactical convenience; between the elect and the damned, the liberators and the oppressed, the question of mutual acceptance of rights to sovereignty or independence does not arise.

What has been called the Grotian or internationalist tradition stands between the realist tradition and the universalist tradition. The Grotian tradition describes international politics in terms of a society of states or international society. As against the Hobbesian tradition, the Grotians contend that states are not engaged in simple struggle, like gladiators in an arena, but are limited in their conflicts with one another by common rules and institutions. But as against the Kantian or universalist perspective the Grotians accept the Hobbesian premise that sovereigns or states are the principal reality in international politics; the immediate members of international society are states rather than individual human beings. International politics, in the Grotian understanding, expresses neither complete conflict of interest between states nor complete identity of interest; it resembles a game that is partly distributive but also partly productive. The particular international activity which, on the Grotian view, best typifies international activity as a whole is neither war between states, nor horizontal conflict cutting across the boundaries of states, but trade—or, more generally, economic and social intercourse between one country and another.

The Grotian prescription for international conduct is that all states, in their dealings with one another, are bound by the rules and institutions of the society they form. As against the view of the Hobbesians, states in the Grotian view are bound not only by rules of prudence or expediency but also by imperatives of morality and law. But, as against the view of the universalists, what these imperatives enjoin is not the overthrow of the system of states and its replacement by a universal community of mankind, but rather acceptance of the requirements of coexistence and co-operation in a society of states.

Each of these traditions embodies a great variety of doctrines about international politics; among which there exists only a loose connection. In different periods each pattern of thought appears in a different idiom and in relation to different issues and preoccupations. This is not the place to explore further the connections and distinctions within each tradition. Here we have only to take account of the fact that the Grotian idea of international society has always been present in thought about the states system, and to indicate in broad terms the metamorphoses which, in the last three to four centuries, it has undergone.

ORDER VERSUS JUSTICE IN WORLD POLITICS

Order is not merely an actual or possible condition or state of affairs in world politics, it is also very generally regarded as a value. But it is not the only value in relation to which international conduct can be shaped, nor is it necessarily an overriding one. At the present time, for example, it is often said that whereas the Western powers, in the justifications they offer of their policies, show themselves to be primarily concerned with order, the states of the Third World are primarily concerned with the achievement of justice in the world community, even at the price of disorder. Professor Ali Mazrui, one of the few contemporary writers on international relations to have thought deeply about this question, has said that the Western powers, the principal authors of the United Nations Charter, wrote it in such a way that peace and security are treated as the primary objectives of the organisation, and the promotion of human rights as a secondary objective, whereas the African and Asian states are dedicated to reversing this order of priority.

How far Professor Mazrui is correct in characterising in this way the conflict of policy between the Western powers and the African and Asian states, I shall consider later. My purpose in this chapter is to raise some deeper questions that underlie this contemporary conflict of policy, as they have underlain other such conflicts in the past, concerning the place of order in the hierarchy of human values. In particular I propose to examine the contending claims of order and the other human value most frequently contrasted with it, justice. To this end I shall consider:

(i) What meaning or meanings can we give to the idea of justice in world politics?
(ii) How is order in world politics related to justice? How far are order and justice compatible or mutually reinforcing ends of policy, and how far are they conflicting or even mutually exclusive?
(iii) To the extent that order and justice are conflicting or alternative goals of policy, which should have priority?

In the discussion of questions such as these there is a danger of lapsing into subjectivity or policy prescription. Moreover, it would be naive to imagine that such questions, stated in these general terms, could be answered conclusively or authoritatively. But it should be possible, while avoiding subjectivism and the canvassing of solutions, at least to clarify the questions and to achieve a deeper understanding of the considerations that lie behind the various answer to them.

THE MEANING OF 'JUSTICE'

Unlike order, justice is a term which can ultimately be given only some kind of private or subjective definition. I do not propose to set out any private vision of what just conduct in world politics would be, nor to embark upon any philosophical analysis of the criteria for recognizing it. My starting-point is simply that there are certain ideas or beliefs as to what justice involves in world politics, and that demands formulated in the name of these ideas play a role in the course of events.

Clearly, ideas about justice belong to the class of moral ideas, ideas which treat human actions as right in themselves and not merely as a means to an end, as categorically and not merely hypothetically imperative. Considerations of justice, accordingly, are to be distinguished from considerations of law, and from considerations of the dictates of prudence, interest or necessity.

In thinking about justice there are certain distinctions, familiar in theoretical analyses of the idea, which it is helpful to bear in mind. First, there is the distinction between what has been called 'general' justice, justice as identical with virtuous or righteous conduct in general, and 'particular' justice, justice as one species of right conduct among others. The term 'justice' is sometimes used interchangeably with 'morality' or 'virtue', as if to say an action is just were simply another way of saying that it is morally right. It is often argued, however, that ideas about justice constitute a particular sub-category of moral ideas, as we imply when we say that justice should be tempered with mercy, or that states in their dealings with one another are capable of justice but not of charity. It has often been contended that justice is especially to do with equality in the enjoyment of rights and privileges, perhaps also to do with fairness or reciprocity; that, whatever the substance of the rights or privileges in question, demands for justice are demands for the equal enjoyment of them as between persons who are different from one another in some respect but should be treated in respect of these rights as if they were the same.

Demands for justice in world politics are often of this form; they are demands for the removal of privilege or discrimination, for equality in the distribution or in the application of rights as between the strong and the weak, the large and the small, the rich and the poor, the black and the white, the nuclear and the nonnuclear, or the victors and the vanquished. It is important to distinguish between 'justice' in this special sense of equality of rights and privileges, and 'justice' in the sense in which we are using it interchangeably with 'morality'.

A second important distinction is between 'substantive' and 'formal' justice, the former lying in the recognition of rules conferring certain specified rights and duties—political, social, or economic—and the latter lying in the like application of these rules to like persons, irrespective of what the substantive content of the rules may be. Demands for 'equality before the law', demands that legal rules be applied in a fair or equal manner to like persons or classes of persons, are demands for 'formal justice' in this sense, although such demands arise in relation to all rules, legal and non-legal: that like groups of people should be treated in a like manner is entailed in the very notion of a rule of any kind. Demands for 'justice' in world politics are frequently demands for formal justice in this sense: that some legal rule, such as that requiring states not to interfere in one another's domestic affairs, or some moral rule, such as that which confers on all nations a right of self-determination, or some operational rule or rule of the game, such as that which requires the great powers to respect one another's spheres of influence, should be applied fairly or equally as between one state and another.

A third distinction is between 'arithmetical justice', in the sense of equal rights and duties, and 'proportionate justice', or rights and duties which may not be equal but which are distributed according to the end in view. Equality may be envisaged as the enjoyment by a class of like persons or groups of the same rights and duties. But it is obvious that equality in this sense will often fail to satisfy other criteria of justice. For one thing, given that persons and groups are sometimes unequal in their capacities or in their needs, a rule that provides them with the same rights and duties may have the effect simply of further underlining their inequality; as Aristotle wrote, 'injustice arises when equals are treated unequally and also when unequals are treated equally'. Marx's principle 'from each according to his capacity, to each according to his need' embodies a preference for 'proportionate' over 'arithmetical' justice in relation to the end of a just distribution of wealth. In world politics certain basic rights and duties, such as the right of states to sovereign independence and the duty of states not to interfere in one another's domestic affairs, generally held to apply equally to all states, exemplify 'arithmetical justice', while the doctrine that the use of force in war or reprisals should be in proportion to the injury that has been suffered may be taken to illustrate 'proportionate justice'.

A fourth distinction, closely connected with the latter, is between 'commutative' or reciprocal justice, and 'distributive' justice, or justice assessed in the light of the common good or common interest of society as a whole. 'Commutative' justice lies in the recognition of rights and duties by a process of exchange or bargaining, whereby one individual or group recognises the rights of others in return for their recognition of his or its own. To the extent that the bargaining strength of individuals and groups is equal, this reciprocal process is likely to result in what we have called 'arithmetical justice' or equal rights. 'Distributive justice', by contrast, comes about not through a process of bargaining among individual members of the society in question, but by decision of the society as a whole, in the light of consideration of its common good or interest. It is clear that 'distributive justice' in this sense may often result in justice which is 'proportionate' rather than 'arithmetical', requiring for example that the rich pay higher taxes than the poor, or that the strong perform more labour than the weak. World politics in the present era is principally a process of conflict and co-operation among states having only the most rudimentary sense of the common good of the world as a whole, and is therefore the domain pre-eminently of ideas of 'commutative' rather than 'distributive' justice. The main stuff of contention about justice in international affairs is to be found in the attempt of sovereign states, through a process of claim and counter-claim, to iron out among themselves what rights and duties will be recognised and how they will be applied. But ideas of 'distributive' justice also play a part in the discussion of world politics, and are exemplified by the idea that justice requires a transfer of economic resources from rich countries to poor.

In applying all these distinctions it is important to consider in what agents or actors in world politics moral rights or duties are taken to be vested. Here one may distinguish what may be called international or interstate justice; individual or human justice; and cosmopolitan or world justice.

▉▉▉▉

COMPATIBILITY OF ORDER AND JUSTICE

It is obvious that the existing framework of international order fails to satisfy some of the most deeply felt and powerfully supported of these aspirations for justice. Not only is it true of the contemporary international scene, as noted by Professor Mazrui, that it is marked by conflict between those states that are concerned chiefly to preserve order and those that give priority to the achievement of just change, if necessary at the expense of order; there is also an inherent tension between the order provided by the system and society of states, and the various aspirations for justice that arise in world politics, which is persistently expressed in one way or another.

It is true that justice, in any of its forms, is realisable only in a context of order; it is only if there is a pattern of social activity in which elementary or primary goals of social life are in some degree provided for, that advanced or secondary goals can be secured. It is true *a fortiori,* that international society, by providing a context of order of some kind, however rudimentary, may be regarded as paving the way for the equal enjoyment of rights of various kinds. It is true also that international society at present, through such nearly universal organs as the United Nations and its specialised agencies, is formally committed to much more than the preservation of minimum order or coexistence: it espouses ideas of international or interstate justice, and of individual or human justice, and even takes some account, through its endorsement of the idea of the transfer of resources from rich to poor countries, of goals of world justice; and it facilitates intergovernmental co-operation in many fields to promote the realisation of these ideas.

But, to begin with, the framework of international order is quite inhospitable to projects for the realisation of cosmopolitan or world justice. If the idea of the world common good were to be taken seriously, it would lead to the consideration of such questions as how the immigration policies of states throughout the world should be shaped in the general interest, which countries or which areas of the world have the most need of capital and which the least, how trade and fiscal policies throughout the world should be regulated in accordance with a common set of priorities, or what outcomes of a host of violent civil and international conflicts throughout the world best conformed to the general interests of mankind.

These are of course the very issues over which governments have control, and do not seem likely to be willing to relinquish control, in the absence of vast changes in human society. The position which governments occupy as custodians of the perceived interests of limited sections of mankind imposes familiar obstacles to their viewing themselves simply as so many agencies jointly responsible for the implementation of the world common good. It is sometimes said that the commitment of the donor countries through aid and trade policies to the objective of a minimum level of economic welfare throughout the world implies and presupposes acceptance of the idea of the interests of the community of mankind. Kenneth Boulding, for example, argues that since the transfer of resources from rich to poor countries is wholly one-sided or non-reciprocal it means that the rich see themselves as part of the same community with the poor. 'If A gives B something without expecting anything in return the inference must be drawn that B is "part" of A, or that A and B together are part of a larger system of interests and organisations.' It may be argued that the idea of the community of mankind provides a better rationale for the transfer of resources than others that are sometimes given: better, for example, than the idea sometimes put forward in Western countries that aid to the poor is necessary to promote order or stability (in the sense of a pattern that secures Western-preferred values), or to forestall an incipient revolt of the 'have-nots' against the 'haves'; or the idea prominent in the rhetoric of poor countries that it is necessary so that the rich can expiate the guilt of their past wrongs. It is not clear, however, that the idea of the community of mankind does actually underlie the enterprise of the transfer of resources to any important degree; or indeed that the transfer of resources yet has a secure and established position as part of the permanent business of international society, assailed as it is on the one side by the idea that the rich countries should reduce their involvement in the Third World to the minimum, and on the other side by the doctrine that aid is essentially a means of perpetuating domination and exploitation and hence prejudicial to the true interests of the 'have-nots'.

Ideas of world or cosmopolitan justice are fully realisable, if at all, only in the context of a world or cosmopolitan society. Demands for world justice are therefore demands for the transformation of the system and society of states, and are inherently revolutionary. World justice may be ultimately reconcilable with world order, in the sense that we may have a vision of a world or cosmopolitan society that provides for both. But to pursue the idea of world justice in the context of the system and society of states is to enter into conflict with the devices through which order is at present maintained.

The framework of international order is inhospitable also to demands for human justice, which represent a very powerful ingredient in world politics at the present time. International society takes account of the notion of human rights and duties that may be asserted against the state to which particular human beings belong, but it is inhibited from giving effect to them, except selectively and in a distorted way. If international society were really to treat human justice as primary and coexistence as secondary,—if, as Professor Mazrui says, the African and Asian states want, the United Nations Charter were to give pride of place to human rights rather than to the preservation of peace and security—then in a situation in which there is no agreement as to what human rights are or in what hierarchy of priorities they should be arranged, the result could only be to undermine international order. It is here that the society of states—including, I should say, despite what Professor Mazrui says, African and Asian states—displays its conviction that international order is prior to human justice. African and Asian states, I believe, like other states, are willing to subordinate order to human justice in particular cases closely affecting them, but they are no more willing than the Western states or the states of the Soviet bloc to allow the whole structure of international coexistence to be brought to the ground.

There is another obstacle to the realisation of human justice within the present framework of international order. When questions of human justice achieve a prominent place on the agenda of world political discussion, it is because it is the policy of particular states to raise them. The world after the First World War heard about the war guilt of the Kaiser, and after the Second World War witnessed the trial and punishment of German and Japanese leaders and soldiers for war crimes and crimes against the peace. It did not witness the trial and punishment of American, British and Soviet leaders and soldiers who *prima facie* might have been as much or as little guilty of disregarding their human obligations as Goering, Yamamoto and the rest. This is not to say that the idea of the trial and punishment of war criminals by international procedure is an unjust or unwise one, only that it operates in a selective way. That these men and not others were brought to trial by the victors was an accident of power politics.

In the same way the world has heard of the human rights of non-European persons in Southern Africa, and may even come to see redress of the wrongs they have suffered, because it is the policy of black African states and others to take up this issue, just as the world once heard of the rights of the Christian subjects of the Sultan of Turkey because it was the policy of certain European powers to uphold them. But the rights of Africans in black African states, or of intellectuals in the Soviet Union, or of Tibetans in China or Nagas in India or communists in Indonesia are less likely to be upheld by international action because it is not the policy of any prominent group of states to protect them. The international order does not provide any general protection of human rights, only a selective protection that is determined not by the merits of the case but by the vagaries of international politics.

There is a further obstacle. Even in cases where, as the consequence of these vagaries of international politics, international society permits action directed towards the realisation of human justice, the action taken does not directly impinge upon individual human beings but takes place through the mediation of sovereign states, who shape this action to their own purposes. Take the case of world economic justice, towards the realisation of which the transfer of resources from the rich to the poor countries is bent. The ultimate moral object of this process is to improve the material standard of life of individual human beings in poor Asian, African and Latin American countries. But the donor countries and international organisations concerned transfer resources not directly to these individuals but to the governments of the countries of which they are citizens. As Julius Stone points out, it is left to these governments to determine the criteria according to which the resources will be distributed to individuals, or indeed to distribute them arbitrarily or not distribute them at all. As he says, the unspoken assumption of the business of transfer of resources is that the actual claimants and beneficiaries of what he calls the 'justice constituency' are not individual human beings but governments. The doubts which donor countries entertain about the way in which the governments of recipient countries distribute or fail to distribute the resources transferred to them of course constitute one of the principal disincentives to foreign aid. Yet one has also to agree with Stone's conclusion that although the transfer of resources, as it takes place at present, necessarily falls short of the realisation of what I have called human justice, it is inevitable, given the present nature of international society, that it should do so: donor countries and organisations cannot determine the way in which recipient governments distribute their resources (although they can sometimes lay down conditions for the distribution of resources transferred) without violating the most fundamental norms of the compact of coexistence.

If international society is quite inhospitable to notions of cosmopolitan justice, and able to give only a selective and ambiguous welcome to ideas of human justice, it is not basically unfriendly to notions of interstate or international justice. The structure of international coexistence, as I have argued, itself depends on norms or rules conferring rights and duties upon states—not necessarily moral rules, but procedural rules or rules of the game which in modern international society are stated in some cases in international law. Whereas ideas of world justice may seem entirely at odds with the structure of international society, and notions of human justice to entail a possible threat to its foundations, ideas of interstate and international justice may reinforce the compact of coexistence between states by adding a moral imperative to the imperatives of enlightened self-interest and of law on which it rests.

Yet international order is preserved by means which systematically affront the most basic and widely agreed principles of international justice. I do not mean simply that at the present time there are states and nations which are denied their moral rights or fail to fulfil their moral responsibilities, or that there is gross inequality or unfairness in their enjoyment of these rights, or exercise of responsibilities. This is of course the case, but it has always been the case, and it is the normal condition of any society. What I have in mind is rather that the institutions and mechanisms which sustain international order, even when they are working properly, indeed especially when they are working properly, or fulfilling their functions—their working is reviewed in Part 2 of this study—necessarily violate ordinary notions of justice.

Consider, for example, the role that is played in international order by the institution of the balance of power. Here is an institution which offends against everyday notions of justice by sanctioning war against a state whose power threatens to become preponderant, but which has done no legal or moral injury; by sacrificing the interests of small states, which may be absorbed or partitioned in the interests of the balance; or—in the case of its contemporary variant, the 'balance of terror'—by magnifying and exploiting the risk of destruction. Yet this is an institution whose role in the preservation of order in the international system, in the past and at present, is a central one.

Or consider the role of another institution: war. War also plays a central role in the maintenance of international order in the enforcement of international law, the preservation of the balance of power and the effecting of changes which a consensus maintains are just. But war at the same time may be the instrument of overthrowing rules of international law, of undermining the balance of power and of preventing just changes or effecting changes that are unjust. It is at the same time an instrument which once employed, whether for just or unjust causes, may develop a momentum of its own so that it ceases to be an instrument of those who began it, but transforms them and the situation in which they find themselves beyond recognition.

Consider, again, international law. It is not merely that international law sanctifies the *status quo* without providing for a legislative process whereby the law can be altered by consent and thus causes the pressures for change to consolidate behind demands that the law should be violated in the name of justice. It is also that when the law is violated, and a new situation is brought about by the triumph not necessarily of justice but of force, international law accepts this new situation as legitimate, and concurs in the means whereby it has been brought about. As Mazrui writes, international law condemns aggression, but once aggression has been successful it ceases to be condemned. The conflict between international law and international justice is endemic because the situations from which the law takes its point of departure are a series of *faits accomplis* brought about by force and the threat of force, legitimised by the principle that treaties concluded under duress are valid.

Moreover, contrary to much superficial thinking on this subject, it is not as if this tendency of international law to accommodate itself to power politics were some unfortunate but remediable defect that is fit to be removed by the good work of some high-minded professor of international law or by some ingenious report of the International Law Commission. There is every reason to think that this feature of international law, which sets it at loggerheads with elementary justice, is vital to its working; and that if international law ceased to have this feature, it would so lose contact with international reality as to be unable to play any role at all.

Or consider the role that is played in the maintenance of international order by the special position of the great powers. Great powers contribute to international order by maintaining local systems of hegemony within which order is imposed from above, and by collaborating to manage the global balance of power and, from time to time, to impose their joint will on others. But the great powers, when they perform these services to international order, do so at the price of systematic injustice to the rights of smaller states and nations, the injustice which has been felt by states which fall within the Soviet hegemony in Eastern Europe or the American hegemony in the Caribbean, the injustice which is written into the terms of the United Nations Charter which prescribe a system of collective security that cannot be operated against great powers, the injustice from which small powers always suffer when great ones meet in concert to strike bargains at their expense.

There is no general incompatibility as between order in the abstract, in the sense in which it has been defined, and justice in any of the meanings that have been reviewed. We may imagine, in other words, a society in which there is a pattern of activity that sustains elementary or primary goals of social life, and also provides for advanced or secondary goals of justice or equality, for states, for individuals and in terms of the world common good. There is no *a priori* reason for holding that such a society is unattainable, or that there is any inconsistency in pursuing both world order and world justice. There is, however, incompatibility as between the rules and institutions that now sustain order within the society of states, and demands for world justice, which imply the destruction of this society, demands for human justice, which it can accommodate only in a selective and partial way, and demands for interstate and international justice, to which it is not basically hostile, but to which also it can provide only limited satisfaction.

THE QUESTION OF PRIORITY

Given that the framework of international society fails to satisfy these various ideas of justice, what would be the effects upon international order of attempts to realise them? Can justice in world politics, in its various senses, be achieved only by jeopardising international order? And if this is so, which should take priority?

Chapter Three

Idealism

"When I despair, I remember that all through history the way of truth and love has always won." *Mahatma Gandhi.*

"The ultimate weakness of violence is that it is a descending spiral, begetting the very thing it seeks to destroy . . . . Darkness cannot drive out darkness; only light can do that. Hate cannot drive out hate; only love can do that." Martin Luther King, Jr.

"Washing one's hands of the conflict between the powerful and the powerless means to side with the powerful." *Paulo Friere*

Although *power* and philosophies of *freedom* are crucial to understanding the subject of international politics, there is also a strong idealist strain in the Western tradition that will be seen in the words of the selections in this chapter. Starting with the Ancient Greeks, we briefly consider the questions that were asked and why they might fall under this idealist paradigm. We then move to a variety of arguments and institutional efforts that have as their common theme: "This is how the world ought to be." In the case of many idealists, the argument is made in an effort to convince the reader that change ought to be made, not only in the name of *justice*, but also for mutually benefiting "rational" reasons.

Ancient Greek Contributions to Idealism

It is important to keep in mind that the Greek city-state *(polis)* and Greek ideas of democracy *(demokratia)* occurred well before the development of the Roman Empire. By the seventh-century BCE Greek city-states were prospering around the *acropolis,* and the

Olympic games were already being held, even before Rome was said to be founded by Romulus and Remus.[132] The Ancient Greek philosophers, to which we refer to most, are of this pre-*pax romana* period (i.e., pre-Roman rule): Socrates (470–399 BCE); Plato (428–348 BCE); and Aristotle (384–322 BCE). Recall that Thucydides' account of the Peloponnesian War (431–404 BCE) during the Age of Pericles, to which we referred in Chapter 2, takes place around this time as well. The Ancient Greeks only begin to lose their political power, relative to others in the region, after the defeat of the Athenians and following the adventures of Alexander of Macedon (356–323 BCE), a.k.a. "Alexander the Great."[133]

It is during this time of relevant prosperity, now threatened in the struggle with Sparta, that the aforementioned Athenian political philosophers emerge. However, the achievement of democratic practice occurred in Greek city-states *before* the ideas of these Ancient Greek philosophers were debated (i.e., as is so often the case in history, "reflection followed achievement").[134] Nevertheless, the culture in which these democratic practices and ideas did emerge emphasized the art of conversation and, generally, of modern rhetoric (*rhetorike*)—the art of speaking or writing effectively. It was an atmosphere that, in the words of George Sabine "almost forced the Greek to think of what would now be called comparative government."[135]

Prior to (and during) the rivalry between the Athenians and the Spartans, there existed a constant threat of violence from the Persians to the East. Herodotus, considered by many to be the "father of history," wrote of the history of conflict between the Persians and the Greeks in his seminal book, *The Persian Wars,* ca. 440 BCE.[136] It is not a philosophical book, and its historical accuracy has been challenged (i.e., Herodotus seems to be describing Ancient Greek realities more than those of Persia). In one passage, for example, the Persians are said to be debating the merits of monarchy, aristocracy, and democracy.[137] This passage, according to Sabine, ". . . is a genuine Greek touch which Herodotus certainly did not learn in Persia."[138] We do know that this kind of open debate over the merits of different political systems was now regularly taking place in Ancient Greece using the "Socratic Method," wherein Socrates would guide discussions among his students using cross questioning, rather than simply providing "answers" to their questions. Among Socrates' students was Plato, who has become the world's primary spokesman for his humanist teacher, as Socrates did not leave us with any written work.[139]

---

[132] "Acropolis" refers to the "high place of the town." The traditional date for the founding of Rome is 753 BCE, based on the legend of Romulus and Remus.

[133] The Romans do not formally *rule* Greece until 146 BCE. See: Agnes Savill, *Alexander the Great and His Time* (New York: Barnes & Noble, 1993).

[134] This argument is made by Sabine (1966), p. 21. He argues that prior to Plato, the Ancient Greeks were not reading or writing many books and that, even if there were any treaties written, very little has been preserved.

[135] Ibid. Of the Ancient Greek philosophers, Aristotle is generally considered to be the "father" of comparative politics.

[136] Herodotus, *The Persian Wars* (New York: The Modern Library, 1947).

[137] Book III, 80–82, cited in Sabine (1966), p. 22.

[138] Ibid., p. 23.

[139] That Socrates was a great humanist is suggested by I. F. Stone, *The Trial of Socrates* (Boston: Little, Brown, 1988). We may never know the truth, as it is difficult to disentangle his true opinions from what Aristophanes, Xenophon, and Plato wrote about him. See: Michael Grant, *The Founders of the Western World: A History of Greece and Rome* (New York: Charles Scribner's Sons, 1991), p. 92. Sabine comments, simply: "What exactly were Socrates's conclusions about politics is not known. . . . But in general the implications of identifying virtue with knowledge are too clear to be missed." Sabine (1966), p. 33.

Plato's work has been interpreted in a variety of ways, from being behind everything from communism, totalitarianism, social contract theory, dualism, to elitism.[140] It is likely for this reason that his work is generally left out of the "categories" of realist, idealist, or other paradigms of thought. Nevertheless, Plato did contemplate many of the questions that European philosophers would later continue to debate in many of the social sciences. As with Socrates, it seems that Plato agreed that there must be "an objectively good life, both for individuals and for states, which may be the object of study . . ."[141] For this reason, it is said that Plato believed in both the practical need for, and virtue in, the intellectual pursuit of human behavior in politics.

As a young man, Plato had contemplated a career in politics. But he became disillusioned with the idea after witnessing the turn of events under the rule of the Thirty, which followed the defeat of Athens by Sparta. Although he was put off by the corruption and brutality of political leadership during this period, it was only following the hypocritical trial of his mentor, Socrates, that he completely gave up on a career in politics. In fact, Plato left Athens to continue to study mathematics with Euclid (the "father of geometry") and later to Egypt to study astronomy and mathematics with Theodorus. It was during this time that Plato wrote many of his ideas, including his interpretations of what Socrates had taught him. He developed, for example, the belief that democracy could, in fact, be dangerous and argued that the best political leaders ruled by learned wisdom. Writing in 353 BCE, echoing statements he would make in the *Republic,* Plato argued

> . . . the human race will not see better days until either the stock of those who rightly and genuinely follow philosophy acquire political authority, or else the class who have political control be led by some dispensation of providence to become real philosophers.[142]

It may well have been due to his frustrations with Dionysius that Plato developed these views. Years earlier, in 367–361 BCE, Plato made his famous journeys to Syracuse, at the request of Dionysius's uncle, Dion, to help educate and guide the young king Dionysius. The task that Plato took on was virtually impossible. Although Dionysius' had a horrible reputation and truly unlimited power, Plato still pushed forward, idealistically attempting to teach political philosophy and reason with the youthful ruler. Famously, Plato's effort to educate Dionysius as a "philosopher king" completely backfired. If anything, Dionysius grew to despise political philosophy and, further, claimed that Plato and his uncle were plotting to overthrow him.[143]

Despite the unfortunate turn of events in Sicily with Dionysius, Plato continued to be an advocate of the idea that political leaders should have some "knowledge of the good." And this aspect of Plato's writing, found in the *Republic,* is clearly idealist. As it is described by Sabine, the *Republic* "defies classification" as it deals "with the whole human life."[144] He continues: "It has to do with the *good man* and the *good life,* which for Plato connoted life in a *good state.*"[145] For Plato, "the good" was something that was objectively

---

[140] See: David Denby, *Great Books: My Adventures with Homer, Rousseau, Woolf and Other Indestructible Writers of the Western World* (New York: Simon & Schuster, 1997), pp. 64–75; 92–105.

[141] Sabine (1966), p. 36.

[142] Plato, Letter VII, cited in Sabine (1966), p. 37.

[143] Dionysius may well have been right about his uncle, who later invaded Syracuse, causing Dionysius to flee to Corinth. Having returned to Athens, Plato felt obliged to explain his circumstances, to make it clear to all that he was not involved in this plot.

[144] Sabine (1966), p. 39.

[145] Ibid.

real, and it ought to be realized "not because men want it but because it is good." Quoting Sabine:

> From this it follows that the man who knows—the philosopher or scholar or scientist—ought to have decisive power in government and that it is his knowledge alone which entitles him to this. This is the belief which underlies everything else in the *Republic* and causes Plato to sacrifice every aspect of the state that cannot be brought under the principle of enlightened despotism.[146]

To understand why Plato may have thought this, one has to understand that the order of the day was, in fact, disorder; that most politicians of the day were highly incompetent and ignorant. It is this dilemma that Plato aimed to resolve through his support of "philosopher kings." And again, it was his belief that there can exist a knowledge of "the good" that made him an idealist, as if somehow, through dialogue, this is something that we can ultimately identify.[147] For this reason, although Plato's ideas can be viewed as setting the stage for "republican" ideals, one often hears of "Platonic Idealism."[148]

How can we distinguish our next Ancient Greek philosopher, Aristotle, from Plato? First, it is said that Plato respected his pupil's encyclopedic knowledge, nicknaming him "the reader." Aristotle was one of Plato's most capable students. Second, Aristotle was much less of an idealist and much more of an empiricist. Whereas Plato focused his intellectual energies on identification of the "ideal state," Aristotle aimed at the more practical pursuit of the "best possible form of government."[149] Following the death of Plato, in an effort to apply his more practical ideas, Aristotle famously tutored Alexander the Great of Macedon. What is most ironic about this is that Alexander's exploits mark the true end of the Greek *polis.*[150]

Like Plato, Aristotle did believe that the quest for better understanding, for knowledge, is linked to virtue. Later Roman thinkers, such as Cicero, would argue much the same. In classical Greco-Roman thinking, then, few questioned the worth of intellectual quests. In *Nicomachean Ethics,* for example, Aristotle started with the statement: "Every art and every scientific inquiry, and similarly every action and purpose, may be said to aim at some good."[151] It is this idealist strain, attributed to the Ancient Greeks, that is so often linked to the Western intellectual tradition. The argument, which would be used by so many Enlightenment thinkers hundreds of years later, was that the human struggle was one that generally aimed at achievement of "the good." The birth of Western political philosophy, ac-

---

[146] Ibid., p. 41.

[147] It is for this position that Plato takes on the identification of "the good" that some have said that Socrates similarly had an "absolute standard" of right and wrong. As indicated earlier, we can never really know for certain. See: Grant (1991), pp. 92–97.

[148] See Denby (1999), p. 117. "Neo-platonism" refers to "the omnipresent, transcendental Good," derived from Plato's *Parmenides.* Simon Blackburn, *The Oxford Dictionary of Philosophy* (New York: Oxford University Press, 1996), p. 258.

[149] Nelson (1996), p. 51.

[150] The Macedonian Empire ". . . came to encompass most of the known civilized world, and the Greek city-states lost their autonomy and self-sufficiency. They were absorbed by a new political entity that Aristotle had never even considered. The comparatively intimate governments of the city-states were replaced by a distant emperor ruling over a seemingly limited expanse of peoples who had nothing in common except their new government." Nelson (1996), pp. 69–70.

[151] This line varies somewhat among the translations of the original. Similar logic was used by Mahatma Gandhi (i.e., that the more powerful force in the world, that is expressed by the efforts of individuals, is leading us all (despite the fact that not all intend to do "good") to a better position in the world).

cording to this view, coincides with the Greek vision of growing humanism, visible as early as the tragedies of Homer (ca. 800 BCE) and Sophocles (496–406 BCE).[152]

What Aristotle does have in common with other Ancient Greek thinkers is the assumption that there is "an underlying rational unity and order that exists within the flux and variety of the world."[153] Further, Aristotle does agree that intellectual efforts may well aim at "some good." But, importantly, he does not believe in the identification of an objective morality. For example, referring again to *Nicomachean Ethics,* Aristotle relied less on Plato's idealism and more on "observable phenomena" (i.e., he considered the empirically sound to be more useful). Although open debate led to learning, and perhaps better ideas, the discussion had to remain within the realm of observable reality.

In Chapter 2 we saw that the earliest Roman philosophies borrowed many ideas from the Ancient Greeks. The Romans, through Cicero and later Justinian, left us with some idealist notions, including the quest for an ever-improving body of governing law. Rightly or wrongly, Justinian promoted the idealist view that Roman law was an attempt to determine what *justice* entails and, generally, what is "right." Hence, the Roman lawyer was considered a "priest of justice, the practitioner of a true philosophy . . ."[154] And the Roman law preserved the spirit of Cicero's phrase: "We are the servants of the law in order that we may be free."[155]

In the eyes of some, law itself can be viewed as part of the idealist pursuit to identify what Aristotle ultimately refused to accept: objective morality. The critic of law's objectivity might point out, for example, that currently in the world there are three widespread legal systems: **Common Law** (of the Anglo-American legal tradition), **Islamic Sharia** (with references to the Koran), and **Roman Law** (also referred to as "Civil Law," later carried forward by the Napoleonic Code and found today in most of Europe and many formerly colonized states of Europe). The efforts of Hugo Grotius to make a rational argument for the very existence of an "international law" during both *war* and *peace* are considered in the next passage.

---

[152] Homer's work, like that of many Ancient Greeks afterwards, maintained the sense of "a moral order governing the cosmos." Richard Tarnas, *The Passion of The Western Mind* (New York: Ballantine, 1991), p. 19.

[153] Ibid.

[154] Celsus, quoted in Sabine (1966), p. 170.

[155] Cicero, quote in ibid., p. 172.

READING 6: HUGO GROTIUS

Dutch jurist Hugo Grotius is often referred to as the "father of international law." For that reason—as all proponents of international law can be—he is sometimes labeled as an idealist. During his lifetime Grotius worked for the Dutch East India Company, was for a time a political prisoner, and was charged with treason. Following the publication of *De Jure Belli Ac Pacis* in 1648, Grotius remained in exile from Holland. He eventually became the Swedish Ambassador to France and helped to negotiate for an end to the Thirty Years War. Grotius is said to have died of exhaustion, declaring on his deathbed: "By understanding many things I have accomplished nothing."

Hugo Grotius,

On the Law of War and Peace, 1648

What is Lawful in War

I. HAVING, in the preceding books, considered by what persons, and for what causes, war may be justly declared and undertaken, the subject necessarily leads to an inquiry into the circumstances, under which war may be undertaken, into the extent, to which it may be carried, and into the manner, in which its rights may be enforced. Now all these matters may be viewed in the light of privileges resulting simply from the law of nature and of nations, or as the effects of some prior treaty of promise. But the actions, which are authorised by the law of nature, are those that are first entitled to attention.

II. In the first place, as it has occasionally been observed, the means employed in the pursuit of any object must, in a great degree, derive the complexion of their moral character from the nature of the end to which they lead. It is evident therefore that we may justly avail ourselves of those means, provided they be lawful, which are necessary to the attainment of any right. RIGHT in this place means what is strictly so called, signifying the moral power of action, which any one as a member of society possesses. On which account, a person, if he has no other means of saving his life, is justified in using any forcible means of repelling an attack, though he who makes it, as for instance, a soldier in battle, in doing so, is guilty of no crime. For this is a right resulting not properly from the crime of another, but from the privilege of self-defence, which nature grants to every one. Besides, if any one has SURF and UNDOUBTED grounds to apprehend imminent danger from any thing belonging to another, he may seize it without any regard to the guilt or innocence of that owner. Yet he does not by that seizure become the proprietor of it. For that is not necessary to the end he has in view. He may DETAIN it as a precautionary measure, till he can obtain satisfactory assurance of security.

Upon the same principle any one has a natural right to seize what belongs to him, and is unlawfully detained by another: or, if that is impracticable, he may seize something of equal value, which is nearly the same as recovering a debt. Recoveries of this kind establish a property in the things so reclaimed; which is the only method of restoring the equality and repairing the breaches of violated justice. So too when punishment is lawful and just, all the means absolutely necessary to enforce its execution are also lawful and just, and every act that forms a part of the punishment, such as destroying an enemy's property and country by fire or any other way, falls within the limits of justice proportionable to the offence.

III. In the second place, it is generally known that it is not the ORIGIN only of a just war which is to be viewed as the principal source of many of our rights, but there may be causes growing out of that war which may give birth to additional rights. As in proceedings at law, the sentence of the court may give to the successful litigant other rights besides those belonging to the original matter of dispute. So those who join our enemies, either as allies or subjects, give us a right of defending ourselves against THEM also. So too a nation engaging in an unjust war, the injustice of which she knows and ought to know, becomes liable to make good all the expences and losses incurred, because she has been guilty of occasioning them. In the same manner those powers, who become auxiliaries in wars undertaken without any reasonable grounds, contract a degree of guilt and render themselves liable to punishment in proportion to the injustice of their measures. Plato approves of war conducted so far, as to compel the aggressor to indemnify the injured and the innocent.

IV. In the third place, an individual or belligerent power may, in the prosecution of a lawful object, do many things, which were not in the contemplation of the original design, and which in THEMSELVES it would not be lawful to do. Thus in order to obtain what belongs to us, when it is impossible to recover the specific thing, we may take more than our due, under condition of repaying whatever is above the real value. For the same reason it is lawful to attack a ship manned by pirates, or a house occupied by robbers, although in that ship, or that house there may be many innocent persons, whose lives are endangered by such attack.

But we have had frequent occasion to remark, that what is conformable to right taken in its strictest sense is not always lawful in a moral point of view. For there are many instances, in which the law of charity will not allow us to insist upon our right with the utmost rigour. A reason for which it will be necessary to guard against things, which fall not within the original purpose of an action, and the happening of which might be foreseen: unless indeed the action has a tendency to produce advantages, that will far outweigh the consequences of any accidental calamity, and the apprehensions of evil are by no means to be put in competition with the sure hopes of a successful issue. But to determine in such cases requires no ordinary penetration and discretion. But wherever there is any doubt, it is always the safer-way to decide in favour of another's interest, than to follow the bent of our own inclination. "Suffer the tares to grow, says our divine teacher least in rooting up the tares you root up the wheat also."

The general destruction, which the Almighty, in right of his supreme Majesty, has sometimes decreed and executed, is not a rule, which we can presume to follow. He has not invested men, in the exercise of power, with those transcendent sovereign rights. Yet he himself, notwithstanding the unchangeable nature of his sovereign will, was inclined to spare the most wicked cities, if ten righteous persons could be found therein. Examples like these may furnish us with rules to decide, how far the rights of war against an enemy may be exercised or relaxed.

V. It frequently occurs as a matter of inquiry, how far we are authorised to act against those, who are neither enemies, nor wish to be thought so, but who supply our enemies with certain articles. For we know that it is a point, which on former and recent occasions has been contested with the greatest animosity; some wishing to enforce with all imaginary rigour the rights of war, and others standing up for the freedom of commerce.

In the first place, a distinction must be made between the commodities themselves. For there are some, such as arms for instance, which are only of use in war; there are others again, which are of no use in war, but only administer to luxury; but there are some articles, such as money, provisions, ships and naval stores, which are of use at all times both in peace and war.

As to conveying articles of the first kind, it is evident that any one must be ranked as an enemy, who supplies an enemy with the means of prosecuting hostilities. Against the conveyance of commodities of the second kind, no just complaint can be made.—And as to articles of the third class, from their being of a doubtful kind, a distinction must be made between the times of war and peace. For if a power can not defend itself, but by intercepting the supplies sent to an enemy, necessity will justify such a step, but upon condition of making restoration, unless there be some additional reasons to the contrary. But if the conveyance of goods to an enemy tends to obstruct any belligerent power in the prosecution of a lawful right, and the person so conveying them possesses the means of knowing it; if that power, for instance, is besieging a town, or blockading a port, in expectation of a speedy surrender and a peace, the person, who furnishes the enemy with supplies, and the means of prolonged resistance, will be guilty of an aggression and injury towards that power. He will incur the same guilt, as a person would do by assisting a debtor to escape from prison, and thereby to defraud his creditor. His goods may be taken by way of indemnity, and in discharge of the debt. If the person has not yet committed the injury, but only intended to do so, the aggrieved power will have a right to detain his goods, in order to compel him to give future security, either by putting into his hands hostages, or pledges; or indeed in any other way. But if there are evident proofs of injustice in an enemy's conduct the person who supports him in such a case, by furnishing him with succours, will be guilty not barely of a civil injury, but his giving assistance will amount to a crime as enormous, as it would be to rescue a criminal in the very face of the judge. And on that account the injured power may proceed against him as a criminal, and punish him by a confiscation of his goods.

These are the reasons, which induce belligerent powers to issue manifestoes, as an appeal to other states, upon the justice of their cause, and their probable hopes of ultimate success.

This question has been introduced under the article, which refers to the law of nature, as history supplies us with no precedent to deduce its establishment from the voluntary law of nations.

We are informed by Polybius, in his first book, that the Carthaginians seized some of the Romans, who were carrying supplies to their enemies, though they afterwards gave them up, upon the demand of the Romans. Plutarch says that when Demetrius had invested Attica, and taken the neighbouring towns of Eleusis and Rhamnus, he ordered the master and pilot of a ship, attempting to convey provisions into Athens, to be hanged, as he designed to reduce that city by famine: this act of rigour deterred others from doing the same, and by that means he made himself master of the city.

VI. Wars, for the attainment of their objects, it cannot be denied, must employ force and terror as their most proper agents. But a doubt is sometimes entertained, whether stratagem may be lawfully used in war. The general sense of mankind seems to have approved of such a mode of warfare. For Homer commends his hero, Ulysses, no less for his ability in military stratagem, than for his wisdom. Xenophon, who was a philosopher as well as a soldier and historian, has said, that nothing can be more useful in war than a well-timed stratagem, with whom Brasidas, in Thucydides agrees, declaring it to be the method from which many great generals have derived the most brilliant reputation. And in Plutarch, Agesilaus maintains, that deceiving an enemy is both just and lawful. The authority of Polybius may be added to those already named; for he thinks, that it shows greater talent in a general to avail himself of some favourable opportunity to employ a stratagem, than to gain an open battle. This opinion of poets, historians, and philosophers is supported by that of Theologians. For Augustin has said that, in the prosecution of a just war, the justice of the cause is no way affected by the attainment of the end, whether the object be accomplished by stratagem or open force, and Chrysostom, in his beautiful little treatise on the priestly office, observes, that the highest praises are bestowed on those generals, who have practised successful stratagems. Yet there is one circumstance, upon which the decision of this question turns more than upon any opinion even of the highest authority, and that is, whether stratagem ought to be ranked as one of those evils, which are prohibited under the maxim OF NOT DOING EVIL, THAT GOOD MAY ENSUE, or to be reckoned as one of those actions, which, though evil IN THEMSELVES, may be so modified by particular occasions, as to lose their criminality in consideration of the good, to which they lead.

■■■

ON JUST OR SOLEMN WAR ACCORDING TO THE LAW OF NATIONS ON DECLARATIONS OF WAR

I. IN THE first book of this treatise it was observed, that according to the best writers, a war is defined to be just, not on account of the CAUSES solely, in which it originates, nor on account of the MAGNITUDE of its objects, but from certain, peculiar, effects of right, with which it is attended.

But to what kind of war such an appellation most duly belongs will be best understood by considering the definition, which the Roman lawyers have given of a PUBLIC or NATIONAL enemy. Those, *says Pomponius,* are PUBLIC and LAWFUL ENEMIES, with whose STATE our own is engaged in war: but enemies of every other description, come under the denomination of pirates and robbers. With that opinion Ulpian entirely accords, making an additional observation, that "if any one be taken by robbers, as he is not a lawful prisoner of war, he cannot claim of his own state the right of postliminium. But if he be taken prisoner by a public enemy of the state, being considered as a prisoner of war, he is entitled by the right of postliminium to be restored to his former condition."

These opinions are supported by that of Paulus, who maintains, that persons captured by pirates still continue free, that is, are not to be considered as prisoners, for whom an exchange may be demanded. So that by the opinion of the roman lawyers it is evident, that no war is considered to be lawful, regular, and formal, except that which is begun and carried on by the sovereign power of each country. Cicero, in his fourth Philippic, describes "a public and authorised enemy to be the person, who possesses the civil and military powers of the state, who can command the treasury, and the services of the people in support of his measures, and who, as occasions offer, has power to conclude treaties of peace and amity."

II. A state, though it may commit some act of aggression, or injustice, does not thereby lose its political capacity, nor can a band of pirates or robbers ever become a state, although they may preserve among themselves that degree of subordination, which is absolutely necessary to the subsistence of all society. For with the latter, the commission of crime is the SOLE bond of union, whereas the former, though not always free from blame, but occasionally deviating from the laws of, nature, which in many cases have been in a great measure obliterated, still regulate their conduct by the treaties, which they have made, and certain customs that have been established, being united among themselves for the mutual support of lawful rights, and connected with foreign states by known rules of standing polity.

The Scholiast, upon Thucydides, remarks that the Greeks, at the time when piracy was reckoned lawful, forebore committing massacres, or nightly depredations, and carrying off the oxen that were necessary for the plough. We are informed by Strabo, that other nations too, who lived by plunder, after they had returned home from their predatory voyages, sent messages to the owners, whom they had plundered, to know if they would redeem the captures at a fair price.

In morals, the whole system often derives its name from some one of the principal parts, as Cicero remarks, in the fifth book of his BOUNDS of GOOD and EVIL, and Galen observes that a mixture is often called by the name of its chief ingredient. So that Cicero is not altogether correct in saying, that a state is not merely diseased, but entirely destroyed, by the injustice of its component and leading members. For a morbid body is still a body, and a state, though dreadfully diseased, is still a political being, as long as its laws and tribunals and other necessary parts of its constitution remain, to administer justice and give redress to foreigners, no less than to private subjects in their actions against each other.

III. But to make a war just, according to this meaning, it must not only be carried on by the sovereign authority on both sides, but it must also be duly and formally declared, and declared in such a manner, as to be known to each of the belligerent powers. Cicero, in the first book of his offices, points out "the equity of the rules prescribed by the Roman Law for the declaration of war, from whence it may be concluded that no war is regular or just, but such as is undertaken to compel restitution, and to procure indemnity for injuries, and that too accompanied with a formal declaration." Livy also in the same manner deems an observance of these rules requisite to form the characteristic of a just war. And describing an incursion of the Acarnanians into Attica, and their ravaging the country, he says that "those acts of irritation ended in a declaration Of JUST and REGULAR war on both sides."

■ ■ ■ ■

ON THE RIGHT TO LAY WASTE AN ENEMY'S COUNTRY, AND CARRY OFF HIS EFFECTS

I. CICERO, in the third book of his offices, has said that there is nothing repugnant to the LAW OF NATURE in spoiling the effects of an enemy, whom by the same law we are authorized to kill. Wherefore it is not surprising that the same things should be allowed by the LAW OF NATIONS. Polybius, for this reason, in the fifth book of his history, maintains, that the laws of war authorise the destruction of an enemy's forts, harbours, and fleets, the seizure of his men, or carrying off the produce of his country, and every thing of that description And we find from Livy that there are certain rights of war, by which an enemy must expect to suffer the calamities, which he is allowed to inflict, such as the burning of corn, the destruction of houses, and the plunder of men and cattle. Almost every page of history abounds in examples of entire cities being destroyed, walls levelled to the ground, and even whole countries wasted by fire and sword. Even in cases of surrender, towns have sometimes been destroyed, while the inhabitants were spared—an example of which is given by Tacitus, in the taking of Artaxata by the Romans; the inhabitants opened their gates and were spared, but the town was devoted to the flames.

II. Nor does the law of nations, in itself, considered apart from other duties, which will be mentioned hereafter, make any exemption in favour of things deemed sacred. For when places are taken by an enemy, all things without exception, whether sacred or not, must fall a sacrifice. For which it is assigned as a reason, that things which are called sacred, are not actually excepted from all human uses, but are a kind of public property, called sacred indeed from the general purposes, to which they are more immediately devoted. And as a proof of this, it is usual, when one nation surrenders to another state or sovereign, to surrender, along with other rights, every thing of a sacred kind, as appears by the form cited from Livy in a former part of this treatise.

And therefore Ulpian says, that the public have a property in sacred things. Conformably to which Tacitus says, that "in the Italian towns all the temples, the images of the Gods, and every thing connected with religion belonged of right to the Roman people." For this reason a nation, as the Lawyers, Paulus and Venuleius openly maintain, may, under a change of circumstances, convert to secular uses things, that have before been consecrated: and an overruling necessity may justify the hand, which has formerly consecrated the object in employing it as one of the resources and instruments of war. A thing which Pericles once did under a pledge of making restitution: Mago did the same in Spain, and the Romans in the Mithridatic war. We read of the same actions done by Sylla, Pompey, Caesar, and others. Plutarch in his life of Tiberius Gracchus says that nothing is so sacred and inviolable, as divine offerings: yet no one can hinder these from being removed or applied to other purposes at the pleasure of the state. Thus Livy mentions the ornaments of the temples, which Marcellus brought from Syracuse to Rome, as acquisitions made by the right of war.

III. What has been said of sacred things and edifices applies also to another kind of solemn fabrics, and those are sepulchral structures, which may be considered not merely as repositories of the dead, but as monuments belonging to the living, whether families or states. For this reason Pomponius has said, that these, like all other sacred places, when taken by an enemy may lose their inviolability, and Paulus is of the same opinion, observing that we are not restrained by any religious scruple from using the sepulchers of an enemy: for the stones, taken from thence, may be applied to any other purpose. But this right does not authorise wanton insult, offered to the ashes of the dead. For that would be a violation of the solemn rights of burial, which, as it was shewn in a preceding part of this work, were introduced and established by the law of nations.

IV. Here it may be briefly observed, that, according the law of nations any thing, belonging to an enemy, may be taken not only by open force, but by stratagem, provided it be unaccompanied with treachery.

■■■■

ON THE RIGHT OVER PRISONERS OF WAR

I. BY THE law of nature, in its primaeval state; apart from human institutions. and customs, no men can be slaves: and it is in this sense that legal writers maintain the opinion that slavery is repugnant to nature. Yet in a former part of this treatise, it was shewn that there is nothing repugnant to natural justice, in deriving the origin of servitude from human actions, whether founded upon compact or crime.

But the law of nations now under consideration is of wider extent both in its authority over persons, and its effects. For, as to persons, not only those, who surrender their rights, or engage themselves to servitude, are considered in the light of slaves, but all, who are taken prisoners in public and solemn war, come under the same description from the time that they are carried into the places, of which the enemy is master.

Nor is the commission of crime requisite to reduce them to this condition, but the fate of all is alike, who are unfortunately taken within the territories of an enemy, upon the breaking out of war.

II. and **III.** In ancient times, while slavery was permitted to exist, the offspring, born during captivity or servitude, continued in the same condition as the parents.—The consequences of such rules were of wide extent; there was no cruelty, which masters might not inflict upon their slaves;—there was no service, the performance of which they might not compel;—the power even of life and death was in their hands. However the Roman laws at length set bounds to such wanton power, at least to the exercise of it within the Roman territories.

Every thing too, found upon the prisoner's person, became a lawful prize to the captor. For as Justinian observes, one who was entirely in the power of another could have no property of his own.

IV. and **V.** Incorporeal rights, gained by the enemy, along with the person so captured, cannot be considered in the light of primary and original acquisitions. And there are some rights so purely personal in their nature, that they cannot be lost even by captivity, nor the duties attached thereto ever be relinquished. Of such a nature was the paternal right among the Romans. For rights of this kind cannot exist but immediately with the person to whom they originally belonged.

All these rights to prizes, which were introduced by the law of nations, were intended as an inducement to captors to refrain from the cruel rigour of putting prisoners to death; as they might hope to derive some advantage from sparing and saving them. From hence Pomponius deduces the origin of the word, SERVUS, or SLAVE, being one, who might have been put to death, but from motives of interest or humanity had been saved.

VI. (being the IX. of the original.) It has long been a maxim, universally received among the powers of Christendom, that prisoners of war cannot be made slaves, so as to be sold, or compelled to the hardships and labour attached to slavery. And they have with good reason embraced the latter principle. As it would be inconsistent with every precept of the law of charity, for men to refuse abandoning a cruel right, unless they might be allowed to substitute another, of great, though somewhat inferior rigour, in its place.

And this, as Gregoras informs us, became a traditionary principle among all who professed one common religion; nor was it confined to those, who lived under the authority of the Roman empire, but prevailed among the Thesalians the Illyrians, the Triballians, and Bulgarians. Though such an abolition of slavery, and mitigation of captivity may be considered as of trivial import, yet they were effects produced by the introduction of the Christian religion, especially upon recollection that Socrates tried, but without effect, to prevail upon the Greeks to forbear making slaves of each other.

In this respect the Mahometans act towards each other in the same manner as Christians do. Though it is still the practice among Christian powers to detain prisoners of war, till their ransom be paid, the amount of which depends upon the will of the Conqueror, unless it has been settled by express treaty. The right of detaining such prisoners has sometimes been allowed to the individuals, who took them, except where the prisoners were personages of extraordinary rank, who were always considered as prisoners of war to the state.

CONCLUSION

I. HERE seems to be the proper place to bring this work to a conclusion, without in the least presuming that every thing has been said, which might be said on the subject: but sufficient has been produced to lay a foundation, on which another, if he pleases, may raise a more noble and extensive edifice, an addition and improvement that will provoke no jealousy, but rather be entitled to thanks.

Before entirely dismissing the subject, it may be necessary to observe, that, as in laying down the true motives and causes, that alone will justify war, every possible precaution at the same time was taken to state the reasons for which it should be avoided; so now a few admonitions will not be deemed superfluous, in order to point out the means of preserving good faith in war, and maintaining peace, after war is brought to a termination, and among other reasons for preserving good faith the desire of keeping alive the hope of peace, even in the midst of war, is not the least important. For good faith, in the language of Cicero, is not only the principal hold by which all governments are bound together, but is the key-stone by which the larger society of nations is united. Destroy this, says Aristotle, and you destroy the intercourse of mankind.

In every other branch of justice there is something of obscurity, but the bond of faith is clear in itself, and is used indeed to do away the obscurity of all transactions. The observance of this is a matter of conscience with all lawful kings and sovereign princes, and is the basis of that reputation by which the honour and dignity of their crowns are maintained with foreign nations.

II. In the very heat of war the greatest security and expectation of divine support must be in the unabated desire, and invariable prospect of peace, as the only end for which hostilities can be lawfully begun. So that in the prosecution of war we must never carry the rage of it so far, as to unlearn the nature and dispositions of men.

III. These and these alone would be sufficient motives for the termination of war, and the cultivation of peace. But apart from all considerations of humanity, the INTERESTS of mankind would inevitably lead us to the same point. In the first place it is dangerous to prolong a contest with a more powerful enemy. In such a case some sacrifices should be made for the sake of peace, as in a storm goods are sometimes thrown overboard to prevent a greater calamity, and to save the vessel and the crew.

IV. Even for the stronger party, when flushed with victory, peace is a safer expedient, than the most extensive successes. For there is the boldness of despair to be apprehended from a vanquished enemy, dangerous as the bite of a ferocious animal in the pangs of death.

V. If indeed both parties are upon an equal footing, it is the opinion of Caesar, that it is the most favourable moment for making peace, when each party has confidence in itself.

VI. On whatever terms peace is made, it must be absolutely kept. From the sacredness of the faith pledged in the engagement, and every thing must be cautiously avoided, not only savouring of treachery, but that may tend to awaken and inflame animosity. For what Cicero has said of private friendships may with equal propriety be applied to public engagements of this kind, which are all to be religiously and faithfully observed, especially where war and enmity have ended in peace and reconciliation.

VII. And may God, to whom alone it belongs to dispose the affections and desires of sovereign princes and kings, inscribe these principles upon their hearts and minds, that they may always remember that the noblest office, in which man can be engaged, is the government of men, who are the principal objects of the divine care.

READING 7: IMMANUEL KANT

Immanuel Kant was born in Königsberg, Germany, taught at the University of Königsberg, where he had originally studied, and died in Königsberg. Kant's work inspired a great many German idealists after him, including Fichte, Hegel, and Schopenhauer. One of Kant's primary concerns was to prove the existence of God in an effort to define an objective understanding of *morality*. Although Kant agreed that the existence of God could not be proven through formal logic, he nevertheless argued that God expressed himself through moral means on this Earth. He concluded that the postulates of morality (what he referred to as the "categorical imperative") did exist, as did freedom of the will and immortality of the soul. Part of his frustration was the *dualist* strain of thought (that, as indicated in Chapter 2, is normally attributed to Plato) that emphasized a duality between *spirit* and *matter*. Like other social scientists, Kant aimed at bridging the gap between spirit and matter and to "harmonize the physical and moral laws."[156]

---

[156] Paul Johnson, *The Birth of the Modern* (New York: Harper Collins, 1992), pp. 551 et seq.

Immanuel Kant,

From Political Writings, eighteenth century

On the Relationship of Theory to Practice in Political Right
(Against Hobbes)

Among all the contracts by which a large group of men unites to form a society *(pactum sociale)*, the contract establishing a *civil constitution (pactum unionis civilis)* is of an exceptional nature. For while, so far as its execution is concerned, it has much in common with all others that are likewise directed towards a chosen end to be pursued by joint effort, it is essentially different from all others in the principle of its constitution *(constitutionis civilis)*. *In all social contracts, we find a union of many individuals for some common end which they all* share. But a union as an end in itself which they all *ought to share* and which is thus an absolute and primary duty in all external relationships whatsoever among human beings (who cannot avoid mutually influencing one another), is only found in a society in so far as it constitutes a civil state, i.e. a commonwealth. And the end which is a duty in itself in such external relationships, and which is indeed he highest formal condition *(conditio sine qua non)* of all other external duties, is the *right* of men *under coercive public laws* by which each can be given what is due to him and secured against attack from any others. But the whole concept of an external right is derived entirely from the concept of *freedom* in the mutual external relationships of human beings, and has nothing to do with the end which all men have by nature (i.e. the aim of achieving happiness) or with the recognised means of attaining this end. And thus the latter end must on no account interfere as a determinant with the laws governing external right. *Right* is the restriction of each individual's freedom so that it harmonises with the freedom of everyone else (in so far as this is possible within the terms of a general law). And *public right* is the distinctive quality of the *external laws* which make this constant harmony possible. Since every restriction of freedom through the arbitrary will of another party is termed *coercion,* it follows that a civil constitution is a relationship among *free* men who are subject to coercive laws, while they retain their freedom within the general union with their fellows. Such is the requirement of pure reason, which legislates *a priori,* regardless of all empirical ends (which can all be summed up under the general heading of happiness). *Men have different views on the empirical end of happiness and what it consists of, so that as far as happiness is concerned, their will cannot be brought under any common principle* nor thus under any external law harmonising with the freedom of everyone.

The civil state, regarded purely as a lawful state, is based on the following *a priori* principles:

1. The *freedom* of every member of society as a *human being.*
2. The *equality* of each with all the others as a *subject.*
3. The *independence* of each member of a commonwealth as a *citizen.*

These principles are not so much laws given by an already established state, as laws by which a state can alone be established in accordance with pure rational principles of external human right. Thus:

1. Man's *freedom* as a human being, as a principle for the constitution of a commonwealth, can be expressed in the following formula. No-one can compel me to be happy in accordance with his conception of the welfare of others, for each may seek his happiness in whatever way he sees fit, so long as he does not infringe upon the freedom of others to pursue a similar end which can be reconciled with the freedom of everyone else within a workable general law—i.e. he must accord to others the same right as he enjoys himself. A government might be established on the principle of benevolence towards the people, like that of a father towards his children. Under such a *paternal government (imperium paternale),* the subjects, as immature children who cannot distinguish what is truly useful or harmful to themselves, would be obliged to behave purely passively and to rely upon the judgement of the head of state as to how they *ought* to be happy, and upon his kindness in willing their happiness at all. Such a government is the greatest conceivable *despotism,* i.e. a constitution which suspends the entire freedom of its subjects, who thenceforth have no rights whatsoever. The only conceivable government for men who are capable of possessing rights, even if the ruler is benevolent, is not a *paternal* but a *patriotic* government *(imperium non paternale, sed patrioticum).* A *patriotic* attitude is one where everyone in the state, not excepting its head, regards the commonwealth as a maternal womb, or the land as the paternal ground from which he himself sprang and which he must leave to his descendants as a treasured pledge. Each regards himself as authorised to protect the rights of the commonwealth by laws of the general will, but not to submit it to his personal use at his own absolute pleasure. This right of freedom belongs to each member of the commonwealth as a human being, in so far as each is a being capable of possessing rights.

2. Man's *equality* as a subject might be formulated as follows. Each member of the commonwealth has rights of coercion in relation to all the others, except in relation to the head of state. For he alone is not a member of the commonwealth, but its creator or preserver, and he alone is authorised to coerce others without being subject to any coercive law himself. But all who are subject to laws are the subjects of a state, and are thus subject to the right of coercion along with all other members of the commonwealth; the only exception is a single person (in either the physical or the moral sense of the word), the head of state, through whom alone the rightful coercion of all others can be exercised. For if he too could be coerced, he would not be the head of state, and the hierarchy of subordination would ascend infinitely. But if there were two persons exempt from coercion, neither would be subject to coercive laws, and neither could do to the other anything contrary to right, which is impossible.

This uniform equality of human beings as subjects of a state is, however, perfectly consistent with the utmost inequality of the mass in the degree of its possessions, whether these take the form of physical or mental superiority over others, or of fortuitous external property and of particular rights (of which there may be many) with respect to others. Thus the welfare of the one depends very much on the will of the other (the poor depending on the rich), the one must obey the other (as the child its parents or the wife her husband), the one serves (the labourer) while the other pays, etc. Nevertheless, they are all equal as subjects before the law, which, as the pronouncement of the general will, can only be single in form, and which concerns the form of right and not the material or object in relation to which I possess rights. For no-one can coerce anyone else other than through the public law and its executor, the head of state, while everyone else can resist the others in the same way and to the same degree. No-one, however, can lose this authority to coerce others and to have rights towards them except through committing a crime. And no-one can voluntarily renounce his rights by a contract or legal transaction to the effect that he has no rights but only duties, for such a contract would deprive him of the right to make a contract, and would thus invalidate the one he had already made.

From this ideal of the equality of men as subjects in a commonwealth, there emerges this further formula: every member of the commonwealth must be entitled to reach any degree of rank which a subject can earn through his talent, his industry and his good fortune. And his fellow-subjects may not stand in his way by *hereditary* prerogatives or privileges of rank and thereby hold him and his descendants back indefinitely.

All right consists solely in the restriction of the freedom of others, with the qualification that their freedom can co-exist with my freedom within the terms of a general law; and public right in a commonwealth is simply a state of affairs regulated by a real legislation which conforms to this principle and is backed up by power, and under which a whole people live as subjects in a lawful state *(status iuridicus)*. This is what we call a civil state, and it is characterised by equality in the effects and counter-effects of freely willed actions which limit one another in accordance with the general law of freedom. Thus the *birthright* of each individual in such a state (i.e. before he has performed any acts which can be judged in relation to right) is absolutely *equal* as regards his authority to coerce others to use their freedom in a way which harmonises with his freedom. Since birth is not an act on the part of the one who is born, it cannot create any inequality in his legal position and cannot make him submit to any coercive laws except in so far as he is a subject, along with all the others, of the one supreme legislative power. Thus no member of the commonwealth can have a hereditary privilege as against his fellow-subjects; and no-one can hand down to his descendants the privileges attached to the rank he occupies in the commonwealth, nor act as if he were qualified as a ruler by birth and forcibly prevent others from reaching the higher levels of the hierarchy (which are *superior* and *inferior*, but never *imperans* and *subiectus*) through their own merit. He may hand down everything else, so long as it is material and not pertaining to his person, for it may be acquired and disposed of as property and may over a series of generations create considerable inequalities in wealth among the members of the commonwealth (the employee and the employer, the landowner and the agricultural servants, etc.). But he may not prevent his subordinates from raising themselves to his own level if they are able and entitled to do so by their talent, industry and good fortune. If this were not so, he would be allowed to practise coercion without himself being subject to coercive counter-measures from others, and would thus be more than their fellow-subject. No-one who lives within the lawful state of commonwealth can forfeit this equality other than through some crime of his own, but never by contract or through military force *occupatio bellica*). For no legal transaction on his part or on that of anyone else can make him cease to be his own master. He cannot become like a domestic animal to be employed in any chosen capacity and retained therein without consent for any desired period, even with the reservation (which is at times sanctioned by religion, as among the Indians) that he may not be maimed or killed. He can be considered happy in any condition so long as he is aware that, if he does not reach the same level as others, the fault lies either with himself (i.e. lack of ability or serious endeavour) or with circumstances for which he cannot blame others, and not with the irresistible will of any outside party. For as far as right is concerned, his fellow-subjects have no advantage over him.

3. The *independence (sibisufficientia)* of a member of the commonwealth as a *citizen*, i.e. as a co-legislator, may be defined as follows. In the question of actual legislation, all who are free and equal under existing public laws may be considered equal, but not as regards the right to make these laws. Those who are not entitled to this right are nonetheless obliged, as members of the commonwealth, to comply with these laws, and they thus likewise enjoy their protection (not as *citizens* but as co-beneficiaries of this protection). For all right depends on laws. But a public law which defines for everyone that which is permitted and prohibited by right, is the act of a public will, from which all right proceeds and which must not therefore itself be able to do an injustice to any one. And this requires no less than the will of the entire people (since all men decide for all men and each decides for himself). For only towards oneself can one never act un-

justly. But on the other hand, the will of another person cannot decide anything for someone without injustice, so that the law made by this other person would require a further law to limit his legislation. Thus an individual will cannot legislate for a commonwealth. For this requires freedom, equality and *unity* of the will of *all* the members. And the prerequisite for unity, since it necessitates a general vote (if freedom and equality are both present), is independence. The basic law, which can come only from the general, united will of the people, is called the *original contract*.

Anyone who has the right to vote on this legislation is a *citizen (citoyen,* i.e. citizen of a state, not *bourgeois* or citizen of a town). The only qualification required by a citizen (apart, of course, from being an adult male) is that he must be his *own master (sui iuris),* and must have some *property* (which can include any skill, trade, fine art or science) to support himself. In cases where he must earn his living from others, he must earn it only by *selling* that which is his, and not by allowing others to make use of him; for he must in the true sense of the word *serve* no-one but the commonwealth. In this respect, artisans and large or small landowners are all equal, and each is entitled to one vote only. As for landowners, we leave aside the question of how anyone can have rightfully acquired more land than he can cultivate with his own hands (for acquisition by military seizure is not primary acquisition), and how it came about that numerous people who might otherwise have acquired permanent property were thereby reduced to serving someone else in order to live at all. It would certainly conflict with the above principle of equality if a law were to grant them a privileged status so that their descendants would always remain feudal landowners, without their land being sold or divided by inheritance and thus made useful to more people; it would also be unjust if only those belonging to an arbitrarily selected class were allowed to acquire land, should the estates in fact be divided. The owner of a large estate keeps out as many smaller property owners (and their votes) as could otherwise occupy his territories. He does not vote on their behalf, and himself has only *one* vote. It should be left exclusively to the ability, industry and good fortune of each member of the commonwealth to enable each to acquire a part and all to acquire the whole, although this distinction cannot be observed within the general legislation itself. The number of those entitled to vote on matters of legislation must be calculated purely from the number of property owners, not from the size of their properties.

Those who possess this right to vote must agree *unanimously* to the law of public justice, or else a legal contention would arise between those who agree and those who disagree, and it would require yet another higher legal principle to resolve it. An entire people cannot, however, be expected to reach unanimity, but only to show a majority of votes (and not even of direct votes, but simply of the votes of those delegated in a large nation to represent the people). Thus the actual principle of being content with majority decisions must be accepted unanimously and embodied in a contract; and this itself must be the ultimate basis on which a civil constitution is established.

CONCLUSION

This, then, is an *original contract* by means of which a civil and thus completely lawful constitution and commonwealth can alone be established. But we need by no means assume that this contract *(contractus originarius* or *pactum sociale),* based on a coalition of the wills of all private individuals in a nation to form a common, public will for the purposes of rightful legislation, actually exists as a *fact,* for it cannot possibly be so. Such an assumption would mean that we would first have to prove from history that some nation, whose rights and obligations have been passed down to us, did in fact perform such an act, and handed down some authentic record or legal instrument, orally or in writing, before we could regard ourselves as bound by a pre-existing civil constitution. It is in fact merely an *idea* of reason, which nonetheless has undoubted practical reality; for it can oblige every legislator to frame

his laws in such a way that they could have been produced by the united will of a whole nation, and to regard each subject, in so far as he can claim citizenship, as if he had consented
within the general will. This is the test of the rightfulness of every public law. For if the law is
such that a whole people could not *possibly* agree to it (for example, if it stated that a certain
class of *subjects* must be privileged as a hereditary *ruling class*), it is unjust; but if it is at least
possible that a people could agree to it, it is our duty to consider the law as just, even if the
people is at present in such a position or attitude of mind that it would probably refuse its
consent if it were consulted. But this restriction obviously applies only to the judgement of
the legislator, not to that of the subject. Thus if a people, under some existing legislation,
were asked to make a judgement which in all probability would prejudice its happiness, what
should it do? Should the people not oppose the measure? The only possible answer is that
they could do nothing but obey. For we are not concerned here with any happiness which
the subject might expect to derive from the institutions or administration of the commonwealth, but primarily with the rights which would thereby be secured for everyone. And this
is the highest principle from which all maxims relating to the commonwealth must begin, and
which cannot be qualified by any other principles. No generally valid principle of legislation
can be based on happiness. For both the current circumstances and the highly conflicting
and variable illusions as to what happiness is (and no-one can prescribe to others how they
should attain it) make all fixed principles impossible, so that happiness alone can never be a
suitable principle of legislation. The doctrine that *salus publica suprema civitatis lex est* retains its value and authority undiminished; but the public welfare which demands *first* consideration lies precisely in that legal constitution which guarantees everyone his freedom
within the law, so that each remains free to seek his happiness in whatever way he thinks
best, so long as he does not violate the lawful freedom and rights of his fellow subjects at
large. If the supreme power makes laws which are primarily directed towards happiness (the
affluence of the citizens, increased population etc.), this cannot be regarded as the end for
which a civil constitution was established, but only as a means of *securing the rightful state,*
especially against external enemies of the people. The head of state must be authorised to
judge for himself whether such measures are necessary for the commonwealth's prosperity,
which is required to maintain its strength and stability both internally and against external enemies. The aim is not, as it were, to make the people happy against its will, but only to ensure its continued existence as a commonwealth. The legislator may indeed err in judging
whether or not the measures he adopts are *prudent,* but not in deciding whether or not the
law harmonises with the principle of right. For he has ready to hand as an infallible *a priori*
standard the idea of an original contract, and he need not wait for experience to show
whether the means are suitable, as would be necessary if they were based on the principle
of happiness. For so long as it is not self-contradictory to say that an entire people could
agree to such a law, however painful it might seem, then the law is in harmony with right. But
if a public law is beyond reproach (i.e. *irreprehensible*) with respect to right, it carries with it
the authority to coerce those to whom it applies, and conversely, it forbids them to resist the
will of the legislator by violent means. In other words, the power of the state to put the law
into effect is also *irresistible,* and no rightfully established commonwealth can exist without a
force of this kind to suppress all internal resistance. For such resistance would be dictated by
a maxim which, if it became general, would destroy the whole civil constitution and put an
end to the only state in which men can possess rights.

It thus follows that all resistance against the supreme legislative power, all incitement of the
subjects to violent expressions of discontent, all defiance which breaks out into rebellion, is the
greatest and most punishable crime in a commonwealth, for it destroys its very foundations. This
prohibition is *absolute.* And even if the power of the state or its agent, the head of state, has violated the original contract by authorising the government to act tyrannically, and has thereby, in

the eyes of the subject, forfeited the right to legislate, the subject is still not entitled to offer counter-resistance. The reason for this is that the people, under an existing civil constitution, has no longer any right to judge how the constitution should be administered. For if we suppose that it does have this right to judge and that it disagrees with the judgement of the actual head of state, who is to decide which side is right? Neither can act as judge of his own cause. Thus there would have to be another head above the head of state to mediate between the latter and the people, which is self-contradictory.—Nor can a right of necessity *(ius in casu necessitatis)* be invoked here as a means of removing the barriers which restrict the power of the people; for it is monstrous to suppose that we can have a right to do wrong in the direst (physical) distress. For the head of state can just as readily claim that his severe treatment of his subjects is justified by their insubordination as the subjects can justify their rebellion by complaints about their unmerited suffering, and who is to decide? The decision must rest with whoever controls the ultimate enforcement of the public law, i.e. the head of state himself. Thus no-one in the commonwealth can have a right to contest his authority.

Nonetheless, estimable men have declared that the subject is justified, under certain circumstances, is using force against his superiors. I need name only Achenwall, who is extremely cautious, precise and restrained in his theories of natural right. He says: 'If the danger which threatens the commonwealth as a result of long endurance of injustices from the head of state is greater than the danger to be feared from taking up arms against him, the people may then resist him. It may use this right to abrogate its contract of subjection and to dethrone him as a tyrant.' And he concludes: 'The people, in dethroning its ruler, thus returns to the state of nature.'

I well believe that neither Achenwall nor any others of the worthy men who have speculated along the same lines as he would ever have given their advice or agreement to such hazardous projects if the case had arisen. And it can scarcely be doubted that if the revolutions whereby Switzerland, the United Netherlands or even Great Britain won their much admired constitutions had failed, the readers of their history would regard the execution of their celebrated founders as no more than the deserved punishment of great political criminals. For the result usually affects our judgement of the rightfulness of an action, although the result is uncertain, whereas the principles of right are constant. But it is clear that these peoples have done the greatest degree of wrong in seeking their rights in this way, even if we admit that such a revolution did no injustice to a ruler who had violated a specific basic agreement with the people, such as the *Joyeuse Entrée*. For such procedures, if made into a maxim, make all lawful constitutions insecure and produce a state of complete lawlessness *(status naturalis)* where all rights cease at least to be effectual. In view of this tendency of so many right-thinking authors to plead on behalf of the people (and to its own detriment), I will only remark that such errors arise in part from the usual fallacy of allowing the principle of happiness to influence the judgement, wherever the principle of right is involved; and partly because these writers have assumed that the idea of an original contract (a basic postulate of reason) is something which must have taken place *in reality,* even where there is no document to show that any contract was actually submitted to the commonwealth, accepted by the head of state, and sanctioned by both parties. Such writers thus believe that the people retains the right to abrogate the original contract at its own discretion, if, in the opinion of the people, the contract has been severely violated.

It is obvious from this that the principle of happiness (which is not in fact a definite principle at all) has ill effects in political right just as in morality, however good the intentions of those who teach it. The sovereign wants to make the people happy as he thinks best, and thus becomes a despot, while the people are unwilling to give up their universal human desire to seek happiness in their own way, and thus become rebels. If they had first of all asked what is lawful (in terms of *a priori* certainty, which no empiricist can upset), the idea of a social contract would retain its authority undiminished. But it would not exist as a fact (as Danton would have it, declaring that since it does not actually exist, all property and all rights under the existing civil constitution are null and void), but only as a rational principle for judging any lawful public constitution whatsoever. And it would then be seen that, until the general will is there, the people has no coercive right against its ruler, since it can apply coercion legally only through him. But if the will is there, no force can be applied to the ruler by the people, otherwise the people would be the supreme ruler. Thus the people can never possess a right of coercion against the head of state, or be entitled to oppose him in word or deed.

We can see, furthermore, that this theory is adequately confirmed in practice. In the British constitution, of which the people are so proud that they hold it up as a model for the whole world, we find no mention of what the people are entitled to do if the monarch were to violate the contract of 1688. Since there is no law to cover such a case, the people tacitly reserve the right to rebel against him if he should violate the contract. And it would be an obvious contradiction if the constitution included a law for such eventualities, entitling the people to overthrow the existing constitution, from which all particular laws are derived, if the contract were violated. For there would then have to be a *publicly constituted* opposing power, hence a second head of state to protect the rights of the people against the first ruler, and then yet a third to decide which of the other two had right on his side. In fact, the leaders (or guardians—call them what you will) of the British people, fearing some such accusation if their plans did not succeed, *invented* the notion of a voluntary abdication by the monarch they forced out, rather than claim a right to depose him (which would have made the constitution self-contradictory).

While I trust that no-one will accuse me of flattering monarchs too much by declaring them inviolable, I likewise hope that I shall be spared the reproach of claiming, too much for the people if I maintain that the people too have inalienable rights against the head of state, even if these cannot be rights of coercion.

Hobbes is *of the opposite opinion. According to him* (*De Cive*, Chap. 7, §14), *the head of state has no contractual obligations towards the people; he can do no injustice to a citizen, but may act towards him as he pleases.* This proposition would be perfectly correct if injustice were taken to mean any injury which gave the injured party a *coercive right* against the one who has done him injustice. But *in its general form, the proposition [is quite terrifying.]*

The non-resisting subject must be able to assume that his ruler has no *wish* to do him injustice. And everyone has his inalienable rights, which he cannot give up even if he wishes to, and about which he is entitled to make his own judgements. But if he assumes that the ruler's attitude is one of good will, any injustice which he believes he has suffered can only have resulted through error, or through ignorance of certain possible consequences of the laws which the supreme authority has made. Thus the citizen must, with the approval of the ruler, be entitled to make public his opinion on whatever of the ruler's measures seem to him to constitute an injustice against the commonwealth. For to assume that the head of state can neither make mistakes nor be ignorant of anything would be to imply that he receives divine inspiration and is more than a human being. *Thus* freedom of the pen *is the only safeguard of the rights of the people, although it must not transcend the bounds of respect and devotion towards the existing constitution,* which should itself create a liberal attitude of mind among the subjects. To try to deny the citizen this freedom does not only mean, as Hobbes maintains, that the subject can claim no rights against the supreme ruler. It also means withholding from the ruler all knowledge of those matters which, if he knew about them, he would himself rectify, so that he is thereby put into a self-stultifying position. For his will issues commands to his subjects (as citizens) only in so far as he represents the general will of the people. But to encourage the head of state to fear that independent and public thought might cause political unrest is tantamount to making him distrust his own power and feel hatred towards his people.

The general principle, however, according to which a people may judge negatively whatever it believes was *not decreed* in good will by the supreme legislation, can be summed up as follows: *Whatever a people cannot impose upon itself cannot be imposed upon it by the legislator either.*

For example, if we wish to discover whether a law which declares permanently valid an ecclesiastical constitution (itself formulated at some time in the past) can be regarded as emanating from the actual will or intention of the legislator, we must first ask whether a people is *authorised* to make a law for itself whereby certain accepted doctrines and outward forms of religion are declared permanent, and whether the people may thus prevent its own descendants from making further progress in religious understanding or from correcting any past mistakes. It is clear that any original contract of the people which established such a law would in itself be null and void, for it would conflict with the appointed aim and purpose of mankind. Thus a law of this kind cannot be regarded as the actual will of the monarch, to whom counter-representations may accordingly be made. In all cases, however, where the supreme legislation did nevertheless adopt such measures, it would be permissible to pass general and public judgements upon them, but never to offer any verbal or active resistance.

In every commonwealth, there must be *obedience* to generally valid coercive laws within the mechanism of the political constitution. There must also be a *spirit of freedom,* for in all matters concerning universal human duties, each individual requires to be convinced by reason that the coercion which prevails is lawful, otherwise he would be in contradiction with himself. Obedience without the spirit of freedom is the effective cause of all *secret societies.* For it is a natural vocation of man to communicate with his fellows, especially in matters affecting mankind as a whole. Thus secret societies would disappear if freedom of this kind were encouraged. And how else can the government itself acquire the knowledge it needs to further its own basic intention, if not by allowing the spirit of freedom, so admirable in its origins and effects, to make itself heard?

Nowhere does practice so readily bypass all pure principles of reason and treat theory so presumptuously as in the question of what is needed for a good political constitution. The reason for this is that a legal constitution of long standing gradually makes the people accustomed to judging both their happiness and their rights in terms of the peaceful *status quo.* Conversely, it does not encourage them to value the existing state of affairs in the light of those concepts of happiness and right which reason provides. It rather makes them prefer this passive state to the dangerous task of looking for a better one, thus bearing out the saying which Hippocrates told physicians to remember: *iudicium anceps, experimentum periculosum.* Thus all constitutions which have lasted for a sufficiently long time, whatever their inadequacies and variations, produce the same result: the people remain content with what they have. If we therefore consider the *welfare of the people,* theory is not in fact valid, for everything depends upon practice derived from experience.

But reason provides a concept which we express by the words *political right.* And this concept has binding force for human beings who coexist in a state of antagonism produced by their natural freedom, so that it has an objective practical reality, irrespective of the good or ill it may produce (for these can only be known by experience). Thus it is based on *a priori* principles, for experience cannot provide knowledge of what is right, and there is a *theory* of political right to which practice must conform before it can be valid.

The only objection which can be raised against this is that, although men have in their minds the idea of the rights to which they are entitled, their intractability is such that they are incapable and unworthy of being treated as their rights demand, so that they can and ought to be kept under control by a supreme power acting purely from expediency. But this counsel of desperation *(salto mortale)* means that, since there is no appeal to right but only to force, the people may themselves resort to force and thus make every legal constitution insecure. If there is nothing which commands immediate respect through reason, such as the basic rights of man, no influence can prevail upon man's arbitrary will and restrain his freedom. But if both benevolence and right speak out in loud tones, human nature will not prove too debased to listen to their voice with respect. *Tum pietate gravem meritisque si forte virum quem Conspexere, silent arrectisque auribus adstant* (Virgil).

READING 8: WOODROW WILSON

Woodrow Wilson was the son of a Presbyterian minister, a fact that some historians argue impacted his thinking about his place in politics.[157] Born in 1856 in Virginia, he was raised in Augusta, Georgia, during the Civil War and Reconstruction period. After graduation from Princeton and the University of Virginia Law School, Wilson pursued his doctorate at Johns Hopkins University. Following his formal studies he advanced rapidly as a conservative professor of political science to eventually become president of Princeton University. His interpretation of politics during this period was as "a war of causes; a jousting of principles. Government is too serious a matter to admit of meaningless courtesies."[158] His seriousness of purpose was picked up by members of the Democratic Party, and they eventually urged Wilson to become involved in politics. It was as a conservative Democrat that he campaigned, first as Governor of New Jersey, and later U.S. President. Nominated for president at the 1912 Democratic Convention, Wilson vigorously campaigned for his New Freedom vision, which stressed individual rights and the renewal of small business competition. He resided over the establishment of the U.S. Federal Reserve, prohibition of child labor, and the eight-hour workday for railroad workers. Running for reelection in 1916 he campaigned against U.S. involvement in World War I. But after the election, Wilson concluded that the United States could not stay out of the war. To clarify America's war aims, Wilson made the Fourteen Points speech before Congress in January 1918.

[157] Richard Hofstadter, *The American Political Tradition: And the Men Who Made It* (New York: HBJ, 1948, 1989), Ch. 10: "Woodrow Wilson: The Conservative as Liberal."

[158] Wilson, cited in ibid., p. 310.

WOODROW WILSON,

"FOURTEEN POINTS SPEECH", 1918

THE WORLD MUST BE MADE SAFE FOR DEMOCRACY

I have called the Congress into extraordinary session because there are serious, very serious, choices of policy to be made, and made immediately, which it was neither right nor constitutionally permissible that I should assume the responsibility of making.

On the third of February last I officially laid before you the extraordinary announcement of the Imperial German Government that on and after the first day of February it was its purpose to put aside all restraints of law or of humanity and use its submarines to sink every vessel that sought to approach either the ports of Great Britain and Ireland or the western coasts of Europe or any of the ports controlled by the enemies of Germany within the Mediterranean. That had seemed to be the object of the German submarine warfare earlier in the war, but since April of last year the Imperial Government had somewhat restrained the commanders of its undersea craft in conformity with its promise then given to us that passenger boats should not be sunk and that due warning would be given to all other vessels which its submarines might seek to destroy, when no resistance was offered or escape attempted, and care taken that their crews were given at least a fair chance to save their lives in their open boats. The precautions taken were meager and haphazard enough, as was proved in distressing instance after instance in the progress of the cruel and unmanly business, but a certain degree of restraint was observed. The new policy has swept every restriction aside. Vessels of every kind, whatever their flag, their character, their cargo, their destination, their errand, have been ruthlessly sent to the bottom without warning and without thought of help or mercy for those on board, the vessels of friendly neutrals along with those of belligerents. Even hospital ships and ships carrying relief to the sorely bereaved and stricken people of Belgium, though the latter were provided with safe conduct through the proscribed areas by the German Government itself and were distinguished by unmistakable marks of identity, have been sunk with the same reckless lack of compassion or of principle.

I was for a little while unable to believe that such things would in fact be done by any government that had hitherto subscribed to the humane practices of civilized nations. International law had its origin in the attempt to set up some law which would be respected and observed upon the seas, where no nation had right of dominion and where lay the free highways of the world. By painful stage after stage has that law been built up, with meager enough results, indeed, after all was accomplished that could be accomplished, but always was a clear view, at least, of what the heart and conscience of mankind demanded. This minimum of right the German Government has swept aside under the plea of retaliation and necessity and because it had no weapons which it could use at sea except these which it is impossible to employ as it is employing them without throwing to the winds all scruples of humanity or of respect for the understandings that were supposed to underlie the intercourse of the world. I am not now thinking of the loss of property involved, immense and serious as that is, but only of the wanton and wholesale destruction of the lives of noncombatants, men, women, and children, engaged in pursuits which have always, even in the darkest periods of modern history, been deemed innocent and legitimate. Property can be paid for; the lives of peaceful and innocent people cannot be. *The present German submarine warfare against commerce is a warfare against mankind.*

It is a war against all nations. American ships have been sunk, American lives taken, in ways which it has stirred us very deeply to learn of, but the ships and people of other neutral and friendly nations have been sunk and overwhelmed in the waters in the same way. There has been no discrimination. The challenge is to all mankind. Each nation must decide for itself how it will meet it. The choice we make for ourselves must be made with a moderation of counsel and a temperateness of judgment befitting our character and our motives as a nation. We must put excited feeling away. Our motive will not be revenge or the victorious assertion of the physical might of the nation, but only the vindication of right, of human right, of which we are only a single champion.

When I addressed the Congress on the twenty-sixth of February last I thought that it would suffice to assert our neutral rights with arms, our right to use the seas against unlawful interference, our right to keep our people safe against unlawful violence. But armed neutrality, it now appears, is impracticable. . . . There is one choice we cannot make, we are incapable of making: we will not choose the path of submission and suffer the most sacred rights of our Nation and our people to be ignored or violated. The wrings against which we now array ourselves are no common wrongs; they cut to the very roots of human life.

With a profound sense of the solemn and even tragical character of the step I am taking and of the grave responsibilities which it involves, but in unhesitating obedience to what I deem my constitutional duty, I advise that the Congress declare the recent course of the *Imperial German Government to be in fact nothing less than war against the Government and people of the United States;* that it formally accept the status of belligerent which has thus been thrust upon it; and that it take immediate steps not only to put the country in a more thorough state of defense but also to exert all its power and employ all its resources to bring the Government of the German Empire to terms and end the war. . . .

While we do these things, these deeply momentous things, let us be very clear, and make very clear to all the world what our motives and our objects are. My own thought has not been driven from its habitual and normal course by the unhappy events of the last two months, and I do not believe that the thought of the Nation has been altered or clouded by them. I have exactly the same things in mind now that I had in mind when I addressed the Senate on the twenty-second of January last; the same that I had in mind when I addressed the Congress on the third of February and on the twenty-sixth of February. Our object now, as then, is to vindicate the principles of peace and justice in the life of the world as against selfish and autocratic power and to set up amongst the really free and self-governed peoples of the world such a concert of purpose and of action as will henceforth insure the observance of those principles. Neutrality is no longer feasible or desirable where the peace of the world is involved and the freedom of its peoples, and the menace to that peace and freedom lies in the existence of autocratic governments backed by organized force which is controlled wholly by their will, not by the will of their people. We have seen the last of neutrality in such circumstances. We are at the beginning of an age in which it will be insisted that the same standards of conduct and of responsibility for wrong done shall be observed among nations and their governments that are observed among the individual citizens of civilized states.

We have no quarrel with the German people. We have no feeling towards them but one of sympathy and friendship. It was not upon their impulse that *their government acted in entering the war.* It was not with their previous knowledge or approval. It was a war determined upon as wars used to be determined upon in the old, unhappy days when people were nowhere consulted by their rulers and wars were provoked and waged in the interest of dynasties or of little groups of ambitious men who were accustomed to use their fellow men as pawns and tools. Self-governed nations do not fill their neighbor states with spies or set the course of intrigue to bring about some critical posture of affairs which will give them an opportunity to strike and make conquest. Such designs can be successfully worked out only under cover and where no one has the right to ask questions. Cunningly contrived plans of deception or aggression, carried, it may be, from generation to generation, can be worked out and kept from the light only within the privacy of courts or behind the carefully guarded confidences of a narrow and privileged class. They are happily impossible where public opinion commands and insists upon full information concerning all the nation's affairs.

A steadfast concert for peace can never be maintained except by a partnership of democratic nations. No autocratic government could be trusted to keep faith within it or observe its covenants. It must be a league of honor, a partnership of opinion. Intrigue would eat its vitals away; the plottings of inner circles who could plan what they would and render account to no one would be a corruption seated at its very heart. Only free peoples can hold their purpose and their honor steady to a common end and prefer the interests of mankind to any narrow interest of their own. . . .

▮▮▮▮

THE FOURTEEN POINTS

We entered this war because violations of right had occurred which touched us to the quick and made the life of our own people impossible unless they were corrected and the world secured once and for all against their recurrence. *What we demand in this war, therefore, is nothing peculiar to ourselves. It is that the world be made fit and safe to live in;* and particularly that it be made safe for every peace-loving nation which, like our own, wishes to live its own life, determine its own institutions, be assured of justice and fair dealing by the other people of the world as against force and selfish aggression. All the peoples of the world are in effect partners in this interest, and for our own part we see very clearly that unless justice be done to others it will not be done to us. The program of the world's peace, therefore, is our program; and that program, the only possible program, as we see it, is this:

I. *Open covenants of peace, openly arrived at, after which there shall be no private international understandings of any kind but diplomacy shall proceed always frankly and in the public view.*

II. *Absolute freedom of navigation upon the seas,* outside territorial waters, alike in peace and in war, except as the seas may be closed in whole or in part by international action for the enforcement of international covenants.

III. The removal, so far as possible, of all economic barriers and the establishment of an equality of trade conditions among all the nations consenting to the peace and associating themselves for its maintenance.

IV. *Adequate guarantees given and taken that national armaments will be reduced to the lowest point consistent with domestic safety.*

V. *A free, open-minded, and absolutely impartial adjustment of all colonial claims,* based upon a strict observance of the principle that in determining all such questions of sovereignty the interests of the populations concerned must have equal weight with the equitable claims of the government whose title is to be determined.

VI. The evacuation of all Russian territory and such a settlement of all questions affecting Russia as will secure the best and freest cooperation of the other nations of the world in obtaining for her an unhampered and unembarrassed opportunity for the independent determination of her own political development and national policy and assure her of a sincere welcome into the society of free nations under institutions of her own choosing; and, more than a welcome, assistance also of every kind that she may need and may herself desire. The treatment accorded Russia by her sister nations in the months to come will be the acid test of their good will, of their comprehension of her needs as distinguished from their own interests, and of their intelligent and unselfish sympathy.

VII. Belgium, the whole world will agree, must be evacuated and restored, without any attempt to limit the sovereignty which she enjoys in common with all other free nations. No other single act will serve as this will serve to restore confidence among the nations in the laws which they have themselves set and determined for the government of their relations with one another. Without this healing act the whole structure and validity of international law is forever impaired.

VIII. All French territory should be freed and the invaded portions restored, and the wrong done to France by Prussia in 1871 in the matter of Alsace-Lorraine, which has unsettled the peace of the world for nearly fifty years, should be righted, in order that peace may once more be made secure in the interest of all.

IX. A readjustment of the frontiers of Italy should be effected along clearly recognizable lines of nationality.

X. The peoples of Austria-Hungary, whose place among the nations we wish to see safeguarded and assured, should be accorded the freest opportunity of autonomous development.

XI. Rumania, Serbia, and Montenegro should be evacuated; occupied territories restored; Serbia accorded free and secure access to the sea; and the relations of the several Balkan states to one another determined by friendly counsel along historically established lines of allegiance and nationality; and international guarantees of the political and economic independence and territorial integrity of the several Balkan states should be entered into.

XII. The Turkish portions of the present Ottoman Empire should be assured a secure sovereignty, but the other nationalities which are now under Turkish rule should be assured an undoubted security of life and an absolutely unmolested opportunity of autonomous developments, and the Dardanelles should be permanently opened as a free passage to the ships and commerce of all nations under international guarantees.

XIII. An independent Polish state should be erected which should include the territories inhabited by indisputably Polish populations, which should be assured a free and secure access to the sea, and whose political and economic independence and territorial integrity should be guaranteed by international covenant.

XIV. A general association of nations must be formed under specific covenants for the purpose of affording mutual guarantees of political independence and territorial integrity to great and small states alike.

In regard to these essential rectifications of wrong and assertions of right we feel ourselves to be intimate partners of all the governments and peoples associated together against the imperialists. We cannot be separated in interest or divided in purpose. We stand together until the end.

For such arrangements and covenants we are willing to fight and to continue to fight until they are achieved; but only because we wish the right to prevail and desire a just and stable peace such as can be secured only by removing the chief provocations to war, which this program does remove. We have no jealousy of German greatness, and there is nothing in this program that impairs it. We grudge her no achievement or distinction of learning or of pacific enterprise such as have made her record very bright and very enviable. We do not wish to injure her or to block in any way her legitimate influence or power. We do not wish to fight her either with arms or with hostile arrangements of trade if she is willing to associate herself with us and the other peace-loving nations of the world in covenants of justice and law and fair dealing. We wish her only to accept a place of equality among the peoples of the world—the new world in which we now live—instead of a place of mastery.

Neither do we presume to suggest to her any alteration or modification of her institutions. But it is necessary, we must frankly say, and necessary as a preliminary to any intelligent dealings with her on our part, that we should know whom her spokesmen speak for when they speak to us, whether for the Reichstag majority or for the military party and the men whose creed is imperial domination.

We have spoken now, surely, in terms too concrete to admit of any further doubt or question. An evident principle runs through the whole program I have outlined. It is the principle of justice to all peoples and nationalities, and their right to live on equal terms of liberty and safety with one another, whether they be strong or weak. Unless this principle be made its foundation no part of the structure of international justice can stand. The people of the United States could act upon no other principle; and to the vindication of this principle they are ready to devote their lives, their honor, and everything that they possess. The moral climax of this the culminating and final war for human liberty has come and they are ready to put their own strength, their own highest purpose, their own integrity and devotion to the test.

READING 9: NIEO, BEDJAOUI AND PARKINSON

The New International Economic Order (NIEO) was an immediate result of the many new sovereign states that had achieved independence in the 1950s and 1960s and who were now, as participating members of the United Nations General Assembly, making demands. Frustrated with the lack of concrete change following the United Nations Conference on Trade and Development (UNCTAD) and encouraged by the financial gains made by the developing world states participating in the Organization of Petroleum Exporting Countries (OPEC), the NIEO was viewed by its supporters as the only rational path for the future of international politics.

This section on the New International Economic Order (NIEO) is divided into three parts: (a) "U.N. Declaration on the Establishment of a NIEO," 1974; (b) Mohammed Bedjaoui, "Poverty of the International Order," in *Towards a New International Economic Order* (Paris: UNESCO, 1979); and (c) F. Parkinson, "Latin America, Her Newly Industrialising Countries and the NIEO," *Journal of Latin American Studies*, 1984.

A) NIEO

OFFICIAL DOCUMENTS

UNITED NATIONS GENERAL ASSEMBLY DECLARATION ON THE ESTABLISHMENT OF A NEW INTERNATIONAL ECONOMIC ORDER RESOLUTION 3201 (S-VII)[1]

The General Assembly
Adopts the following Declaration:

Declaration on the Establishment of a New International Economic Order

We, the members of the United Nations,
Having convened a special session of the General Assembly to study for the first time the problems of raw materials and development, devoted to the consideration of the most important economic problems facing the world community,
Bearing in mind the spirit, purposes and principles of the Charter of the United Nations to promote the economic advancement and social progress of all peoples,
Solemnly proclaim our united determination to work urgently for

The Establishment of a New International Economic Order

based on equity, sovereign equality, interdependence, common interest and co-operation among all States, irrespective of their economic and social systems, which shall correct inequalities and redress existing injustices, make it possible to eliminate the widening gap between the developed and the developing countries and ensure steadily accelerating economic and social development in peace and justice for present and future generations.

1. The greatest and most significant achievement during the last decades has been the independence from colonial and alien domination of a large number of peoples and nations which has enabled them to become members of the community of free peoples. Technological progress has also been made in all spheres of economic activities in the last three decades, thus providing a solid potential for improving the well-being of all peoples. However, the remaining vestiges of alien and colonial domination, foreign occupation, racial discrimination, *apartheid* and neo-colonialism in all its forms continue to be among the greatest obstacles to the full emancipation and progress of the developing countries and all the peoples involved. The benefits of technological progress are not shared equitably by all members of the international community. The developing countries, which constitute 70 per cent of the world population, account for only 30 per cent of the world's income. It has proved impossible to achieve an even and balanced development of the international community under the existing international economic order. The gap between the developed and the developing countries continues to widen in a system which was established at a time when most of the developing countries did not even exist as independent States and which perpetuates inequality.

From *United Nations General Assembly Declaration on the Establishment of a New International Economic Order,* Resolution 2301. Reprinted by permission of the United Nations.

[1] Adopted without vote at the Sixth Special Session, 2229th plenary meeting, May 1, 1974. At the same meeting, the General Assembly adopted, also without vote, resolution 3202(S-VI), *Programme of Action on the Establishment of a New Economic Order.* 70 DEPT. STATE BULL. 574 (1974); 13 ILM 720 (1974).

2. The present international economic order is in direct conflict with current developments in international political and economic relations. Since 1970, the world economy has experienced a series of grave crises which have had severe repercussions, especially on the developing countries because of their generally greater vulnerability to external economic impulses. The developing world has become a powerful factor that makes its influence felt in all fields of international activity. These irreversible changes in the relationship of forces in the world necessitate the active, full and equal participation of the developing countries in the formulation and application of all decisions that concern the international community.

3. All these changes have thrust into prominence the reality of interdependence of all the members of the world community. Current events have brought into sharp focus the realization that the interests of the developed countries and the interests of the developing countries can no longer be isolated from each other; that there is close interrelationship between the prosperity of the developed countries and the growth and development of the developing countries, and that the prosperity of the international community as a whole depends upon the prosperity of its constituent parts. International co-operation for development is the shared goal and common duty of all countries. Thus the political, economic and social well-being of present and future generations depends more than ever on co-operation between all members of the international community on the basis of sovereign equality and the removal of the disequilibrium that exists between them.

4. The new international economic order should be founded on full respect for the following principles:

   (a) Sovereign equality of States, self-determination of all peoples, inadmissibility of the acquisition of territories by force, territorial integrity and noninterference in the internal affairs of other States;

   (b) Broadest co-operation of all the member States of the international community, based on equity, hereby the prevailing disparities in the world may be banished and prosperity secured for all;

   (c) Full and effective participation on the basis of equality of all countries in the solving of world economic problems in the common interest of all countries, bearing in mind the necessity to ensure the accelerated development of all the developing countries, while devoting particular attention to the adoption of special measures in favor of the least developed, land-locked and island developing countries as well as those developing countries most seriously affected by economic crises and natural calamities, without losing sight of the interests of other developing countries;

   (d) Every country has the right to adopt the economic and social system that it deems to be the most appropriate for its own development and not to be subjected to discrimination of any kind as a result;

   (e) Full permanent sovereignty of every State over its natural resources and all economic activities. In order to safeguard these resources, each State is entitled to exercise effective control over them and their exploitation with means suitable to its own situation, including the right to nationalization or transfer of ownership to its nationals, this right being an expression of the full permanent sovereignty of the State. No State may be subjected to economic, political or any other type of coercion to prevent the free and full exercise of this inalienable right;

   (f) All States, territories and peoples under foreign occupation, alien and colonial domination of *apartheid* have the right to restitution and full compensation for the exploitation and depletion of, and damages to, the natural and all other resources of those States, territories and peoples;

   (g) Regulation and supervision of the activities of transnational corporations by taking measures in the interest of the national economies of the countries where such transnational corporations operate on the basis of the full sovereignty of those countries;

(h) Right of the developing countries and the peoples of territories under colonial and racial domination and foreign occupation to achieve their liberation and to regain effective control over their natural resources and economic activities;

(i) Extending of assistance to developing countries, peoples and territories under colonial and alien domination, foreign occupation, racial discrimination or *apartheid* or which are subjected to economic, political or any other type of measures to coerce them in order to obtain from them the subordination of the exercise of their sovereign rights and to secure from them advantages of any kind, and to neo-colonialism in all its forms and which have established or are endeavouring to establish effective control over their natural resources and economic activities that have been or are still under foreign control;

(j) Just and equitable relationship between the prices of raw materials, primary products, manufactured and semi-manufactured goods exported by developing countries and the prices of raw materials, primary commodities, manufactures, capital goods and equipment imported by them with the aim of bringing about sustained improvement in their unsatisfactory terms of trade and the expansion of the world economy;

(k) Extension of active assistance to developing countries by the whole international community, free of any political or military conditions;

(l) Ensuring that one of the main aims of the reformed international monetary system shall be the promotion of the development of the developing countries and the adequate flow of real resources to them;

(m) Improving the competitiveness of natural materials facing competition from synthetic substitutes;

(n) Preferential and non-reciprocal treatment for developing countries wherever feasible, in all fields of international economic co-operation, wherever feasible;

(o) Securing favourable conditions for the transfer of financial resources to developing countries;

(p) To give to the developing countries access to the achievements of modern science and technology, to promote the transfer of technology and the creation of indigenous technology for the benefit of the developing countries in forms and in accordance with procedures which are suited to their economies;

(q) Necessity for all States to put an end to the waste of natural resources, including food products;

(r) The need for developing countries to concentrate all their resources for the cause of development;

(s) Strengthening—through individual and collective actions—of mutual economic, trade, financial and technical co-operation among the developing countries mainly on a preferential basis;

(t) Facilitating the role which producers associations may play, within the framework of international co-operation, and in pursuance of their aims, *inter alia,* assisting in promotion of sustained growth of world economy and accelerating development of developing countries.

5. The unanimous adoption of the International Development Strategy for the Second Development Decade was an important step in the promotion of international economic co-operation on a just and equitable basis.[1] The accelerated implementation of obligations and commitments assumed by the international community within the framework of the Strategy, particularly those concerning imperative development needs of developing countries, would contribute significantly to the fulfillment of the aims and objectives of the present Declaration.

---

[1] General Assembly resolution 2626(XXV). [Footnote in original.]

6. The United Nations as a universal organization should be capable of dealing with the problems of international economic co-operation in a comprehensive manner and ensuring equally the interests of all countries. It must have an even greater role in the establishment of a new international economic order. The Charter of Economic Rights and Duties of States, for the preparation of which this Declaration will provide an additional source of inspiration, will constitute a significant contribution in this respect. All the States members of the United Nations are therefore called upon to exert maximum efforts with a view to securing the implementation of this Declaration, which is one of the principal guarantees for the creation of better conditions for all peoples to reach a life worthy of human dignity.

7. This Declaration on the Establishment of a New International Economic Order shall be one of the most important bases of economic relations between all peoples and all nations.

B) Mohammed Bedjaoui

Poverty of the International Order

Traditional international law is derived from the laws of the capitalist economy and the liberal political system. From these two sources it derives the elements and factors of a certain consistency to be found in its theoretical construction and in the terms of its actual rules.

The judicial order set up by the former international society gave the impression of neutrality or indifference. But the laisser-faire and easy-going attitude which it thus sanctioned led in reality to legal non-intervention, which favoured the seizure of the wealth and possessions of weaker peoples. Classic international law in its apparent indifference was *ipso facto* permissive. It recognized and enforced a 'right of dominion' for the benefit of the 'civilized nations'. This was a colonial and imperial right, institutionalized at the 1885 Berlin Conference on the Congo.

In addition to ratifying the European countries' right to conquer and occupy the territories concerned, international law recognized the validity of 'unequal treaties', essentially leonine, whereby the weaker peoples for a long time delivered up their natural wealth on terms imposed on them by the stronger States. Neutral or indifferent, international law was thus also a formalistic law, attached to the semblance of equality which barely hid the flagrant inequalities of the relationships expressed in these leonine treaties.

It was also a law eminently suited to the protection of the 'civilized countries' privileges, through the interests of their nationals. By virtue of diplomatic protection and intervention, the law enabled the nationals of the countries concerned to obtain, in certain States, advantages which were not even awarded to the citizens of those States.

International law made use of a series of justifications and excuses to create legitimacy for the subjugation and pillaging of the Third World, which was pronounced uncivilized. As we shall see, these justifications were dropped as and when they had fulfilled their allotted function of mystification.

However, the consistency of the system required that the freedom of action allotted by international law to a 'civilized' State should be matched by the same freedom for any other civilized State. This accepted international law was thus obliged to assume the essential function of reconciling the freedom of every State belonging to the family of 'civilized nations' with the freedom of all the other States in the same family.

To keep in line with the predatory economic order, this international law was thus obliged simultaneously to assume the guise of: (a) an *oligarchic law* governing the relations between civilized States members of an exclusive club; (b) a *plutocratic law* allowing these States to exploit weaker peoples; (c) a *non-interventionist law* (to the greatest possible extent), carefully drafted to allow a wide margin of laisser-faire and indulgence to the leading States in the club, while at the same time making if possible to reconcile the total freedom allowed to each of them. However, this matter of controlling rival appetites was not taken very far.

Until the League of Nations came into being, this international law was simply a European law, arising from the combination of regional fact with material power, and transposed as a law dominating all international relations. The European States thus projected their power and their law on to the world as a whole. Here we come to the real nature of the so-called 'international' law, to its substance and even to the reality of its existence. As it had been formed historically on the basis of regional acts of force, it could not be an international law established by common accord, but an international law given to the whole world by one or two dominant groups. This is how it was able to serve as a legal basis for the various political and economic aspects of imperialism.

This classic international law thus consisted of a set of rules with a geographical basis (it was a European law), a religious-ethical inspiration (it was a Christian law), an economic motivation (it was a mercantilist law) and political aims (it was an imperialist law).

Until the recent period of successive decolonizations, there was no perceptible change in this law as a backing for imperialism, apart from the fact that the emergence of the two super-great powers eclipsed the European influence and provoked a large-scale revision of the boundaries of spheres of influence in the world.

An Oligarchic International Law

The adjective 'international' was invented by Jeremy Bentham in 1780. He thought it wiser to call the collection of rules governing the official relations between European States at that time 'international law' rather than 'law of nations' in his Principles of Morals and Legislation. This law was obviously international only in name.

The 'Christian kingdoms of Europe' turned into independent, indomitable empires, each trying to create for its own benefit, through unbridled, unlimited sovereignty, a Roman-type universal monarchy. The Treaties of Westphalia in 1648 put a stop to these efforts and marked a new trend in international relations. Under the system introduced by the Peace of Westphalia, the 'European system of States' replaced the uneasy coexistence of the Christian countries. It rested on a balance (the equilibrium of the Peace of Westphalia) between the individual sovereignty of each State and the plurality of Europe, involving the need for each European State to respect the status of others. The Peace of Utrecht (1713) clearly illustrated this principle of equilibrium between European States.

The New World was to be europeanized and evangelized, which meant that the European system of international law was not radically changed by its geographical extension to other continents. There was a law of the European system which both governed the European States' interrelations and acted as a regulator in their extra-European relations aimed at the domination of the rest of the world. As part of Asia had *grosso modo* eluded direct European domination, unlike Latin America and Africa, the relations between Asia and Europe were systematized in a sort of minor and marginal form of international law.

The American Declaration of Independence in 1776 marked a new step forward with the replacement of the legal system of the European States by that of the States of 'Christian civilization'. For Europe, however, the conception of an oligarchic law was no whit changed because of this geographical enlargement. For Europe, the international community was reduced to the galaxy of States making up that continent, and having the same culture and the same religion. International law was applicable only among these European powers, or to the United States then emerging.

In the law governing relations between European and other States, the former tended, in the nineteenth century, not to recognize the latter as States, and in fact to deny them this distinction. As we shall see later, the doctrine was not clear on the subject of the States composing the 'community of the law of nations'. The latter, which was particularly limited, was passing through a historical stage corresponding to a 'closed community' kind of organization directed by the European Club. States emerged only if willed by the Concert of Europe, and on the conditions imposed by it. Thus Bismarck asserted in 1878, on behalf of the Congress of Berlin, that 'Europe alone has the right to sanction independence; she must therefore consider under what conditions she will take this important decision'.

In short, Europe alone was qualified to issue the birth certificate of any new State. Recognition of the State was not merely declaratory, i.e. depending on the simple fact of the State's existence. It had become constitutive, as the European States had laid down who should compose the community of the law of nations, to which they held the key. Recognition of the existence of a State outside the European Club, and its recognition as a civilized State, was exclusively a matter for Europe under its discretionary powers, having no connection with the political and legal position of the State concerned.

A very large number of works have emphasized the European and imperialist basis of traditional international law. Some authors, investigating the historical role of the Concert of Europe, have reached the obvious conclusion that this areopagus was not acting in the interests of the law.[1] The whole Concert of Europe, which outlasted the Holy Alliance, was based on the concept of European common good or common good of Europe.[2] At the time of triumphant European egocentrism, the common good of Europe was identified with the common good of civilized humanity.

As an imperial system of law based on inequality, corresponding to a given pattern of world organization, it was clearly international only in name. Gradually built up over four centuries by and for Europe, applying only to the European countries, to the exclusion of colonies, protectorates and 'uncivilized' countries, it was purely conceived for the European community, inspired by European civilization and values, symbolizing an epoch, a hegemony and a network of economic and other interests. The influence of the overseas expansion and economic development of the Netherlands on Grotius is well-known.[3]

Professor Verzijl writes: 'There is no denying or even doubting the fact that international law, as it is at present, is the product of the European mind, and that it originated in a common source of European beliefs. In both these aspects, it remains primarily of European origin.' Richard Falk noted that the law was regarded both as 'a law for civilized countries and a civilized law', and that 'the notion of civilization was partly conceived of as embracing Christendom and

---

[1] René Dupuis, 'Aperçu des Relations Internationales en Europe, de Charlemagne à nos Jours', *Collected Courses of The Hague Academy of International Law,* 1939, Vol. II.

[2] See Maurice Bourquin, 'La Sainte-Alliance. Un Essai d'Organisation Européenne', *Collected Courses of The Hague Academy of International Law,* 1953, Vol. II, p. 454.

[3] Grotius, living in the midst of this seafaring people, brought up amongst the international trade of the Hollanders of those days, ought he not to have had a keener vision than a jurist of any non-trading, non-cosmopolitan country?' (Van Der Mandere, 'Grotius and International Society Today', *American Political Science Review,* 1925, Vol. 19, p. 806).
George Wolfskill writes, for his part: 'Everyone knows that the immortal work of Grotius on the law of nations arose out of an incident concerning his country's commercial development and overseas expansion. . . . International trade was, perhaps, in some way responsible for the success of Grotius' system.' (George Wolfskill, 'Is Modern International Law "Modern"!', *Journal of Public Law,* vol. 7, 1958 (pp. 362–77, p. 365). He adds: 'Clearly, that is why the bourgeoisie became the dominant class; it was a legal system admirably suited to the economic needs of that class whose members were closely connected and interdependent. The 19th century was the golden age of international law because national and international society had been refashioned in the image of bourgeois capitalism' (ibid., p. 370).

partly conceived of as including all States powerful enough to exert an independent influence'.[4] Wolfgang Friedmann observes that 'the existing rules of international law have been overwhelmingly developed by the nations that today are in the position of the "haves" and therefore tend to favor a position which the economically underprivileged states of today seek to modify'.[5] Röling flatly states that 'law serves first and foremost the interests of power'. European international law, the international law of nations, is no exception to this rule.[6]

A law of domination by exclusion from the 'international community'

The above analysis shows that any civilized State—and only a civilized State—could belong to the 'international community' as it was organized and recognized by the European States. Conversely, any State not belonging to this exclusive club was not a civilized State, and its territory could be occupied by a State that was a member (i.e. a European State), become a protectorate of that State or be absorbed into its sphere of influence. In other words, simply because the other political groupings in the world were not organized in conformity with the canons and models of nineteenth century Europe, in particular as regards the organization of the State, they were merely barbarous States or 'non-States'—for the purposes of European law—to which the right of conquest or occupation could apply.

Von Liszt explained that only civilized States formed part of the international community: 'In all its relations with non-civilized communities, the international community can exercise the power it wields: it is bound only by moral principles prescribed by Christian feeling and humanity.[7]

Heffter spoke of 'European public law'. According to the European doctrine, especially in Germany and Switzerland, the European States' relations with other States were regarded simply as 'special arrangements based on natural law, apart from the European law of nations'. Weaton explained that 'public law, with a few exceptions, has always been and still is limited to the civilized, Christian peoples of Europe, or those of European origin'.

For the application of European international law, Lorimer in 1883–84 classified humanity under three categories: 'civilized', 'barbarian' and 'savage'; Von Liszt, in turn, classified them as 'civilized', 'half-civilized' and 'uncivilized'. European international law dealt with the civilized, and it was not surprising that they were limited to the Christian States of Europe and the extra-European Christian States. The common denominator was still religion. The dependencies and colonies of these European States were not protected by international law, but it was applied there to protect the European States where necessary.

Von Liszt's 'half-civilized' and Lorimer's 'barbarians' were such countries as China, Persia, Siam, Morocco or Afghanistan which were not part of the international community as defined by Europe, but to which a marginal international law, mainly of conventional origin, was applicable in their relations with Europe and in the strictly defined areas governed by treaties concluded between them and Europe.

---

[4] Richard A. Falk, 'The New States and International Legal Order', *Collected Courses of The Hague Academy of International Law*, Vol. 118, 1966, II.

[5] Wolfgang Friedmann, 'The Position of Underdeveloped Countries and the Universality of International Law', *Columbia Journal of Transnational Law*, 1963 (p. 76–86).

[6] B. V. A. Röling, *International Law in an Expanded World*, Amsterdam, 1960.

[7] Von Liszt, *Le Droit International*, p. 6, translation by Gilbert Gidel of the German edition of 1913, Paris, 1927.

The uncivilized or barbarian populations were 'beyond the pale'. Any special, benevolent treatment accorded to them was said to be granted on Christian, humanitarian grounds. This being so, it could be said that all the 'non-Christian' countries were 'outside the law', i.e. subject to the law of 'might is right'. The conquering Europe of the nineteenth century could thus claim a legitimate right to subjugate and pillage the Third World countries, labeled as 'uncivilized'. A conventional decision was needed to make an exception for Turkey and place it under the protection of European international law. It was stated in Article 7 of the Treaty of Paris of 30 March 1856 that 'the Sublime Porte was authorized to share in the benefits of European public law and the Concert of Europe'.

But Turkey's entry into the international community by no means signified a decisive turning point affecting the preconceived ideas held with regard to non-European countries, which were still regarded as culturally inferior and politically underdeveloped. Furthermore, Turkey was obliged to accept the 'capitulations', which represented tremendous inroads on her sovereignty.

One author of the time wanted to know:

> What exactly is the 'community of the law of nations'? In what circumstances is a State considered to belong to the community of the law of nations or not? What is the situation of a State which accepts most of the provisions of the law of nations and rejects a few others? . . . Other societies in fact remain outside the community of the law of nations and are nevertheless States worthy of respect; such as the situation o the American States at the time of the Spanish Conquest.[8]

The inferior status of the non-European States in the eighteenth and nineteenth centuries by comparison with the European States must be made quite clear. The standards set by European international law had effects on two entirely different planes. Relations *inter se*—ones limited to the European States among themselves—were governed by the international law, which reciprocally guaranteed their sovereignty and independence, as well as all a State's legal capacities. This field of geographical application *inter se* of the European international law determined at the same time the extent of the community of the law of nations.

However, this European international law did not recognize the same safeguards for other States. It allowed the European States to do whatever they liked wherever they liked outside the area of the community of the law of nations. This permissive law was at once a negation of the independent existence of the other States, and a licence for rivalry and competition between the European States. The implications of this international law of European imperialism have been summed up by one writer as follows: 'In the absence of agreement, no exclusive competence; there only remain competitive rival competences, and areas where international law does not prohibit any State from performing any acts it desires; however, it does not make this faculty

---

[8] Remarks by Engelhardt at the 1888 Lausanne session of the Institute of International Law (Annuaire de l'Institut, 1888–89, p. 177 and 178). The discussion had been opened on 'territorial occupations', and a draft paper presented by de Martitz contained the following in its first article: 'Shall be considered as *territroium nullius* any region which is not actually covered by the sovereignty or protectorate of one of the States forming the community of the law of nations; it matters little whether that region is or is not inhabited.' This definition, which faithfully reflects the practice of the European States, needs no comment. The Institute adopted the draft on territorial occupations, but made no attempt to define *terra nullius*, i.e. the very territory to be occupied.

F. de Martens wrote at this time: 'The only lands that can be occupied are ones belonging to no-one and inhabited by barbaric tribes'. (F. de Martens, *Traité de Droit International*, Paris, 1886, vol. A, p. 464). In other words the inhabitants of such territories were 'non-persons' under European international law.

a legal power, protected from interferences by others.'[9] And again: 'Any Christian State was free to do anything anywhere.'[10]

This view was not appreciably modified, even at the time when Europe developed its relations with States of such ancient tradition and culture as Japan, China, Siam or Persia which had, for example, taken part in the 1899 Conference at The Hague, side by side with the European States that were the exclusive founders of the Community of the law of nations.

Each age invents its own excuses and camouflage. Thus Europe acquired colonies in the sixteenth century under the pretext of combating the infidels and evangelizing them, whereas it was in actual fact to reduce them to slavery and exploit their wealth. Later on, colonies were taken in order to bring the inhabitants the enlightenment of civilization and dispense its benefits.

From this point of view, everyone is somebody else's 'savage' if he does not share the proselytizer's ethical, political, philosophical or religious systems of reference. If it is decreed that the territory concerned should be allotted to the colonial power desiring it, the native inhabitants must clearly be rendered incapable of running and ruling the country. They must therefore be pronounced unfit for its administration. As a finishing touch, if the 'savages' are unable to manage their public affaire unaided, it is because they are even incapable of discerning what is for their own good and their own salvation. They are reduced to the condition of minors, who will fortunately one day be educated up to the age of reason and responsibility by the colonial power.

Whatever may be the moral justifications, and whatever legal arguments may have been advanced, the oligarchic European international law, when applied outside that continent, has always served to support the law of the big stick. For this purpose, certain 'justifications' have been invented in the course of time, amounting in every period to the camouflaging of the power relationships by legal quibbles. These various 'justifications' correspond to different phases in this law of conquest and occupation, and to the stages of its progress in an international legal edifice rendered increasingly complicated by its internal contradictions and the keen appetites of the major European powers. This law was distorted owing to the extraordinary capacity of the conduct of the European States whose enterprises, and more particularly their colonial expeditions, were hidden under a smokescreen.

Such is the cosmogony of international relations as seen by the dominant European States, simple and strictly logical in its imperialism. The limitless readiness for war, the 'occupation-conquests', the exploitation and domination of other peoples, were backed by grandiose and bloody, prestigious and cruel enforcements, physically powerful and ethically weak, which are inscribed for ever in the annals of human history, and which history can only accept as the expression of one of the ages of man entangled in the misdirected power and absurd vanity of his undertakings.

It should, however, be noted that with the passage of time, Europe began to harbour a deep-seated belief in the sanctity of traditional law. This belief was no doubt founded on a proper appreciation of economic and other interests to be preserved. But that was obscured and sublimated by the firmly rooted conviction that this law was really the international law *par excellence*. Detached from their economic context, the European values which inspired it gradually acceded to universality.

Such, very briefly, is this European law which reduced the international community to an exclusive European club made up of civilized nations. Not until the United Nations Charter was adopted could an open community replace the closed one, and the expression 'peace-loving States' be substituted for 'civilized nations' in the wording of Article 4, paragraph 1 of the Charter.

---

[9] A. Decencière-Ferrandière, 'Essai Historique et Critique sur l'Occupation comme Mode d'Acquérir les Territoires en Droit International', *Revue de Droit International*, 1937, p. 661 and 662.
[10] Ibid., p. 371.

C) F. PARKINSON

LATIN AMERICA, HER NEWLY INDUSTRIALISING COUNTRIES AND THE NEW INTERNATIONAL ECONOMIC ORDER

The New International Economic Order is an ill-defined concept which is nonetheless of considerable political importance. Non-existing in present-day international reality, it represents a vision, especially on the part of developing countries, of a future in which the latter will be an integral part of the world economy, instead of existing at its margins. As an idea, the New International Economic Order was given formal expression in 1974, though its historical roots go back to at least 1960.

As an economic concept, the New International Economic order has no autonomous basis as there is no agreement on its precise substance and shape beyond the broadest outlines. In so far as it consists of a catalogue of complaints voiced by the developing countries, it can be likened to the grievances contained in the *cahiers de doléance* presented to the Bourbon rulers on the eve of the French Revolution.[1] As a political concept, the New International Economic Order may be viewed as a weapon wielded by the developing countries in pressing their claims against the developed ones, whether in the context of co-operation or conflict.[2]

As a strategic concept intended to bring about a transformation of the old into a new economic world order, the notion of a New International Economic Order, however inarticulate at first, has guided the United Nations Economic Commission for Latin America, especially under the chairmanship of Raúl Prebisch, in elaborating a set of propositions (*ideología cepalina*) which was to be internationally applicable. When in 1963 Prebisch was appointed Executive-Secretary of the United Nations Conference on Trade and Development (UNCTAD), an institution in which, despite its universal and heterogeneous membership, the developing countries organised in the so-called 'Group of 77' countries provide the driving force, the substance of the *ideología cepalina* became the conventional wisdom of UNCTAD.

THE DEBATE ON DEVELOPMENTAL STRATEGY

Among developing continents, Latin America has been the pioneer of the two premier development strategies of import-substitution and export-led development. Dominant in the 1950s and 1960s, ECLA's recipe of joint industrialisation by collective import-substitution was applied in the Central American Common Market, in the Latin American Free Trade Association and in the Andean Group before doubts were beginning to be cast on its continuing validity in the 1970s.

Proceeding from the assumption that the terms of trade between developing and developed countries would always favour the latter, and that industrialisation was the appropriate remedy for redressing that imbalance, Prebisch urged the adoption of the following international measures: (i) financial aid; (ii) preferential tariffs; (iii) commodity agreements; and (iv) the integration of markets. Formulated in the early 1960s, Prebisch's theses have lost little of their powers of conviction, even though the master has had to alter their emphasis somewhat in the light of experience.[3] The vigorous criticisms expressed by a group of writers subsumed under the name of *de-*

[1] E. Hill and L. Tomassini (eds.), *América Latina y el Nuevo Orden Económico Internacional* (Santiago, Corporación de Promoción Universitaria, 1979), p. 6.

[2] Roberto Russell and Teresa Carballal, in *ibid.,* pp. 148–150.

[3] For relevant excerpts form a report presented by Prebisch at the meeting of ECLA at Mar del Plata, Argentina, in May 1963, see P. E. Sigmund (ed.), *The Ideologies of the Developing Nations,* 2nd. ed. (New York and London, Praeger, 1967), pp. 367–82. For Prebisch's recent shift of emphasis, see pp. 29–33 of *South* (London), January 1981.

pendencia[4] have made more impact in the academic world than among practical decision-makers of Latin America. Still, some committed 'developmentalists' of the Prebisch school (sometimes referred to as the Latin American 'structuralist' school), like Enrique V. Iglesias, head of ECLA, while rehearsing the familiar arguments in favour of industrialisation and the integration of Latin American markets[5] have had to admit that Prebisch's idea of inserting Latin America into the world economic system has had some negative consequences. Some writers have gone further. W. Baer insists that, far from reducing the margin of external dependency, the strategy of import-substitution has merely changed its nature,[6] and Aldo Ferrer has added point to this criticism by noting that Prebisch's original policy recommendations have proved palliatives, since they merely served to relieve the political pressures for change building up at the 'periphery'.[7]

What has emerged in recent years, however, is the rising degree of acceptance of Fernando Henrique Cardoso's explanatory theory of 'dependent development',[8] put in a nutshell by Argentina's former Minister of Finance (1970–71), Aldo Ferrer, as development in which 'the periphery grew in the margin of the capitalist world market'.[9]

It would be fair to say that Cardoso's contribution to the debate has given it an open character, in which new directions are sought and explored. Thus Eduardo Hill and Luciano Tomassini have investigated the implications of (i) reform (ii) revolution, and (iii) incorporation into the old international economic order as a possible means of escape from present strategic dilemmas. It is characteristic of the open-mindedness of the present debate that they have failed to settle on a single course of strategy that could be regarded as both desirable and credible. Of the three options examined, their findings show that (i) reform would require solidarity on a world scale, (ii) revolution would lead to the fragmentation of the world economy, and (iii) incorporation was ineligible as having been tried in the past and found wanting. As to tactics, Hill and Tomassini, tired of mere 'rhetorical positions', have opted for greater emphasis on 'what is possible than what is desirable', favouring the seeking out of areas of common interest in the present dialogue between developing and developed countries, in preference of posing unrealistic demands for the unilateral transfer of resources.[10]

Some authors would carry this newly fashionable pragmatism a stage further by their insistance on the overriding need for maintaining the momentum of an economic development, requiring close relationships with (i) world capital markets, (ii) international public financial agencies, and (iii) transnational corporations, to keep up direct investments and the flow of technology into the region.[11]

OVERHAULING ECLA?

Inevitably the question must be raised whether the hallowed *ideología cepalina* is now due for a general overhaul. Iglesias has argued that while Prebisch's original findings were sound, ECLA's very success has rendered its underlying conceptions out of date.[12] According to Iglesias, eco-

---

[4] For a brief comprehensive analysis, see F. Parkinson, *The Philosophy of International Relations* (Beverly Hills and London, *Sage,* 1977), pp. 123–6.

[5] P. 168 in Hill and Tomassini, *op. cit.*

[6] W. Baer, in J. Grunwald (ed.), *Latin America and World Economy: A Changing International Order* (Beverly Hills and London, *Sage,* 1978), p. 159.

[7] P. 82 in Hill and Tomassini, *op. cit.*

[8] P. 80 in *ibid.*

[9] For a presentation of Cardoso's theory, see F. H. Cardoso and E. Faletto, *Dependencia y desarrollo en América Latina* (Mexico City, Siglo Veintiuno, 1971).

[10] P. 8 in Hill and Tomassini, *op. cit.*

[11] Grunwald, *op. cit.,* p. 12.

[12] On this point see O. Rodríguez, *La teoría de subdesarrollo de la CEPAL* (Mexico City, Siglo Veintiuno, 1980).

nomic change affecting Latin America has been so rapid as to make past models seem irrelevant. To support his contention, he cites the fourfold increase in the national product of the region during the period between 1950 and 1975, in which rates of growth exceeded the most optimistic expectations, producing a situation in which industrial manufactures not only take up 20% of the region's total exports, but have also created the internal capacity to produce intermediate and capital goods previously imported.[13]

A Case of Mistaken Identity and the Urgent Need for a Rediscovery of Latin America's sub-NICs

However, the calls for the abandonment of ECLA's traditional strategy of industrialisation by import-substitution and joint development *(desarrollo adentro)* in favour of export-led development *(desarrollo afuera)* proceed from two unarticulated assumptions of (i) the harmony of economic interests throughout the region and (ii) the area's uniform progress in economic development. Both of these are grounded in massive fallacies that should not be allowed to go unchallenged.

In the first place, the indiscriminate equation of the interests of the Newly Industrialising Countries (NICs) with those of the sub-NICs, and the confusion of progress made in the NICs and sub-NICs alike, represents no less than a case of mistaken identity. It would be foolish to dispute the relative progress made by Latin America's sub-NICs since 1950. Central America represents a case in point. Applying ECLA's strategic prescriptions on a broad front, the Central American Common Market managed to register spectacular progress towards industrialisation—albeit, as it turned out, at the price of 'dependent industrialisation'.[14] It would nonetheless be rash to advise Central America's economic decision-makers to adopt a strategy of *desarrollo afuera*, which, by exposing the area to the inclement climate of world competition, would jeopardise the gains made. Far from being obsolescent, ECLA's time-honoured strategy of *desarrollo adentro* would seem to retain its full validity for that area, and for Latin America's sub-NICs in general.

In the second place one would have to voice considerable doubt as to the availability of the option of *desarrollo afuera* in an economic world climate of contraction, even for Latin America's NICs, since a buoyant world market may be an indispensable requisite for export-led development. It was not for nothing that at the onset of the Great Depression of 1930 Latin America was compelled to abandon export-led development in favour of import-substitution. The premature adoption of a strategy of *desarrollo afuera* may therefore not only prove detrimental to the economies of the sub-NICs, but in present circumstances have a rebounding effect on the NICs also.

While, fascinated by the spectacular progress made by Latin America's NICs, some writers dealing with the region's international economic relations have tended to treat the area's sub-NICs as Cinderellas, others have shown a salutary awareness of the need to separate NICs and sub-NICs in their assessment of economic development. Thus, it has been proposed that where a switch from *desarrollo adentro* to *desarrollo afuera* is contemplated, it should be made with circumspection and collectively, within a wide range of variations on the plane of 'countries with a similar level of development'.[15] This is a pointer in the right direction, but many conscious efforts will be required in the way of the rediscovery of the area's sub-NICs and a heightened awareness brought to bear regarding the economic differentials now in existence before balanced judgments can be arrived at as to the choice of strategies of economic development.

---

[13] Pp. 171–2 in Hill and Tomassini, *op. cit.*

[14] R. Harvey, 'Central America: A Potential Vietnam?', *The World Today*, no. 38, (July–August 1982), pp. 282–287.

[15] R. Ffrench-Davis and E. Tironi (eds.), *Latin America and the New International Economic Order* (London, Macmillan in association with St Antony's College, Oxford, 1982), p. 240.

THE POLARISATION OF LATIN AMERICA

Lenin accepted the 'uneven development' of capitalism as a permanent condition.[16] In the case of Latin America, discrepancies in size and economic endowment between countries, accentuated over time by the uneven incidence of industrialisation, have inflicted a cleavage between the NICs and sub-NICs. The point was alluded to discreetly by Iglesias, who noted that 'inequalities between the countries of the Latin-American region have deepened'.[17] Indeed, some of them—Brazil, Argentina, Mexico—may have reached 'taking-off' point to autonomous industrialisation. Brazil has diversified its economy to the stage where half its exports are of manufactured goods.[18] The sharp discrepancy in economic development between Latin America's NICs and sub-NICs is reflected in the rate of growth in the export of manufactures from the area as a whole from 3% in 1960 to over 18% in 1978, but with the three main NICs of the region registering an equivalent rate from 5 to 30%![19] The world's NICs collectively have achieved a momentum of economic development that is strikingly attested by their capture of 10% of world exports—almost equal to Japan's gigantic share.[20]

The process has reached a point at which Latin America's NICs and sub-NICs must be wondering whether they have more in common with their socio-economic counterparts in Asia and Africa than with each other within Latin America. Consequently, the region's NICs appear to have lost their sense of direction and belonging. The position would not be so bad if the NICs worldwide had found a suitable institutional framework in which to articulate their material interests in the manner in which the OECD has been doing for the fully industrialised countries[21] and the 'Group of 77' for the world's sub-NICs. For the time being, it seems, Latin America's NICs are retaining their membership of the 'Group of 77', and Brazil is trying to escape from the dilemma of growing ambivalence by aspiring to political leadership of that Group.[22]

Yet, that Latin America was becoming critically heterogeneous in terms of uneven economic development was first implicitly recognised as far back as 1964, when ECLA advised Latin America's representatives to UNCTAD not to form a caucus of their own but to join interest groups from other continents in conformity with their respective levels of economic development.[23] This advice was disregarded as Latin America refused to disaggregate in the manner suggested in favour of merging *en bloc* with the sub-NICs of Asia and Africa in the 'Group of 77'.

The full implications of Latin America's growing economic polarisation have as yet hardly been grasped by Latin Americanists. On the contrary, in the majority of cases the conclusion is drawn that rapidly developing Latin America is moving away from the rest of the developing world into a category of its own. Thus, it has been claimed that the difference between Latin America and other developing areas lies in its higher degree of industrialisation[24] and 'middle income group' status,[25] as if Latin America were now composed of a solid mass of NICs. From these confident assertions one would suppose that the 'trickle-down' theory, whereby dynamic

---

[16] For the historical background, see F. Parkinson, *op. cit.*, pp. 118–19.

[17] P. 176 in Hill and Tomassini, *op. cit.*

[18] Ffrench and Tironi, *op. cit.*, p. 8.

[19] *Ibid.*

[20] *Financial Times,* 28 July 1982; *The Economist,* 20 November 1982.

[21] For a general treatment of the phenomenon of the NICs, see L. Turner and others, *Living with the Newly Industrializing Countries* (London, Royal Institute of International Affairs, 1980).

[22] It was on Brazil's initiative that the so-called 'framework group' was set up by the Trade Negotiating Committee of the Tokyo Round of GATT negotiations in November 1976, with a view to dealing with areas of particular relevance to developing countries.

[23] For a general treatment of ECLA, see ECLA, *Development Problems in Latin America* (Austin, University of Texas Press, 1970).

[24] Grunwald, *op. cit.*, p. 15.

[25] F. Orrego and I. Lavados, in Hill and Tomassini, *op. cit.*, pp. 107 and 293 respectively.

economic growth would spread its benefits both domestically and across the frontiers, was still alive and kicking, instead of having been buried over a decade ago. 'Social development must not be seen simply as a spontaneous by-product of economic growth'. Latin America certainly does not seem to have benefited from the supposed effects of 'trickle-down'.[26]

Latin America must be seen not in isolation but as a microcosm of the developing world in all its diversities. What, in those circumstances, ought to be the proper international affiliation of her NICs? Two acute Argentine observers can do little by way of clarification in suggesting the consolidation of their ties with the developing world on the one hand, or the incorporation—alas! a subordinate one—in the 'closed circle of industrialised countries'.[27]

The dilemma stemming from Latin America's polarisation will remain, and so will the feelings of ambivalence experienced by the NICs. Moreover, the dilemma is likely to deepen. Procrastination will solve nothing. The problem ought to be recognised by Latin Americanists the world over in all its depth, and its various implications investigated fearlessly and, if need be, ruthlessly.

NICs and sub-NICs: Can Prebisch Bridge the Gulf?

Prebisch's original policy recommendations ought now to be reappraised in the light of the widening gulf between Latin America's NICs and sub-NICs. Of the four policy prescriptions made by Prebisch, two—international financial aid, and preferential tariffs—have been taken care of in several mechanisms set up by agencies of the United Nations.[28] One—an international régime for the stabilisation of commodities—has led to the creation of an appropriate mechanism, but second thoughts as to its underlying assumptions have prevented it from operating.[29] The last of Prebisch's recommendations—the merger of the markets of developing countries on a regional scale—has been left to the appropriate regions to implement.

Though there is evidence to show that the Generalised System of Preferences operated by the General Agreement on Tariffs and Trade (GATT) since 1971 has resulted in disproportionate gains accruing to the NICs selected as beneficiaries under that scheme, the present paper will confine itself to a discussion of the polarising effects produced or likely to be produced in the spheres of commodity trade and regional economic integration.

(A)   Commodities

Prebisch's main contention concerning the price level of commodities in world trade was their proclivity to decline in relation to trade in manufactured goods.[30] Since, almost by definition, most developing countries are primarily dependent on the export of their commodities for the bulk of their revenues, this condition must be rated one of the prime reasons for their state of underdevelopment.

However, it has been claimed that it is 'not possible to formulate a law à la Prebisch valid for all countries at all times'.[31] Ernesto Tironi, for instance, maintains that Latin America has taken effective control of its commodity-producing bases by substituting the agency of the State for that of the transnational corporation. Two objections may be made. In the first place, while it is true that most of Latin America's NICs have done so, most sub-NICs have not, no doubt because of

---

[26] Russell and Carballal in *ibid.*, pp. 157–8.

[27] *Ibid.*

[28] As part of the Second Development Strategy of the United Nations (1971–81).

[29] F. Parkinson, 'The United Nations Integrated Programme for Commodities', *Current Legal Problems*, no. 34, 1981), pp. 259–77.

[30] J. Spraos, *Inequalising Trade? A Study of Traditional North–South Specialisation in the Context of Terms of Trade Concepts* (London, Oxford University Press, 1983).

[31] R. Junguito and D. Pizano, in Ffrench-Davis and Tironi, *op. cit.*, p. 52.

lack of political strength. In the second place, exports from Latin America of practically all basic commodities are 'dominated by a few countries', which are mainly NIC.[32] The implications are obvious.

Attempts to stabilise and defend world commodity prices have, at least since 1945, taken the form of cooperative schemes between producers and consumers. It has recently been suggested that empirical studies be undertaken to determine whether for Latin America the creation of international producers' associations might not be 'preferable initiatives',[33] especially since Latin America has been in the forefront in pioneering the establishment of such associations as an alternative to mixed producer-consumer based agreements, witness the late Pérez Alfonzo's initiative in founding OPEC in 1960, and the joint Frei-Kaunda initiative in 1966 in setting up CIPEC.[34]

The idea of a 'trade union'-type pressure groups formed by commodity producers on an international scale came to the fore *pari passu* with the notion of a New International Economic Order. While numerous associations of this kind have sprung up in recent years,[35] it is well to recall that in the absence of a world famine of commodities, the pressures exerted can be fully felt only where a small number of producers is capable of achieving oligopolistic effects.[36] However, Latin American producers would be well placed in this respect, since phosphate, bauxite, tin and oil are all to be found in this category. Whether specifically Latin American associations of producers would before long be dominated by the NICs—such as Brazil in the case of coffee— thereby accentuating the effect of polarisation even while defending Latin American interests as a whole in that sphere, is difficult to determine at the moment.

(B) REGIONAL ECONOMIC INTEGRATION

It is impossible not to be struck by the correlation between the rapid rise of the NICs and the flagging momentum of the movement towards the economic integration of Latin America. The fate of LAFTA presents a case in point. The growing diversity of economic interests within it, and the disproportionately large benefits accruing to the NICs, resulted in the welling up of dissatisfaction on the part of the sub-NICs and eventually led to the unworkability of LAFTA's institutions. The enterprise in its erstwhile form had to be abandoned, and in 1980 LAFTA was replaced by the diverse and loosely structured Latin American Integration Association (LAIA) which makes express provision for autonomous preferential trading areas within economically homogeneous subregions within it.[37] Outside LAIA, both the Central American Common market—now partially defunct for political reasons—and the Andrean Group have both been organised on the principle of economic homogeneity and done well. At first sight, the establishment of the Pan-Latin American *Sistema Económico Latinoamericano* (SELA) in October 1975 would appear to run counter to the trend towards disintegration until it is realised that its purpose is the strengthening of *interdependence*, rather than the promotion of *integration*.[38]

---

[32] S. Teitel, in *ibid.,* p. 117.

[33] Junguito and Pizano, in *ibid.,* pp. 62–7.

[34] Conseil Intergouvernemental des Pays Exportateurs de Cuivre.

[35] G. Martner, *Producers Exporter Associations of Developing Countries: An Instrument for the Establishment of a New International Economic Order* (Geneva, IFDA, 1979). See also L. B. Francis, 'Producers' Associations in Relation to the New International Economic Order', *International and Comparative Law Quarterly,* no. 30 (1981), pp. 745–54.

[36] B. Lietaer, *Europe and Latin America and the Transnationals* (Westmead, Farnborough, Saxon House, 1979), p. 66.

[37] Text in *Integración Latinoamericana,* June 1980.

[38] On SELA, see Manfred Mols, in M. Mols (ed.), *Integration und Kooperation in Lateinamerika* (Paderborn, Schöningh, 1981), pp. 249–310.

It is therefore difficult to escape the conclusion that international economic integration in Latin America makes sense only among partners of roughly equal economic strength on a sub-regional, rather than a regional plane, and that any realistic assessment of the process must start with the crucial criterion of the comparative distribution of benefits. Any other approach would lead to a further widening of the rift between NICs and sub-NICs of the area.

(c)   TRANSNATIONAL CORPORATIONS: THE NEW FACTOR

One dimension left out of Prebisch's original policy prescriptions related to the activities and impact of transnational corporations on the economic development of Latin America. While their great importance was soon appreciated both by him and his critics, what has long gone unrecognised is the deeply divisive effects of the transnationals. These require investigation.

(i)   FOREIGN INVESTMENTS: DIVISION AND DEPENDENCE?

Of the two principal functions of transnational corporations in the economic development of Latin America—the provision of foreign capital and the purveyance of technology—the former is now capable of being dispensed with by the NICs, which are in a position to generate sufficient capital by their own efforts to cover their own development needs, mainly from ploughed-back profits.[39] Always the favoured recipients of transnational investments, foreign capital has been heavily concentrated in them, with Brazil, Mexico, Argentina and Venezuela accounting for over 80% of all foreign investments in the manufacturing sector.[40] Furthermore, the activities of transnational corporations have accounted for 43% of the manufactured exports of Brazil, and between 25 and 30% of Mexico, with similar levels applying to Argentina and Colombia.[41] The sub-NICs have naturally been of a far lesser attraction to foreign capital, and their benefits have consequently been fewer. It is therefore downright absurd for the president of the giant transnational corporation International Machines Bull (IMB) to claim that transnationals act as the 'great equaliser among countries'.[42] Latin America's experience would prompt one to draw the directly opposite conclusion.

In spite of the manifestly positive effects of the activities of the transnational on the NICs, there has been some eyebrow-raising in respect of a new kind of dependency of those NICs on the transnationals. Thus, attention has been drawn to the 'commanding position of the transnational enterprises within the Brazilian economy',[43] and note has been taken that in spite of a policy of 'Mexicanisation' of some vintage, the major control of joint ventures in Mexico has remained in foreign hands.[44] It has been claimed that, though constituting only 10 per cent of total investment, foreign investment in Brazil is dominating the dynamic sectors of the economy making it more dependent on foreigners than ever before.[45]

However these warnings are interpreted, they would seem to provide sustenance to Cardoso's explanatory theory of 'dependent development'.

---

[39] On transnational corporations in general, see United Nations Center on Transnational Corporations, *Transnational Corporations* (New York, 1980).

[40] Lietaer, *op. cit.,* p. 20.

[41] Ffrench-Davis and Tironi, *op. cit.,* p. 9.

[42] Lietaer, *op. cit.,* p. 35.

[43] P. Evans in R. R. Fagen (ed.), *Capitalism and the State in U.S.–Latin American Relations* (Stanford, Stanford University Press, 1979), p. 303.

[44] R. Montavon and others, *The Role of Transnational Companies in Latin America: A Case Study of Mexico* (Westmead, Farnborough, Saxon House, 1979), p. 13.

[45] Grunwald, *op. cit,* p. 13.

(II) TECHNOLOGY: LAST BASTION OF DEPENDENCE IN THE NICS?

While the NICs may be a large be able to stand on their own feet in the sphere of capital-generation, this seems to be far from being the case in the field of technology, an item more coveted than foreign capital. The pace of progress in technology tends to defeat even the most advanced NICs.[46] Mexico, for one, has remained the epitomy of technological dependence and given up hope of being self-sufficient in this sphere in the near future, concentrating instead on enhancing her bargaining power during negotiations for contracts for the transfer of technology. There would appear to exist some optimism in regarding the rise of a new class of Latin American *técnicos* that is fast acquiring the requisite skills.[47]

TRANSNATIONAL CORPORATIONS: LATIN AMERICA'S RESPONSES

(A) DOMESTICATION

The response of Latin American countries to the overwhelming influence of the transnational corporations operating in the region has been varied. There is little doubt, however, that the NICs are in a much better position than the sub-NICs to cope by taking countervailing measures to contain the power of the transnationals within acceptable limits.

Trotsky once argued that, in the absence of a robust middle class, the industrialisation of Russia would have to be carried out by the Bolshevik State, and one writer insists that the absence of a 'national bourgeoisie' in Latin America places a similarly heavy burden on the State.[48] Thus, in Mexico the State has since 1972 pursued policies designed to promote co-existence without friction with the transnationals.[49] State action has, however, gone furthest in Brazil in this respect, where the 'domestication' of the transnationals is being accomplished by ensnaring them within the so-called 'triple alliance' composed of *(a)* the government, represented by the *Conselho de Desenvolvimento Industrial* charged with the task of seeking out suitable areas for joint development, *(b)* 'national' capital, organised in the increasingly influential *Associão Brasileira pelo Desenvolvimento de Indústria de Base,* as well as *(c)* the transnationals themselves. By all intents and purposes the transnational corporations concerned appear to be settling down to the new situation with surprising ease.[50]

(B) MULTINATIONAL ENTERPRISES

What the NICs are capable of doing in the way of mustering countervailing power to match the mounting influence of transnational corporations on an individual level, the sub-NICs can only hope to achieve by collective action. In their case, the formation of countervailing power in the shape of multinational enterprises may be seen as a fitting response.

Though often semantically confused with transnational corporations, their opponents, multinational enterprises have been accurately defined as resulting 'through formal and permanent agreement between two or more developing countries (or nationals of those countries)'.[51] A log-

---

[46] The late Professor H. G. Johnson has argued that it was presumably cheaper to transplant an already known technology to a different environment to which it is not appropriate than to develop a technology appropriate to it. See H. G. Johnson, *Technology and Economic Dependence* (London, Macmillan, 1975), p. 76. The crucial choice then seems to lie between expensive adaptation to avoid significant social and economic distortions or uncritical but relatively cheap transplantation of technology. See Lietaer, *op. cit.,* p. 36.

[47] The United Nations is willing to offer a helping hand. See United Nations, *Measures Strengthening the Negotiating Capacity of Governments in their Relations with Transnational Corporations: Regional integration cum/versus Corporate Integration* (New York, 1982).

[48] Evans in Fagen, *op. cit.,* pp. 304–5.

[49] Montavon, *op. cit.,* p. 110.

[50] Evans in Fagen, *op. cit.,* pp. 306–7.

[51] Felipe Herrera in Grunwald, *op. cit.,* p. 130.

ically consistent and politically successful attempt in this direction has been made within the context of the Andean Group in Decisions 46 and 169, passed by the *junta* in 1971 and 1982 respectively. The *Sistema Económico Latinoamericano* (SELA) similarly has been anxious to encourage the formation of multinational enterprises throughout the region.[52]

The point about multinational enterprises is that in addition to being pitted against the transnationals they are also capable of performing important functions in the joint industrialisation of sub-regions in Latin America, thus pulling their weight against the prevailing trend towards polarisation.

Unfortunately, the operation of multinationals requires the application of complex legal controls, and it is to be feared that only the NICs have developed a bureaucratic apparatus sufficiently sophisticated to handle those controls effectively. It is perhaps for this reason that the hopes entertained in the sub-NICs regarding the smooth and rapid creation of multinational enterprises have come no nearer to fulfillment. On the contrary, while their draftsmen have been busy devising elaborate schemes for the operation of multinationals, some NICs have advanced sufficiently far on the road of industrialisation to launch transnational corporations of their own. Bráspetro, the foreign arm of the Brazilian State-operated oil concern Petrobrás, represents a case in point, as does the steel corporation Río Vale Doce, also of Brazil.

Sadly, the prospects of the sub-NICs in this respect seem to be bleak also.

(c)   *Inter-transnational Competition*

The third countervailing strategy available to Latin America is to promote competition among the transnational corporations active in the region, and it has been suggested that new entrants among the species are on that account to be welcomed.[53]

Theoretically, major benefits should accrue to the Latin American host States from keen competition among the transnationals. In some areas that competition appears to exist. However, a strategy of this sort imports the danger of inviting the formation of inter-transnational cartels, possibly on a region-wide scale, such as was confidently predicted on a world scale by Karl Kautsky, the Austro-Marxist theoretician, during the second decade of this century.

However beneficial, at least initially, the adoption of this strategic countervailing option to the NICs, it seems almost impossible to imagine that the sub-NICs could benefit from it, since it has been empirically established that not only the 'traditional' transnational corporations operating in Latin America, but also Japanese[54] and West European new entrants among them prefer to concentrate on the NICs.[55]

The New International Economic Order: The Prospects for Latin America

Growing diversity in economic development and the resulting discrepancies in economic, and ultimately political power, have led to a marked differentiation among the countries of Latin America, and the possibility of a *marginalização* of her sub-NICs.

Several consequences are flowing from those trends. In the field of commodities, Latin American countries must now take seriously the suggestion of participating either in intra-continental or inter-continental producer associations in defence of world commodity prices, while at the same time watching the power exercised by some of their own major producer-exporters, to prevent imbalances of power from arising within their own ranks.

---

[52] Grunwald, *op. cit.*, p. 234.

[53] Ffrench-Davis and Tironi, *op. cit.*, p. 177.

[54] P. K. Hall, 'Avance des transnacionalismo japonés y América latina', *Foro Internacional*, January–March 1983, pp. 287–304.

[55] Lietaer, *op. cit.*, p. 18.

Ambitious schemes for the economic integration of Latin America as a whole, or the largest part of it, comprising the NICs, must now be abandoned as impractical. To be effective, schemes of this nature should henceforth be confined to manageable geoeconomic sub-regions and have the double purpose of containing the influence of transnational corporations on the one hand, and matching the economic strength of Latin America's NICs on the other.

The meteoric rise of the transnational corporations the world over, but especially in Latin America, has provoked the initiation of a number of counter-measures. Where this has happened in the NICs, they stand a good chance of achieving the intended objective of controlling the transnationals, but where the region's sub-NICs have attempted this, their chances of success must be rated as slim. New techniques might have to be devised to relieve their plight in this respect.

The progressive articulation of the implications of the New International Economic Order is a task for which Latin America's intellectuals are specially fitted. From Carlos Calvo in the nineteenth century to Raúl Prebisch in the twentieth, Latin American scholars and diplomats have been in a straight line of tradition in criticising the older international economic order and calling for fundamental change. This is a source of justified pride and a tradition worthy of being maintained. What is required of them now is the elaboration of new theoretical conceptions catering for the new circumstances that have arisen in Latin America as a result of differentiation in the prevailing levels of economic development. This would rule out any attempts to treat the region as economically homogeneous in favour of a duality of standards of judgment in relation to NICs and sub-NICs that alone can do justice to the heterogeneous character of present-day Latin America.

READING 10: RICHARD FALK

Professor emeritus of international law at Princeton University, Richard Falk has supported the development of international law for decades. In the 1970s he was one of the supporters of the World Order Models Project (WOMP). As we see in the following two excerpts, Falk has often found himself on the defensive.

RICHARD FALK,

A STUDY OF FUTURE WORLDS, 1975

WORLD ORDER BARGAINS AND BARGAINING
Formal international cooperation is increasingly required to efficiently handle a vast array of functional issues with global dimensions. An erstwhile laissez-faire confidence in "the invisible hand," harmonizing world community interests with the separate interests of national policy-makers,

seems to be vanishing in all portions of the world.[1] Even the most powerful state actors require reliable international norms, procedures and regimes, in order to achieve desired levels of predictability and stability.[2] The United States has a particularly high stake in promoting dependable forms of international cooperation, because its essential activities are spread out far beyond its own "jurisdiction" (i.e., its territorial domain), and its domestic equilibrium depends in intricate ways upon the dynamics of global interdependence.

In many areas of international life, including important economic relations, strong governments are at least temporarily less able and less eager than formerly to use direct action as a prime means of imposing their wills on the weak, even with respect to legal claims based on property rights.[3] When France and Great Britain attempted to enforce their economic claims on Egypt after Nasser expropriated the Suez Canal Company in 1956, the U.S. opposition to this military effort indicated a real shift in tactics. At the same time, the hostile U.S. reaction to radical regimes in Latin America and concomitant efforts to thwart their success suggest that we should not over-estimate the significance of this shift. The present world structure of economic dependency provides the United States with potent nonmilitary levers of influence, which bear on credit terms, foreign aid, tax schedules for exports and imports, and freezing foreign-held accounts and other assets.

In some contexts, however, this leverage is limited by a paramount interest in maintaining cooperative links with foreign governments in matters of security and basic ideological orientation.

For instance, the United States government is reluctant to push its claims that Ecuador is illegally seizing and fining U.S. fishing vessels off its shores, because of its overriding interest in maintaining solidarity with respect to hemispheric security and geopolitical affiliation.[4] Thus, the United States government has so far preferred to have its own taxpayers reimburse American owners of captured fishing vessels, rather than attempt even indirectly to coerce these governments into accepting the American position on territorial jurisdiction over ocean activity.

Similarly, government officials in the United States charged with halting the international flow of heroin, and aware that Thai officials are not taking steps to prevent heroin production on their

---

[1] More important than the interplay of national and global well-being is the link between national behavior and species adaptability. The ecological challenge of the present era, unlike earlier challenges which altered man's behavioral patterns and relation to his environment, is man-caused and of global scope.[50] The appropriate line of response, then, needs to be of comparable scope in order to remove the threats now mounting against the species. It is our special contention that unlike earlier ecological challenges, the present one calls for a response centered around a movement for rapid global reform.

[2] A more dependable international legal order does not signify a more equitable one. Legal arrangements reflect political arrangements, and the former will be as coercive and exploitative as the latter dictates. Therefore, an expanded role for international law is not necessarily consistent with global reform as we have specified it. Its consistency will depend on whether a neo-Darwinian or humanistic ethos prevails in the relations of states and peoples, or whether some kind of "mix" emerges. In the likely event of a "mix" it becomes more essential than ever for international lawyers to become more alert to the value implications of given proposals for legal development. It might be helpful to assess systematically the annual output of the International Court of Justice, the International Law Commission, and other bodies of the United Nations from the perspective of probable impacts on WOMP goals.

[3] It is exceedingly doubtful that this renunciation of force by the strong would withstand real pressures on their interests, e.g., if the United States economy were as pressed in the 1970's by Arab manipulation of the market conditions for oil, as Japan was pressed in the 1930's by Euro-American manipulation of world trade conditions. Japan's military quest for control over resources essential to its national economy suggests the degree to which even a country with a relatively isolationist tradition can be induced to adopt an imperial strategy.

[4] What is suggestive here is the bargaining potential of weak governments when the military sanctions of strong governments are rendered inoperative either by self-restraint (i.e., renunciation of force for nondefensive purposes) or by offsetting considerations (i.e., fear of provoking domestic radicalization or geopolitical defection). In this regard, even the puppet ends up pulling some of the strings, as the United States discovered in its anguished relations with the Saigon regime under both Diem and Thieu and in its relations with the Chiang regime on Taiwan.

territory, have opposed legislative efforts to penalize Thailand by cutting off $100 million in foreign aid. In a setting like this, the diverse interests of governments may conflict, even in the face of shared nominal and rhetorical commitments to halting heroin use. As evidence has shown, foreign government officials may themselves benefit from the heroin trade, or may regard export sales as an essential source of scarce foreign exchange; it may even be (as has been convincingly alleged) that the CIA or other segments of the U.S. government do not really favor implementing the official national policy.

Air piracy, or hijacking, is another problem which illustrates how interdependence, statist constraints, and diverse perceived interests can interact to offset one another. Nongovernmental actors with no positive interest in intergovernmental stability can all too easily block efforts to reach an effective world order bargain. Hijacking is also a metaphor for the growing vulnerability of the emerging world public order system to disruption by any group with deep grievances that are not susceptible to peaceful, orderly satisfaction. This vulnerability provides the ruling groups with a rationale and rationalization for repressive tactics, ranging from police prerogatives to intrusions on privacy. The complexity of the United States, the surfacing discontent of change-oriented groups, and the traditions of personal liberty and social contract, make our society a likely arena for the enactment of this drama in a form that has wider than national significance.

The domestic response to hijacking, and the related questions of kidnapping high diplomatic and business officials, are separate from the effort of the United States to strike a world order bargain. With regard to hijacking, the United States has strong incentives to strike a bargain: its interests are so spread around the globe that secure air travel and unimpeded diplomatic and business intercourse are crucial, intrinsically as well as symbolically. Can such a bargain be struck? Are there genuine common interests that enable the negotiation of an effective world procedure? The more militant Arab governments have actually joined in celebrating successful hijackings and other acts of terror organized by extremist wings of Palestinian liberation groups; indeed, these disruptive undertakings are popularly viewed in the Middle East as spectacular exploits of courage and their perpetrators are treated as heroes. While much of the world was shocked by terror against Israeli athletes participating in the 1972 Olympic Games in Munich, the Black Septembrists who died there were brought to Libya to be buried amid exultant crowds. Obviously, such governments would be reluctant to commit themselves to an effective international anti-hijacking code. As long as there are deep-seated human conflicts in the world arena, those governments and groups who identify with the goals of the hijackers would not be inclined to adopt, much less support, a program designed to discourage hijackings. Israel might not be ready to cooperate with a procedure that compelled the return of hijackers to the country of origin; what if the hijackers happened to be Soviet Jews seeking to emigrate to Israel?

In certain contexts a procedure has been tacitly accepted whereby planes and ransom money are returned but the hijacker is granted asylum. Cuba and Algeria have apparently adopted this intermediate position, but these governments have mixed interests. In the Beirut Raid of December, 1968, Israel demonstrated that she was prepared to retaliate against Arab commercial air capabilities, as a way of punishing and deterring the support Arab governments had allegedly given to anti-Israel hijacking activities. Clearly, there are some objective conditions of vulnerability to various types of hijacking, a vulnerability increased by the diverse governmental attitudes toward the particular political *motives* involved. In any event, by definition, an intergovernmental bargain would not altogether prevent hijacking or kidnapping. The United States has been able only to reduce but not to eliminate domestic hijacking, despite a unified national policy of surveillance, regulation, and punishment. Indeed, a fully satisfactory world order bargain may not be possible in such an area. The competitive logic of S_1 (and the nature of the act itself) may virtually preclude an international solution.

The United States government would like to negotiate world order "bargains" that create reciprocal obligations by foreign governments in exchange for undertakings by the United States. Naturally, these bargains must be based on "tradeoffs" between governments that have diverse perceived interests. The Treaty on Non-Proliferation of Nuclear Weapons (1968) is an excellent example of an effort to strike such a world order bargain; the non-nuclear powers renounce their option to develop nuclear weaponry, and in exchange receive technical assistance to enable their development of peaceful nuclear technology and energy facilities. Whether this trade-off continues to be mutually beneficial over time depends on a number of uncertain factors, such as the overall character of world order, decisions made by non-signatory governments regarding their own nuclear status, the willingness of nuclear powers to denuclearize world politics, and satisfaction with the way the nuclear powers fulfill their pledge to render nonmilitary assistance. An existing treaty obligation indicates only that a bargain has been struck at one point in time, not that an accord will be maintained indefinitely. The Non-Proliferation Treaty explicitly recognized the conditional effectiveness of treaty arrangements by providing governments with a three-month right of withdrawal for unilaterally determined reasons of supreme national interest.[5]

We think the United States government should seek a series of world order bargains in this world of independent states and interdependent interests, because conditions of reciprocity need to be perceived by governments, and then established and sustained. Where reciprocity cannot be negotiated, the United States is faced with a series of options; the options range from deference to foreign claims, to the coercive use of military power. Obviously, nonviolent, collective means of persuasion are preferred strategies, in contexts where world order bargains are prevented either because interests diverge too sharply, or because the relevant governmental actors cannot negotiate mutually reasonable tradeoffs.

It is possible to complement world order bargains with unilateral nonmilitary sanctions which might be both effective and beneficial for community welfare. For instance, it seems desirable to encourage cooperative arrangements for protecting endangered species such as great whales and polar bears, by prohibiting the sale of product imports in American markets. Similarly, national legislation to prohibit foreign SST's from landing on American air fields seems like a desirable way to discourage further development of ecologically destructive and dangerous technology. Such "unilateralism" would exert American power on behalf of widely shared community values.

Efforts like the Hickenlooper Amendment represent another brand of unilateralism—the desire to impose special American policy on foreign governments in an area of legitimate diversity. (In this case, national law specifies the terms of compensation that a foreign government must give an expropriated American investor; if proper compensation is not made, the President is authorized to cut off foreign aid.)[6] The Hickenooper enactment was a response to corporate pressure, and thus the North American *legislative* definition of international legal requirements bears little resemblance to the requirements of either world justice or of existing rules of international law.

The area of foreign investment illustrates a much more general problem with unilateral approaches to world order bargaining. The United States government's capacity to represent the enlightened self-interest of the nation as a whole is seriously affected by the differential access

---

[5] Such conditional effectiveness of treaty obligations on the continuation of perceived advantage to participating governments is a natural consequence of S_1 logic and dynamics. A particular government may, for egocentric reasons, conclude that its general interests in stability are better sustained by respecting a disadvantageous obligation of international law. However, this general sentiment is weak in world affairs, especially as dominant actors do not seem often to accord such general respect.

[6] Unilateral efforts to coerce compliance by others with dubious international norms (especially norms repudiated as expressions of nonvoluntary creations, as in the foreign investment area) encourage retaliatory acts and embitter international relationships. Reliable law in S_1 is based on voluntary contracts among participating governments; imposed contracts, such as peace treaties, have not fared well when the imposing power is removed; they characteristically inspire disrespect that is popularly supported.

which some special interest groups have to influential policy-makers. International positions are skewed toward the outlooks of well-organized and well-financed lobbies both inside and outside of government. For example, in connection with the attempt to establish a global code for governing the exploitation of offshore oil resources, the oil industry has influenced the U.S. government to put forward an apparently non-negotiable offer which, if accepted, will virtually assure a statist competitive scramble. As a result, an excellent opportunity to experiment with supranational arrangements for control and development of ocean activity has been jeopardized, and perhaps lost altogether.

A series of questions are raised about the capacity of governments, including our own, to reach and sustain satisfactory world order bargains that must simultaneously embody the reciprocal interests of many governments. Experience with this bargaining capacity will one way or another influence the American policy-making elites' general perception of the feasibility of world order reforms and adjustments within the confines of S_1. In any area where "national security" is at stake, such as assured access to oil, the "national solutions" argument is likely to prevail. Thus, despite expected environmental harm, the United States has decided to go ahead with the development of the North Pine Slope oil fields and the trans-Alaska pipeline, in order to reduce its increasing dependence on oil imports.[7] It is always difficult to distinguish special pleading (e.g., a "national security" cover for concern over company profits) from honest expression of the self-reliance ethic which girds the belief system of most power-wielders in S_1.

Can S_1 forms of order prevent destructive competition in nonmilitary realms, when its underlying structure so heavily depends on the war system and a wasteful, perilous arms race? When confronting critical functional problems, can an American government hope to crystallize bargaining positions that genuinely reflect its own national interests in world order stability, much less provide reasonable incentives to diversely oriented foreign governments?[8] Will foreign governments, especially those that are most sovereignty-oriented—either because of totalitarian tendencies toward exclusive control, or national self-assertion during a period of domestic nation-building—be capable of realistic world order bargaining? That is, even if the United States develops its side of the bargain in a reasonable manner, will enough other principal actors perceive the offer as "reasonable," or make a counter-offer that the United States government perceives (or should perceive) as reasonable?

We fear that the United States is not likely to develop reasonable proposals where critical world order bargains need to be struck and that, in any case, shared perceptions of reasonableness will not be forthcoming to sustain important forms of international cooperation. In this event, the problem-solving capacities of S^1 will appear obsolete even without consideration of the war system, and receptivity to S_2 type thinking is likely to increase.[9] Testing grounds for reform potential are likely to arise early in t_1, most probably with regard to negotiations on world monetary and trade relations, a global regime for the exploitation of ocean resources, the protection of ocean quality, and satellite broadcasting. These negotiations will probably fail unless

---

[7] Indeed, President Nixon's principal response to the American energy crisis, aggravated by an Arab oil embargo, had been to move deeper into S_1 patterns by proclaiming Project Independence for realization in 1980, i.e., making the United States independent of external supplies. In the European context, Henry Kissinger has taken a second line of approach, proposing in a preliminary way the shared management of energy supplies among developed non-Communist societies.

[8] In effect, this question asks whether special interest perspectives can be sufficiently neutralized so that the national position reflects the overall well-being of the United States. The evidence is not encouraging in critical areas where significant business opportunities exist.

[9] There is already some elite receptivity to an S_2 approach to global reform, but its character is *hegemonial* rather than *egalitarian, elitist* rather than *equitable*. The sort of humanistic approaches to S_2 embodied in WOMP are not present in government or corporate visions of the future.

dominant political consciousness in this and other critical national arenas proceeds at least to a mid-t_1 position of receptivity to $S_{2(WOMP)}$.[10] "Failure" in this context can occur because no bargain can be reached, or because only a nominal bargain with minimal behavioral consequences is negotiated. In other words, failure constitutes an inability to strike a world order bargain that achieves a generally satisfactory functional solution of global scope.

To date, the international economic system has been fragmented along ideological lines. What is generally described as "world trade relations" or the "world monetary system" has in reality been limited to relations among non-Communist actors. It remains unclear whether economic relations will be universalized by revived "balance of power thinking," the rise of inter-bloc trade, the presence of China in the United Nations, the decline of ideological politics in the main world capitals, the Sino-Soviet split, a shared rich-country consensus about the boundaries of their respective spheres of influence, and a statist ordering of world relations.

A major uncertainty surrounds the multinational corporation as world actor—whether it opts or is co-opted into a position of support for concert politics of principal governments, or whether it opposes neo-statist trends and seeks, on a relatively autonomous basis, to organize economic markets around its own interests.[11] The United States has a particular relationship to the global role of the MNC. As Robert Gilpin notes in an important study of the link between the MNC and American national interests, "In large measure, the term 'multinational corporation' or MNC is a euphemism for the outward expression of America's giant national corporations." Contrary to some popular impressions, the bulk of this investment has been in the industrial sector of the world economy, mainly Western Europe and Canada, although increasingly in Japan as well. Between 1946 and 1970, American direct foreign investment increased at a remarkable pace: from $7 billion to $80 billion. Europe and Canada have become very agitated about "the American challenge," and have felt that their national independence was being eroded, if not threatened, by the growing influence of American export capital in their societies.

Gilpin raises important complementary questions about the extent to which American state interests have been served by the outflow of capital, and the related tendency to substitute foreign investment for exports. His basic conclusion is that our national tax law provides American business with an extra incentive to make foreign investments. In the course of a sophisticated discussion of economic consequences, Gilpin persuasively contends that this basic pattern of exporting productivity (via investment) rather than goods is producing a *rentier* position for the United States. This position implies both a kind of parasitism vis-à-vis foreign productivity, and extreme vulnerability to changes in foreign investment circumstances. The extent of this vulnerability has been vividly demonstrated in the area of oil production. Gilpin also suggests that the national economy is being hurt by the insufficient rate of domestic investment, a diminished emphasis on increasing profits via technological innovation in domestic industry, and the ten-

---

[10] It is a curious paradox that given present levels of governmental consciousness, reformist potentialities in S_1 depend greatly on an increasing acceptance of WOMP goals. This dependence reflects the fact that reformism requires the voluntary accommodation of unequally placed governments increasingly aware of their real situation. Even reactionary governments such as Brazil adopt a Third World outlook in world order bargaining situations to maximize the interests of their national elites.

[11] See Chapter VI, p. 381 for a discussion of the multinational corporation as actor in S_1. The ability of the corporate interests to deny anti-MNC individuals and groups access to national power will be major influence on whether an independent $S_{2(MNC)}$ becomes a serious possibility. There is no doubt that the resources at the disposal of world business interests are so great that the MNC's preferences will either be realized or its autonomy destroyed by government regulation. Either governments will become captives of multinational business, or the other way around. At the present time, the split between corporate and sovereign perspectives has a healthy effect of dissolving the identity of interests that has united business and political elites in this country for several decades, producing a kind of state capitalism which combines some of the worst ingredients of socialist and capitalist arrangements.

dency to deprive labor of its normal share of the economic fruits of increasing productivity. Therefore, the harm done to this country by the MNC arises mainly from its failure to allow the nation as a whole to enjoy the benefits of economic growth, and from the instability that may result from having such a large stake in maintaining a favorable investment climate abroad. It should be emphasized that Gilpin is not arguing the case against the MNC from a radical perspective. On the contrary, he is contending that a pro-foreign investment tax credit has allowed the MNC to acquire an overly large share of American capital activities, and that new regulatory approaches are needed to restore balance. In effect, foreign antagonists of American economic penetration by means of the MNC, and domestic critics of the Gilpin variety, arrive at the same conclusion—namely, that the loss of government control over domestic economic well-being has harmful effects and risks.

A related uncertainty involves how the Third World will react to the challenge of the international economy: by bargaining for marginal improvements in *terms* of participation, or by seeking a new *structure* that bends toward greater equality of participation and benefits.[12] Because of their size and stature, the attitudes of China and India on these issues will be critically important. It is likely that marginalists and structuralists will do battle in these countries in the years ahead.

For the United States, the search for viable world order bargains will be determined by the overall relation of social forces within domestic society. In the event that a progressive coalition takes shape, and is not thwarted by a reactionary coup, the United States will be likely to seek world order bargains that move in the direction of $S_{2(WOMP)}$ rather than $S_{2(CONCERT)}$, $S_{2(MNC)}$, or $S_{2(IMP)}$. Early in such a period, it will be difficult to decide whether to treat a particular action as an S_1 reform, or as a transition step toward $S_{2(WOMP)}$. In isolation an act may partake of both tendencies within S_1. By t_2, such ambiguity will largely be eliminated, and S_1 reformers will be aligned against $S_{2(WOMP)}$ planners, as well as against other categories of S_2 advocates.

If a progressive coalition does not acquire power in the United States by the 1970's, either a concert or market outlook, or possibly an amalgam of the two, is likely to become paramount in government thinking. Given the strains of managing a world of severe inequity, intense interdependence, and ecological fragility, the prospects are for more explicit structures of domination within the United States and in the world as a whole. In this sense, the drift toward an S_2 solution will appear as increasingly inevitable, but if t_1 is never completed the United States is likely to become a leading participant in the creation of a regressive, coercive variant of S_2 that seeks to sustain America's relative power, control, and wealth, but involves a conformist nightmare at home and abroad.[13]

---

[12] There is no reason, of course, to expect a consistent strategy of reform on the part of Third World governments. Their present orientations toward global reform are very diverse, as are their antagonisms toward one another. However, a pattern may emerge as issues involving global management grow more crystallized. The basic choice, then, would become whether to increase their relative position in S_1, or to pursue an S_2 option that seemed to promote their particular interests in global reform, assuming a consensus could be reached on such an option during the course of t_1.

[13] We are arguing, in effect, that there is a continuity between domestic and global politics, that it is impossible to pursue a neo-Darwinian global strategy and a humanist domestic strategy, especially in an overall world situation of deepening ecological and social crisis. Why? It will prove impossible to sustain a domestic consensus based on such a discontinuity. One of the consequences of humanism is to reject artificial confines of national boundaries as the proper orbit of empathy. Thus, the very success of a humanistic approach within the nation will lead to a repudiation of neo-Darwinianism as a global strategy. Also, the degree of global awareness arising from technological innovation and economic interdependence will make it increasingly uncomfortable to wallow in wealth while most others languish in misery; the split condition will induce severe spiritual depressions and might provide fertile territory for a religious revival of really potent force. But suppose the scale of world poverty grows so acute that the only apparent choice is between islands of affluent dignity and an ocean of shared misery? This condition was characteristic for all civilizations prior to the industrial revolution and provided an underpinning for institutions of slavery and the like that was indeed supported by a domestic consensus that embraced most ethically sensitive members of society.

SOME DOMESTIC YARDSTICKS OF GLOBAL REFORM PROSPECTS

Value changes, including shifts in attitudes toward world order and global reform, are likely to be best understood in domestic arenas. In our special framework, an assessment of t_1—its depth and its counter-tendencies—can be most successfully made by considering the debates, behavioral patterns, and interrelation of social, economic, and political forces within the United States. One useful focus would be upon the links between discussions of domestic and global dimensions of the war system; this could be done by comparing the treatment of arms control, arms spending and arms use in foreign policy, with such domestic matters as gun control, prison reform, and crime control. Above all, we should acknowledge our reliance on a "war system" to maintain domestic law and order. Our confidence in democratic processes critically depends on whether governmental authority can administer peaceful procedures fast enough to overcome perceived grievances and deprivations, and whether groups with grievances accept the system's legitimacy.[14] In the United States there has been a recent decline in the legitimacy of governing institutions, stemming from a combination of the Indochina War, "the benign neglect" of minority grievances, and the mounting evidence of official lawlessness.[15] This decline has generated an offsetting series of populist demands for police protection against "those who take the law into their own hands." Is Father Daniel Berrigan, as civil disobedient, a servant of grace and inspiration, or an arrogant and destructive fool?[57] Both interpretations are so ardently held by different portions of the society, that there is virtually no possibility of a social contract between the government and the citizenry. Contradictions between authority and justice induce repression to sustain the ruler's imperative, while stimulating disobedience and resistance by an aggrieved citizenry.

Prevailing ethical attitudes in the United States support domestic reliance on the war system. The failure of Congress to enact effective legislation prohibiting hand gun sales is indicative, as in public support for brutal police responses to unruly anti-war demonstrations during the latter phase of the Indochina War. By an uncomfortably large margin, public opinion felt that the National Guard was justified in using live ammunition against unarmed student demonstrators at Kent State University in the Spring of 1970, even though four students died as a result. Similarly, the public approved Governor Rockefeller's authorization of lethal force to restore order at Attica Prison in 1971, despite the bloodshed that resulted. These instances disclose a public enthusiasm for violence, provided it is directed against those who seem to militantly oppose the established order.[16] This approval of violence also embraced the public acceptance

---

[14] Perhaps even more important in the United States, will mildly advantaged or less disadvantaged groups regard themselves as victimized by the excessive concern displayed by more advantaged groups for those who are, in socioeconomic respects, the most disadvantaged segments of American society? Blue-collar hostility toward welfare programs directed at the ghetto poor is one manifestation of this phenomenon. Middle American responses to the Woodstock ethos is another. In effect, we can see a kind of anti-liberal insistence that the poorest groups get ahead according to the American work and competitive ethic (i.e., the neo-Darwinian obstacle course which only the fittest can complete). This ethical premise makes welfare payments seem both corrupting to the poor, and unfair to those who work hard to avoid being poor. It is easy to grasp the link between neo-Darwinism of this variety, and its global expression. Our main point here is that among those who can become aggrieved when compassionate politics gain widespread support are those who perceive themselves as victims of their own self-reliance.

[15] The other side of official illegitimacy—that is, ineffectiveness—is also manifested by increasing self-reliance on the part of urban groups threatened by rampant criminality. Since the government is unable or unwilling to enforce the law and provide its citizenry with personal security, the citizens are inclined to arm themselves and pursue strategies of self-help.

[16] Reliance on disruptive and illegal tactics by white parents to prevent school busing generated quite opposite sentiments in the general public. The unpopularity of busing designed to achieve racial integration (as contrasted with the acceptance in the South of busing to thwart integration) led to widespread acceptance of parental rights to engage in resistance activities that were viewed by the same citizens with such disfavor, when engaged in by draft-age students during the Indochina War. Thus, the critical feature is not law abidingness, but the acceptability of the social objective sought by protest.

year after year of the cruel and senseless bombardment of Indochina. Many Americans evidently believe that a show of force by the rich and privileged will intimidate change-oriented militancy wherever it occurs.[17]

The emerging national debate on "amnesty" for Indochina draft resisters will also be indicative of public morality in the United States. It is interesting that no one in mainstream politics talks about "amnesty" for the war-makers, but only for those young people who refused—out of moral scruples, or possibly out of concern for their own safety—to participate in a cruel and remote war.[18] Admittedly, complicated problems are raised by the amnesty issue. Many young soldiers may have contemplated or unsuccessfully sought amnesty, or wished they had, but may have wound up maimed or dead instead after tours of military service which they reluctantly accepted as their duty. This issue of comparative virtue is poignantly embodied in the Mel Tillis song "Ruby, Don't Take Your Love to Town":[19]

> It wasn't me that started that ole crazy Asian war
> But I was proud to go and do my patriotic chore
> . . . .
> It's hard to love a man whose legs are bent and paralyzed

The maimed veteran's appeal for love is a pathetic reminder of the costs borne by conscripted citizens and their families. Obviously, bitterness will be present, and those who refused to bear such costs—the draft evaders—will, at the very least, be regarded as unpatriotic, as having defaulted, in the song's terms, on their "patriotic chore."

Amnesty claimants are not "victims" or opponents of the system in the same way as the militant blacks. Reconciliation with the blacks is being sought in ways that do not vindicate disrespect for positive law or governmental authority. "Deserters," even if comparably motivated, are unlikely to receive as considerate national treatment, because their constituency is much more likely to encompass reference groups that are already excluded from the dominant consensus. The "boy next door" is not likely to be a deserter, even though in numerical terms the number of deserters surpasses the number of pre-induction draft resisters or evaders.

The amnesty debate is a world order issue because, as we have argued already, the earliest bearers of world order change will be those who pursue domestic goals which enhance individual and group dignity, social and economic justice, peace, and ecological balance.[20] The application of WOMP values to domestic social, economic, and political exigencies is itself a desirable contribution to global reform. The "law and order" struggle has profound implications for voluntary government—government which sustains its legitimacy primarily by engendering respect and affection. Voluntary government resorts to force only against those whose "deviance" exploits the polity or injures its members, or those who are so "unreasonably" impatient about ad-

---

[17] Moral confusion in America can be discerned also in the efforts to prohibit pornography rather than ultra-violence. Movie ratings are also indicative: an X-rating usually denotes explicit sexuality, not depravity of mind and spirit as exhibited by violent behavior or by the exploitation of those who are weak and helpless.

[18] Why should young Americans accept orders or laws so risky to life and limb, when no convincing rationale based on national well-being or personal responsibility is provided? Solicitude for one's own safety is a sign of psychic health; a citizenry that allows itself to be led to slaughter by its rulers abandons its own most solemn prerogatives and responsibilities.

[19] Mel Tillis, "Ruby, Don't Take Your Love to Town," © Copyright 1966—Cedarwood Publishing Co., Inc., 815 16th Ave., S., Nashville, Tenn. 37203. Reprinted by permission.

[20] Of course, honest disagreements may exist among adherents of various belief systems. The invocation of value referents does not settle the issue of normative impact. We are here avowing an anti-Darwinian value creed that is fundamentally humanist in character.

justment and change that they resort to dangerous violence. A "reasonable" definition of deviance is as a complex sociological and philosophical problem. We believe that any such definition should be sensitive to the views of those who are now societal "victims" by reason of poverty, discrimination, or privation. As the old structures of power and control grow less able to satisfy public expectations, the "victimized" sector of society expands, although the perception of "victimhood" may be delayed and even resisted. Indeed, under such conditions of systemic decline, the victim's identity is defined partially by a condition of alienation; this condition characteristically tends, in turn, to blind individuals to their own social situation. The American labor movement—upholding such leaders of its own betrayal as George Meany and James Hoffa, and demonstrating beneath placards proclaiming "God Bless the Establishment"—exemplifies basic alienation from the objective interests of the average worker in the United States.

The government in the United States, aware of its declining capacity to solve human problems in accordance with its own creed, acts to prevent the mass of people from comprehending the true state of affairs. Therefore, the government's reliance upon secrecy and deception vis-à-vis its own citizenry takes on emblematic importance. Hostility toward a free press and the impulse to "manage the news"—properly held up to scorn when they occur in a totalitarian society—are increasingly prevalent here at home. Hence, the furor over the release of the *Pentagon Papers,* and Agnew's pre-Watergate onslaughts against the media, are weather-vane tendencies; the expanded reliance on surveillance and secret inquisitorial grand jury proceedings also demonstrate concerted government efforts to destroy the seeds of an $S_{2(WOMP)}$ ethos among change-oriented domestic groups.[21]

This authoritarian orientation is also congruent with the search in world affairs for a moderate variant of the regressive structure of S_1, or an equivalent S_2 option. The United States government would like to maintain present relations of privilege and dominance by neutralizing its "victims"—with alienating techniques if possible, by intimidation and force if necessary. The Nixon-Kissinger-Brezhnev pursuit of concert politics represents a clever move to strike a gigantic world order bargain among "the top dogs." This international approach perfectly complements the domestic governing strategy: our leaders are attempting to base international stability on structures of dominance and exploitation, which can then be reinforced by the capacity and willingness of the powerful to deal brutally with challenges from below.

The reality of the mailed fist is thinly veiled by the increasingly questionable assertion that even poor countries can expect steady increases in living standards, provided only that they organize their economies to sustain indefinite growth. Besides being pre-ecological in its reliance on indefinite expansion of GNP, the myth neglects "the systematic underdevelopment" that results from existing world economic and political structures, as well as the degree to which net increases in GNP benefit only the upper stratum of society or are diverted to accommodate a growing population and an expanding defense budget. In essence, part of the government's mystification of mainstream America consists in its assertion that the affluence and power of the United States are in no way responsible for the inequality, poverty, and misery which riddle the present world order system.[22] Although at this point there is not much evidence that the general public would object to a more candid disclosure of the American role in the world, there nevertheless seems to be a tendency for managers of a cruel system to disguise its nature, even if the manipulators themselves wind up enmeshed in the web of their own deception. One has the

---

[21] The Watergate disclosures provide especially blatant evidence of this assertion, although they may spuriously suggest that the repressive tendency is a matter of political pathology confined to members of the original Nixon entourage. In actuality, the Mitchell-Haldeman-Ehrlichman-Dean mentality was merely an extreme case of recently solidifying Presidential attitudes and policies.

[22] Indeed, American apologists make the opposite point—that the poor would be poorer without the existence of the rich (by losing markets, jobs, capital, goods), whereas the rich do not depend nearly so much on the poor.

impression that American policy-makers are themselves largely unaware of these realities. Hence, they are unable to perceive very clearly the latent dangers embedded in a world order design which further fragments the potential community of mankind by superimposing a politico-economic structure of dominance upon the already existing hierarchy of states.

World order dialogue has failed to consider the main options for global reform. This failure results from an interplay between the general public's false comprehension of the objective situation, and the elite's self-interested effort to maintain its own advantages by refusing to confront its apparent role in consigning most of humanity to a life of misery. Such selfishness and complacency is characteristic of a colonial situation, where ignorance takes the place of innocence or willingness to risk change. Given the dynamics of world relations, we believe that false consciousness imperils the future of America as well as the world, and underestimates the prospects and benefits of a global reform movement built around WOMP values. This case for global reform must be made throughout the United States early in t_1, although even its very statement will generate intense hostility, and any evidence of its serious acceptance on the part of the general public is likely to occasion a repressive movement of considerable virulence. An early domestic formulation of the case for global reform along the lines of $S_{2(WOMP/USA)}$ may concentrate upon the quest for a more survival-oriented world order bargain than is provided by the prospect of a five-power world. Such a bargain would have to depend on a minimal acceptance of human solidarity and the oneness of the earth; on this basis, an American understanding of the need to work for equity and ecological equilibrium on a global scale could begin to take effective shape. Such a movement for global reform could also appeal to the positive side of the American past, to its role as beacon on the hill, as innovator and benefactor of mankind; in this spirit, the quest for appropriate global reform might help America reconcile its goals in world society with those it professes for itself.[23]

THE POSITIVE POTENTIAL OF THE UNITED STATES FOR GLOBAL REFORM

Value changes and favorable shifts in consciousness are occurring at a rapid rate in the United States. Indeed, some cultural commentators have made "future shock" the main focus of their appraisal of the country. Given WOMP criteria, these changes are moving in contradictory directions.

Some positive factors can be identified. The ending in relative failure of the Indochina War has encouraged American leaders to redefine the country's role in the world, and to explore more carefully the possibilities for global reform. This process of redefinition has also been encouraged by the muting of East-West tensions, and the exacerbation of the Sino-Soviet conflict.

By posing world order issues in new contexts, ecological strains have further exposed the inadequacy of S_1 responses and the need for an S_2 approach. The ecological dimension of many global problems can, if aptly interpreted, provide a crucial learning experience relevant to global reform.[24]

NASA's Apollo Program of moon landings has helped stimulate a visual appreciation of the wholeness and oneness of the planet. Such imagery fosters an understanding of the artificiality of the statist boundaries and loyalties which have divided mankind into warring nationalities. The earth, as seen from the moon, is emblematic for the new world order awareness which will be

---

[23] Global reform may provide the indispensable context for domestic reforms compatible with goals of peacefulness, dignity, equity, and ecological regard, rather than the other way around. There is, at least, a dialectic between principal areas wherein issues of social policy are resolved; different constituencies can have beneficial or harmful learning experiences in different areas, or even contradictory learning experiences in the same area.

[24] The ecological dimension encourages a holistic, unified approach to human problems; by encouraging synthetic and integrative procedures of inquiry, it offsets to some extent the analytic, fractionalizing procedures of inquiry associated with empiricism and behavioral methodologies.

required by a post-statist phase of global politics. Although this awareness has not yet exerted any political influence, it has created unprecedented receptivity to globalist thinking. Excessive infatuation with technological progress has given rise to a "counter-culture" which questions the basic commitments of American society. New attitudes toward people, and even toward artifacts that respect human dignity, engender a sensitivity to social and political relations that is necessarily reformist. The ease of communication and travel, the mobility of ideas and people, give many national elite groups an increasingly transnational and cosmopolitan identity. Individuals often feel a closer identification with their counterparts in transnational reference groups than with their fellow-citizens; these wider symbolic networks of respect, affection, and affiliation erode the state system's narrow ideology of national patriotism.[25] The market imperatives of world business enterprise are responsible for a nonterritorial S_2 world order design and executive life-style which are increasingly at odds with the economic artificiality and distortion caused by persisting national prerogatives of economic regulation and planning (for instance, a national goal of full employment is increasingly incompatible with economic efficiency). The millenarian context of the year 2000 encourages organic interpretations of world history, and arouses reformist hopes that human energies will be both renewed and refocused.

In addition to these broader currents oriented toward positive change, there are several explicit reform movements now underway in the United States which could be easily linked to a global reform movement based on an $S_{2(WOMP/USA)}$ program.

CONSUMER CONSCIOUSNESS

The efforts of Ralph Nader are both symbolically and inherently significant. Nader has taken on issues that affect the lives of all Americans—auto safety, food quality, building codes—and has demonstrated to large segments of the public that corporations are callous and the government complicit. Nader has dispelled the bland belief that we can trust official institutions to protect our most basic human interests, or that we can expect large corporations to be motivated by goodwill and conscience. The consumer movement encourages a healthy overall skepticism about governmental solutions to human problems; it vividly demonstrates the need for citizen action and personal responsibility.[26]

Furthermore, Nader's success as a catalyst of relevant awareness suggests the extent to which change can be stimulated, in fact, *must* be stimulated, by private actions. It also suggests that mass adult education is best conducted outside school buildings. Perhaps, like any successful educational program, it involves a combination of thought and action which is virtually impossible to obtain within most formal educational institutions, given their stress on abstract knowledge, value neutrality, "objectivity," and the separation of thought and action.

The experience with consumer consciousness provides some insight into the direction that a humanist movement for global reform must take, namely: the objective situation must be accurately and precisely described; these ideas must be carried into the realm of action at some personal risk (thereby manifesting the seriousness of the reform commitment); the program of reform must concern itself with the underlying structures of wealth and power that caused the problems or dislocations in the first place.

---

[25] In earlier periods the boundaries of the state set the limits of most networks of human interaction. Individual experiences were bounded in the same way as were national societies. The new transnational nature of much human activity now means that leading citizens typically participate in a series of human networks whose boundaries are wider than the limits of their states.

[26] Such a mood sets the tone for a global populist movement in which the needs and aspirations of people, not the interests of governments, are accorded priority.

FEMININE CONSCIOUSNESS

It is difficult to interpret the prospects of the women's movement in the United States at the present time. Nevertheless, there are important indications that women's liberation is a positive development, fully compatible with wider goals of equity, dignity, and nonviolence. For one thing, the cutting edge of feminist ideology involves a challenge directed at the world as structured by male dominance. Hence, there is a strong undertow of antiwar, social justice sentiment in the movement's literature, despite some deviation from the humanist mainstream as a result of factionalism, and an over-liberated insistence by some spokeswomen on issuing sexual manifestos that appear to transcend the biological identity and existential yearnings of most women.

Women have clearly mounted a formidable challenge on such bread-and-butter issues as job discrimination and access to power. However, "access to power" is interpreted by the movement to mean more than equal opportunity; there is an insistence that female perspectives be given a major influence in realms of power and authority. Therefore, it is not only a matter of allowing women to compete on an equal basis, so that they might become "prime minister" or members of the National Security Council. The main point is that women should be granted participation in the formulation of policy and transformation of power structures, to enable the pursuit of different societal objectives. Movement leaders such as Bella Abzug, Gloria Steinem, and Betty Friedan have adopted a progressive orientation toward American society and politics that could usefully be complemented by a global or world dimension. It is doubtful, though perhaps not important, whether women can become "the new proletariat" impelling revolutionary change, because their socioeconomic interests crosscut the structure of society to a very great degree. At the same time it does seem significant, as Kate Millet emphasizes, that male-dominated liberation and revolutionary movements have been deeply flawed by their unwillingness to end the exploitation of women.[27]

It seems clear that the women's movement will gain increasing access to mainstream political areas in the years ahead and, hence, will have various opportunities to advocate a distinctive vision of the future. Indeed, it seems quite possible that there will be a serious woman Vice-Presidential or Presidential candidate by 1976. If such a woman has a WOMP-oriented outlook on human affairs, her candidacy might not only provide the first opportunity to challenge basic domestic and world structures, but would materially improve the chances of creating a significant political base for a humanist movement of global reform.[28]

LABOR CONSCIOUSNESS

An important possible source of support for humanist global reform is the American labor movement, despite its regressive record on many key issues, especially in the area of foreign policy.[29]

---

[27] That is, in the past men have carried their regressive attitudes toward women right into the new revolutionary situation. These attitudes are a virus that afflicts prospects for renewal. In this sense, a global reform movement that hopes to achieve peace and justice should seek to purify its own attitudes toward human relations during its consciousness-raising phase. Such purification involves additional exploitative attitudes often embedded in self-righteous reform ideologies: for instance, attitudes toward the young and the old, attitudes toward unborn generations, attitudes toward non-human co-tenants of the planet, and possibly attitudes toward co-tenants of the galaxy and universe.

[28] The explicitness of the ideological discussions of reform that characterizes the women's movement in America increases the possibility that a woman who is a product of the movement will seek something more than access to high political power. This *something more* would relate to values that have been underplayed as a consequence of the peculiar orientation of male consciousness; it would very likely include heightened sensitivity to the grievances of other groups in the society, as well as a serious questioning of the war system mentality.

[29] Unfortunately, the labor movement as a whole cannot now be depended upon to consistently support even domestic reformist goals associated with equity, human dignity, and peace. A status quo conservativism has led union leaders and their rank-and-file to oppose liberalization in American society, partly because their stake in the system has increased and partly because they have been the principal victims of ghetto frustrations and criminality.

However, the technological progress of American society is likely to provoke a wide-ranging crisis regarding the dignity of work and workers in post-industrial settings. This crisis may deepen if the multinational corporation stimulates a flight of capital from the high labor costs of domestic production. However, we cannot predict whether this crisis will develop soon, and/or whether it will generate a new kind of labor leader who seeks broad sociopolitical value changes in addition to *ad hoc* socioeconomic bargains with big business. In any event, those who represent the dominant concerns of organized labor will undoubtedly be raising new kinds of questions. Of course, ruling groups will rely on their largely successful tactics of producing a sufficient economic surplus to give labor a material stake in system-maintenance, and of rewarding "pacified" labor leaders with elite status within the system.

We anticipate, however, that domestic strains will begin to split the labor movement into genuine and pacified factions. The beginning of this process may be already evident in the failure of the AFL/CIO Executive Board either to support McGovern's candidacy for President in 1972 or to repudiate America's involvement in the Indochina War.[30] It remains to be seen whether the present labor leadership will be confronted by a value-based challenge that offers a coherent alternative interpretation of exploitation in American society. Such an interpretation would have to be both post-Marxist and anti-Stalinist in character, and it would have to link the self-realization of American workers with U.S. participation in the world system.

Herbert Marcuse writes that

> the working class remains the potentially revolutionary class, although it would be a class of different composition and with a different consciousness. . . . The impulses for radical change would be rooted, not primarily in material privation but in human degradation . . . in the awareness that it can be otherwise, here and now; that technical progress can become human liberation, that the fatal union of growing productivity and growing destruction can be broken. New needs are becoming a material force; the need for self-determination, for a non-repressive organization of work; the need for a life that has not only to be "earned" but is made an end in itself . . . the new radical consensus is still largely repressed, diffuse; it is articulated mainly among the oppressed racial minorities, among students, women. But it is spreading among labor itself, especially among young workers.

With this new spirit in mind, the tendencies of American labor leaders to stabilize their privileged position must be exposed as inconsistent with the longer term well-being of American workers. Instead, a labor commitment to reformism of the sort implied by WOMP values would greatly help to transform consciousness in the American domestic arena during t_1. Indeed, such a shift in outlook by the American labor movement may be an indispensable ingredient for completing t_1 and initiating t_2.

LINKAGE AND DECOUPLING STRATEGIES

America' economic and political role in the world has led it to ally with a series of governments that abuse their own populations. These alliances sometimes require an endorsement of or involvement in brutal policies that are repudiated within our own society. At present, the United States government lends its active support to a whole series of regimes which torture and otherwise abuse their political opponents. Can we, as a society, endorse policies in foreign countries that contradict our most minimal concepts of decency, without incurring serious consequences? Put differently, can geopolitical opportunism altogether neglect foreign abuses of human rights? The issues are often complex. The search for world peace may lead to a détente which would

---

[30] Offsetting these positions, to an unclear extent, is the commitment made by the leadership of organized labor to make a substantial effort to unseat Richard Nixon by impeachment proceedings.

be jeopardized by U.S. insistence upon Soviet liberalization of its domestic approach to civil liberties. On the other hand, official indifference to torture, genocide, or apartheid indicates a lack of concern about the rights of individuals which will probably—given any pressure—translate itself into abuse of American rights. The Indochina/Watergate revelations have amply shown how lawless violence in a foreign setting sets the tone for domestic politics. Furthermore, the potential realities of human brotherhood, and a shared destiny that joins all men and women together in the struggle to sustain life and achieve human development on this planet, constitute the moral basis for WOMP-oriented global reform. The international protection of human rights as a genuine national priority is of utmost significance in linking our concern with the plight of others, wherever they may be.

The Nixon Administration has sustained its commitments to repressive regimes abroad. Indeed, in the post-Vietnam period it has moved to make these commitments viable by reducing those costs which, if perceived by American citizens, might otherwise have generated opposition. The idea is to pursue counterrevolutionary aims without huge outlays of American resources or lives. Its execution depends on building up foreign counterinsurgency capabilities, and backing these capabilities with American air and naval power if necessary. The main thrust of this Nixonian effort is to decouple foreign policy from domestic concerns, so that policymakers can pursue the former without real accountability to the American electorate.

Decoupling strategies rest on a house of cards. In particular, they minimize the dangers of ecological and economic interdependence, thereby making it seem as if the United States can remain prosperous and free, while somehow absolved from responsibility toward the poor and deprived two-thirds of the world's population.

Linkage strategies have so far aimed at a foreign policy that sustains American dominance by controlling critical foreign resources, personnel, and policy. These interventionary approaches are being pursued by low-profile (covert, secret, indirect) tactics, to avoid agitating the domestic polity. To the extent that the domestic population is treated as a potentially hostile audience which must be deceived, the results are negative for the United States. The process of deception tends to destroy the democratic ethos, shatters the social contract underlying the consent of the governed, and vindicates deviant behavior that seeks to keep faith with earlier promises and expectations. These dynamics contribute to a vicious cycle of rebellion and repression that threatens to transform the foundation of "law and order" in America from voluntary respect for the rights of others into the efficiency of the police.

One apparent way to break the cycle is for the United States to attempt a kind of isolationist withdrawal from world involvement—in effect, to break the linkage by having no other foreign policy commitments than our own territorial defense. This repudiation of interventionary diplomacy is healthy, but it understates the realities of interdependence and misses the significance of active participation by the United States in this period of inevitable transition to a more unified system of world order. Therefore, as a nation, we need to pursue a foreign policy that takes account of our domestic ideals, and that explicitly associates the linkage between domestic and global arenas with the prospects for $S_1 \rightarrow S_{2(WOMP/USA)}$. It is here that public education must be made a matter of highest priority. At first, such an educational mission can and will be attempted only at the margins of policy-formation, but hopefully the cogency of its interpretation will gain ever-widening influence.

The bicentennial celebration planned for 1976 could provide an initial focus for American recovery of national pride and confidence. This pride and confidence can exist only if our domestic creed of constitutionalism and human rights is convincingly reconciled with our role as a leading actor in the world. This reconciliation cannot be accomplished by marginal, Nixonian adjustments of imperial policies. Nor will it be attained by any kind of neo-isolationist pretension that, in a disintegrating world order system in which we are the richest and most powerful actor, we can somehow devise self-contained solutions to our domestic problems. The first positive step in t_1 may be to frame the American foreign policy debate around this kind of Hobson's choice. Subsequent steps will be influenced by many factors, including the outcome of parallel debates in other principal foreign societies. Only at the end of t_1 will it be plausible to implement a new foreign policy that reflects a serious American commitment to $S_1 \rightarrow S_{2(WOMP/USA)}$.

It should be remembered that t_1 may never end, if elites in the United States and elsewhere succeed in pacifying, neutralizing, and repressing counter-elites who favor S_2 options in the spirit of WOMP. If t_1 doesn't end, the $S_1 \rightarrow S_2$ is likely to be traumatic and demonic in transition and regressive in outcome. We believe that the momentous uncertainty surrounding transition will be gradually removed by political developments in the United States during the 1970's. These developments will in turn be significantly influenced by whether current American adherence to prevailing S_1/S_2 lines of reform can avoid perceived breakdowns in the realms of economic, ecological, and security policy. As a nation we are unlikely to learn basic world order lessons except through experiences of adversity,[31] and unless we manage to produce a coherent ideology of drastic global reform that embodies humanist values in its transition and design. Our national resistance to this kind of massive world order educational effort reflects in part the absence of any experience with foreign war in which hardship and bloodshed penetrate the boundaries of the state and the citizenry witness at first-hand the awesome brutality and general suffering of war. World Wars I and II, Korea, and Indochina were all in foreign theaters; there were no foreign conquerors in our land, and the domestic social and political fabric was never torn asunder.[32]

---

[31] The energy crisis may have important potential as a world order learning experience, because its impact is so directly related to daily life. It seems very important that global reform groups seize this occasion to provide a WOMP-oriented interpretation of the problem and its most beneficial solution.

[32] Such assertions are not meant to overlook the sufferings of participants and their families that resulted from these wars. We draw a distinction in national experience between going off to fight a war on foreign territory, and fighting a foreign invader on national territory.

Chapter Four

Liberalism

"Though the earth and all inferior creatures be common to all men, yet every man has a property in his own person; this nobody has any right to but himself." *John Locke*

"We seek a free flow of information. . . . We are not afraid to entrust the American people with unpleasant facts, foreign ideas, alien philosophies, and competitive values. For a nation that is afraid to let its people judge the truth and falsehood in an open market is a nation that is afraid of its people." *John F. Kennedy*

"We hold these truths to be self-evident, that all men are created equal. That they are endowed by their Creator with certain unalienable Rights, that among these are Life, Liberty and the pursuit of Happiness." *U.S. Constitution*

The explanatory rift that was perhaps most evident during the Cold War, yet lingers to this day, is between theories of historical materialism and those that emphasize battles of ideas. The Western tradition has tended to focus on the latter. That is, through open, free, and rigorous debate it is hoped that better ideas and, ultimately, better policies will result. In Chapter 3, we saw that this was an essential assumption for the Ancient Greek philosophers, as it was for Georg Hegel, who influenced Karl Marx (Chapter 5), and it can be seen in the words of modern-day politics. Consider, for example, the words of former CIA Director, James Woolsey, who has argued: "Under the First Amendment of the Constitution, prior restraint of speech is extremely difficult and this freedom generally serves us very well, not only because we like to say what we want, but because free exchange of ideas is the best way for us to correct our mistakes."[159]

---

[159] ABC News transcript of interview with James Woolsey, former director of the CIA (1993–95), October 11, 2001. Woolsey is currently a partner at the Washington-based law firm Shea & Gardner. (http://www.abc.com).

From this classically liberal perspective, political change in history is due to better ideas "breaking through." There is clearly an appeal to the gradual improvement of ideas and policies through time, what has been termed Social Darwinism (i.e., it is comforting to know that open debate of ideas has led, in Western history, to improvement).[160] The advent of the French and American Revolutions can be interpreted, in this way, as people opting for "better ideas" and rebelling against an older order with ideas that are of less merit. It is for this reason that the Western tradition does hold high this ideal of open debate (Liberalism) while "reform" is sometimes held in check by the more practical goals emphasized by political realists (Realism). That is, as we saw with Cicero in Chapter 2, the realist is generally more resistant to any changes of the status quo. The classic use of the term liberalism, as we shall see, is similarly quite conservative.

"Classic" Political Liberalism

In the political science classroom, the term *liberalism* generally refers to the classic meaning of the term, stemming from the ideas of the Enlightenment that are addressed in the writings of John Locke, Baron de Montesquieu, François-Marie Arouet Voltaire, and others. For the Enlightenment writers, liberal referred to *liberty,* tied to notions of *individualism.* The meaning of "classic" liberalism, it must be acknowledged, is distinct from the more modern American usage of the term *liberal* that refers to the use of the welfare state in an effort to resolve social inequities. When referring to the liberalism of Locke and Smith, below, we are referring to their respective arguments for freedom.

In Locke's case, the argument was being made against Sir Robert Filmer's political philosophy of "divine right." In seventeenth-century England, two political philosophies dominated—that of Thomas Hobbes, discussed in Chapter 2, and arguments that tied the political authority of the king to the will of God. In *Two Treatises on Government,* Locke argues that individuals have the right to rebel. In so doing, he also gives us an Enlightenment interpretation of what political liberalism entails. His work was particularly influential to Thomas Jefferson and the logic behind *The Declaration of Independence.* Other liberal thinkers include John Stuart Mill, who wrote his seminal text, *On Liberty* (1859), and John Rawls, *Political Liberalism* (1993).[161]

---

[160] This argument is made by Richard Hofstadter, *Social Darwinism in American Thought* (New York: Beacon Press, 1992).

[161] John Rawls is perhaps better known for his earlier publications, *A Theory of Justice* (Cambridge, MA: Harvard University Press, 1971); *Political Liberalism* (New York: Columbia University Press, 1993).

READING 11: JOHN LOCKE

John Locke,

Two Treatises on Government, 1690

Chapter I

1. It having been shown in the foregoing discourse:

(1) That Adam had not, either by natural right of fatherhood or by positive donation from God, any such authority over his children or dominion over the world as is pretended.

(2) That if he had, his heirs yet had no right to it.

(3) That if his heirs had, there being no law of nature nor positive law of God that determines which is the right heir in all cases that may arise, the right of succession, and consequently of bearing rule, could not have been certainly determined.

(4) That if even that had been determined, yet the knowledge of which is the eldest line of Adam's posterity being so long since utterly lost, that in the races of mankind and families of the world there remains not to one above another the least pretence to be the eldest house, and to have the right of inheritance.

All these premises having, as I think, been clearly made out, it is impossible that the rulers now on earth should make any benefit or derive any the least shadow of authority from that which is held to be the fountain of all power: Adam's private dominion and paternal jurisdiction; so that he that will not give just occasion to think that all government in the world is the product only of force and violence, and that men live together by no other rules but that of beasts, where the strongest carries it, and so lay a foundation for perpetual disorder and mischief, tumult, sedition, and rebellion—things that the followers of that hypothesis so loudly cry out against—must of necessity find out another rise of government, another original of political power, and another way of designing and knowing the persons that have it than what Sir Robert Filmer hath taught us.

2. To this purpose, I think it may not be amiss to set down what I take to be political power; that the power of a magistrate over a subject may be distinguished from that of a father over his children, a master over his servants, a husband over his wife, and a lord over his slave. All which distinct powers happening sometimes together in the same man, if he be considered under these different relations, it may help us to distinguish these powers one from another, and show the difference betwixt a ruler of a commonwealth, a father of a family, and a captain of a galley.

3. Political power, then, I take to be a right of making laws with penalties of death and, consequently, all less penalties for the regulating and preserving of property, and of employing the force of the community in the execution of such laws, and in the defence of the commonwealth from foreign injury, and all this only for the public good.

Chapter II

Of the State of Nature

4. To understand political power right, and derive it from its original, we must consider what state all men are naturally in, and that is a state of perfect freedom to order their actions and dispose of their possessions and persons as they think fit, within the bounds of the law of nature, without asking leave or depending upon the will of any other man.

A state also of equality, wherein all the power and jurisdiction is reciprocal, no one having more than another; there being nothing more evident than that creatures of the same species

John Locke, *Two Treatises of Government,* (Hafner Library of Classics, 1947).

and rank, promiscuously born to all the same advantages of nature and the use of the same faculties, should also be equal one amongst another without subordination or subjection; unless the lord and master of them all should, by any manifest declaration of his will, set one above another, and confer on him by an evident and clear appointment an undoubted right to dominion and sovereignty.

5. This equality of men by nature the judicious Hooker[1] looks upon as so evident in itself and beyond all question that he makes it the foundation of that obligation to mutual love amongst men on which he builds the duties we owe one another, and from whence he derives the great maxims of justice and charity. His words are:

> The like natural inducement hath brought men to know that it is no less their duty to love others than themselves; for seeing those things which are equal must needs all have one measure; if I cannot but wish to receive good, even as much as every man's hands as any man can wish unto his own soul, how should I look to have any part of my desire herein satisfied unless myself be careful to satisfy the like desire, which is undoubtedly in other men, being of one and the same nature? To have anything offered them repugnant to this desire must needs in all respects grieve them as much as me; so that, if I do harm, I must look to suffer, there being no reason that others should show greater measure of love to me than they have by me showed unto them; my desire therefore to be loved of my equals in nature, as much as possibly may be, imposeth upon me a natural duty of bearing to them-ward fully the like affection; from which relation of equality between ourselves and them that are as ourselves, what several rules and canons natural reason hath drawn, for direction of life, no man is ignorant. (*Eccl. Pol.* lib. i.).

6. But though this be a state of liberty, yet it is not a state of licence; though man in that state have an uncontrollable liberty to dispose of his person or possessions, yet he has not liberty to destroy himself, or so much as any creature in his possession, but where some nobler use than its bare preservation calls for it. The state of nature has a law of nature to govern it which obliges every one; and reason, which is that law, teaches all mankind who will but consult it that, being all equal and independent, no one ought to harm another in his life, health, liberty, or possessions; for men being all the workmanship of one omnipotent and infinitely wise Maker—all the servants of one sovereign master, sent into the world by his order, and about his business—they are his property whose workmanship they are, made to last during his, not one another's, pleasure; and being furnished with like faculties, sharing all in one community of nature, there cannot be supposed any such subordination among us that may authorize us to destroy another, as if we were made for one another's uses as the inferior ranks of creatures are for ours. Every one, as he is bound to preserve himself and not to quit his station wilfully, so by the like reason, when his own preservation comes not in competition, ought he, as much as he can, to preserve the rest of mankind, and may not, unless it be to do justice to an offender, take away or impair the life, or what tends to the preservation of life: the liberty, health, limb, or goods of another.

7. And that all men may be restrained from invading others' rights and from doing hurt to one another, and the law of nature be observed which willeth the peace and preservation of all mankind, the execution of the law of nature is, in that state, put into every man's hands, whereby

---

[1] ["The judicious Hooker" (1554–1600) was the celebrated English ecclesiastic who defended the Reformation settlements and wrote the famous *Lawes of Ecclesiasticall Politie*, of which Books I to V appeared from 1594 to 1597, and Books VI to VIII were published posthumously in 1648. While defending the monarchy, he rested it on a doctrine of social contract. He was a precursor of Locke in that, while living in a monarchical government, he was not a defender of divine right, and took, on the whole, a constitutional position. Celebrated for moderation and balance, Richard Hooker possessed some of the same virtues possessed by Locke himself.]

everyone has a right to punish the transgressors of that law to such a degree as may hinder its violation; for the law of nature would, as all other laws that concern men in this world, be in vain, if there were nobody that in the state of nature had a power to execute that law and thereby preserve the innocent and restrain offenders. And if any one in the state of nature may punish another for any evil he has done, every one may do so; for in that state of perfect equality where naturally there is no superiority or jurisdiction of one over another, what any may do in prosecution of that law, every one must needs have a right to do.

8. And thus in the state of nature one man comes by a power over another; but yet no absolute or arbitrary power to use a criminal, when he has got him in his hands, according to the passionate heats or boundless extravagancy of his own will; but only to retribute to him, so far as calm reason and conscience dictate, what is proportionate to his transgression, which is so much as may serve for reparation and restraint; for these two are the only reasons why one man may lawfully do harm to another, which is that we call punishment. In transgressing the law of nature, the offender declares himself to live by another rule than that of reason and common equity, which is that measure God has set to the actions of men for their mutual security; and so he becomes dangerous to mankind, the tie which is to secure them from injury and violence being slighted and broken by him. Which being a trespass against the whole species and the peace and safety of it provided for by the law of nature, every man upon this score, by the right he hath to preserve mankind in general, may restrain, or, where it is necessary, destroy things noxious to them, and so may bring such evil on any one who hath transgressed that law, as may make him repent the doing of it and thereby deter him, and by his example others, from doing the like mischief. And in this case, and upon this ground, *every man hath a right to punish the offender and be executioner of the law of nature.*

9. I doubt not but this will seem a very strange doctrine to some men; but before they condemn it, I desire them to resolve me by what right any prince or state can put to death or punish any alien for any crime he commits in their country. It is certain their laws, by virtue of any sanction they receive from the promulgated will of the legislative, reach not a stranger; they speak not to him, nor, if they did, is he bound to hearken to them. The legislative authority, by which they are in force over the subjects of that commonwealth, hath no power over him. Those who have the supreme power of making laws in England, France, or Holland, are to an Indian but like the rest of the world, men without authority; and therefore, if by the law of nature every man hath not a power to punish offences against it as he soberly judges the case to require, I see not how the magistrates of any community can punish an alien of another country, since, in reference to him, they can have no more power than what every man naturally may have over another.[2]

10. Besides the crime which consists in violating the law and varying from the right rule of reason, whereby a man so far becomes degenerate and declares himself to quit the principles of human nature and to be a noxious creature, there is commonly injury done to some person or other, and some other man receives damage by his transgression; in which case he who hath received any damage has, besides the right of punishment common to him with other men, a

---

[2] [Locke's point here rests in fact on a somewhat shaky foundation, since authority could well be based on sovereignty over territory, and so over all those who found themselves within it, whether by birth, by immigration, or by temporary visit. Moreover, while it might lead back to a natural law of consent, the position could be argued that a stranger put himself under a country's laws by entering its domain. Locke here was actually assuming the duties of hospitality to, and respect for, the persons of strangers frequently found in early societies; or he was arguing the normal right of extraterritoriality. In some earlier civilizations, as indeed in Greece and Rome, foreigners were under the protection of some local and accepted resident of their country who had to guarantee their obedience to its laws, though they did not acquire personal rights thereunder.]

particular right to seek reparation from him that has done it; and any other person, who finds it just, may also join with him that is injured and assist him in recovering from the offender so much as may make satisfaction for the harm he has suffered.

11. From these two distinct rights—the one of punishing the crime for restraint and preventing the like offence, which right of punishing is in everybody; the other of taking reparation, which belongs only to the injured party—comes it to pass that the magistrate, who by being magistrate hath the common right of punishing put into his hands, can often, where the public good demands not the execution of the law, remit the punishment of criminal offences by his own authority, but yet cannot remit the satisfaction due to any private man for the damage he has received. That he who has suffered the damage has a right to demand in his own name, and he alone can remit; the damnified person has this power of appropriating to himself the goods or service of the offender by right of self-preservation, as every man has a power to punish the crime to prevent its being committed again, by the right he has of preserving all mankind, and doing all reasonable things he can in order to that end; and thus it is that every man, in the state of nature, has a power to kill a murderer, both to deter others from doing the like injury, which no reparation can compensate, by the example of the punishment that attends it from everybody, and also to secure men from the attempts of a criminal who, having renounced reason—the common rule and measure God hath given to mankind—hath, by the unjust violence and slaughter he hath committed upon one, declared war against all mankind; and therefore may be destroyed as a lion or a tiger, one of those wild savage beasts with whom men can have no society nor security. And upon this is grounded that great law of nature, "Whoso sheddeth man's blood, by man shall his blood be shed." And Cain was so fully convinced that every one had a right to destroy such a criminal that, after the murder of his brother, he cries out, "Every one that findeth me, shall slay me;" so plain was it writ in the hearts of mankind.

12. By the same reason may a man in the state of nature punish the lesser breaches of that law. It will perhaps be demanded: with death? I answer: Each transgression may be punished to that degree and with so much severity as will suffice to make it an ill bargain to the offender, give him cause to repent, and terrify others from doing the like. Every offence that can be committed in the state of nature may in the state of nature be also punished equally, and as far forth as it may in a commonwealth; for though it would be beside my present purpose to enter here into the particulars of the law of nature, or its measures of punishment, yet it is certain there is such a law, and that, too, as intelligible and plain to a rational creature and a studier of that law as the positive laws of commonwealths, nay, possibly plainer, as much as reason is easier to be understood than the fancies and intricate contrivances of men, following contrary and hidden interests put into words; for so truly are a great part of the municipal laws of countries, which are only so far right as they are founded on the law of nature, by which they are to be regulated and interpreted.

13. To this strange doctrine—viz., that in the state of nature every one has the executive power of the law of nature—I doubt not but it will be objected that it is unreasonable for men to be judges in their own cases, that self-love will make men partial to themselves and their friends, and, on the other side, that ill-nature, passion, and revenge will carry them too far in punishing others, and hence nothing but confusion and disorder will follow; and that therefore God hath certainly appointed government to restrain the partiality and violence of men. I easily grant that civil government is the proper remedy for the inconveniences of the state of nature, which must certainly be great where men may be judges in their own case; since it is easy to be imagined that he who was so unjust as to do his brother an injury will scarce be so just as to condemn himself for it; but I shall desire those who make this objection to remember that absolute monarchs are but men, and if government is to be the remedy of those evils which necessarily follow from men's being judges in their own cases, and the state of nature is therefore not to be endured, I desire to know what kind of government that is, and how much better it is than the state of nature, where one man commanding a multitude has the liberty to be judge in his own

case, and may do to all his subjects whatever he pleases, without the least liberty to any one to question or control those who execute his pleasure, and in whatsoever he doth, whether led by reason, mistake, or passion, must be submitted to? Much better it is in the state of nature, wherein men are not bound to submit to the unjust will of another; and if he that judges, judges amiss in his own or any other case, he is answerable for it to the rest of mankind.

14. It is often asked as a mighty objection, "Where are or ever were there any men in such a state of nature?" To which it may suffice as an answer at present that, since all princes and rulers of independent governments all through the world are in a state of nature, it is plain the world never was, nor ever will be, without numbers of men in that state. I have named all governors of independent communities, whether they are, or are not, in league with others; for it is not every compact that puts an end to the state of nature between men, but only this one of agreeing together mutually to enter into one community and make one body politic; other promises and compacts men may make one with another and yet still be in the state of nature. The promises and bargains for truck, etc., between the two men in the desert island, mentioned by Garcilasso de la Vega, in his *History of Peru*,[3] or between a Swiss and an Indian, in the woods of America, are binding to them, though they are perfectly in a state of nature in reference to one another; for truth and keeping of faith belongs to men as men, and not as members of society.

15. To those that say there were never any men in the state of nature, I will not only oppose the authority of the judicious Hooker, *Eccl. Pol.*, lib. i., sect. 10, where he says,

> The laws which have been hitherto mentioned, (*i.e.*, the laws of nature) do bind men absolutely, even as they are men, although they have never any settled fellowship, never any solemn agreement amongst themselves what to do, or not to do; but forasmuch as we are not by ourselves sufficient to furnish ourselves with competent store of things needful for such a life as our nature doth desire, a life fit for the dignity of man; therefore to supply those defects and imperfections which are in us, as living singly and solely by ourselves, we are naturally induced to seek communion and fellowship with others. This was the cause of men's uniting themselves at first in politic societies.

But I, moreover, affirm that all men are naturally in that state and remain so till by their own consents they make themselves members of some politic society; and I doubt not in the sequel of this discourse to make it very clear.

■ ■ ▮ ■ ▮

Chapter III

Of Property

16. Whether we consider natural reason, which tells us that men, being once born, have a right to their preservation, and consequently to meat and drink and such other things as nature affords for their subsistence; or revelation, which gives us an account of those grants God made of the world to Adam, and to Noah and his sons; it is very clear that God, as King David says (Psal. cxv. 16), "has given the earth to the children of men," given it to mankind in common. But this being supposed, it seems to some a very great difficulty how any one should ever come to have a property in anything. I will not content myself to answer that if it be difficult to make out property upon a supposition that God gave the world to Adam and his posterity in common, it is im-

---

[3] [Garcilasso de la Vega (1535–1616), called *el Inca*, was a historian of Peru and the first South American in Spanish literature. His most famous books are: *La Florida del Inca* (1605) and his history of Peru, *Commentarios reales que tartan del origin de los Incas* (Lisbon, Part I, 1609; Part II, 1617).]

possible that any man but one universal monarch should have any property upon a supposition that God gave the world to Adam and his heirs in succession, exclusive of all the rest of his posterity. But I shall endeavour to show how men might come to have a property in several parts of that which God gave to mankind in common, and that without any express compact of all the commoners.

17. God, who hath given the world to men in common, hath also given them reason to make use of it to the best advantage of life and convenience. The earth and all that is therein is given to men for the support and comfort of their being. And though all the fruits it naturally produces and beasts it feeds belong to mankind in common, as they are produced by the spontaneous hand of nature; and nobody has originally a private dominion exclusive of the rest of mankind in any of them, as they are thus in their natural state; yet, being given for the use of men, there must of necessity be a means to appropriate them some way or other before they can be of any use or at all beneficial to any particular man. The fruit or venison which nourishes the wild Indian, who knows no enclosure and is still a tenant in common, must be his, and so his, *i.e.,* a part of him, that another can no longer have any right to it before it can do him any good for the support of his life.

18. Though the earth and all inferior creatures be common to all men, yet every man has a property in his own person; this nobody has any right to but himself. The labour of his body and the work of his hands, we may say, are properly his. Whatsoever then he removes out of the state that nature hath provided and left it in, he hath mixed his labour with, and joined to it something that is his own, and thereby makes it his property. It being by him removed from the common state nature hath placed it in, it hath by this labour something annexed to it that excludes the common right of other men. For this labour being the unquestionable property of the labourer, no man but he can have a right to what that is once joined to, at least where there is enough and as good left in common for others.

19. He that is nourished by the acorns he picked up under an oak, or the apples he gathered from the trees in the wood, has certainly appropriated them to himself. Nobody can deny but the nourishment is his. I ask, then, when did they begin to be his? when he digested? or when he ate? or when he boiled? or when he brought them home? or when he picked them up? And it is plain, if the first gathering made them not his, nothing else could. That labour put a distinction between them and common; that added something to them more than nature, the common mother of all, had done; and so they became his private right. And will anyone say he had no right to those acorns or apples he thus appropriated, because he had not the consent of all mankind to make them his? Was it a robbery thus to assume to himself what belonged to all in common? If such a consent as that was necessary, man had starved, notwithstanding the plenty God had given him. We see in commons, which remain so by compact, that it is the taking any part of what is common and removing it out of the state nature leaves it in which begins the property, without which the common is of no use. And the taking of this or that part does not depend on the express consent of all the commoners. Thus the grass my horse has bit, the turfs my servant has cut, and the ore I have digged in any place where I have a right to them in common with others, become my property without the assignation or consent of anybody. The labour that was mine, removing them out of that common state they were in, hath fixed my property in them.

20. By making an explicit consent of every commoner necessary to any one's appropriating to himself any part of what is given in common, children or servants could not cut the meat which their father or master had provided for them in common without assigning to every one his peculiar part. Though the water running in the fountain be every one's, yet who can doubt but that in the pitcher is his only who drew it out? His labour hath taken it out of the hands of nature, where it was common and belonged equally to all her children, and hath thereby appropriated it to himself.

21. Thus this law of reason makes the deer that Indian's who hath killed it; it is allowed to be his goods who hath bestowed his labour upon it, though before it was the common right of

every one. And amongst those who are counted the civilized part of mankind, who have made and multiplied positive laws to determine property, this original law of nature, for the beginning of property in what was before common, still takes place; and by virtue thereof what fish any one catches in the ocean, that great and still remaining common of mankind, or what ambergris any one takes up here, is, by the labour that removes it out of that common state nature left it in, made his property who takes that pains about it. And even amongst us, the hare that anyone is hunting is thought his who pursues her during the chase; for, being a beast that is still looked upon as common and no man's private possession, whoever has employed so much labour about any of that kind as to find and pursue her has thereby removed her from the state of nature wherein she was common, and hath begun a property.

22. It will perhaps be objected to this that "if gathering the acorns, or other fruits of the earth, etc., makes a right to them, then anyone may engross as much as he will." To which I answer: not so. The same law of nature that does by this means give us property does also bound that property, too. "God has given us all things richly" (I Tim. vi. 17), is the voice of reason confirmed by inspiration. But how far has he given it us? To enjoy. As much as any one can make use of to any advantage of life before it spoils, so much he may by his labour fix a property in; whatever is beyond this is more than his share, and belongs to others. Nothing was made by God for man to spoil or destroy. And thus, considering the plenty of natural provisions there was a long time in the world, and the few spenders, and to how small a part of that provision the industry of one man could extend itself and engross it to the prejudice of others, especially keeping within the bounds set by reason of what might serve for his use, there could be then little room for quarrels or contentions about property so established.

23. But the chief matter of property being now not the fruits of the earth and the beasts that subsist on it, but the earth itself, as that which takes in and carries with it all the rest, I think it is plain that property in that, too, is acquired as the former. As much land as a man tills, plants, improves, cultivates, and can use the product of, so much is his property. He by his labour does, as it were, enclose it from the common. Nor will it invalidate his right to say everybody else has an equal title to it, and therefore he cannot appropriate, he cannot enclose, without the consent of all his fellow commoners—all mankind. God, when he gave the world in common to all mankind, commanded man also to labour, and the penury of his condition required it of him. God and his reason commanded him to subdue the earth, *i.e.*, improve it for the benefit of life, and therein lay out something upon it that was his own, his labour. He that in obedience to this command of God subdued, tilled, and sowed any part of it, thereby annexed to it something that was his property, which another had no title to, nor could without injury take from him.

24. Nor was this appropriation of any parcel of land by improving it any prejudice to any other man, since there was still enough and as good left, and more than the yet unprovided could use. So that, in effect, there was never the less left for others because of his enclosure for himself; for he that leaves as much as another can make use of does as good as take nothing at all. Nobody could think himself injured by the drinking of another man, though he took a good draught, who had a whole river of the same water left him to quench his thirst; and the case of land and water, where there is enough for both, is perfectly the same.

25. God gave the world to men in common; but since he gave it them for their benefit and the greatest conveniences of life they were capable to draw from it, it cannot be supposed he meant it should always remain common and uncultivated. He gave it to the use of the *industrious and rational*—and labour was to be his title to it—*not to the fancy or covetousness of the quarrelsome and contentious.* He that had as good left for his improvement as was already taken up needed not complain, ought not to meddle with what was already improved by another's labour; if he did, it is plain he desired the benefit of another's pains which he had no right to, and not the ground which God had given him in common with others to labour on, and whereof there was as good left as that already possessed, and more than he knew what to do with, or his industry could reach to.

26. It is true, in land that is common in England or any other country where there is plenty of people under government who have money and commerce, no one can enclose or appropriate any part without the consent of all his fellow-commoners; because this is left common by compact, *i.e.,* by the law of the land, which is not to be violated. And though it be common in respect of some men, it is not so to all mankind, but is the joint property of this country or this parish. Besides, the remainder after such enclosure would not be as good to the rest of the commoners as the whole was when they could all make use of the whole; whereas in the beginning and first peopling of the great common of the world it was quite otherwise. The law man was under was rather for appropriating. God commanded, and his wants forced, him to labour. That was his property which could not be taken from him wherever he had fixed it. And hence subduing or cultivating the earth and having dominion, we see, are joined together. The one gave title to the other. So that God; by commanding to subdue, gave authority so far to appropriates and the condition of human life which requires labour and material, to work on necessarily introduces private possessions.

27. The measure of property nature has well set by the extent of men's labour and the conveniences of life. No man's labour could subdue or appropriate all, nor could his enjoyment consume more than a small part; so that it was impossible for any man, this way, to entrench upon the right of another, or acquire to himself a property to the prejudice of his neighbour, who would still have room for as good and as large a possession—after the other had taken out his—as before it was appropriated. This measure did confine every man's possession to a very moderate proportion, and such as he might appropriate to himself without injury to anybody in the first ages of the world, when men were more in danger to be lost by wandering from their company in the then vast wilderness of the earth than to be straitened for want of room to plant in. And the same measure may be allowed still without prejudice to anybody, as full as the world seems; for supposing a man or family in the state they were at first peopling of the world by the children of Adam or Noah, let him plant in some inland, vacant places of America, we shall find that the possessions he could make himself, upon the measures we have given, would not be very large, nor, even to this day, prejudice the rest of mankind, or give them reason to complain or think themselves injured by this man's encroachment, though the race of men have now spread themselves to all the corners of the world and do infinitely exceed the small number which was at the beginning. Nay, the extent of ground is of so little value without labour that I have heard it affirmed that in Spain itself a man may be permitted to plough, sow, and reap, without being disturbed, upon land he has no other title to but only his making use of it. But, on the contrary, the inhabitants think themselves beholden to him who by his industry on neglected and, consequently, waste land has increased the stock of corn which they wanted. But be this as it will, which I lay no stress on, this I dare boldly affirm—that the same rule of propriety, viz., that every man should have as much as he could make use of, would hold still in the world without straitening anybody, since there is land enough in the world to suffice double the inhabitants, had not the invention of money and the tacit agreement of men to put a value on it introduced—by consent—larger possessions and a right to them; which, how it has done, I shall by-and-by show more at large.

28. This is certain, that in the beginning, before the desire of having more than man needed had altered the intrinsic value of things which depends only on their usefulness to the life of man, or had agreed that a little piece of yellow metal which would keep without wasting or decay should be worth a great piece of flesh or a whole heap of corn, though men had a right to appropriate, by their labour, each one to himself as much of the things of nature as he could use, yet this could not be much, nor to the prejudice of others, where the same plenty was still left to those who would use the same industry. To which let me add that he who appropriates land to himself by his labour does not lessen but increase the common stock of mankind; for the provisions serving to the support of human life produced by one acre of enclosed and cultivated land are—to speak much within compass—ten times more than those which are yielded by an acre of

land of an equal richness lying waste in common. And therefore he that encloses land, and has a greater plenty of the conveniences of life from ten acres than he could have from a hundred left to nature, may truly be said to give ninety acres to mankind; for his labour now supplies him with provisions out of ten acres which were by the product of a hundred lying in common. I have here rated the improved land very low in making its product but as ten to one, when it is much nearer a hundred to one; for I ask whether in the wild woods and uncultivated waste of America, left to nature, without any improvement, tillage, or husbandry, a thousand acres yield the needy and wretched inhabitants as many conveniences of life as ten acres equally fertile land do in Devonshire, where they are well cultivated.

Before the appropriation of land, he who gathered as much of the wild fruit, killed, caught, or tamed as many of the beasts as he could; he that so employed his pains about any of the spontaneous products of nature as any way to alter them from the state which nature put them in, by placing any of his labour on them, did thereby acquire a propriety in them; but, if they perished in his possession without their due use, if the fruits rotted or the venison putrified, before he could spend it, he offended against the common law of nature, and was liable to be punished; he invaded his neighbor's share, for he had no right farther than his use called for any of them, and they might serve to afford him conveniences of life.

29. The same measures governed the possession of land, too: whatsoever he tilled and reaped, laid up and made use of before it spoiled, that was his peculiar right; whatsoever he enclosed and could feed and make use of, the cattle and product was also his. But if either the grass of his enclosure rotted on the ground, or the fruit of his planting perished without gathering and laying up, this part of the earth, notwithstanding his enclosure, was still to be looked on as waste, and might be the possession of any other. Thus, at the beginning, Cain might take as much ground as he could till and make it his own land, and yet leave enough to Abel's sheep to feed on; a few acres would serve for both their possessions. But as families increased and industry enlarge their stocks, their possessions enlarged with the need of them; but yet it was commonly without any fixed property in the ground they made use of till they incorporated, settled themselves together, and built cities; and then, by consent, they came in time to set out the bounds of their distinct territories, and agree on limits between them and their neighbours, and by laws within themselves settled the properties of those of the same society; for we see that in that part of the world which was first inhabited, and therefore like to be best peopled, even as low down as Abraham's time they wandered with their flocks and their herds, which was their substance, freely up and down; and this Abraham did in a country where he was a stranger. Whence it is plain that at least a great part of the land lay in common; that the inhabitants valued it not, nor claimed property in any more than they made use of. But when there was not room enough in the same place for their herds to feed together, they, by consent, as Abraham and Lot did (Gen. xiii. 5), separated and enlarged their pasture where it best liked them. And for the same reason Esau went from his father and his brother and planted in Mount Seir (Gen. xxxvi. 6).

30. And thus, without supposing any private dominion and property in Adam over all the world exclusive of all other men, which can no way be proved, nor any one's property be made out from it; but supposing the world given, as it was, to the children of men in common, we see how labour could make men distinct titles to several parcels of it for their private uses, wherein there could be no doubt of right, no room for quarrel.

31. Nor is it so strange, as perhaps before consideration it may appear, that the property of labour should be able to overbalance the community of land; for it is labour indeed that put the difference of value on everything; and let any one consider what the difference is between an acre of land planted with tobacco or sugar, sown with wheat or barley, and let any one consider what the difference is between an acre of land planted with tobacco or sugar, sown with wheat or barley, and an acre of the same land lying in common, without any husbandry upon it, and he will find that the improvement of labour makes the far greater part of the value. I think it will be but a very modest computation to say that, of the products of the earth useful to the life of man,

nine-tenths are the effects of labour; nay, if we will rightly estimate things as they come to our use and cast up the several expenses about them, what in them is purely owing to nature, and what to labour, we shall find that in most of them ninety-nine hundredths are wholly to be put on the account of labour.

32. There cannot be a clearer demonstration of anything than several nations of the Americans are of this, who are rich in land and poor in all the comforts of life; whom nature having furnished as liberally as any other people with the materials of plenty, *i.e.,* a fruitful soil, apt to produce in abundance what might serve for food, raiment, and delight, yet for want of improving it by labour have not one-hundredth part of the conveniences we enjoy. And a king of a large and fruitful territory there feeds, lodges, and is clad worse than a day-labourer in England.

33. To make this a little clear, let us but trace some of the ordinary provisions of life through their several progresses before they come to our use and see how much of their value they receive from human industry. Bread, wine, and cloth are things of daily use and great plenty; yet, notwithstanding, acorns, water, and leaves, or skins must be our bread, drink, and clothing, did not labour furnish us with these more useful commodities; for whatever bread is more worth than acorns, wine than water, and cloth or silk than leaves, skins, or moss, that is wholly owing to labour and industry: the one of these being the food and raiment which unassisted nature furnishes us with; the other, provisions which our industry and pains prepare for us, which how much they exceed the other in value when any one hath computed, he will then see how much labour makes the far greatest part of the value of things we enjoy in this world. And the ground which produces the materials is scarce to be reckoned in as any, or at most but a very small, part of it; so little that even amongst us land that is left wholly to nature, that hath no improvement of pasturage, tillage, or planting, is called, as indeed it is, "waste"; and we shall find the benefit of it amount to little more than nothing.

This shows how much numbers of men are to be preferred to largeness of dominions; and that the increase of lands and the right of employing of them is the great art of government; and that prince who shall be so wise and godlike as by established laws of liberty to secure protection and encouragement to the honest industry of mankind, against the oppression of power and narrowness of party, will quickly be too hard for his neighbours; but this by the bye.

To return to the argument in hand.

34. An acre of land that bears here twenty bushels of wheat, and another in America which with the same husbandry would do the like, are, without doubt, of the same natural intrinsic value; but yet the benefit mankind receives from the one in a year is worth £5, and from the other possibly not worth a penny if all the profit an Indian received from it were to be valued and sold here; at least, I may truly say, not one-thousandth. It is labour, then, which puts the greatest part of the value upon land, without which it would scarcely be worth anything; it is to that we owe the greatest part of all its useful products; for all that the straw, bran, bread of that acre of wheat is more worth than the product of an acre of as good land which lies waste is all the effect of labour. For it is not barely the ploughman's pains, the reaper's and thresher's toil, and the baker's sweat is to be counted into the bread we eat; the labour of those who broke the oxen, who digged and wrought the iron and stones, who felled and framed the timber employed about the plough, mill, oven, or any other utensils, which are a vast number requisite to this corn, from its being seed to be sown to its being made bread, must all be charged on the account of labour, and received as an effect of that; nature and the earth furnished only the almost worthless materials as in themselves. It would be a strange "catalogue of things that industry provided and made use of about every loaf of bread," before it came to our use, if we could trace them: iron, wood, leather, bark, timber, stone, bricks, coals, lime, cloth, dyeing, drugs, pitch, tar, masts, ropes, and all the materials made use of in the ship that brought any of the commodities used by any of the workmen to any part of the work; all which it would be almost impossible, at least too long, to reckon up.

35. From all which it is evident that, though the tings of nature are given in common, yet man, by being master of himself and proprietor of his own person and the actions of labour of it, had still in himself the great foundation of property; and that which made up the greater part

of what he applied to the support or comfort of his being, when invention and arts had improved the conveniences of life, was perfectly his own and did not belong in common to others.

36. Thus labour, in the beginning, gave a right of property wherever anyone was pleased to employ it upon what was common, which remained a long while the far greater part and is yet more than mankind makes use of. Men, at first, for the most part contented themselves with what unassisted nature offered to their necessities; and though afterwards, in some parts of the world—where the increase of people and stock, with the use of money, had made land scarce and so of some value—the several communities settled the bounds of their distinct territories and, by laws within themselves, regulated the properties of the private men of their society, and so, by compact and agreement, settled the property which labour and industry began. And the leagues that have been made between several states and kingdoms either expressly or tacitly disowning all claim and right to the land in the others' possession have, by common consent, given up their pretences to their natural common right which originally they had to those countries, and so have, by positive agreement, settled a property amongst themselves in distinct parts and parcels of the earth; yet there are still great tracts of ground to be found which—the inhabitants thereof not having joined with the rest of mankind in the consent of the use of their common money—lie waste, and are more than the people who dwell on it do or can make use of, and so still lie in common; though this can scarce happen amongst that part of mankind that have consented to the use of money.

37. The greatest part of things really useful to the life of man, and such as the necessity of subsisting made the first commoners of the world look after, as it doth the Americans now, are generally things of short duration, such as, if they are not consumed by use, will decay and perish of themselves; gold, silver, and diamonds are things that fancy or agreement hath put the value on, more than real use and the necessary support of life. Now of those good things which nature hath provided in common, every one had a right, as hath been said, to as much as he could use, and property in all that he could effect with his labour; all that his industry could extend to, to alter from the state nature had put it in, was his. He that gathered a hundred bushels of acorns or apples had thereby a property in them; they were his goods as soon as gathered. He was only to look that he used them before they spoiled, else he took more than his share and robbed others. And indeed it was a foolish thing, as well as dishonest, to hoard up more than he could make use of. If he gave away a part to anybody else so that it perished not uselessly in his possession, these he also made use of. And if he also bartered away plums that would have rotted in a week for nuts that would last good for his eating a whole year, he did no injury; he wasted not the common stock, destroyed no part of the portion of the goods that belonged to others, so long as nothing perished uselessly in his hands. Again, if he would give his nuts for a piece of metal, pleased with its colour, or exchange his sheep for shells, or wool for a sparkling pebble or a diamond, and keep those by him all his life, he invaded not the right of others; he might heap as much of these durable things as he pleased; the exceeding of the bounds of his just property not lying in the largeness of his possession, but the perishing of anything uselessly in it.

38. And thus came in the use of money—some lasting thing that men might keep without spoiling, and that by mutual consent men would take in exchange for the truly useful but perishable supports of life.

39. And as different degrees of industry were apt to give men possessions in different proportions, so this invention of money gave them the opportunity to continue and enlarge them; for supposing an island, separate from all possible commerce with the rest of the world, wherein there were but a hundred families, but there were sheep, horses, and cows, with other useful animals, wholesome fruits, and land enough for corn for a hundred thousand times as many, but nothing in the island, either because of its commonness or perishableness, fit to supply the place of money; what reason could any one have there to enlarge his possessions beyond the use of his family and a plentiful supply to its consumption, either in what their own industry produced or they could barter for like perishable, useful commodities with others? Where there is not something both lasting and scarce, and so valuable to be hoarded up, there men will not be

apt to enlarge their possessions of land were it ever so rich, ever so free for them to take. For, I ask, what would a man value ten thousand or a hundred thousand acres of excellent land, ready cultivated and well stocked, too, with cattle, in the middle of the inland parts of America where he had no hopes of commerce with other parts of the world to draw money to him by the sale of the product? It would not be worth the enclosing, and we should see him give up again to the wild common of nature whatever was more than would supply the conveniences of life to be had there for him and his family.

40. Thus in the beginning all the world was America, and more so than that is now; for no such thing as money was anywhere known. Find out something that hath the use and value of money amongst his neighbours, you shall see the same man will begin presently to enlarge his possessions.

41. But since gold and silver, being little useful to the life of man in proportion to food, raiment, and carriage, has its value only from the consent of men, whereof labour yet makes, in great part, the measure, it is plain that men have agreed to a disproportionate and unequal possession of the earth, they having, by a tacit and voluntary consent, found out a way how a man may fairly possess more land than he himself can use the product of, by receiving in exchange for the overplus gold and silver which may be hoarded up without injury to any one, these metals not spoiling or decaying in the hands of the possessor. This partage of things in an inequality of private possessions men have made practicable out of the bounds of society and without compact, only by putting a value on gold and silver, and tacitly agreeing in the use of money; for, *in governments, the laws regulate the right of property,* and the possession of land is determined by positive constitutions.

42. And thus, I think, it is very easy to conceive how labour could at first begin a title of property in the common things of nature, and how the spending it upon our uses bounded it. So that there could then be no reason of quarrelling about title, nor any doubt about the largeness of possession it gave. Right and convenience went together; for as a man had a right to all he could employ his labour upon, so he had no temptation to labour for more than he could make use of. This left no room for controversy about the title, nor for encroachment on the right of others; what portion a man carved to himself was easily seen, and it was useless, as well as dishonest, to carve himself too much or take more than he needed.

Economic Liberalism

In the earliest years of the industrial process, when specialization of labor was being emphasized by capitalists in an effort to provide more efficient production outcomes, Adam Smith observed the functioning of a pin factory. This he described in great detail in *The Wealth of Nations*. Unlike another observer of the industrial process, Karl Marx, who interpreted the same industrial process as exploitation of labor, Smith and economic liberals were deeply impressed with what could now be achieved. If anything, the specialization of labor was seen as something that was miraculous.[162] Not only was it best for the produc-

---

[162] Later observers of the industrial process, such as Emile Durkheim, argued that specialization of labor was the most moral arrangement for any industrial society. See: Emile Durkheim, *On Morality and Society* (Chicago: The University of Chicago Press, 1973) and *The Division of Labor in Society* (Glencoe, IL: Free Press, 1947, first published in 1893).

tion of goods in domestic societies, but also economic liberals expanded the logic of specialization to trade between states.

As with Locke before him, Smith was arguing against the restriction on individual freedoms that existed in society. Smith argued that the prevailing wisdom of mercantilism was wrongheaded and that mutually beneficial, or absolute gains, could be made through trade with other states. In other words, trade was not simply a zero-sum game where the world had only a limited amount of wealth and it was up to state leaders to determine how to acquire it. Rather, Smith argued that trade should be thought of as a positive-sum game, where both parties to trade can benefit. Left to their own devices the "invisible hand" of the free market would help guide society to the best, most efficient use of its limited resources. Further, borrowing from the French *physiocrats* Smith argued that the most efficient path for all was "laissez-faire" (i.e., the removal of the burden of the state). Some time later, British economist David Ricardo made a similar but improved argument regarding the benefits of free trade. Ricardo's primary concern was the British Corn Laws (1815–64) that aimed at protecting British agriculturalists, which Ricardo saw as a violation of Smith's "laissez-faire" principle. Ricardo's argument focused on the comparative advantage of states. By comparing the inputs of labor into the production of goods, Ricardo argued that states should focus on the production and trade of those goods for which they had a comparative advantage. That is, if Portugal could provide five barrels of wine with ten units of labor, and Britain could provide five barrels of wine with twelve units of labor, then Portugal had a comparative advantage in wine. Portugal, therefore, should specialize in the production and export of wine over Britain. In this way, he argued, global welfare could be increased. The assumption, of course, was that every trading state had a comparative advantage of some kind, an assumption that continues to this day. Modern proponents of this view include international liberals, who are proponents of free trade, and neoconservative economists, such as Milton Friedman and Jagdish Bhagwati.[163]

---

[163] Milton Friedman had a strong impact on economic policy in the 1980s and is a proponent of supply-side economics. He is also a supporter of free trade. See: Milton Friedman, *Free to Choose* (New York: HBJ, 1980). Columbia University Professor Jagdish Bhagwati has become one of the most outspoken proponents of free trade in recent years. He is regularly cited in the popular press and has published several books on the subject, including: *Free-Trade Today* (Princeton, NJ: Princeton University Press, 2001) and *World Trade System at Risk* (Princeton, NJ: Princeton University Press, 1991).

■ ▮ ■ ▮ ■ ▮ ■ ▮ ■ ▮ ■ ■ ▮ ■ ▮ ■ ▮ ■ ▮ ■ ▮ ■ ▮ ■ ■ ▮ ■ ■ ▮ ■ ▮ ■ ▮ ■ ▮ ■ ▮ ■

READING 12: ADAM SMITH

ADAM SMITH,

THE WEALTH OF NATIONS, 1776

CHAPTER IV
*OF RESTRAINTS UPON THE IMPORTATION FROM FOREIGN COUNTRIES
OF SUCH GOODS AS CAN BE PRODUCED AT HOME*

By restraining, either by high duties, or by absolute prohibitions, the importation of such goods from foreign countries as can be produced at home, the monopoly of the home market is more

---

Adam Smith, *The Wealth of Nations,* (Modern Library, 1965).

or less secured to the domestic industry employed in producing them. Thus the prohibition of importing either live cattle[1] or salt provisions from foreign countries secures to the graziers of Great Britain the monopoly of the home market for butcher's meat. The high duties upon the importation of corn,[2] which in times of moderate plenty amount to a prohibition, give a like advantage to the growers of that commodity. The prohibition of the importation of foreign woollens is equally favourable to the woollen manufacturers.[3] The silk manufacture, though altogether employed upon foreign materials, has lately obtained the same advantage.[4] The linen manufacture has not yet obtained it, but is making great strides towards it.[5] Many other sorts of manufacturers[6] have, in the same manner, obtained in Great Britain, either altogether, or very nearly a monopoly against their countrymen. The variety of goods of which the importation into Great Britain is prohibited, either absolutely, or under certain circumstances, greatly exceeds what can easily be suspected by those who are not well acquainted with the laws of the customs.[7]

That this monopoly of the home-market frequently gives great encouragement to that particular species of industry which enjoys it, and frequently turns towards that employment a greater share of both the labour and stock of the society than would otherwise have gone to it, cannot be doubted. But whether it tends either to increase the general industry of the society, or to give it the most advantageous direction, is not, perhaps, altogether so evident.[8]

The general industry of the society never can exceed what the capital of the society can employ. As the number of workmen that can be kept in employment by any particular person must bear a certain proportion to his capital, so the number of those that can be continually employed by all the members of a great society, must bear a certain proportion to the whole capital of that society, and never can exceed that proportion. No regulation of commerce can increase the quantity of industry in any society beyond what its capital can maintain. It can only divert a part of it into a direction into which it might not otherwise have gone; and it is by no means certain that this artificial direction is likely to be more advantageous to the society than that into which it would have gone of its own accord.

Every individual is continually exerting himself to find out the most advantageous employment for whatever capital he can command. It is his own advantage, indeed, and not that of the society, which he has in view. But the study of his own advantage naturally, or rather necessarily leads him to prefer that employment which is most advantageous to the society.

First, every individual endeavours to employ his capital as near home as he can, and consequently as much as he can in the support of domestic industry; provided always that he can thereby obtain the ordinary, or not a great deal less than the ordinary profits of stock.

Thus, upon equal or nearly equal profits, every wholesale merchant naturally prefers the home-trade to the foreign trade of consumption, and the foreign trade of consumption to the carrying trade. In the home-trade his capital is never so long out of his sight as it frequently is in the foreign trade of consumption. He can know better the character and situation of the persons whom he trusts, and if he should happen to be deceived, he knows better the laws of the country from which he must seek redress. In the carrying trade, the capital of the merchant is, as it were, divided between two foreign countries, and no part of it is ever necessarily brought home,

---

[1] See above, p. 394.

[2] See below, pp. 502, 503.

[3] 11 and 12 Ed. III., c. 3; 4 Ed. IV., c. 7.

[4] 6 Geo. III., c. 28.

[5] By the additional duties, 7 Geo. III., c. 28.

[6] Misprinted "manufactures" in ed. 5.

[7] This sentence appears first in Additions and Corrections and ed. 3.

[8] Ed. 1 reads "certain."

or placed under his own immediate view and command. The capital which an Amsterdam merchant employs in carrying corn from Konnigsberg to Lisbon, and fruit and wine from Lisbon to Konnigsberg, must generally be the one-half of it at Konnigsberg and the other half at Lisbon. No part of it need ever come to Amsterdam. The natural residence of such a merchant should either be at Konnigsberg or Lisbon, and it can only be some very particular circumstances which can make him prefer the residence of Amsterdam. The uneasiness, however, which he feels at being separated so far from his capital, generally determines him to bring part both of the Konnigsberg goods which he destines for the market of Lisbon, and of the Lisbon goods which he destines for that of Konnigsberg, to Amsterdam: and though this necessarily subjects him to a double charge of loading and unloading, as well as to the payment of some duties and customs, yet for the sake of having some part of his capital always under his own view and command, he willingly submits to this extraordinary charge; and it is in this manner that every country which has any considerable share of the carrying trade, becomes always the emporium, or general market, for the goods of all the different countries whose trade it carries on. The merchant, in order to save a second loading and unloading, endeavours always to sell in the home-market as much of the goods of all those different countries as he can, and thus, so far as he can, to convert his carrying trade into a foreign trade of consumption. A merchant, in the same manner, who is engaged in the foreign trade of consumption, when he collects goods for foreign markets, will always be glad, upon equal or nearly equal profits, to sell as great a part of them at home as he can. He saves himself the risk and trouble of exportation, when, so far as he can, he thus converts his foreign trade of consumption into a home-trade. Home is in this manner the center, if I may say so, round which the capitals of the inhabitants of every country are continually circulating, and towards which they are always tending, though by particular causes they may sometimes be driven off and repelled from it towards more distant employments. But a capital employed in the home-trade, it has already been shown,[9] necessarily puts into motion a greater quantity of domestic industry, and gives revenue and employment to a greater number of the inhabitants of the country, than an equal capital employed in the foreign trade of consumption: and one employed in the foreign trade of consumption has the same advantage over an equal capital employed in the carrying trade. Upon equal, or only nearly equal profits, therefore, every individual naturally inclines to employ his capital in the manner in which it is likely to afford the greatest support to domestic industry, and to give revenue and employment to the greatest number of[10] people of his own country.

Secondly, every individual who employs his capital in the support of domestic industry, necessarily endeavours so to direct that industry, that its produce may be of the greatest possible value.

The produce of industry is what it adds to the subject or materials upon which it is employed. In proportion as the value of this produce is great or small, so will likewise be the profits of the employer. But it is only for the sake of profit that any man employs a capital in the support of industry; and he will always, therefore, endeavour to employ it in the support of that industry of which the produce is likely to be of the greatest value, or to exchange for the greatest quantity either of money or of other goods.

But the annual revenue of every society is always precisely equal to the exchangeable value of the whole annual produce of its industry, or rather is precisely the same thing with that exchangeable value. As every individual, therefore, endeavours as much as he can both to employ his capital in the support of domestic industry, and so to direct that industry that its produce may be of the greatest value; every individual necessarily labours to render the annual revenue of the society as great as he can. He generally, indeed, neither intends to promote the public interest,

---

[9] Above, pp. 349–353.
[10] Ed. 1 reads "the" here.

nor knows how much he is promoting it. By preferring the support of domestic to that of foreign industry, he intends only his own security; and by directing that industry in such a manner as its produce may be of the greatest value, he intends only his own gain, and he is in this, as in many other cases, led by an invisible hand to promote an end which was no part of his intention. Nor is it always the worse for the society that it was no part of it. By pursuing his own interest he frequently promotes that of the society more effectually than when he really intends to promote it. I have never known much good done by those who affected to trade for the public good. It is an affectation, indeed, not very common among merchants, and very few words need be employed in dissuading them from it.

What is the species of domestic industry which his capital can employ, and of which the produce is likely to be of the greatest value, every individual, it is evident, can, in his local situation, judge much better than any statesman or lawgiver can do for him. The statesman, who should attempt to direct private people in what manner they ought to employ their capitals, would not only load himself with a most unnecessary attention, but assume an authority which could safely be trusted, not only to no single person, but to no council or senate whatever, and which would nowhere be so dangerous as in the hands of a man who had folly and presumption enough to fancy himself fit to exercise it.

To give the monopoly of the home-market to the produce of domestic industry, in any particular art or manufacture, is in some measure to direct private people in what manner they ought to employ their capitals, and must, in almost all cases, be either a useless or a hurtful regulation. If the produce of domestic can be brought there as cheap as that of foreign industry, the regulation is evidently useless. If it cannot, it must generally be hurtful. It is the maxim of every prudent master of a family, never to attempt to make at home what it will cost him more to make than to buy. The taylor does not attempt to make his own shoes, but buys them of the shoemaker. The shoemaker does not attempt to make his own clothes, but employs a taylor. The farmer attempts to make neither the one nor the other, but employs those different artificers. All of them find it for their interest to employ their whole industry in a way in which they have some advantage over their neighbours, and to purchase with a part of its produce, or what is the same thing, with the price of a part of it, whatever else they have occasion for.

What is prudence in the conduct of every private family, can scarce be folly in that of a great kingdom. If a foreign country can supply us with a commodity cheaper than we ourselves can make it, better buy it of them with some part of the produce of our own industry, employed in a way in which we have some advantage. The general industry of the country, being always in proportion to the capital which employs it, will not thereby be diminished, no more than that of the above-mentioned artificers; but only left to find out the way in which it can be employed with the greatest advantage. It is certainly not employed to the greatest advantage, when it is thus directed towards an object which it can buy cheaper than it can make. The value of its annual produce is certainly more or less diminished, when it is thus turned away from producing commodities evidently of more value than the commodity which it is directed to produce. According to the supposition, that commodity could be purchased from foreign countries cheaper than it can be made at home. It could, therefore, have been purchased with a part only of the commodities, or, what is the same thing, with a part only of the price of the commodities, which the industry employed by an equal capital would have produced at home, had it been left to follow its natural course. The industry of the country, therefore, is thus turned away from a more, to a less advantageous employment, and the exchangeable value of its annual produce, instead of being increased, according to the intention of the lawgiver, must necessarily be diminished by every such regulation.

By means of such regulations, indeed, a particular manufacture may sometimes be acquired sooner than it could have been otherwise, and after a certain time may be made at home as cheap or cheaper than in the foreign country. But though the industry of the society may be thus carried with advantage into a particular channel sooner than it could have been otherwise, it will by no means follow that the sum total, either of its industry, or of its revenue, can ever be augmented by any such regulation. The industry of the society can augment only in proportion as its capital augments, and its capital can augment only in proportion to what can be gradually saved out of its revenue. But the immediate effect of every such regulation is to diminish its revenue, and what diminishes its revenue is certainly not very likely to augment its capital faster than it would have augmented of its own accord, had both capital and industry been left to find out their natural employments.

Though for want of such regulations the society should never acquire the proposed manufacture, it would not, upon that account, necessarily be the poorer in any one period of its duration. In every period of its duration its whole capital and industry might still have been employed, though upon different objects, in the manner that was most advantageous at the time. In every period its revenue might have been the greatest which its capital could afford, and both capital and revenue might have been augmented[11] with the greatest possible rapidity.

The natural advantages which one country has over another in producing particular commodities are sometimes so great, that it is acknowledged by all the world to be in vain to struggle with them. By means of glasses, hotbeds, and hotwalls, very good grapes can be raised in Scotland, and very good wine too can be made of them at about thirty times the expence for which at least equally good can be brought from foreign countries. Would it be a reasonable law to prohibit the importation of all foreign wines, merely to encourage the making of claret and burgundy in Scotland? But if there would be a manifest absurdity in turning towards any employment, thirty times more of the capital and industry of the country, than would be necessary to purchase from foreign countries an equal quantity of the commodities wanted, there must be an absurdity, though not altogether so glaring, yet exactly of the same kind, in turning towards any such employment a thirtieth, or even a three hundredth part more of either. Whether the advantages which one country has over another, be natural or acquired, is in this respect of no consequence. As long as the one country has those advantages, and the other wants them, it will always be more advantageous for the latter, rather to buy of the former than to make. It is an acquired advantage only, which one artificer has over his neighbour, who exercises another trade; and yet they both find it more advantageous to buy of one another, than to make what does not belong to their particular trades.

Merchants and manufacturers are the people who derive the greatest advantage from this monopoly of the home-market. The prohibition of the importation of foreign cattle, and of salt provisions, together with the high duties upon foreign corn, which in times of moderate plenty amount to a prohibition,[12] are not near so advantageous to the graziers and farmers of Great Britain, as other regulations of the same kind are to its merchants and manufacturers. Manufactures, those of the finer kind especially, are more easily transported from one country to another than corn or cattle. It is in the fetching and carrying manufactures, accordingly, that foreign trade is chiefly employed. In manufactures, a very small advantage will enable foreigners to undersell our own workmen, even in the home market. It will require a very great one to enable them to do so in the rude produce of the soil. If the free importation of foreign manufactures were[13] permitted, several of the home manufactures would probably suffer, and some of them, perhaps, go to ruin altogether, and a considerable part of the stock and industry at present employed in them, would be forced to find out some other employment. But the freest importation of the rude produce of the soil could have no such effect upon the agriculture of the country.

If the importation of foreign cattle, for example, were made ever so free, so few could be imported, that the grazing trade of Great Britain could be little affected by it. Live cattle are, perhaps,

---

[11] Ed. 1 reads "augmenting," which seems more correct.

[12] Above, p. 420, and below, pp. 502, 503.

[13] Eds. 1–3 read "was" here and six lines lower down.

the only commodity of which the transportation is more expensive by sea than by land. By land they carry themselves to market. By sea, not only the cattle, but their food and their water too, must be carried at no small expence and inconveniency. The short sea between Ireland and Great Britain, indeed, renders the importation of Irish cattle more easy. But though the free importation of them, which was lately permitted only for a limited time, were rendered perpetual, it could have no considerable effect upon the interest of the graziers of Great Britain. Those parts of Great Britain which border upon the Irish sea are all grazing countries. Irish cattle could never be imported for their use, but must be drove through those very extensive countries, at no small expence and inconveniency, before they could arrive at their proper market. Fat cattle could not be drove so far. Lean cattle, therefore, only could be imported, and such importation could interfere, not with the interest of the feeding or fattening countries, to which, by reducing the price of lean cattle, it would rather be advantageous, but with that of the breeding countries only. The small number of Irish cattle imported since their importation was permitted, together with the good price at which lean cattle still continue to sell, seem to demonstrate that even the breeding countries of Great Britain are never likely to be much affected by the free importation of Irish cattle. The common people of Ireland, indeed, are said to have sometimes opposed with violence the exportation of their cattle. But if the exporters had found any great advantage in continuing the trade, they could easily, when the law was on their side, have conquered this mobbish opposition.

Feeding and fattening countries, besides, must always be highly improved, whereas breeding countries are generally uncultivated. The high price of lean cattle, by augmenting the value of uncultivated land, is like a bounty against improvement. To any country which was highly improved throughout, it would be more advantageous to import its lean cattle than to breed them. The province of Holland, accordingly, is said to follow this maxim at present. The mountains of Scotland, Wales, and Northumberland, indeed, are countries not capable of much improvement, and seem destined by nature to be the breeding countries of Great Britain. The freest importation of foreign cattle could have no other effect than to hinder those breeding countries from taking advantage of the increasing population and improvement of the rest of the kingdom, from raising their price to an exorbitant height, and from laying a real tax upon all the more improved and cultivated parts of the country.

The freest importation of salt provisions, in the same manner, could have as little effect upon the interest of the graziers of Great Britain as that of live cattle. Salt provisions are not only a very bulky commodity, but when compared with fresh meat, they are a commodity both of worse quality, and as they cost more labour and expence, of higher price. They could never, therefore, come into competition with the fresh meat, though they might with the salt provisions of the country. They might be used for victualling ships for distant voyages, and such like uses, but could never make any considerable part of the food of the people. The small quantity of salt provisions imported from Ireland since their importation was rendered free, is an experimental proof that our graziers have nothing to apprehend from it. It does not appear that the price of butcher's-meat has ever been sensibly affected by it.

Even the free importation of foreign corn could very little affect the interest of the farmers of Great Britain. Corn is a much more bulky commodity than butcher's-meat. A pound of wheat at a penny is as dear as a pound of butcher's-meat at fourpence. The small quantity of foreign corn imported even in times of the greatest scarcity, may satisfy our farmers that they can have nothing to fear from the freest importation. The average quantity imported one year with another, amounts only, according to the very well informed author of the tracts upon the corn trade, to twenty-three thousand seven hundred and twenty-eight quarters of all sorts of grain, and does not exceed the five hundredth and seventy-one part of the annual consumption.[14] but as the

---

[14] Charles Smith, *Three Tracts on the Corn-Trade and Corn-Laws*, pp. 144–145. The same figure is quoted below, p. 501.

bounty upon corn occasions a greater exportation in years of plenty, so it must of consequence occasion a greater importation in years of scarcity, than in the actual state of tillage[15] would otherwise take place. By means of it, the plenty of one year does not compensate the scarcity of another, and as the average quantity exported is necessarily augmented by it, so must likewise, in the actual state of tillage, the average quantity imported. If there were[16] no bounty, as less corn could be exported, so it is probable that, one year with another, less would be imported than at present. The corn merchants, the fetchers and carriers of corn between Great Britain and foreign countries, would have much less employment, and might suffer considerably; but the country gentlemen and farmers could suffer very little. It is in the corn merchants accordingly, rather than in the country gentlemen and farmers, that I have observed the greatest anxiety for the renewal and continuation of the bounty.

Country gentlemen and farmers are, to their great honour, of all people, the least subject to the wretched spirit of monopoly. The undertaker of a great manufactory is sometimes alarmed if another work of the same kind is established within twenty miles of him. The Dutch undertaker of the woollen manufacture at Abbeville[17] stipulated, that no work of the same kind should be established within thirty leagues of that city. Farmers and country gentlemen, on the contrary, are generally disposed rather to promote than to obstruct the cultivation and improvement of their neighbours farms and estates. They have no secrets, such as those of the greater part of manufacturers, but are generally rather fond of communicating to their neighbours, and of extending as far as possible any new practice which they have found to be advantageous. *Pius Questus,* says old Cato, *stabilissimusque, minimeque invidiosus; minimeque male cogitantes sunt, qui in eo studio occupati sunt.*[18] Country gentlemen and farmers, dispersed in different parts of the country, cannot so easily combine as merchants and manufacturers, who being collected into towns, and accustomed to that exclusive corporation spirit which prevails in them, naturally endeavour to obtain against all their countrymen, the same exclusive privilege which they generally possess against the inhabitants of their respective towns. They accordingly seem to have been the original inventors of those restraints upon the importation of foreign goods, which secure to them the monopoly of the home-market. It was probably in imitation of them, and to put themselves upon a level with those who, they found, were disposed to oppress them, that the country gentlemen and farmers of Great Britain so far forgot the generosity which is natural to their station, as to demand the exclusive privilege of supplying their countrymen with corn and butcher's-meat. They did not perhaps take time to consider, how much less their interest could be affected by the freedom of trade, than that of the people whose example they followed.

To prohibit by a perpetual law the importation of foreign corn and cattle, is in reality to enact, that the population and industry of the country shall at no time exceed what the rude produce of its own soil can maintain.

There seem, however, to be two cases in which it will generally be advantageous to lay some burden upon foreign, for the encouragement of domestic industry.

The first is, when some particular sort of industry is necessary for the defence of the country. The defence of Great Britain, for example, depends very much upon the number of its sailors and shipping. The act of navigation,[19] therefore, very properly endeavours to give the sailors and

---

[15] Ed. 1 does not contain the words "in the actual state of tillage."

[16] Eds. 1–3 read "was."

[17] Joseph Van Robais in 1669.—John Smith, *Memoirs of Wool,* vol. ii., pp. 426, 427, but neither John Smith nor Charles King, *British Merchant,* 1721, vol. ii., pp. 93, 94, gives the particular stipulation mentioned.

[18] Cato, *De re rustica, ad init.,* but "*Questus*" should of course be "*quæstus.*"

[19] 12 Car. II., c. 18, "An act for the encouraging and increasing of shipping and navigation."

shipping of Great Britain the monopoly of the trade of their own country, in some cases, by absolute prohibitions, and in others by heavy burdens upon the shipping of foreign countries. The following are the principal dispositions of this act.

First, all ships, of which the owners, masters, and three-fourths of the mariners are not British subjects, are prohibited, upon pain of forfeiting ship and cargo, from trading to the British settlements and plantations, or from being employed in the coasting trade of Great Britain.[20]

Secondly, a great variety of the most bulky articles of importation can be brought into Great Britain only, either in such ships as are above described, or in ships of the country where those goods are produced, and of which the owners, masters, and three-fourths of the mariners, are of that particular country; and when imported even in ships of this latter kind, they are subject to double aliens duty. If imported in ships of any other country, the penalty is forfeiture of ship and goods.[21] When this act was made, the Dutch were, what they still are, the great carriers of Europe, and by this regulation they were entirely excluded from being the carriers to Great Britain, or from importing to us the goods of any other European country.

Thirdly, a great variety of the most bulky articles of importation are prohibited from being imported, even in British ships, from any country but that in which they are produced; under pain of forfeiting ship and cargo.[22] This regulation too was probably intended against the Dutch. Holland was then, as now, the great emporium for all European goods, and by this regulation, British ships were hindered from loading in Holland the goods of any other European country.

Fourthly, salt fish of all kinds, whale-fins, whale-bone, oil, and blubber, not caught by and cured on board British vessels, when imported into Great Britain, are subjected to double aliens duty.[23] The Dutch, as they are still the principal, were then the only fishers in Europe that attempted to supply foreign nations with fish. By this regulation, a very heavy burden was laid upon their supplying Great Britain.

When the act of navigation was made, though England and Holland were not actually at war, the most violent animosity subsisted between the two nations. It had begun during the government of the long parliament, which first framed this act,[24] and it broke out soon after in the Dutch wars during that of the Protector and of Charles the Second. It is not impossible, therefore, that some of the regulations of this famous act may have proceeded from national animosity. They are as wise, however, as if they had all been dictated by the most deliberate wisdom. National animosity at that particular time aimed at the very same object which the most deliberate wisdom would have recommended, the diminution of the naval power of Holland, the only naval power which could endanger the security of England.

The act of navigation is not favourable to foreign commerce, or to the growth of that opulence which can arise from it. The interest of a nation in its commercial relations to foreign nations is, like that of a merchant with regard to the different people with whom he deals, to buy as cheap and to sell as dear as possible. But it will be most likely to buy cheap, when by the most perfect freedom of trade it encourages all nations to bring to it the goods which it has occasion to purchase; and, for the same reason, it will be most likely to sell dear, when its markets

---

[20] §§ 1 and 6.

[21] §§ 8 and 9. Eds. 1 and 2 read "ship and cargo." The alteration was probably made in order to avoid wearisome repetition of the same phrase in the three paragraphs.

[22] § 4, which, however, applies to all such goods of foreign growth and manufacture as were forbidden to be imported except in English ships, not only to bulky goods. The words "great variety of the most bulky articles of importation" occur at the beginning of the previous paragraph, and are perhaps copied here by mistake.

[23] § 5.

[24] In 1651, by "An act for the increase of shipping and encouragement of the navigation of this nation," p. 1,449 in the collection of Commonwealth Acts.

are thus filled with the greatest number of buyers. The act of navigation, it is true, lays no burden upon foreign ships that come to export the produce of British industry. Even the ancient aliens duty, which used to be paid upon all goods exported as well as imported, has, by several subsequent acts, been taken off from the greater part of the articles of exportation.[25] But if foreigners, either by prohibitions or high duties, are hindered from coming to sell, they cannot always afford to come to buy; because coming without a cargo, they must lose the freight from their own country to Great Britain. By diminishing the number of sellers, therefore, we necessarily diminish that of buyers, and are thus likely not only to buy foreign goods dearer, but to sell our own cheaper, than if there was a more perfect freedom of trade. As defence, however, is of much more importance than opulence, the act of navigation is, perhaps, the wisest of all the commercial regulations of England.

The second case, in which it will generally be advantageous to lay some burden upon foreign for the encouragement of domestic industry, is, when some tax is imposed at home upon the produce of the latter. In this case, it seems reasonable that an equal tax should be imposed upon the like produce of the former. This would not give the monopoly of the home market to domestic industry, nor turn towards a particular employment a greater share of the stock and labour of the country, than what would naturally go to it. It would only hinder any part of what would naturally go to it from being turned away by the tax, into a less natural direction, and would leave the competition between foreign and domestic industry, after the tax, as nearly as possible upon the same footing as before it. In Great Britain, when any such tax is laid upon the produce of domestic industry, it is usual at the same time, in order to stop the clamorous complaints of our merchants and manufacturers, that they will be undersold at home, to lay a much heavier duty upon the importation of all foreign goods of the same kind.

This second limitation of the freedom of trade according to some people should, upon some occasions, be extended much farther than to the precise foreign commodities which could come into competition with those which had been taxed at home. When the necessaries of life have been taxed in any country, it becomes proper, they pretend, to tax not only the like necessaries of life imported from other countries, but all sorts of foreign goods which can come into competition with any thing that is the produce of domestic industry. Subsistence, they say, becomes necessarily dearer in consequence of such taxes; and the price of labour must always rise with the price of the labourers subsistence. Every commodity, therefore, which is the produce of domestic industry, though not immediately taxed itself, becomes dearer in consequence of such taxes, because the labour which produces it becomes so. Such taxes, therefore, are really equivalent, they say, to a tax upon every particular commodity produced at home. In order to put domestic upon the same footing with foreign industry, therefore, it becomes necessary, they think, to lay some duty upon every foreign commodity, equal to this enhancement of the price of the home commodities with which it can come into competition.

Whether taxes upon the necessaries of life, such as those in Great Britain upon[26] soap, salt, leather, candles, &c. necessarily raise the price of labour, and consequently that of all other commodities, I shall consider hereafter,[27] when I come to treat of taxes. Supposing, however, in the mean time, that they have this effect, and they have it undoubtedly, this general enhancement of the price of all commodities, in consequence of that of labour, is a case which differs in the

---

[25] By 25 Car. II., c. 6, § 1, except on coal. The plural "acts" may refer to renewing acts. Anderson, *Commerce,* A.D. 1672.

[26] Ed. 1 contains the words "malt, beer" here.

[27] Below, pp. 821–826.

two following respects from that of a particular commodity, of which the price was enhanced by a particular tax immediately imposed upon it.

First, it might always be known with great exactness how far the price of such a commodity could be enhanced by such a tax: but how far the general enhancement of the price of labour might affect that of every different commodity about which labour was employed, could never be known with any tolerable exactness. It would be impossible, therefore, to proportion with any tolerable exactness the tax upon every foreign, to this enhancement of the price of every home commodity.

Secondly, taxes upon the necessaries of life have nearly the same effect upon the circumstances of the people as a poor soil and a bad climate. Provisions are thereby rendered dearer in the same manner as if it required extraordinary labour and expence to raise them. As in the natural scarcity arising from soil and climate, it would be absurd to direct the people in what manner they ought to employ their capitals and industry, so is it[28] likewise in the artificial scarcity arising from such taxes. To be left to accommodate, as well as they could, their industry to their situation, and to find out those employments in which, notwithstanding their unfavourable circumstances, they might have some advantage either in the home or in the foreign market, is what in both cases would evidently be most for their advantage. To lay a new tax upon them, because they are already overburdened with taxes, and because they already pay too dear for the necessaries of life, to make them likewise pay too dear for the greater part of other commodities, is certainly a most absurd way of making amends.

Such taxes, when they have grown up to a certain height, are a curse equal to the barrenness of the earth and the inclemency of the heavens; and yet it is in the richest and most industrious countries that they have been most generally imposed. No other countries could support so great a disorder. As the strongest bodies only can live and enjoy health, under an unwholesome regimen; so the nations only, that in every sort of industry have the greatest natural and acquired advantages, can subsist and prosper under such taxes. Holland is the country in Europe in which they abound most, and which from peculiar circumstances continues to prosper, not by means of them, as has been most absurdly supposed, but in spite of them.

As there are two cases in which it will generally be advantageous to lay some burden upon foreign, for the encouragement of domestic industry; so there are two others in which it may sometimes be a matter of deliberation; in the one, how far it is proper to continue the free importation of certain foreign goods; and in the other, how far, or in what manner, it may be proper to restore that free importation after it has been for some time interrupted.

The case in which it may sometimes be a matter of deliberation how far it is proper to continue the free importation of certain foreign goods, is, when some foreign nation restrains by high duties or prohibitions the importation of some of our manufactures into their country. Revenge in this case naturally dictates retaliation, and that we should impose the like duties and prohibitions upon the importation of some or all of their manufactures into ours. Nations accordingly seldom fail to retaliate in this manner. The French have been particularly forward to favour their own manufactures by restraining the importation of such foreign goods as could come into competition with them. In this consisted a great part of the policy of Mr. Colbert, who, notwithstanding his great abilities, seems in this case to have been imposed upon by the sophistry of merchants and manufacturers, who are always demanding a monopoly against their countrymen. It is at present the opinion of the most intelligent men in France that his operations of this kind have not been beneficial to his country. That minister, by the tariff of 1667, imposed very high duties upon a great number of foreign manufactures. Upon his refusing to moderate

---

[28] Ed. 1 reads "it is."

them in favour of the Dutch, they in 1671 prohibited the importation of the wines, brandies and manufactures of France. The war of 1672 seems to have been in part occasioned by this commercial dispute. The peace of Nimeguen put an end to it in 1678, by moderating some of those duties in favour of the Dutch, who in consequence took off their prohibition. It was about the same time that the French and English began mutually to oppress each other's industry, by the like duties and prohibitions, of which the French, however, seem to have set the first example. The spirit of hostility which has subsisted between the two nations ever since, has hitherto hindered them from being moderated on either side. In 1697 the English prohibited the importation of bonelace, the manufacture of Flanders. The government of that country, at that time under the dominion of Spain, prohibited in return the importation of English woollens. In 1700, the prohibition of importing bonelace into England, was taken off upon condition that the importation of English woollens into Flanders should be put on the same footing as before.[29]

There may be good policy in retaliations of this kind, when there is a probability that they will procure the repeal of the high duties or prohibitions complained of. The recovery of a great foreign market will generally more than compensate the transitory inconveniency of paying dearer during a short time for some sorts of goods. To judge whether such retaliations are likely to produce such an effect, does not, perhaps, belong so much to the science of a legislator, whose deliberations ought to be governed by general principles which are always the same, as to the skill of that insidious and crafty animal, vulgarly called a statesman or politician, whose councils are directed by the momentary fluctuations of affairs. When there is no probability that any such repeal can be procured, it seems a bad method of compensating the injury done to certain classes of our people, to do another injury ourselves, not only to those classes, but to[30] almost all the other classes of them. When our neighbours prohibit some manufacture of ours, we generally prohibit, not only the same, for that alone would seldom affect them considerably, but some other manufacture of theirs. This may no doubt give encouragement to some particular class of workmen among ourselves, and by excluding some of their rivals, may enable them to raise their price in the home-market. Those workmen, however, who suffered by our neighbours' prohibition will not be benefited by ours. On the contrary, they and almost all the other classes of our citizens will thereby be obliged to pay dearer than before for certain goods. Every such law, therefore, imposes a real tax upon the whole country, not in favour of that particular class of workmen who were injured by our neighbours' prohibition, but of some other class.

The case in which it may sometimes be a matter of deliberation, how far, or in what manner, it is proper to restore the free importation of foreign goods, after it has been for some time interrupted, is, when particular manufactures, by means of high duties or prohibitions upon all foreign goods which can come into competition with them, have been so far extended as to employ a great multitude of hands. Humanity may in this case require that the freedom of trade should be restored only by slow gradations, and with a good deal of reserve and circumspection. Were those high duties and prohibitions taken away all at once, cheaper foreign goods of the same kind might be poured so fast into the home market, as to deprive all at once many thousands of our people of their ordinary employment and means of subsistence. The disorder which this would occasion might no doubt be very considerable. It would in all probability, however, be much less than is commonly imagined, for the two following reasons:

First, all those manufactures, of which any part is commonly exported to other European countries without a bounty, could be very little affected by the freest importation of foreign

---

[29] The importation of bone lace was prohibited by 13 and 14 Car. II., c. 13, and 9, and 10 W. III., c. 9, was passed to make the prohibition more effectual. By 11 and 12 W. III., c. 11, it was provided that the prohibition should cease three months after English woollen manufactures were readmitted to Flanders.

[30] Ed. 1 reads "injury ourselves, both to those classes and to."

goods. Such manufactures must be sold as cheap abroad as any other foreign goods of the same quality and kind, and consequently must be sold cheaper at home. They would still, therefore, keep possession of the home market, and though a capricious man of fashion might sometimes prefer foreign wares, merely because they were foreign, to cheaper and better goods of the same kind that were made at home, this folly could, from the nature of things, extend to so few, that it could make no sensible impression upon the general employment of the people. But a great part of all the different branches of our woollen manufacture, of our tanned leather, and of our hard-ware, are annually exported to other European countries without any bounty, and these are the manufactures which employ the greatest number of hands. The silk, perhaps, is the manufacture which would suffer the most by this freedom of trade, and after it the linen, though the latter much less than the former.

Secondly, though a great number of people should, by thus restoring the freedom of trade, be thrown all at once out of their ordinary employment and common method of subsistence, it would by no means follow that they would thereby be deprived either of employment or subsistence. By the reduction of the army and navy at the end of the late war, more than a hundred thousand soldiers and seamen, a number equal to what is employed in the greatest manufactures, were all at once thrown out of their ordinary employment; but, though they no doubt suffered some inconveniency, they were not thereby deprived of all employment and subsistence. The greater part of the seamen, it is probable, gradually betook themselves to the merchant-service as they could find occasion, and in the meantime both they and the soldiers were absorbed in the great mass of the people, and employed in a great variety of occupations. Not only no great convulsion, but no sensible disorder arose from so great a change in the situation of more than a hundred thousand men, all accustomed to the use of arms, and many of them to rapine and plunder. The number of vagrants was scarce any-where sensibly increased by it, even the wages of labour were not reduced by it in any occupation, so far as I have been able to learn, except in that of seamen in the merchant-service. But if we compare together the habits of a soldier and of any sort of manufacturer, we shall find that those of the latter do not tend so much to disqualify him from being employed in a new trade, as those of the former from being employed in any. The manufacturer has always been accustomed to look for his subsistence from his labour only: the soldier to expect it from his pay. Application and industry have been familiar to the one; idleness and dissipation to the other. But it is surely much easier to change the direction of industry from one sort of labour to another, than to turn idleness and dissipation to any. To the greater part of manufactures besides, it has already been observed,[31] there are other collateral manufactures of so similar a nature, that a workman can easily transfer his industry from one of them to another. The greater part of such workmen too are occasionally employed in country labour. The stock which employed them in a particular manufacture before, will still remain in the country to employ an equal number of people in some other way. The capital of the country remaining the same, the demand for labour will likewise be the same, or very nearly the same, though it may be exerted in different places and for different occupations. Soldiers and seamen, indeed, when discharged from the king's service, are at liberty to exercise any trade, within any town or place of Great Britain or Ireland.[32] Let the same natural liberty of exercising what species of industry they please, be restored to all his majesty's subjects, in the same manner as to soldiers and seamen; that is, break down the exclusive privileges of corporations, and repeal the statute of apprenticeship, both which are real encroachments upon natural liberty, and add to these the repeal of the law of settlements, so that a poor workman, when thrown out

---

[31] Above, p. 134, 135.

[32] 12 Car. II., c. 16; 12 Ann., st. 1, § 13; 3 Geo. III., c. 8, gave this liberty after particular wars.

of employment either in one trade or in one place, may seek for it in another trade or in another place, without the fear either of a prosecution or of a removal, and neither the public nor the individuals will suffer much more from the occasional disbanding some particular classes of manufacturers, than from that of soldiers. Our manufacturers have no doubt great merit with their country, but they cannot have more than those who defend it with their blood, nor deserve to be treated with more delicacy.

To expect, indeed, that the freedom of trade should ever be entirely restored in Great Britain, is as absurd as to expect that an Oceana or Utopia[33] should ever be established in it. Not only the prejudices of the public, but what is much more unconquerable, the private interests of many individuals, irresistibly oppose it. Were the officers of the army to oppose with the same zeal and unanimity any reduction in the number of forces, with which master manufacturers set themselves against every law that is likely to increase the number of their rivals in the home market; were the former to animate their soldiers, in the same manner as the latter enflame their workmen, to attack with violence and outrage the proposers of any such regulation; to attempt to reduce the army would be as dangerous as it has now become to attempt to diminish in any respect the monopoly which our manufacturers have obtained against us. This monopoly has so much increased the number of some particular tribes of them, that, like an overgrown standing army, they have become formidable to the government, and upon many occasions intimidate the legislature. The member of parliament who supports every proposal for strengthening this monopoly, is sure to acquire not only the reputation of understanding trade, but great popularity and influence with an order of men whose numbers and wealth render them of great importance. If he opposes them, on the contrary, and still more if he has authority enough to be able to thwart them, neither the most acknowledged probity, nor the highest rank, nor the greatest public services, can protect him from the most infamous abuse and detraction, from personal insults, nor sometimes from real danger, arising from the insolent outrage of furious and disappointed monopolists.

The undertaker of a great manufacture, who, by the home markets being suddenly laid open to the competition of foreigners, should be obliged to abandon his trade, would no doubt suffer very considerably. That part of his capital which had usually been employed in purchasing materials and in paying his workmen, might, without much difficulty, perhaps, find another employment. But that part of it which was fixed in workhouses, and in the instruments of trade, could scarce be disposed of without considerable loss. The equitable regard, therefore, to his interest requires that changes of this kind should never be introduced suddenly, but slowly, gradually, and after a very long warning. The legislature, were it possible that its deliberations could be always directed, not by the clamorous importunity of partial interests, but by an extensive view of the general good, ought upon this very account, perhaps, to be particularly careful neither to establish any new monopolies of this kind, nor to extend further those which are already established. Every such regulation introduces some degree of real disorder into the constitution of the state, which it will be difficult afterwards to cure without occasioning another disorder.

How far it may be proper to impose taxes upon the importation of foreign goods, in order, not to prevent their importation, but to raise a revenue for government, I shall consider hereafter when I come to treat of taxes.[34] Taxes imposed with a view to prevent, or even to diminish importation, are evidently as destructive of the revenue of the customs as of the freedom of trade.

---

[33] Ed. 1 reads "Utopea."
[34] Below, pp. 845–850.

Modern Liberalism

When Americans hear the term *liberal* the images that immediately come to mind are of political leaders such as Franklin D. Roosevelt, Hillary Clinton, or Teddy Kennedy or of economists such as John Maynard Keynes or Paul Krugman. Although there is most certainly reason to keep in mind what the term means in the American context, one should not lose sight of the fact that, in international politics, the term is used to denote "classic" understandings of political and economic freedoms. That said, the modern American liberal is a product of the twentieth century.

In economic terms, the American liberal has traditionally fought for a progressive tax system, demand-side economics, and, in times of economic turmoil, deficit spending. The progressive tax system, as well as the establishment of the U.S. Federal Reserve, occurred during the Progressive era in American politics. During the 1920s, American political leaders were determined to make changes to the progressive tax system that they deemed as being a punishment on the rich. U.S. Secretary of the Treasury Andrew Mellon and the 1920s presidents (Warren G. Harding, Calvin Coolidge, and Herbert Hoover) pushed for what has since been termed a "supply-side" economy, wherein the wealthy of society would get additional tax breaks in an effort to create jobs for the masses. Supply-side economic policies have, of course, been a fundamental rift between the Republican and Democratic political parties ever since. The other side of the policy coin, demand-side economics, argues that the path out of an economic slump is to provide tax breaks to the least wealthy of a society. The logic is that the least wealthy of a society will spend virtually all their additional income, thereby increasing consumption and benefiting the economy. Demand-siders argue that, if the rich are given a tax break there is really no guarantee that all the additional income would be spent, and therefore, there would be less impact on economic activity. Finally, deficit spending is something that has become linked to the policies of the American liberal.

The logic of deficit spending is said to come from British economist John Maynard Keynes and is today referred to as Keynesianism. Keynes argued that, in times of economic stagnation, the government could help to get the economy moving along by spending money that it did not yet have. Although this would, in the short term, result in a deficit, the longer-term impact would be to reap benefits from the economic activity that had been started by putting money back into the economy. Keynesianism is sometimes linked to demand-side logic in that it can be another way to get more money into the hands of consumers. Critics of deficit spending argue that it is fiscally irresponsible and, more recently, that the benefits of putting money back into the economy are no longer limited to domestic spending. That is, there is no guarantee that the U.S. government's putting money into the hands of American consumers will benefit the U.S. economy. In fact, the opposite can be true as Americans buy more and more products from abroad.

Another way of thinking about American liberalism is in terms of government spending in the name of social and economic equality. Here, the policies stem from the logic of the 1960s' "War of Poverty" and the entire government welfare system that followed. In the 1980s the term *entitlements* was used in an effort to stem the abuse of the system that had occurred. In other words, it was clear that at least some people were taking advantage of the welfare system and, for some, welfare also created a "culture of dependency." In 1992, under pressure from the Republican-dominated U.S. Congress, President Clinton made the announcement that the time had come for the United States to "end welfare as we know it." Since then, a variety of policy changes have been made in an effort to get welfare-dependent individuals and families into the workforce.

Simultaneously, and using much the same logic, many U.S. politicians have supported dramatic decreases in international aid over the past decade.[164] Arguing that aid simply distorts the development of free markets, Congressmen Phil Crane, Charles Rangel, and Jim McDermott introduced a bill dubbed the "The End of Dependency Act of 1997" (H.R. 4198). It has since moved on to become the African Growth and Opportunity Act (AGOA) and was signed into law on May 18, 2000, as Title 1 of The Trade and Development Act of 2000.[165] In other words, in both domestic and international circles, economic aid—an American liberal policy—has been dramatically altered over the past decade.

International Liberalism

Proponents of international liberalism generally focus on the benefits of economic freedom. "Institutional Liberals" emphasize, for example, the importance of using the Bretton Woods Institutions (IMF, IBRD, and WTO) in an effort to support free-market liberalism.[166] "Orthodox Liberals" have less allegiance to these institutional supports, favoring less state involvement, or "laissez-faire" policies. As conflicts faced by the WTO have demonstrated, support of free-market goals has included the *protection* of trade-related intellectual property rights (TRIPs) and barriers to immigration. In other words, the goal of the free market has proven to be quite complex in an increasingly global economy.

---

[164] Economist Theodore Cohn argues that, due to its belief in free markets, the United States has consistently had the lowest percentage of Net Offical Development Assistance (ODA), in terms of GNP, vis-á-vis other OECD member-states over the past four decades. For the United States it amounts to approximately 0.1 percent of GNP (1999), whereas for other states, such as Denmark, it amounts to 1.01 percent of GNP (1999), i.e., more than ten times the commitment to development aid. See: Cohn, *Global Political Economy* (New York: Pearson-Longman, 2003), p. 405.

[165] Complete, now, with its own website: http://www.agoa.gov.

[166] Stated briefly here, the Bretton Woods Institutions listed support the goals of the free market in a variety of ways: the International Monetary Fund (IMF) supports currency stability; the International Bank for Reconstruction and Development (IBRD or World Bank) supports infrastructural development and poverty alleviation; and the World Trade Organization (WTO) has as its primary goal the removal of barriers to free trade. See: Cohn (2003), Chapter 2.

Chapter Five

Structuralism

"The history of all hitherto existing society is the history of class struggles. Freeman and slave, patrician and plebian, lord and serf, guild-master and journeyman, in a word, oppressor and oppressed, stood in constant opposition to one another. . ."
Karl Marx & Friedrich Engels (1848)

"Bourgeois scholars and publicists usually come out in defence of imperialism in a somewhat veiled form, and obscure its complete domination and its profound roots. . ."
V. I. Lenin (1916)

"There are today no socialist systems in the world-economy any more than there are feudal systems because there is only *one* world-system. It is a world-economy and it is by definition capitalist in form." *Immanuel Wallerstein (1979)*

Whereas political change in the West has generally been attributed to a combination of the ideals contemplated in previous chapters, through rigorous debate and even policy experimentation, the former Soviet bloc (East) has historically relied on the logic of Marxism–Leninism (herein referred to as structuralism). According to the structuralist view, the primary motives for political change in history have been concrete differences of material wealth. This body of literature, stemming from the nineteenth-century works of Karl Marx and Friedrich Engels, is referred to as historical materialism.[167]

---

[167] George Plekhanov, *Essays in Historical Materialism: The Materialist Conception of History* (New York: International Publishers, 1940).

Given today's extreme differences of political power and wealth and the increased ability of all to see these differences, one must not conclude that the ideas of Marx no longer hold sway. It may be premature to say that the Cold War East–West debate has lost all relevance. In fact, it could be argued that a new ideological rift exists between the industrialized North and the materially less-developed South has taken the place of the former East-West rivalry, with similar philosophical and practical governing differences. That is, free-market individualism has now engulfed much of the northern hemisphere whereas many in the southern hemisphere have seemingly adopted the logic of structuralism (i.e., the Cold War debate may have "pivoted" from East-West to North-South). Tragic events during the post-Cold War years remind us that the ideological debate between the merits of free-market individualism and various forms of collectivism remain relevant. The "battle of ideas," therefore, continues and it has, historically, formed the basis for war. For example, ideological differences during the twentieth century—between Communism, Fascism, and Democratic Liberalism—formed the basis for conflict in WWI and WWII. One way to interpret the North-South rift is in terms of a debate of ideas and/or policies. As we saw in the previous chapter, this is how many citizens of the industrialized north would like the debate to take place. Another way is to say that the rift has nothing to do with ideas. That is, following the logic of Marx and of historical materialism, any tension between us has more to do with differences of material wealth.

Certainly, this is the view espoused by the *dependencistas* writers. A seminal thinker of the Dependency School is Raul Prebisch, who was the director of the Economic Commission for Latin America (ECLA). In a paper written in 1950, Prebisch argued that the "Ricardian theory of international trade was not applicable in the context of the existing international division of labor, and instead contributed to trade-generate inequality and structural underdevelopment."[168] As this argument convinced a great many Latin American and other southern hemisphere leaders, many states adopted what is termed Import Substitution Industrialization (ISI) policies.[169] Ultimately, ISI approaches to state development were discredited due to the more successful export-oriented strategies espoused by East Asian economies. But, in the 1950s and 1960s ISI was viewed as one of the only policy alternatives available to struggling "dependent" economies. To this day, interpretations as to how successful these policies were to Latin American states vary. Duncan Green, for example, argues

> By the early 1960s, domestic industry supplied 95 percent of Mexico's and 98 percent of Brazil's consumer goods. From 1950 to 1980 Latin America's industrial output went up six times keeping well ahead of population growth. Infant mortality fell from 107 per 1000 births in 1960 to 69 per 1000 in 1980, life expectancy rose from 52 to 64 years. In the mid 1950s, Latin America's economies were growing faster than those of the industrialized West.[170]

---

[168] As described by Ankie Hoogvelt, *Globalization and the Postcolonial World* (Baltimore, MD: Johns Hopkins University Press, 1997), p. 223.

[169] ISI is also referred to, in the literature, as import *substitutive* industrialization.

[170] Duncan Green, *Silent Revolution, the Rise of Market Economics in Latin America* (London: Cassell & Latin America Bureau, 1995), p. 16, cited in Hoogvelt (1997), p. 224.

READING 13: KARL MARX AND FREDRICH ENGELS

Karl Marx was born in Germany to Jewish parents who converted to Lutheranism when he was only six. Exactly what the impact on Marx might have been is hard to say, but he did make the famous comment that religious belief was "the opiate of the masses." Educated at Bonn and Berlin, he was particularly influenced by the thinking of Georg Hegel. As a young man, Marx worked as a journalist, later moving to Paris and Brussels. Over time, he became increasingly radical, eventually getting involved in the Communist League, for which he cowrote *The Communist Manifesto*. Due to his activities in Belgium, he was forced to leave for London, where he would spend the rest of his life writing. Though poor most of his life, he worked intensely and suffered many personal losses, including the loss of three children. Marx had a radically different view of industrialization from what we saw in the works of Adam Smith. Using the dialectic method of Hegel, Marx interpreted all human history as a struggle between the haves and the have-nots. In his view, industrialization was a far cry from something that can be described as the "miracle of specialization." Rather, the laborer (whom he termed, the Proletariat) was being exploited by the industrial capitalist (whom he termed, the Bourgeoisie). The ideas of Marx can assuredly be said to have influenced the Cold War ideological rivalry between the East and the West. And one must not forget that, to this day, Marx's ideas often prevail where there exist dramatic differences between the rich and the poor.

A) MARX & ENGELS,

THE COMMUNIST MANIFESTO, 1848

BOURGEOIS AND PROLETARIANS[1]

The history of all hitherto existing society[2] is the history of class struggles.

Freeman and slave, patrician and plebeian, lord and serf, guild-master[3] and journeyman, in a word, oppressor and oppressed, stood in constant opposition to one another, carried on an

---

Karl Marx and Freidrich Engels, *The Communist Manifesto* (Penguin Classics, 1987).

[1] By bourgeoisie is meant the class of modern Capitalists, owners of the means of social production and employers of wage labour. By proletariat, the class of modern wage-labourers who, having no means of production of their own, are reduced to selling their labour power in order to live. [*Note by Engels to the English edition of 1888.*]

[2] That is, all *written* history. In 1847, the pre-history of society, the social organization existing previous to recorded history, was all but unknown. Since then, Haxthausen discovered common ownership of land in Russia, Maurer proved it to be the social foundation from which all Teutonic races started in history, and by and by village communities were found to be, or to have been the primitive form of society everywhere from India to Ireland. The inner organization of this primitive Communistic society was laid bare, in its typical form, by Morgan's crowning discovery of the true nature of the *gens* and its relation to the *tribe*. With the dissolution of these primeval communities society begins to be differentiated into separate and finally antagonistic classes. I have attempted to retrace this process of dissolution in: *Der Ursprung der Familie, des Privateigenthums und des Staats (The Origin of the Family, Private Property and the State)*, 2nd edition, Stuttgart 1886. [*Note by Engels to the English edition of 1888.*]

[3] Guild-master, that is, a full member of a guild, a master within, not a head of a guild. [*Note by Engels to the English edition of 1888.*]

uninterrupted, now hidden, now open fight, a fight that each time ended, either in a revolutionary reconstitution of society at large, or in the common ruin of the contending classes.

In the earlier epochs of history, we find almost everywhere a complicated arrangement of society into various orders, a manifold gradation of social rank. In ancient Rome we have patricians, knights, plebeians, slaves; in the Middle Ages, feudal lords, vassals, guild-masters, journeymen, apprentices, serfs; in almost all of these classes, again, subordinate gradations.

The modern bourgeois society that has sprouted from the ruins of feudal society has not done away with class antagonisms. It has but established new classes, new conditions of oppression, new forms of struggle in place of the old ones.

Our epoch, the epoch of the bourgeoisie, possesses, however, this distinctive feature: it has simplified the class antagonisms. Society as a whole is more and more splitting up into two great hostile camps, into two great classes directly facing each other: Bourgeoisie and Proletariat.

From the serfs of the Middle Ages sprang the chartered burghers of the earliest towns. From these burgesses the first elements of the bourgeoisie were developed.

The discovery of America, the rounding of the Cape, opened up fresh ground for the rising bourgeoisie. The East-Indian and Chinese markets, the colonization of America, trade with the colonies, the increase in the means of exchange and in commodities generally, gave to commerce, to navigation, to industry, an impulse never before known, and thereby, to the revolutionary element in the tottering feudal society, a rapid development.

The feudal system of industry, under which industrial production was monopolized by closed guilds, now no longer sufficed for the growing wants of the new markets. The manufacturing system took its place. The guild-masters were pushed on one side by the manufacturing middle class; division of labour between the different corporate guilds vanished in the face of division of labour in each single workshop.

Meantime the markets kept ever growing, the demand ever rising. Even manufacture no longer sufficed. Thereupon, steam and machinery revolutionized industrial production. The place of manufacture was taken by the giant, Modern Industry, the place of the industrial middle class, by industrial millionaires, the leaders of whole industrial armies, the modern bourgeois.

Modern industry has established the world market, for which the discovery of America paved the way. This market has given an immense development to commerce, to navigation, to communication by land. This development has, in its turn, reacted on the extension of industry; and in proportion as industry, commerce, navigation, railways extended, in the same proportion the bourgeoisie developed, increased its capital, and pushed into the background every class handed down from the Middle Ages.

We see, therefore, how the modern bourgeoisie is itself the product of a long course of development, of a series of revolutions in the modes of production and of exchange.

Each step in the development of the bourgeoisie was accompanied by a corresponding political advance of that class. An oppressed class under the sway of the feudal nobility, an armed and self-governing association in the medieval commune;[4] here independent urban republic (as in Italy and Germany), there taxable 'third estate' of the monarchy (as in France), afterwards, in the period of manufacture proper, serving either the semi-feudal or the absolute monarchy as a counterpoise against the nobility, and, in fact, corner-stone of the great monarchies in general, the

---

[4] 'Commune' was the name taken, in France, by the nascent towns even before they had conquered from their feudal lords and masters local self-government and political rights as the 'Third Estate'. Generally speaking, for the economical development of the bourgeoisie, England is here taken as the typical country; for its political development, France. [*Note by Engels to the English edition of 1888.*]

This was the name given their urban communities by the townsmen of Italy and France, after they had purchased or wrested their initial rights of self-government from their feudal lords. [*Note by Engels to the German edition of 1890.*]

bourgeoisie has at last, since the establishment of Modern Industry and of the world market, conquered for itself, in the modern representative State, exclusive political sway. The executive of the modern State is but a committee for managing the common affairs of the whole bourgeoisie.

The bourgeoisie, historically, has played a most revolutionary part.

The bourgeoisie, wherever it has got the upper hand, has put an end to all feudal, patriarchal, idyllic relations. It has pitilessly torn asunder the motley feudal ties that bound man to his 'natural superiors', and has left remaining no other nexus between man and man than naked self-interest, than callous 'cash payment'. It has drowned the most heavenly ecstasies of religious fervour, of chivalrous enthusiasm, of philistine sentimentalism, in the icy water of egotistical calculation. It has resolved personal worth into exchange value, and in place of the numberless indefeasible chartered freedoms, has set up that single, unconscionable freedom—Free Trade. In one word, for exploitation, veiled by religious and political illusions, it has substituted naked, shameless, direct, brutal exploitation.

The bourgeoisie has stripped of its halo every occupation hitherto honoured and looked up to with reverent awe. It has converted the physician, the lawyer, the priest, the poet, the man of science, into its paid wage-labourers.

The bourgeoisie has torn away from the family its sentimental veil, and has reduced the family relation to a mere money relation.

The bourgeoisie has disclosed how it came to pass that the brutal display of vigour in the Middle Ages, which Reactionists so much admire, found its fitting complement in the most slothful indolence. It has been the first to show what man's activity can bring about. It has accomplished wonders far surpassing Egyptian pyramids, Roman aqueducts, and Gothic cathedrals; it has conducted expeditions that put in the shade all former Exoduses of nations and crusades.

The bourgeoisie cannot exist without constantly revolutionizing the instruments of production, and thereby the relations of production, and with them the whole relations of society. Conservation of the old modes of production in unaltered form, was, on the contrary, the first condition of existence for all earlier industrial classes. Constant revolutionizing of production, uninterrupted disturbance of all social conditions, everlasting uncertainty and agitation distinguish the bourgeois epoch from all earlier ones. All fixed, fast-frozen relations, with their train of ancient and venerable prejudices and opinions are swept away, all new-formed ones become antiquated before they can ossify. All that is solid melts into air, all that is holy is profaned, and man is at last compelled to face with sober senses, his real conditions of life, and his relations with his kind.

The need of a constantly expanding market for its products chases the bourgeoisie over the whole surface of the globe. It must nestle everywhere, settle everywhere, establish connexions everywhere.

The bourgeoisie has through its exploitation of the world market given a cosmopolitan character to production and consumption in every country. To the great chagrin of Reactionists, it has drawn from under the feet of industry the national ground on which it stood. All old-established national industries have been destroyed or are daily being destroyed. They are dislodged by new industries, whose introduction becomes a life and death question for all civilized nations, by industries that no longer work up indigenous raw material, but raw material drawn from the remotest zones; industries who products are consumed, not only at home, but in every quarter of the globe. In place of the old wants, satisfied by the productions of the country, we find new wants, requiring for their satisfaction the products of distant lands and climes. In place of the old local and national seclusion and self-sufficiency, we have intercourse in every direction, universal inter-dependence of nations. And as in material, so also in intellectual production. The intellectual creations of individual nations become common property. National one-sidedness and narrow-mindedness become more and more impossible, and from the numerous national and local literatures, there arises a world literature.

The bourgeoisie, by the rapid improvement of all instruments of production, by the immensely facilitated means of communication, draws all, even the most barbarian, nations into civilization. The cheap prices of its commodities are the heavy artillery with which it batters down all Chinese walls, with which it forces the barbarians' intensely obstinate hatred of foreigners to capitulate. It compels all nations, on pain of extinction, to adopt the bourgeois mode of production; it compels them to introduce what it calls civilization into their midst, i.e., to become bourgeois themselves. In one word, it creates a world after its own image.

The bourgeoisie has subjected the country to the rule of the towns. It has created enormous cities, has greatly increased the urban population as compared with the rural, and has thus rescued a considerable part of the population from the idiocy of rural life. Just as it has made the country dependent on the towns, so it has made barbarian and semibarbarian countries dependent on the civilized ones, nations of peasants on nations of bourgeois, the East on the West.

The bouregeoisie keeps more and more doing away with the scattered state of the population, of the means of production, and of property. It has agglomerated population, centralized means of production, and has concentrated property in a few hands. The necessary consequence of this was political centralization. Independent, or but loosely connected, provinces with separate interests, laws, governments and systems of taxation, became lumped together into one nation, with one government, one code of laws, one national class-interest, one frontier and one customs-tariff.

The bourgeoisie, during its rule of scarce one hundred years, has created more massive and more colossal productive forces than have all preceding generations together. Subjection of Nature's forces to man, machinery, application of chemistry to industry and agriculture, steam-navigation, railways, electric telegraphs, clearing of whole continents for cultivation, canalization of rivers, whole populations conjured out of the ground—what earlier century had even a presentiment that such productive forces slumbered in the lap of social labour?

We see then: the means of production and of exchange, on whose foundation the bourgeoisie built itself up, were generated in feudal society. At a certain stage in the development of these means of production and of exchange, the conditions under which feudal society produced and exchanged, the feudal organization of agriculture and manufacturing industry, in one word, the feudal relations of property became no longer compatible with the already developed productive forces; they became so many fetters. They had to be burst asunder; they were burst asunder.

Into their place stepped free competition, accompanied by a social and political constitution adapted to it, and by the economical and political sway of the bourgeois class.

A similar movement is going on before our own eyes. Modern bourgeois society with its relations of production, of exchange and of property, a society that has conjured up such gigantic means of production and of exchange, is like the sorcerer, who is no longer able to control the powers of the nether world whom he has called up by his spells. For many a decade past the history of industry and commerce is but the history of the revolt of modern productive forces against modern conditions of production, against the property relations that are the conditions for the existence of the bourgeoisie and of its rule. It is enough to mention the commercial crises that by their periodical return put on its trial, each time more threateningly, the existence of the entire bourgeois society. In these crises a great part not only of the existing products, but also of the previously created productive forces, are periodically destroyed. In these crises there breaks out an epidemic that, in all earlier epochs, would have seemed an absurdity—the epidemic of overproduction. Society suddenly finds itself put back into a state of momentary barbarism; it appears as if a famine, a universal war of devastation had cut off the supply of every means of subsistence; industry and commerce seem to be destroyed; and why? Because there is too much civilization, too much means of subsistence, too much industry, too much commerce. The productive forces at the disposal of society no longer tend to further the development of the conditions of bourgeois property; on the contrary, they have become too powerful for these conditions, by which they are fettered, and so soon as they overcome these fetters, they bring disorder into the whole of bourgeois society, endanger the existence of bourgeois property. The conditions of bourgeois society are too narrow to comprise the wealth created by them. And how does the bourgeoisie get over these crises? On the one hand by enforced destruction of a mass of productive forces; on the other, by the conquest of new markets, and by the more thorough exploitation of the old ones. That is to say, by paving the way for more extensive and more destructive crises, and by diminishing the means whereby crises are prevented.

The weapons with which the bourgeoisie felled feudalism to the ground are now turned against the bourgeoisie itself.

But not only has the bourgeoisie forged the weapons that bring death to itself; it has also called into existence the men who are to wield those weapons—the modern working class—the proletarians.

In proportion as the bourgeoisie, i.e., capital, is developed, in the same proportion is the proletariat, the modern working class, developed—a class of labourers, who live only so long as they find work, and who find work only so long as their labour increases capital. These labourers, who must sell themselves piecemeal, are a commodity, like every other article of commerce, and are consequently exposed to all the vicissitudes of competition, to all the fluctuations of the market.

Owing to the extensive use of machinery and to division of labour, the work of the proletarians has lost all individual character, and, consequently, all charm for the workman. He becomes an appendage of the machine, and it is only the most simple, most monotonous, and most easily acquired knack, that is required of him. Hence, the cost of production of a workman is restricted, almost entirely, to the means of subsistence that he requires for his maintenance, and for the propagation of his race. But the price of a commodity, and therefore also of labour, is equal to its cost of production. In proportion, therefore, as the repulsiveness of the work increases, the wage decreases. Nay more, in proportion as the use of machinery and division of labour increases, in the same proportion the burden of toil also increases, whether by prolongation of the working hours, by increase of the work exacted in a given time or by increased speed of the machinery, etc.

Modern industry has converted the little workshop of the patriarchal master into the great factory of the industrial capitalist. Masses of labourers, crowded into the factory, are organized like soldiers. As privates of the industrial army they are placed under the command of a perfect hierarchy of officers and sergeants. Not only are they slaves of the bourgeois class, and of the bourgeois State; they are daily and hourly enslaved by the machine, by the overlooker, and, above all, by the individual bourgeois manufacturer himself. The more openly this despotism proclaims gain to be its end and aim, the more petty, the more hateful and the more embittering it is.

The less the skill and exertion of strength implied in manual labour, in other words, the more modern industry becomes developed, the more is the labour of men superseded by that of women. Differences of age and sex have no longer any distinctive social validity for the working class. All are instruments of labour, more or less expensive to use, according to their age and sex.

No sooner is the exploitation of the labourer by the manufacturer, so far, at an end, that he receives his wages in cash, than he is set upon by the other portions of the bourgeoisie, the landlord, the shopkeeper, the pawnbroker, etc.

The lower strata of the middle class—the small trades people, shopkeepers, and retired tradesmen generally, the handicraftsmen and peasants—all these sink gradually into the proletariat, partly because their diminutive capital does not suffice for the scale on which Modern Industry is carried on, and is swamped in the competition with the large capitalists, partly because their specialized skill is rendered worthless by new methods of production. Thus the proletariat is recruited from all classes of the population.

The proletariat goes through various stages of development. With its birth begins its struggle with the bourgeoisie. At first the contest is carried on by individual labourers, then by the workpeople of a factory, then by the operatives of one trade, in one locality, against the individual bourgeois who directly exploits them. They direct their attacks not against the bourgeois conditions of production, but against the instruments of production themselves; they destroy imported wares that compete with their labour, they smash to pieces machinery, they set factories ablaze, they seek to restore by force the vanished status of the workman of the Middle Ages.

At this stage the labourers still form an incoherent mass scattered over the whole country, and broken up by their mutual competition. If anywhere they unite to form more compact bodies, this is not yet the consequence of their own active union, but of the union of the bourgeoisie, which class, in order to attain its own political ends, is compelled to set the whole proletariat in motion, and is moreover yet, for a time, able to do so. At this stage, therefore, the proletarians do not fight their enemies, but the enemies of their enemies, the remnants of absolute monarchy, the landowners, the non-industrial bourgeois, the petty bourgeoisie. Thus the whole historical movement is concentrated in the hands of the bourgeoisie; every victory so obtained is a victory for the bourgeoisie.

But with the development of industry the proletariat not only increases in number; it becomes concentrated in greater masses, its strength grows, and it feels that strength more. The various interests and conditions of life within the ranks of the proletariat are more and more equalized, in proportion as machinery obliterates all distinctions of labour, and nearly everywhere reduces wages to the same low level. The growing competition among the bourgeois, and the resulting commercial crises, make the wages of the workers ever more fluctuating. The unceasing improvement of machinery, ever more rapidly developing, makes their livelihood more and more precarious; the collisions between individual workmen and individual bourgeois take more and more the character of collisions between two classes. Thereupon the workers begin for form combinations (Trades Unions) against the bourgeois; they club together in order to keep up the rate of wages; they found permanent associations in order to make provision beforehand for these occasional revolts. Here and there the contest breaks out into riots.

Now and then the workers are victorious, but only for a time. The real fruit of their battles lies, not in the immediate result, but in the ever-expanding union of the workers. This union is helped on by the improved means of communication that are created by modern industry and that place the workers of different localities in contact with one another. It was just this contact that was needed to centralize the numerous local struggles, all of the same character, into one national struggle between classes. But every class struggle is a political struggle. And that union, to attain which the burghers of the Middle Ages, with their miserable highways, required centuries, the modern proletarians, thanks to railways, achieve in a few years.

This organization of the proletarians into a class, and consequently into a political party, is continually being upset again by the competition between the workers themselves. But it ever rises up again, stronger, firmer, mightier. It compels legislative recognition of particular interests of the workers, by taking advantage of the divisions among the bourgeoisie itself. Thus the Ten Hours bill in England was carried.

Altogether collisions between the classes of the old society further, in many ways, the course of development of the proletariat. The bourgeoisie finds itself involved in a constant battle. At first with the aristocracy; later on, with those portions of the bourgeoisie itself, whose interests have become antagonistic to the progress of industry; at all times, with the bourgeoisie of foreign countries. In all these battles it sees itself compelled to appeal to the proletariat, to ask for its help, and thus, to drag it into the political arena. The bourgeoisie itself, therefore, supplies the proletariat with its own elements of political and general education, in other words, it furnishes the proletariat with weapons for fighting the bourgeoisie.

Further, as we have already seen, entire sections of the ruling classes are, by the advance of industry, precipitated into the proletariat, or are at least threatened in their conditions of existence. There also supply the proletariat with fresh elements of enlightenment and progress.

Finally, in times when the class struggle nears the decisive hour, the process of dissolution going on within the ruling class, in fact within the whole range of old society, assumes such a violent, glaring character, that a small section of the ruling class cuts itself adrift, and joins the revolutionary class, the class that holds the future in its hands. Just as, therefore, at an earlier period, a section of the nobility went over to the bourgeoisie, so now a portion of the bourgeoisie goes over to the proletariat, and in particular, a portion of the bourgeois ideologists, who have raised themselves to the level of comprehending theoretically the historical movement as a whole.

Of all the classes that stand face to face with the bourgeoisie today, the proletariat alone is a really revolutionary class. The other classes decay and finally disappear in the face of modern industry; the proletariat is its special and essential product.

The lower middle class, the small manufacturer, the shopkeeper, the artisan, the peasant, all these fight against the bourgeoisie, to save from extinction their existence as fractions of the middle class. They are therefore not revolutionary, but conservative. Nay more, they are reactionary, for they try to roll back the wheel of history. If by chance they are revolutionary, they are so only in view of their impending transfer into the proletariat, they thus defend not their present, but their future interests, they desert their own standpoint to place themselves at that of the proletariat.

The 'dangerous class', the social scum, that passively rotting mass thrown off by the lowest layers of old society, may, here and there, be swept into the movement by a proletarian revolution; its conditions of life, however, prepare it far more for the part of a bribed tool of reactionary intrigue.

In the conditions of the proletariat, those of old society at large are already virtually swamped. The proletarian is without property; his relation to his wife and children has no longer anything in common with the bourgeois family relations; modern industrial labour, modern subjection to capital, the same in England as in France, in America as in Germany, has stripped him of every trace of national character. Law, morality, religion, are to him so many bourgeois prejudices, behind which lurk in ambush just as many bourgeois interests.

All the preceding classes that got the upper hand sought to fortify their already acquired status by subjecting society at large to their conditions of appropriation. The proletarians cannot become masters of the productive forces of society, except by abolishing their own previous mode of appropriation, and thereby also every other previous mode of appropriation. They have nothing of their own to secure and to fortify; their mission is to destroy all previous securities for, and insurances of, individual property.

All previous historical movements were movements of minorities, or in the interest of minorities. The proletarian movement is the self-conscious, independent movement of the immense majority, in the interest of the immense majority. The proletariat, the lowest stratum of our present society, cannot stir, cannot raise itself up, without the whole superincumbent strata of official society being sprung into the air.

Though not in substance, yet in form, the struggle of the proletariat with the bourgeoisie is at first a national struggle. The proletariat of each country must, of course, first of all settle matters with its own bourgeoisie.

In depicting the most general phases of the development of the proletariat, we traced the more or less veiled civil war, raging within existing society, up to the point where that war breaks out into open revolution, and where the violent overthrow of the bourgeoisie lays the foundation for the sway of the proletariat.

Hitherto, every form of society has been based, as we have already seen, on the antagonism of oppressing and oppressed classes. But in order to oppress a class, certain conditions must be assured to it under when it can, at least, continue its slavish existence. The serf, in the period of serfdom, raised himself to membership in the commune, just as the petty bourgeois, under the yoke of feudal absolutism, managed to develop into a bourgeois. The modern labourer, on the contrary, instead of rising with the progress of industry, sinks deeper and deeper below the conditions of existence of his own class. He becomes a pauper, and pauperism develops more rapidly than population and wealth. And here it becomes evident, that the bourgeoisie is unfit any longer to be the ruling class in society, and to impose its conditions of existence upon society as an overriding law. It is unfit to rule because it is incompetent to assure an existence to its slave within his slavery, because it cannot help letting him sink into such a state, that it has to feed him, instead of being fed by him. Society can no longer live under this bourgeoisie, in other words, its existence is no longer compatible with society.

The essential condition for the existence, and for the sway of the bourgeois class, is the formation and augmentation of capital; the condition for capital is wage labour. Wage labour rests exclusively on competition between the labourers. The advance of industry, whose involuntary promoter is the bourgeoisie, replaces the isolation of the labourers, due to competition, by their revolutionary combination, due to association. The development of Modern Industry, therefore, cuts from under its feet the very foundation on which the bourgeoisie produces and appropriates products. What the bourgeoisie, therefore, produces, above all, is its own grave-diggers. Its fall and the victory of the proletariat are equally inevitable.

■■■■■■■■■■■■■■■■■■■■■■■■■■■■■■■■■

B) KARL MARX,

EARLIER WRITINGS

PRIVATE PROPERTY AND LABOUR

[I] *ad* page XXXVI. The subjective essence of *private* property, private property as activity for itself, as *subject*, as *person,* is labour. It is evident, therefore, that only the political economy which recognized labour as its principle (Adam Smith) and which no longer regarded private property as merely a *condition* external to man, can be considered as both a product of the real *dynamism* and *development* of private property,[1] a product of modern *industry,* and a force which has accelerated and extolled the dynamism and development of industry and has made it a power in the domain of *consciousness.*

Thus, from the viewpoint of this enlightened political economy which has discovered the *subjective* essence of wealth within the framework of private property, the partisans of the monetary system and the mercantilist system, who consider private property as a *purely objective* being for man, are *fetishists* and *Catholics.* Engels is right, therefore, in calling Adam Smith the *Luther of political economy.* Just as Luther recognized religion and *faith* as the essence of the real *world,* and for that reason took up a position against Catholic paganism; just as he annulled *external* religiosity while making religiosity the *inner* essence of man; just as he negated the distinction between priest and layman because he transferred the priest into the heart of the layman; so wealth external to man and independent of him (and thus only to be acquired and conserved from outside) is annulled. That is to say, its *external* and *mindless objectivity* is annulled by the fact that private property is incorporated in man himself, and man himself is recognized as its essence. But as a result, man himself is brought into the sphere of private property, just as, with Luther, he is brought into the sphere of religion. Under the guise of recognizing man, political economy, whose principle is labour, carries to its logical conclusion the denial of man. Man himself is no longer in a condition of external tension with the external substance of private property; he has himself become the tension-ridden being of private property. What was previously a phenomenon of *being external to oneself,* a real external manifestation of man, has now become the act of objectification, of alienation. This political economy seems at first, therefore, to recognize man with his independence, his personal activity, etc. It incorporates private property in the very essence of man, and it is no longer, therefore, conditioned by the local or national *characteristics of private property* regarded as existing outside itself. It manifests a cosmopolitan, universal activity which is destructive of every limit and every bond, and substitutes itself as the *only* policy, the *only* universality, the *only* limit and the *only* bond. But in its further development it is obliged to discard this hypocrisy and to show itself in all its cynicism. It does this, without any regard for the apparent

---

[1] It is the independent movement of private property become conscious of itself; modern industry as Self.

contradictions to which its doctrine leads, by showing in a more one-sided fashion, and thus with greater logic and clarity, that *labour* is the sole *essence of wealth,* and by demonstrating that this doctrine, in contrast with the original conception, has consequences with are *inimical to man.* Finally, it gives the death-blow to *ground rent;* that last individual and natural form of private property and source of wealth existing independently of the movement of labour, which was the expression of feudal property but has become entirely its economic expression and is no longer able to put up any resistance to political economy. (The Ricardo School.) Not only does the *cynicism* of political economy increase from Smith, through Say, to Ricardo, Mill, *et al.* inasmuch as for the latter the consequence of *industry* appeared more and more developed and contradictory; from a positive point of view they become more alienated, and more consciously alienated, from man, in comparison with their predecessors. This is *only* because their science develops with greater logic and truth. Since they make private property in its active form the subject, and since at the same time they make man as a non-being into a being, the contradiction in reality corresponds entirely with the contradictory essence which they have accepted as a principle. The divided [II] *reality* of *industry* is far from refuting, but instead confirms, its *self-divided* principle. Its principle is in fact the principle of this division.

The physiocratic doctrine of Quesnay forms the transition from the mercantilist system to Adam Smith. *Physiocracy* is in a direct sense the *economic* decomposition of feudal property, but for this reason it is equally directly the *economic transformation,* the re-establishment, of this same feudal property; with the difference that its language is no longer feudal but economic. All wealth is reduced to *land* and *cultivation* (agriculture). Land is not yet *capital* but is still a particular mode of existence of capital, whose value is claimed to reside in, and derive from, its natural particularity; but land is none the less a natural and universal *element,* whereas the mercantilist system regarded only precious metals as wealth. The object of wealth, its matter, has, therefore, been given the greatest universality within natural limits—inasmuch as it is also, as nature, directly objective wealth. And it is only by labour, by agriculture, that land exists for man. Consequently, the subjective essence of wealth is already transferred to labour. But at the same time agriculture is the *only productive labour.* Labour is, therefore, not yet taken in its universality and its abstract form; it is still bound to a particular *element of nature as its matter,* and is only recognized in a particular *mode of existence determined by nature.* Labour is still only a *determinate, particular* alienation of man, and its product is also conceived as a determinate part of wealth due more to nature than to labour itself. Land is still regarded here as something which exists naturally and independently of man, and not yet as capital, i.e. as a factor of labour. On the contrary, labour appears to be a factor of *nature.* But since the fetishism of the old external wealth, existing only as an object, has been reduced to a very simple natural element, and since its essence has been partially, and in a certain way, recognized in its subjective existence, the necessary advance has been made in recognizing the *universal nature* of wealth and in raising *labour* in its absolute form, i.e. in abstraction, to the *principle.* It is demonstrated against the Physiocrats that from the economic point of view (i.e. from the only valid point of view) agriculture does not differ from any other industry; and that it is not, therefore, a specific kind of labour, bound to a particular element, or a particular manifestation of labour, but *labour in general* which is the *essence* of wealth.

Physiocracy denies *specific,* external, purely objective wealth, in declaring that labour is its essence. For the Physiocrats, however, labour is in the first place only the *subjective essence* of landed property. (They begin from that kind of property which appears historically as the predominant recognized type.) They merely turn landed property into alienated man. They annul its feudal character by declaring that *industry* (agriculture) is its *essence;* but they reject the industrial world and accept the feudal system by declaring that *agriculture* is the only industry.

It is evident that when the *subjective essence*—industry in opposition to landed property, industry forming itself as industry—is grasped, this essence includes within itself the opposition. For just as industry incorporates the superseded landed property, its subjective essence incorporates the subjective essence of the latter.

Landed property is the first form of private property, and industry first appears historically in simple opposition to it, as a particular form of private property (or rather, as the liberated slave of landed property); this sequence is repeated in the scientific study of the *subjective* essence of private property, and labour appears at first only as *agricultural labour* but later establishes itself as *labour in general.*

[III] All wealth has become *industrial wealth,* the *wealth* of labour, and *industry* is realized labour; just as the *factory system* is the realized essence of *industry* (i.e. of labour), and as *industrial capital* is the realized objective form of private property. Thus we see that it is only at this stage that private property can consolidate its rule over man and become, in its most general form, a world-historical power.

PRIVATE PROPERTY AND COMMUNISM

ad page XXXIX. But the antithesis between *propertylessness* and *property* is still an indeterminate antithesis, which if not conceived in its *active reference* to its intrinsic relations, not yet conceived as a contradiction, so long as it is not understood as an antithesis between *labour* and *capital.* Even without the advanced development of private property, e.g. in ancient Rome, in Turkey, etc. this antithesis may be expressed in a primitive form. In this form it does not yet *appear* as established by private property itself. But labour, the subjective essence of private property as the exclusion of property, and capital, objective labour as the exclusion of labour, constitute *private property* as the developed relation of the contradiction and thus a dynamic relation which drives towards its resolution.

ad ibidem. The supersession of self-estrangement follows the same course as self-estrangement. *Private property* is first considered only from its objective aspect, but with labour conceived as its essence. Its mode of existence is, therefore, *capital* which it is necessary to abolish "as such" (Proudhon). Or else the *specific form* of labour (labour which is brought to a common level, subdivided, and thus unfree) is regarded as the source of the *nocivity* of private property and of its existence alienated from man. Fourier, in accord with the Physiocrats, regards *agricultural labour* as being at least the exemplary kind of labour. Saint-Simon asserts on the contrary that *industrial labour* as such is the essence of labour, and consequently he desires the *exclusive* rule of the industrialists and an amelioration of the condition of the workers. Finally, *communism* is the positive expression of the abolition of private property, and in the first place of universal private property. In taking this relation in its *universal aspect* communism is, in its first form, only the generalization and fulfillment of the relation. As such it appears in a double form; the domination of material property looms so large that it aims to destroy everything which is incapable of being possessed by everyone as private property. It wishes to eliminate talent, etc. by *force.* Immediate physical possession seems to it the unique goal of life and existence. The role of *worker* is not abolished, but is extended to all men. The relation of private property remains the relation of the community to the world of things. Finally, this tendency to oppose general private property to private property is expressed in an animal form; *marriage* (which is incontestably a form of *exclusive private property*) is contrasted with the community of women, in which women become communal and common property. One may say that this idea of the *community of women* is the *open secret* of this entirely crude and unreflective communism. Just as women are to pass from marriage to universal prostitution, so the whole world of wealth (i.e. the objective being of man) is to pass from the relation of exclusive marriage with the private owner to the relation of universal prostitution with the community. This communism, which negates the *personality* of man in every sphere, is only the logical expression of private property, which is this negation. Universal *envy* setting itself up as a power is only a camouflaged form of cupidity which re-establishes itself and satisfies itself in a different way. The thoughts of every individual private property are *at least* directed against any *wealthier* private property, in the form of envy and the desire to reduce everything to a common level; so that this envy and levelling in fact constitute the essence of competition. Crude communism is only the culmination of such envy and levelling-down on the basis of a *preconceived* minimum. How little this abolition of private property represents a genuine appropriation is shown by the abstract negation of the whole world of culture and civilization, and the regression to the *unnatural* [IV] simplicity of the poor and wantless individual who has not only not surpassed private property but has not yet even attained to it.

The community is only a community of work *and of* equality of wages *paid out by the communal capital, by the* community *as universal capitalist. The two sides of the relation are raised to a* supposed *universality;* labour *as a condition in which everyone is placed, and* capital *as the acknowledged universality and power of the community.*

In the relationship with *woman,* as the prey and the handmaid of communal lust, is expressed the infinite degradation in which man exists for himself; for the secret of this relationship finds its *unequivocal,* incontestable, *open* and revealed expression in the relation of man to woman and in the way in which the *direct* and *natural* species-relationship is conceived. The immediate, natural and necessary relation of human being to human being is also the *relation* of *man* to *woman.* In this *natural* species-relationship man's relation to nature is directly his relation to man, and his relation to man is directly his relation to nature, to his own *natural* function. Thus, in this relation is *sensuously revealed,* reduced to an observable *fact,* the extent to which human nature has become nature for man and to which nature has become human nature for him. From this relationship man's whole level of development can be assessed. It follows from the character of this relationship how far *man* has become, and has understood himself as, a *species-being,* a *human being.* The relation of man to woman is the *most natural* relation of human being to human being. It indicates, therefore, how far man's *natural* behaviour has become *human,* and how far his *human* essence has become a *natural* essence for him, how far his *human nature* has become *nature* for him. It also shows how far man's needs have become *human* needs, and consequently how far the other person, as a person, has become one of his needs, and to what extent he is in his individual existence at the same time a social being. The first positive annulment of private property, crude communism, is, therefore, only a *phenomenal form* of the infamy of private property representing itself as positive community.

2. Communism *(a)* still political in nature, democratic or despotic; *(b)* with the abolition of the state, yet still incomplete and influenced by private property, that is, by the alienation of man. In both forms communism is already aware of being the reintegration of man, his return to himself, the supersession of man's self-alienation. But since it has not yet grasped the positive nature of private property, or the *human* nature of needs, it is still captured and contaminated by private property. It has well understood the concept, but not the essence.

3. *Communism* is the *positive* abolition of *private property,* of *human self-alienation,* and thus the real *appropriation* of *human* nature through and for man. It is, therefore, the return of man himself as a *social,* i.e. really human, being, a complete and conscious return which assimilates all the wealth of previous development. Communism as a fully developed naturalism is humanism and as a fully developed humanism is naturalism. *It is the* definitive *resolution of the antagonism between man and nature, and between man and man.* It is the true solution of the conflict between existence and essence, between objectification and self-affirmation, between freedom and necessity, between individual and species. *It is the solution of the riddle of history and knows itself to be this solution.*

[V] Thus the whole historical development, both the *real* genesis of communism (the birth of its empirical existence) and its thinking consciousness, is its comprehended and conscious process of becoming; whereas the other, still undeveloped, communism seeks in certain historical forms opposed to private property a *historical* justification founded upon what already exists, and to this end tears out of their context isolated elements of this development (Cabet[1] and Villegardelle are pre-eminent among those who ride this hobby-horse) and asserts them as proofs of its historical pedigree. In doing so, it makes clear that by far the greater part of this development contradicts its own assertions, and that if it has ever existed its past existence refutes its pretension to *essential being.*

It is easy to understand the necessity which leads the whole revolutionary movement to find its empirical, as well its as theoretical, basis in the development of *private property,* and more precisely of the economic system.

This material, directly *perceptible* private property is the material and sensuous expression of *alienated human* life. Its movement—production and consumption—is the *sensuous* manifestation of the movement of all previous production, i.e. the realization or reality of man. Religion, the family, the state, law,, morality, science, art, etc. are only *particular* forms of production and come under its general law. The positive supersession of *private property,* as the appropriation of *human* life, is, therefore, the positive supersession of all alienation, and the return of man from religion, the family, the state, etc. to his *human,* i.e. social life. Religious alienation as such occurs only in the sphere of *consciousness,* in the inner life of man, but economic alienation is that of *real life* and its supersession, therefore, affects both aspects. Of course, the development in different nations has a different beginning according to whether the actual and *established* life of the people is more in the realm of mind or more in the external world, is a real or ideal life. Communism begins where atheism beings (Owen), but atheism is at the outset still far from being *communism;* indeed it is still for the most part an abstraction.[2]

Thus the philanthropy of atheism is at first only an abstract *philosophical* philanthropy, whereas that of communism is at once *real* and oriented towards *action.*

We have seen how, on the assumption that private property has been positively superseded, man produces man, himself and then other men; how the object which is the direct activity of his personality is at the same time his existence for other men and their existence for him. Similarly, the material of labour and man himself as a subject are the starting-point as well as the result of this movement (and because there must be this starting-point private property is a historical necessity). Therefore, the *social* character is the universal character of the whole movement; *as* society itself produces *man* as *man,* so it is *produced* by him. Activity and mind are social in their content as well as in their *origin;* they are *social* activity and social mind. The *human* significance of nature only exists for *social* man, because only in this case is nature a *bond* with other *men,* the basis of his existence for others and of their existence for him. Only then is nature the *basis* of his own *human* experience and a vital element of human reality. The *natural* existence of man has here become his *human* existence and nature itself has become human for him. Thus *society* is the accomplished union of man with nature, the veritable resurrection of nature, the realized naturalism of man and the realized humanism of nature.

[VI] Social activity and social mind by no means exist *only* in the form of activity or mind which is directly communal. Nevertheless, communal activity and mind, i.e. activity and mind which express and confirm themselves directly in a *real association* with other men, occur everywhere where this direct expression of sociability arises from the content of the activity or corresponds to the nature of mind.

---

[1] Etienne Cabet (1788–1856); author of *Voyage en Icarie* (1840) and founder of a Utopian Community, Icaria, in Illinois. [*Editor's note.*]

[2] Marx inserted a note here which referred back to his discussion of "crude communism": "Prostitution is only a *specific* expression of the *universal* prostitution of the worker, and since prostitution is a relationship which includes both the one who is prostituted and the one who prostitutes (and the latter is much more base), so the capitalist, etc. comes within this category." [*Editor's note.*]

Even when I carry out *scientific* work, etc., an activity which I can seldom conduct in direct association with other men, I perform a *social,* because *human,* act. It is not only the material of my activity—such as the language itself which the thinker uses—which is given to me as a social product. My *own existence* is a social activity. For this reason, what I myself produce I produce for society, and with the consciousness of acting as a social being.

My universal consciousness is only the *theoretical* form of that whose *living* form is the real community, the social entity, although at the present day this universal consciousness is an abstraction from real life and is opposed to it as an enemy. That is why the *activity* of my universal consciousness as such is my *theoretical* existence as a social being.

It is above all necessary to avoid postulating "society" once again as an abstraction confronting the individual. The individual *is* the *social being.* The manifestation of his life—even when it does not appear directly in the form of a communal manifestation, accomplished in association with other men—is, therefore, a manifestation and affirmation of *social life.* Individual human life and species-life are not different things, even though the mode of existence of individual life is necessarily either a more *specific* or a more *general* mode of species-life, or that of species-life a *specific* or more *general* mode of individual life.

In this *species-consciousness* man confirms his real *social life,* and reproduces his real existence in thought; while conversely, species-life confirms itself in species-consciousness and exists for itself in its universality as a thinking being. Though man is a unique individual—and it is just his particularity which makes him an individual, a really *individual* communal being—he is equally the *whole,* the ideal whole, the subjective existence of society as thought and experienced. He exists in reality as the representation and the real mind of social existence, and as the sum of human manifestations of life.

Thought and being are indeed *distinct* but they also form a unity. *Death* seems to be a harsh victory of the species over the individual and to contradict their unity; but the particular individual is only a *determinate species-being* and as such he is mortal.

4. Just as *private property* is only the sensuous expression of the fact that man is at the same time an *objective* fact for himself and becomes an alien and non-human object for himself; just as his manifestation of life is also his alienation of life and his self-realization a loss of reality, the emergence of an *alien* reality; so the positive supersession of private property, i.e. the *sensuous* appropriation of the human essence and of human life, of objective man and of human *creations,* by and for man, should not be taken only in the sense of *immediate,* exclusive *enjoyment,* or only in the sense of *possession* or *having.* Man appropriates his manifold being in an all-inclusive way, and thus as a whole man. All his *human* relations to the world—seeing, hearing, smelling, tasting, touching, thinking, observing, feeling, desiring, acting, loving—in short, all the organs of his individuality, like the organs which are directly communal in form, [VII] are in their objective action (their *action in relation to the object*) the appropriation of this object, the appropriation of human reality. The way in which they react to the object is the confirmation of *human reality.*[3] It is human effectiveness and human *suffering,* for suffering humanly considered is an enjoyment of the self for man.

Private property has made us so stupid and partial that an object is only *ours* when we have it, when it exists for us as capital or when it is directly eaten, drunk, worn, inhabited, etc., in short, *utilized* in some way. But private property itself only conceives these various forms of possession as *means of life,* and the life for which they serve as means is the *life* of *private property*—labour and creation of capital.

Thus *all* the physical and intellectual senses have been replaced by the simple alienation of *all* these senses; the sense of *having.* The human being had to be reduced to this absolute

---

[3] It is, therefore, just as varied as the determinations of human nature and activities are diverse.

poverty in order to be able to give birth to all his inner wealth. (On the category of *having* see Hess in *Einundzwanzig Bogen.*)[4]

The supersession of private property is, therefore, the complete *emancipation* of all the human qualities and senses. It is such an emancipation because these qualities and senses have become *human,* from the subjective as well as the objective point of view. The eye has become a *human* eye when its *object* has become a *human,* social object, created by man and destined for him. The senses have, therefore, become directly theoreticians in practice. They relate themselves to the thing for the sake of the thing, but the thing itself is an *objective human* relation to itself and to man, and vice versa.[5] Need and enjoyment have thus lost their *egoistic* character and nature has lost its mere *utility* by the fact that its utilization has become *human* utilization.

Similarly, the senses and minds of other men have become my *own* appropriation. Thus besides these direct organs, *social* organs are constituted, in the form of society; for example, activity in direct association with others has become an organ for the manifestation of life and a mode of appropriation of *human* life.

It is evident that the human eye appreciates things in a different way from the crude, non-human eye, the human *ear* differently from the crude ear. As we have seen, it is only when the object becomes a *human* object, or objective *humanity,* that man does not become lost in it. This is only possible when man himself becomes a *social* object; when he himself becomes a social being and society becomes a being for him in this object.

On the one hand, it is only when objective reality everywhere becomes for man in society the reality of human faculties, human reality, and thus the reality of his own faculties, that all *objects* become for him the *objectification of himself.* The objects then confirm and realize his individuality, they are *his own* objects, i.e. man himself becomes the object. The *manner in which these objects* become his own depends upon the *nature of the object* and the nature of the corresponding faculty; for it is precisely the *determinate character* of this relation which constitutes the specific *real* mode of affirmation. The object is not the same for the *eye* as for the *ear,* for the ear as for the eye. The *distinctive character* of each faculty is precisely its *characteristic* essence and thus also the characteristic mode of its objectification, of its *objectively real,* living *being.* It is therefore not only in thought, [VIII] but through *all* the senses that man is affirmed in the objective world.

Let us next consider the subjective aspect. Man's musical sense is only awakened by music. The most beautiful music has no meaning for the non-musical ear, is not an object for it, because my object can only be the confirmation of one of my own faculties. It can only be so for me in so far as my faculty exists for itself as a subjective capacity, because the meaning of an object for me extends only as far as the sense extends (only makes sense for an appropriate sense). For this reason, the *senses* of social man are *different* from those of non-social man. It is only through the objectively deployed wealth of the human being that the wealth of subjective *human* sensibility (a musical ear, an eye which is sensitive to the beauty of form, in short, senses which are capable of human satisfaction and which confirm themselves as human faculties) is cultivated or created. For it is not only the five senses, but also the so-called spiritual senses, the practical senses (desiring, loving, etc.), in brief, human sensibility and the human character of the senses, which can only come into being through the existence of *its* object, through humanized nature. The cultivation of the five senses is the work of all previous history. Sense which is subservient to crude needs has only a restricted meaning. For a starving man the human form of food does not exist, but only its abstract character as food. It could just as well exist in the most crude form, and it is impossible to say in what way this feeding-activity would differ from that of

---

[4] *Einundzwanzig Bogen aus der Schweiz,* op. cit., p. 329.

[5] In practice I can only relate myself in a human way to a thing when the thing is related in a human way to man.

animals. The needy man, burdened with cares, has no appreciation of the most beautiful spectacle. The dealer in minerals sees only their commercial value, not their beauty or their particular characteristics; he has no mineralogical sense. Thus, the objectification of the human essence, both theoretically and practically, is necessary in order to *humanize* man's senses, and also to create the *human senses* corresponding to all the wealth of human and natural being.

Just as society at its beginnings finds, through the development of *private property* with its wealth and poverty (both intellectual and material), the materials necessary for this *cultural development,* so the fully constituted society produces man in all the plenitude of his being, the wealthy man endowed with all the senses, as an enduring reality. It is only in a social context that subjectivism and objectivism, spiritualism and materialism, activity and passivity, cease to be antinomies and thus cease to exist as such antinomies. The resolution of the *theoretical* contradictions is possible *only* through practical means, only through the *practical* energy of man. Their resolution is not by any means, therefore, only a problem of knowledge, but is a *real* problem of life which philosophy was unable to solve precisely because it saw there a purely theoretical problem.

It can be seen that the history of *industry* and industry as it *objectively* exists is an *open* book of the *human faculties,* and a human *psychology* which can be sensuously apprehended. This history has not so far been conceived in relation to human *nature,* but only from a superficial utilitarian point of view, since in the condition of alienation it was only possible to conceive real human faculties and *human* species-action in the form of general human existence, as religion, or as history in its abstract, general aspect as politics, art and literature, etc. *Everyday material industry* (which can be conceived as part of that general development; or equally, the general development can be conceived as a specific part of industry since all human activity up to the present has been labour, i.e. industry, self-alienated activity) shows us, in the form of *sensuous useful objects,* in an alienated form, the *essential human faculties* transformed into objects. No psychology for which this book, i.e. the most tangible and accessible part of history, remains closed, can become a *real* science with a genuine content. What is to be though of a science which stays aloof from this enormous field of human labour, and which does not feel its own inadequacy even though this great wealth of human activity means nothing to it except perhaps what can be expressed in the single phrase—"need," "common need"?

The *natural sciences* have developed a tremendous activity and have assembled an ever-growing mass of data. But philosophy has remained alien to these sciences just as they have remained alien to philosophy. Their momentary *rapprochement* was only a *fantastic* illusion. There was a desire for union but the power to effect it was lacking. Historiography itself only takes natural science into account incidentally, regarding it as a factor making for enlightenment, for practical utility and for particular great discoveries. But natural science has penetrated all the more *practically* into human life through industry. It has transformed human life and prepared the emancipation of humanity, even though its immediate effect was to accentuate the dehumanization of man. *Industry* is the actual historical relationship of nature, and thus of natural science, to man. If industry is conceived as the *exoteric* manifestation of the essential human *faculties,* the *human* essence of nature and the *natural* essence of man can also be understood. Natural science will then abandon its abstract materialist, or rather idealist, orientation, and will become the basis of a *human* science, just as it has already become—though in an alienated form—the basis of actual human life. One basis for life and another for science is *a priori* a falsehood. Nature, as it develops in human history, in the act of genesis of human society, is the *actual* nature of man; thus nature, as it develops through industry, though in an *alienated* form, is truly *anthropological* nature.

Sense experience (*see* Feuerbach) must be the basis of all science. Science is only genuine science when it proceeds from sense experience, in the two forms of *sense perception* and *sensuous* need; i.e. only when it proceeds from nature. The whole of history is a preparation for "man" to become an object of *sense* perception, and for the development of human needs (the needs of man as such). History itself is a *real* part of *natural history,* of the development of nature into man. Natural science will one day incorporate the science of man, just as the science of man will incorporate natural science; there will be a *single* science.

Man is the direct object of natural science, because directly *perceptible nature* is for man directly human sense experience (an identical expression) in the form of the *other person* who is directly presented to him in a sensuous way. His own sense experience only exists as human sense experience for himself through the *other person*. But *nature* is the direct object of the *science of man*. The first object for man—man himself—is nature, sense experience; and the particular sensuous human faculties, which can only find objective realization in *natural* objects, can only attain self-knowledge in the science of natural being. The element of thought itself, the element of the living manifestation of thought, language, is sensuous in character. The *social* reality of nature and *human* natural science, or the *natural science of man,* are identical expressions.

It will be seen from this how, in place of the *wealth* and *poverty* of political economy, we have the *wealthy* man and the plentitude of *human* need. The wealthy man is at the same time one who *needs* a complex of human manifestations of life, and whose own self-realization exists as an inner necessity, a *need*. Not only the wealth but also the *poverty* of man acquires, in a socialist perspective, a *human* and thus a social meaning. Poverty is the passive bond which leads man to experience a need for the greatest wealth, the *other* person. The sway of the objective entity within me, the sensuous eruption of my life-activity, is the passion which here becomes the *activity* of my being.

A being does not regard himself as independent unless he is his own master, and he is only his own master when he owes his existence to himself. A man who lives by the favour of another considers himself a dependent being. But I live completely by another person's favour when I owe to him not only the continuance of my life but also *its creation;* when he is its *source.* My life has necessarily such a cause outside itself if it is not my own creation. The idea of *creation* is thus one which it is difficult to eliminate from popular consciousness. This consciousness is *unable to conceive* that nature and man exist on their own account, because such an existence contradicts all the tangible facts of practical life.

The idea of the creation of the *earth* has received a severe blow from the science of geogeny, i.e. from the science which portrays the formation and development of the earth as a process of spontaneous generation. *Generatio aequivoca* (spontaneous generation) is the only practical refutation of the theory of creation.

But it is easy indeed to say to the particular individual what Aristotle said: You are engendered by your father and mother, and consequently it is the coitus of two human beings, a human species-act, which has produced the human being. You see, therefore, that even in a physical sense man owes his existence to man. Consequently, it is not enough to keep in view only one of the two aspects, the *infinite* progression, and to ask further: who engendered my father and my grandfather? You must also keep in mind the *circular movement* which is perceptible in that progression, according to which man, in the act of generation reproduces himself; thus *man* always remains the subject. But you will reply: I grant you this circular movement, but you must in turn concede the progression, which leads ever further to the point where I ask: who created the first man and nature as a whole? I can only reply: your question is itself a product of abstraction. Ask yourself how you arrive at that question. Ask yourself whether your question does not arise from a point of view to which I cannot reply because it is a perverted one. Ask yourself whether that progression exists as such for rational thought. If you ask a question about the creation of nature and man you abstract from nature and man. You suppose them *non-existent* and you want me to demonstrate that they *exist*. I reply: give up your abstraction and at the same time you abandon your question. Or else, if you want to maintain your abstraction, be consistent, and if you think of man and nature as non-existent, [XI] think of yourself too as non-existent, for you are also man and nature. Do not think, do not ask me any questions, for as soon as you think and ask questions your abstraction from the existence of nature and man becomes meaningless. Or are you such an egoist that you conceive everything as non-existent and yet want to exist yourself?

You may reply: I do not want to conceive the nothingness of nature, etc.; I only ask you about the act of its creation, just as I ask the anatomist about the formation of bones, etc.

Since, however, for socialist man, the *whole of what is called world history* is nothing but the creation of man by human labour, and the emergence of nature for man, he, therefore, has the evident and irrefutable proof of his *self-creation,* of his own *origins.* Once the essence of man and of nature, man as a natural being and nature as a human reality, has become evident in practical life, in sense experience, the quest for an *alien* being, a being above man and nature (a quest which is an avowal of the unreality of man and nature) becomes impossible in practice. *Atheism,* as a denial of this unreality, is no longer meaningful, for atheism is a *negation of God* and seeks to assert by this negation the *existence of man.* Socialism no longer requires such a roundabout method; it beings from the *theoretical* and *practical sense perception* of man and nature as essential begins. It is positive human *self-consciousness,* no longer a self-consciousness attained through the negation of religion; just as the *real life* of man is positive and no longer attained through the negation of private property, through *communism.* Communism is the phase of negation of the negation and is, consequently, for the next stage of historical development, a real and necessary factor in the emancipation and rehabilitation of man. Communism is the necessary form and the dynamic principle of the immediate future, but communism is not itself the goal of human development—the form of human society.

■■■■■■■■■■■■■■■ ■ ■■■■■■■■■■■■■■■■■■■■

READING 14: V. I. LENIN

In 1902, at a time when the rapid industrialization of Russia was leading to rapid urbanization, urban strife, increased crime, a growing and visible gap between the rich and poor, and all of the unchecked excesses of industrialism, V. I. Lenin wrote an essay entitled "What Is to Be Done?" Given these historical circumstances, it is clear to see how even the title of Lenin's essay had some appeal to the masses. Lenin thus became a leader of the Bolshevik cause and later the leader of the Bolshevik Revolution (1917). He managed to convince his Russian comrades that communism was the more appropriate, more morally acceptable, developmental path. While capitalist states were struggling through their stage in history, communist states would already be taking the lead. In order to ensure the success of this process, Lenin established what he termed the "Vanguard of the Proletariat" (i.e., a class of government bureaucrats who would act as "Philosopher Kings")—to use Plato's term—that would make more equitable decisions for all of society.

Across the northern hemisphere, where industrialization was rapidly taking hold, one of the primary concerns was how to address the phenomenon of monopoly.[171] Lenin tied the stranglehold of monopolies on domestic state economies to imperialist practices. Having saturated domestic markets, and now eager for new markets, the capitalist had simply—in Lenin's view—"gone international." Lenin argued that Marx's prediction of revolution in a capitalist society was still valid; the revolution was simply being postponed by the capitalists' practices of imperialism—hence the title, Imperialism: the highest (i.e., *last*) stage of capitalism.

---

[171] In the United States, this was an issue for Theodore Roosevelt—hence his reputation as a "Trust Buster"—and for all the progressive leaders, including Woodrow Wilson, whose New Freedom policies aimed at supporting the development of small businesses, in the name of improved competition. Of course, let us not forget that the immensely popular board game, *Monopoly*® was created in 1935.

V. I. Lenin,

Imperialism: The Highest Stage of Capitalism, 1916

Imperialism as a Special Stage of Capitalism

We must now try to sum up and put together what has been said above on the subject of imperialism. Imperialism emerged as the development and direct continuation of the fundamental attributes of capitalism in general. But capitalism only became capitalist imperialism at a definite and very high stage of its development, when certain of its fundamental attributes began to be transformed into their opposites, when the features of a period of transition from capitalism to a higher social and economic system began to take shape and reveal themselves all along the line. Economically, the main thing in this process is the substitution of capitalist monopolies for capitalist free competition. Free competition is the fundamental attribute of capitalism, and of commodity production generally. Monopoly is exactly the opposite of free competition; but we have seen the latter being transformed into monopoly before our very eyes, creating large-scale industry and eliminating small industry, replacing large-scale industry by still larger-scale industry, finally leading to such a concentration of production and capital that monopoly has been and is the result: cartels, syndicates and trusts, and merging with them, the capital of a dozen or so banks manipulating thousands of millions. At the same time monopoly, which has grown out of free competition, does not abolish the latter, but exists over it and alongside of it, and thereby gives rise to a number of very acute, intense antagonisms, friction and conflicts. Monopoly is the transition from capitalism to a higher system.

If it were necessary to give the briefest possible definition of imperialism we should have to say that imperialism is the monopoly stage of capitalism. Such a definition would include what is most important, for, on the one hand, finance capital is the bank capital of a few big monopolist banks, merged with the capital of the monopolist combines of manufacturers; and, on the other hand, the division of the world is the transition from a colonial policy which has extended without hindrance to territories unoccupied by any capitalist power, to a colonial policy of monopolistic possession of the territory of the world which has been completely divided up.

But very brief definitions, although convenient, for they sum up the main points, are nevertheless inadequate, because very important features of the phenomenon that has to be defined have to be especially deduced. And so, without forgetting the conditional and relative value of all definitions, which can never include all the concatenations of a phenomenon in its complete development, we must give a definition of imperialism that will embrace the following five essential features:

1. The concentration of production and capital developed to such a high stage that it created monopolies which play a decisive role in economic life.
2. The merging of bank capital with industrial capital, and the creation, on the basis of this "finance capital," of a "financial oligarchy."
3. The export of capital, which has become extremely important, as distinguished from the export of commodities.
4. The formation of international capitalist monopolies which share the world among themselves.
5. The territorial division of the whole world among the greatest capitalist powers is completed.

Imperialism is capitalism in that stage of development in which the dominance of monopolies and finance capital has established itself; in which the export of capital has acquired pronounced importance; in which the division of the world among the international trusts has begun; in which the division of all territories of the globe among the great capitalist powers has been completed.

We shall see later that imperialism can and must be defined differently if consideration is to be given, not only to the basic, purely economic factors—to which the above definition is limited—but also to the historical place of this stage of capitalism in relation to capitalism in general, or to the relations between imperialism and the two main trends in the working class movement. The point to be noted just now is that imperialism, as interpreted above, undoubtedly represents a special stage in the development of capitalism. In order to enable the reader to obtain as well grounded an idea of imperialism as possible, we deliberately quoted largely from *bourgeois* economists who are obliged to admit the particularly incontrovertible facts regarding modern capitalist economy. With the same object in view, we have produced detailed statistics which reveal the extent to which bank capital, etc., has developed, showing how the transformation of quantity into quality, of developed capitalism into imperialism, has expressed itself. Needless to say, all boundaries in nature and in society are conditional and changeable, and, consequently, it would be absurd to discuss the exact year or the decade in which imperialism "definitely" became established.

In this matter of defining imperialism, however, we have to enter into controversy, primarily, with K. Kautsky, the principal Marxian theoretician of the epoch of the so-called Second International—that is, of the twenty-five years between 1889 and 1914.

Kautsky, in 1915 and even in November 1914, very emphatically attacked the fundamental ideas expressed in our definition of imperialism. Kautsky said that imperialism must not be regarded as a "phase" or stage of economy, but as a policy; a definite policy "preferred" by finance capital; that imperialism cannot be "identified" with "contemporary capitalism"; that if imperialism is to be understood to mean "all the phenomena of contemporary capitalism"—cartels, protection, the domination of the financiers and colonial policy—then the question as to whether imperialism is necessary to capitalism becomes reduced to the "flattest tautology"; because, in that case, "imperialism is naturally a vital necessity for capitalism," and so on. The best way to present Kautsky's ideas is to quote his own definition of imperialism, which is diametrically opposed to the substance of the ideas which we have set forth (for the objections coming from the camp of the German Marxists, who have been advocating such ideas for many years already, have been long known to Kautsky as the objections of a definite trend in Marxism).

Kautsky's definition is as follows:

> "Imperialism is a product of highly developed industrial capitalism. It consists in the striving of every industrial capitalist nation to bring under its control and to annex increasingly big *agrarian*" (Kautsky's italics) "regions irrespective of what nations inhabit those regions."[1]

This definition is utterly worthless because it one-sidedly, *i.e.*, arbitrarily, brings out the national question alone (although this is extremely important in itself as well as in its relation to imperialism), it arbitrarily and *inaccurately* relates this question *only* to industrial capital in the countries which annex other nations, and in an equally arbitrary and inaccurate manner brings out the annexation of agrarian regions.

Imperialism is a striving for annexations—this is what the *political* part of Kautsky's definition amounts to. It is correct, but very incomplete, for politically, imperialism is, in general, a striving towards violence and reaction. For the moment, however, we are interested in the *economic* aspect of the question, which Kautsky *himself* introduced into *his* definition. The inac-

---

[1] *Die Neue Zeit,* 32nd year (1913–14), II, p. 909; *cf.* also 34th year (1915–16), II, p. 107 *et seq.*

curacy of Kautsky's definition is strikingly obvious. The characteristic feature of imperialism is *not* industrial capital, *but* finance capital. It is not an accident that in France it was precisely the extraordinarily rapid development of *finance* capital, and the weakening of industrial capital, that, from 1880 onwards, gave rise to the extreme extension of annexationist (colonial) policy. The characteristic feature of imperialism is precisely that it strives to annex *not only* agricultural regions, but even highly industrialised regions (German appetite for Belgium; French appetite for Lorraine), because 1) the fact that the world is already divided up obliges those contemplating a *new* division to reach out for *any kind* of territory, and 2) because an essential feature of imperialism is the rivalry between a number of great powers in the striving for hegemony, *i.e.,* for the conquest of territory, not so much directly for themselves as to weaken the adversary and undermine *his* hegemony. (Belgium is chiefly necessary to Germany as a base for operations against England; England needs Bagdad as a base for operations against Germany, etc.)

Kautsky refers especially—and repeatedly—to English writers who, he alleges, have given a purely political meaning to the word "imperialism" in the sense that Kautsky understands it. We take up the work by the Englishman Hobson, *Imperialism,* which appeared in 1902, and therein we read:

> "The new imperialism differs from the older, first, in substituting for the ambition of a single growing empire the theory and the practice of competing empires, each motivated by similar lusts of political aggrandisement and commercial gain; secondly, in the dominance of financial or investing over mercantile interests."[2]

We see, therefore, that Kautsky is absolutely wrong in referring to English writers generally (unless he meant the vulgar English imperialist writers, or the avowed apologists for imperialism). We see that Kautsky, while claiming that he continues to defend Marxism, as a matter of fact takes a step backward compared with the *social-liberal* Hobson, who *more correctly* takes into account two "historically concrete" (Kautsky's definition is a mockery of historical concreteness) features of modern imperialism: 1) the competition between *several* imperialisms, and 2) the predominance of the financier over the merchant. If it were chiefly a question of the annexation of agrarian countries by industrial countries, the role of the merchant would be predominant.

Kautsky's definition is not only wrong and un-Marxian. It serves as a basis for a whole system of views which run counter to Marxian theory and Marxian practice all along the line. We shall refer to this again later. The argument about words which Kautsky raises as to whether the modern stage of capitalism should be called "imperialism" or "the stage of finance capital" is of no importance. Call it what you will, it matters little. The fact of the matter is that Kautsky detaches the politics of imperialism from its economics, speaks of annexations as being a policy "preferred" by finance capital, and opposes to it another bourgeois policy which, he alleges, is possible on this very basis of finance capital. According to his argument, monopolies in economics are compatible with non-monopolistic, non-violent, non-annexationist methods in politics. According to his argument, the territorial division of the world, which was completed precisely during the period of finance capital, and which constitutes the basis of the present peculiar forms of rivalry between the biggest capitalist states, is compatible with a non-imperialist policy. The result is a slurring-over and a blunting of the most profound contradictions of the latest stage of capitalism, instead of an exposure of their depth; the result is bourgeois reformism instead of Marxism.

---

[2] J. A. Hobson, *Imperialism—a Study,* London, 1902, p. 324.

Kautsky enters into controversy with the German apologist of imperialism and annexations, Cunow, who clumsily and cynically argues that: imperialism is modern capitalism, the development of capitalism is inevitable and progressive; therefore imperialism is progressive; therefore, we should cringe before and eulogise it. This is something like the caricature of Russian Marxism which the Narodniki drew in 1894–95. They used to argue as follows: if the Marxists believe that capitalism is inevitable in Russia, that it is progressive, then they ought to open a public-house and begin to implant capitalism! Kautsky's reply to Cunow is as follows: imperialism is not modern capitalism. It is only one of the forms of the policy of modern capitalism. This policy we can and should fight; we can and should fight against imperialism, annexations, etc.

The reply seems quite plausible, but in effect it is a more subtle and more disguised (and therefore more dangerous) propaganda of conciliation with imperialism; for unless it strikes at the economic basis of the trusts and banks, the "struggle" against the policy of the trusts and banks reduces itself to bourgeois reformism and pacifism, to an innocent and benevolent expression of pious hopes. Kautsky's theory means refraining from mentioning existing contradictions, forgetting the most important of them, instead of revealing them in their full depth; it is a theory that has nothing in common with Marxism. Naturally, such a "theory" can only serve the purpose of advocating unity with the Cunows.

Kautsky writes: "from the purely economic point of view it is not impossible that capitalism will yet go through a new phase, that of the extension of the policy of the cartels to foreign policy, the phase of ultra-imperialism,"[3] *i.e.,* of a super-imperialism, a union of world imperialisms and not struggles among imperialisms; a phase when wars shall cease under capitalism, a phase of "the joint exploitation of the world by internationally combined finance capital."[4]

We shall have to deal with this "theory of ultra-imperialism" later on in order to show in detail how definitely and utterly it departs from Marxism. In keeping with the plan of the present work, we shall examine the exact economic data on this question. Is "ultra-imperialism" possible "from the purely economic point of view" or is it ultra-nonsense?

If, by purely economic point of view a "pure" abstraction is meant, then all that can be said reduces itself to the following proposition: evolution in proceeding towards monopoly; therefore the trend is towards a single world monopoly, to a universal trust. This is indisputable, but it is also as completely meaningless as is the statement that "evolution is proceeding" towards the manufacture of foodstuffs in laboratories. In this sense the "theory" of ultra-imperialism is no less absurd than a "theory of ultra-agriculture" would be.

If, on the other hand, we are discussing the "purely economic" conditions of the epoch of finance capital as an historically concrete epoch which opened at the beginning of the twentieth century, then the best reply that one can make to the lifeless abstractions of "ultra-imperialism" (which serve an exclusively reactionary aim: that of diverting attention from the depth of *existing* antagonisms) is to contrast them with the concrete economic realities of present-day world economy. Kautsky's utterly meaningless talk about ultra-imperialism encourages, among other things, that profoundly mistaken idea which only brings grist to the mill of the apologists of imperialism, *viz.,* that the rule of finance capital *lessens* the unevenness and contradictions inherent in world economy, whereas in reality it *increases* them.

R. Calwer, in his little book, *An Introduction to World Economics*,[5] attempted to compile the main, purely economic, data required to understand in a concrete way the internal relations of

---

[3] *Die Neue Zeit*, 32nd year (1913–14), II, Sept. 11, 1914, p. 909; *cf.* also 34th year (1915–16), II, p. 107 *et seq.*

[4] *Die Neue Zeit*, 33rd year, II (April 30, 1915), p. 144.

[5] R. Calwer, *Einführung in die Weltwirtschaft*, Berlin, 1906.

world economy at the end of the nineteenth and beginning of the twentieth centuries. He divides the world into five "main economic areas," as follows: 1) Central Europe (the whole of Europe with the exception of Russia and Great Britain); 2) Great Britain; 3) Russia; 4) Eastern Asia; 5) America; he includes the colonies in the "areas" of the state to which they belong and "leaves out" a few countries not distributed according to areas, such as Persia, Afghanistan and Arabia in Asia; Morocco and Abyssinia in Africa, etc.

Here is a brief summary of the economic data he quotes on these regions:

Principal Economic Areas	Area	Pop.	Transport		Trade	Industry		
	Million Sq. Km.	Millions	Railways (Thous. Km.)	Mercantile Fleet (Million Tons)	Imports and Exports (Billion Marks)	Output of Coal (Million Tons)	Output of Pig Iron (Million Tons)	No. of Cotton Spindles (Million)
1) Central European	27.6 (23.6)[6]	388 (146)	204	8	41	251	15	26
2) British	28.9 (28.6)[6]	398 (355)	140	11	25	249	9	51
3) Russian	22	131	63	1	3	16	3	7
4) East Asian	12	389	8	1	2	8	0.02	2
5) American	30	148	379	6	14	245	14	19

[6] The figures in parentheses show the area and population of the colonies.

We notice three areas of highly developed capitalism with a high development of means of transport, of trade and of industry, the Central European, the British and the American areas. Among these are three states which dominate the world: Germany, Great Britain, the United States. Imperialist rivalry and the struggle between these countries have become very keen because Germany has only a restricted area and few colonies (the creation of "Central Europe" is still a matter for the future; it is being born in the midst of desperate struggles). For the moment the distinctive feature of Europe is political disintegration. In the British and American areas, on the other hand, political concentration is very highly developed, but there is a tremendous disparity between the immense colonies of the one and the insignificant colonies of the other. In the colonies, capitalism is only beginning to develop. The struggle for South America is becoming more and more acute.

There are two areas where capitalism is not strongly developed: Russia and Eastern Asia. In the former, the density of population is very low, in the latter it is very high; in the former political concentration is very high, in the latter is does not exist. The partition of China is only beginning, and the struggle between Japan, U.S.A., etc., in connection therewith is continually gaining in intensity.

Compare this reality, the vast diversity of economic and political conditions, the extreme disparity in the rate of development of the various countries, etc., and the violent struggles of the imperialist states, with Kautsky's silly little fable about "peaceful" ultra-imperialism. Is this not the reactionary attempt of a frightened philistine to hide from stern reality? Are not the international cartels which Kautsky imagines are the embryos of "ultra-imperialism" (with as much reason as one would have for describing the manufacture of tabloids in a laboratory as ultra-agriculture in embryo) an example of the division and the *redivision* of the world, the transition from peaceful division to non-peaceful division and *vice versa?* Is not American and other finance capital, which divided the whole world peacefully, with Germany's participation, for example, in the international rail syndicate, or in the international mercantile shipping trust, now engaged in *redividing* the world on the basis of a new relation of forces, which has been changed by methods *by no means* peaceful?

Finance capital and the trusts are increasing instead of diminishing the differences in the rate of development of the various parts of world economy. When the relation of forces is changed, how else, *under capitalism,* can the resolution of contradictions be found, except by resorting to *violence?* Railway statistics[7] provide remarkably exact data on the different rates of development of capitalism and finance capital in world economy. In the last decades of imperialist development, the total length of railways has changed as follows:

Railways *(Thousand Kilometres)*			
	1890	*1913*	*Increase*
Europe	224	346	122
U.S.A.	268	411	143
Colonies (total)	82 ⎫	210 ⎫	128 ⎫
Independent and semi-dependent states of Asia and America	43 ⎬ 125	137 ⎬ 347	94 ⎬ 222
Total	617	1,104	

Thus, the development of railways has been more rapid in the colonies and in the independent (and semi-dependent) states of Asia and America. Here, as we know, the finance capital of the four or five biggest capitalist states reigns undisputed. Two hundred thousand kilometers of new railways in the colonies and in the other countries of Asia and America represent more than 40,000,000,000 marks in capital, newly invested on particularly advantageous terms, with special guarantees of a good return and with profitable orders for steel works, etc., etc.

Capitalism is growing with the greatest rapidity in the colonies and in overseas countries. Among the latter, *new* imperialist powers are emerging (*e.g.,* Japan). The struggle of world imperialism is becoming more acute. The tribute levied by finance capital on the most profitable colonial and overseas enterprises is increasing. In sharing out this "booty," an exceptionally large part goes to countries which, as far as the development of productive forces is concerned, do not always stand on the top of the list. In the case of the biggest countries, considered with their colonies, the total length of railways was as follows (in thousands of kilometres):

---

[7] *Statistisches Jahrbuch für das Deutsche Reich (Statistical Yearbook for the German Empire),* 1915, Appendix pp. 46, 47, *Archiv für Eisenbahnwesen (Railroad Archive),* 1892. Minor detailed figures for the distribution of railways among the colonies of the various countries in 1890 had to be estimated approximately.

	1890	1913	Increase
U.S.A	268	413	145
British Empire	107	208	101
Russia	32	78	46
Germany	43	68	25
France	41	63	22
Total	491	830	339

Thus, about 80 per cent of the total existing railways are concentrated in the hands of the five Great Powers. But the concentration of the *ownership* of these railways, of finance capital, is much greater still: French and English millionaires, for example, own an enormous amount of stocks and bonds in American, Russian and other railways.

Thanks to her colonies, Great Britain has increased the length of "her" railways by 100,000 kilometres, four times as much as Germany. And yet, it is well known that the development of productive forces in Germany, and especially the development of the coal and iron industries, has been much more rapid during this period than in England—not to mention France and Russia. In 1892, Germany produced 4,900,000 tons of pig iron and Great Britain produced 6,800,000 tons; in 1912, Germany produced 17,600,000 tons and Great Britain 9,000,000 tons. Germany, therefore, had an overwhelming superiority over England in this respect.[8] We ask, is there *under capitalism* any means of removing the disparity between the development of productive forces and the accumulation of capital on the one side, and the division of colonies and "spheres of influence" for finance capital on the other side—other than by resorting to war?

---

[8] *Cf.* also Edgar Crummond, "The Economic Relation of the British and German Empires," in *Journal of the Royal Statistical Society,* July 1914, p. 777, *et seq.*

READING 15: THEOTONIO DOS SANTOS

Theotonio Dos Santos is one of the best known of the *dependencistas* from Latin America, a group of dependency theorists who built on the ideas of Argentinian Raul Prebisch, mentioned at the start of this chapter. What is perhaps most remarkable about these Latin American views, that clearly still persist, is that many Latin American leaders—notably Brazil's former president, Henrique Cardoso—abandoned them in favor of structural reform policies. This issue is addressed in further detail in Reading 24. Following is the argument, as it stood in 1970.

---

* This work expands on certain preliminary work done in a research project on the relations of dependence in Latin America, directed by the author at the Center for Socio-Economic Studies of the Faculty of Economic Science of the University of Chile. In order to abridge the discussion of various aspects, the author was obliged to cite certain of his earlier works. The author expresses his gratitude to the researcher Orlando Caputo and Roberto Pizarro for some of the data utilized and to Sergio Ramos for his critical comments on the paper.

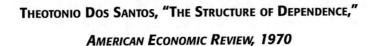

THEOTONIO DOS SANTOS, "THE STRUCTURE OF DEPENDENCE,"

AMERICAN ECONOMIC REVIEW, 1970

This paper attempts to demonstrate that the dependence of Latin American countries on other countries cannot be overcome without a qualitative change in their internal structures and external relations. We shall attempt to show that the relations of dependence to which these countries are subjected conform to a type of international and internal structure which leads them to underdevelopment or more precisely to a dependent structure that deepens and aggravates the fundamental problems of their peoples.

I. *What is Dependence?*

By dependence we mean a situation in which the economy of certain countries is conditioned by the development and expansion of another economy to which the former is subjected. The relation of interdependence between two or more economies, and between these and world trade, assumes the form of dependence when some countries (the dominant ones) can expand and can be self-sustaining, while other countries (the dependent ones) can do this only as a reflection of that expansion, which can have either a positive or a negative effect on their immediate development [7, p. 6].

The concept of dependence permits us to see the internal situation of these countries as part of world economy. In the Marxian tradition; the theory of imperialism has been developed as a study of the process of expansion of the imperialist centers and of their world domination. In the epoch of the revolutionary movement of the Third World, we have to develop the theory of laws of internal development in those countries that are the object of such expansion and are governed by them. This theoretical step transcends the theory of development which seeks to explain the situation of the underdeveloped countries as a product of their slowness or failure to adopt the patterns of efficiency characteristic of developed countries (or to "modernize" or "develop" themselves). Although capitalist development theory admits the existence of an "external" dependence, it is unable to perceive underdevelopment in the way our present theory perceives it, as a consequence and part of the process of the world expansion of capitalism—a part that is necessary to and integrally linked with it.

In analyzing the process of constituting a world economy that integrates the so-called "national economies" in a world market of commodities, capital, and even of labor power, we see that the relations produced by this market are unequal and combined—unequal because development of parts of the system occurs at the expense of other parts. Trade relations are based on monopolistic control of the market, which leads to the transfer of surplus generated in the dependent countries to the dominant countries; financial relations are, from the viewpoint of the dominant powers, based on loans and the export of capital, which permit them to receive interest and profits; thus increasing their domestic surplus and strengthening their control over the economies of the other countries. For the dependent countries these relations represent an export of profits and interest which carries off part of the surplus generated domestically and leads to a loss of control over their productive resources. In order to permit these disadvantageous relations, the dependent countries must generate large surpluses, not in such a way as to create higher levels of technology but rather superexploited manpower. The result is to limit the development of their internal market and their technical and cultural capacity, as well as the moral and physical health of their people. We call this combined development because it is the combination of these inequalities and the transfer of resources from the most backward and dependent sectors to the most advanced and dominant ones which explains the inequality, deepens it, and transforms it into a necessary and structural element of the world economy.

II. HISTORIC FORMS OF DEPENDENCE

Historic forms of dependence are conditioned by:

1. the basic forms of this world economy which has its own laws of development;
2. the type of economic relations dominant in the capitalist centers and the ways in which the latter expand outward; and
3. the types of economic relations existing inside the peripheral countries which are incorporated into the situation of dependence within the network of international economic relations generated by capitalist expansion.

It is not within the purview of this paper to study these forms in detail but only to distinguish broad characteristics of development.

Drawing on an earlier study, we may distinguish:

1. Colonial dependence, trade export in nature, in which commercial and financial capital in alliance with the colonialist state dominated the economic relations of the Europeans and the colonies, by means of a trade monopoly complemented by a colonial monopoly of land, mines, and manpower (serf or slave) in the colonized countries.
2. Financial-industrial dependence which consolidated itself at the end of the nineteenth century, characterized by the domination of big capital in the hegemonic centers, and its expansion abroad through investment in the production of raw materials and agricultural products for consumption in the hegemonic centers. A productive structure grew up in the dependent countries devoted to the export of these products (which Levin labeled export economies [11]; other analysis in other regions [12] [13]), producing what ECLA has called "foreign-oriented development" *(desarrollo hacia afuera)* [4].
3. In the postwar period a new type of dependence has been consolidated, based on multinational corporations which began to invest in industries geared to the internal market of underdeveloped countries. This form of dependence is basically technological-industrial dependence [6].

Each of these forms of dependence corresponds to a situation which conditioned not only the international relations of these countries but also their internal structures: the orientation of production, the forms of capital accumulation, the reproduction of the economy, and, simultaneously, their social and political structure.

III. THE EXPORT ECONOMIES

In forms (1) and (2) of dependence, production is geared to those products destined for export (gold, silver, and tropical products in the colonial epoch; raw materials and agricultural products in the epoch of industrial-financial dependence); i.e., production is determined by demand from the hegemonic centers. The internal productive structure is characterized by rigid specialization and monoculture in entire regions (the Caribbean, the Brazilian Northeast, etc.). Alongside these export sectors there grew up certain complementary economic activities (cattle-raising and some manufacturing, for example) which were dependent, in general, on the export sector to which they sell their products. There was a third, subsistence economy which provided manpower for the export sector under favorable conditions and toward which excess population shifted during periods unfavorable to international trade.

Under these conditions, the existing internal market was restricted by four factors:

1. Most of the national income was derived from export, which was used to purchase the inputs required by export production (slaves, for example) or luxury goods consumed by the hacienda- and mine-owners, and by the more prosperous employees.
2. The available manpower was subject to very arduous forms of superexploitation, which limited its consumption.
3. Part of the consumption of these workers was provided by the subsistence economy, which served as a complement to their income and as a refuge during periods of depression.
4. A fourth factor was to be found in those countries in which land and mines were in the hands of foreigners (cases of an enclave economy): a great part of the accumulated surplus was destined to be sent abroad in the form of profits, limiting not only internal consumption but also possibilities of reinvestment [1].

In the case of enclave economies the relations of the foreign companies with the hegemonic center were even more exploitative and were complemented by the fact that purchases by the enclave were made directly abroad.

IV. THE NEW DEPENDENCE

The new form of dependence, (3) above, is in process of developing and is conditioned by the exigencies of the international commodity and capital markets. The possibility of generating new investments depends on the existence of financial resources in foreign currency for the purchase of machinery and processed raw materials not produced domestically. Such purchases are subject to two limitations: the limit of resources generated by the export sector (reflected in the balance of payments, which includes not only trade but also service relations); and the limitations of monopoly on patents which leads monopolistic firms to prefer to transfer their machines in the form of capital rather than as commodities for sale. It is necessary to analyze these relations of dependence if we are to understand the fundamental structural limits they place on the development of these economies.

1. Industrial development is dependent on an export sector for the foreign currency to buy the inputs utilized by the industrial sector. The first consequence of this dependence is the need to preserve the traditional export sector, which limits economically the development of the internal market by the conservation of backward relations of production and signifies, politically, the maintenance of power by traditional decadent oligarchies. In the countries where these sectors are controlled by foreign capital, it signifies the remittance abroad of high profits, and political dependence on those interests. Only in rare instances does foreign capital not control at least the marketing of these products. In response to these limitations, dependent countries in the 1930's and 1940's developed a policy of exchange restrictions and taxes on the national and foreign export sector; today they tend toward the gradual nationalization of production and toward the imposition of certain timid limitations on foreign control of the marketing of exported products. Furthermore, they seek, still somewhat timidly, to obtain better terms for the sale of their products. In recent decades, they have created mechanisms for international price agreements, and today UNCTAD and ECLA press to obtain more favorable tariff conditions for these products on the part of the hegemonic centers. It is important to point out that the industrial development of these countries is dependent on the situation of the export sector, the continued existence of which they are obliged to accept.

2. Industrial development is, then, strongly conditioned by fluctuations in the balance of payments. This leads toward deficit due to the relations of dependence themselves. The causes of the deficit are three:

a) Trade relations take place in a highly monopolized international market, which tends to lower the price of raw materials and to raise the prices of industrial products, particularly inputs.

In the second place, there is a tendency in modern technology to replace various primary products with synthetic raw materials. Consequently the balance of trade in these countries tends to be less favorable (even though they show a general surplus). The overall Latin American balance of trade from 1946 to 1968 shows a surplus for each of those years. The same thing happens in almost every underdeveloped country. However, the losses due to deterioration of the terms of trade (on the basis of data from ECLA and the International Monetary Fund), excluding Cuba, were $26,383 million for the 1951–66 period, taking 1950 prices as a base. If Cuba and Venezuela are excluded, the total is $15,925 million.

b) For the reasons already given, foreign capital retains control over the most dynamic sectors of the economy and repatriates a high volume of profit; consequently, capital accounts are highly unfavorable to dependent countries. The data show that the amount of capital leaving the country is much greater than the amount entering; this produces an enslaving deficit in capital accounts. To this must be added the deficit in certain services which are virtually under total foreign control—such as freight transport, royalty payments, technical aid, etc. Consequently, an important deficit is produced in the total balance of payments; thus limiting the possibility of importation of inputs for industrialization.

c) The result is that "foreign financing" becomes necessary, in two forms: to cover the existing deficit, and to "finance" development by means of loans for the stimulation of investments and to "supply" an internal economic surplus which was decapitalized to a large extent by the remittance of part of the surplus generated domestically and sent abroad as profits.

Foreign capital and foreign "aid" thus fill up the holes that they themselves created. The real value of this aid, however, is doubtful. If overcharges resulting from the restrictive terms of the aid are subtracted from the total amount of the grants, the average net flow, according to calculations of the Inter-American Economic and Social Council, is approximately 54 percent of the gross flow [5].

If we take account of certain further facts—that a high proportion of aid is paid in local currencies, that Latin American countries make contributions to international financial institutions, and that credits are often "tied"—we find a "real component of foreign aid" of 42.2 percent on a very favorable hypothesis and of 38.3 percent on a more realistic one [5, II-33]. The gravity of the situation becomes even clearer if we consider that these credits are used in large part to finance North American investments, to subsidize foreign imports which compete with national products, to introduce technology not adapted to the needs of underdeveloped countries, and to invest in low-priority sectors of the national economies. The hard truth is that the underdeveloped countries have to pay for all of the "aid" they receive. This situation is generating an enormous protest movement by Latin American governments seeking at least partial relief from such negative relations.

3. Finally, industrial development is strongly conditioned by the technological monopoly exercised by imperialist centers. We have seen that the underdeveloped countries depend on the importation of machinery and raw materials for the development of their industries. However, these goods are not freely available in the international market; they are patented and usually belong to the big companies. The big companies do not sell machinery and processed raw materials as simple merchandise: they demand either the payment of royalties, etc., for their utilization or, in most cases, they convert these goods into capital and introduce them in the form of their own investments. This is how machinery which is replaced in the hegemonic centers by more advanced technology is sent to dependent countries as capital for the installation of affiliates. Let us pause and examine these relations, in order to understand their oppressive and exploitative character.

The dependent countries do not have sufficient foreign currency, for the reasons given. Local businessmen have financing difficulties, and they must pay for the utilization of certain patented techniques. These factors oblige the national bourgeois governments to facilitate the entry of foreign capital in order to supply the restricted national market, which is strongly protected by high tariffs in order to promote industrialization. Thus, foreign capital enters with all the advantages: in many cases, it is given exemption from exchange controls for the importation of machinery; financing of sites for installation of industries is provided; government financing agencies facilitate industrialization; loans are available from foreign and domestic banks, which prefer such clients; foreign aid often subsidizes such investments and finances complementary public investments; after installation, high profits obtained in such favorable circumstances can be reinvested freely. Thus it is not surprising that the data of the U.S. Department of Commerce reveal that the percentage of capital brought in from abroad by these companies is but a part of the total amount of invested capital. These data show that in the period from 1946 to 1967 the new entries of capital into Latin America for direct investment amounted to $5,415 million, while the sum of reinvested profits was $4,424 million. On the other hand, the transfers of profits from Latin America to the United States amounted to $14,775 million. If we estimate total profits as approximately equal to transfers plus reinvestments we have the sum of $18,983 million. In spite of enormous transfers of profits to the United States, the book value of the United States's direct investment in Latin America went from $3,045 million in 1946 to $10,213 million in 1967. From these data it is clear that: (1) Of the new investments made by U.S. companies in Latin America for the period 1946–67, 55 percent corresponds to new entries of capital and 45 percent to reinvestment of profits; in recent years, the trend is more marked, with reinvestments between 1960 and 1966 representing more than 60 percent of new investments. (2) Remittances remained at about 10 percent of book value throughout the period. (3) The ratio of remitted capital to new flow is around 2.7 for the period 1946–67; that is, for each dollar that enters $2.70 leaves. In the 1960's this ratio roughly doubled, and in some years was considerably higher.

The *Survey of Current Business* data on sources and uses of funds for direct North American investment in Latin America in the period 1957–64 show that, of the total sources of direct investment in Latin America, only 11.8 percent came from the United States. The remainder is in large part, the result of the activities of North American firms in Latin America (46.4 percent net income, 27.7 percent under the heading of depreciation), and from "sources located abroad" (14.1 percent). It is significant that the funds obtained abroad that are external to the companies are greater than the funds originating in the United States.

V. EFFECTS ON THE PRODUCTIVE STRUCTURE

It is easy to grasp, even if only superficially, the effects that this dependent structure has on the productive system itself in these countries and the role of this structure in determining a specified type of development, characterized by its dependent nature.

The productive system in the underdeveloped countries is essentially determined by these international relations. In the first place, the need to conserve the agrarian or mining export structure generates a combination between more advanced economic centers that extract surplus value from the more backward sectors, and also between internal "metropolitan" centers and internal interdependent "colonial" centers [10]. The unequal and combined character of capitalist development at the international level is reproduced internally in an acute form. In the second place the industrial and technological structure responds more closely to the interests of the multinational corporations than to internal developmental needs (conceived of not only in terms of the overall interests of the population, but also from the point of view of the interests of a national capitalist development). In the third place, the same technological and economic-financial concentration of the hegemonic economies is transferred without substantial alteration to very different economies and societies, giving rise to a highly unequal productive structure, a high concentration of incomes, underutilization of installed capacity, intensive exploitation of existing markets concentrated in large cities, etc.

The accumulation of capital in such circumstances assumes its own characteristics. In the first place, it is characterized by profound differences among domestic wage-levels, in the context of a local cheap labor market, combined with a capital-intensive technology. The result, from the point of view of relative surplus value, is a high rate of exploitation of labor power. (On measurements of forms of exploitation, see [3].)

This exploitation is further aggravated by the high prices of industrial products enforced by protectionism, exemptions and subsidies given by the national governments, and "aid" from hegemonic centers. Furthermore, since dependent accumulation is necessarily tied into the international economy, it is profoundly conditioned by the unequal and combined character of international capitalist economic relations, by the technological and financial control of the imperialist centers by the realities of the balance of payments, by the economic policies of the state, etc. The role of the state in the growth of national and foreign capital merits a much fuller analysis than can be made here.

Using the analysis offered here as a point of departure, it is possible to understand the limits that this productive system imposes on the growth of the internal markets of these countries. The survival of traditional relations in the countryside is a serious limitation on the size of the market, since industrialization does not offer hopeful prospects. The productive structure created by dependent industrialization limits the growth of the internal market.

First, it subjects the labor force to highly exploitative relations which limit its purchasing power. Second, in adopting a technology of intensive capital use, it creates very few jobs in comparison with population growth, and limits the generation of new sources of income. These two limitations affect the growth of the consumer goods market. Third, the remittance abroad of profits carries away part of the economic surplus generated within the country. In all these ways limits are put on the possible creation of basic national industries which could provide a market for the capital goods this surplus would make possible if it were not remitted abroad.

From this cursory analysis we see that the alleged backwardness of these economies is not due to a lack of integration with capitalism but that, on the contrary, the most powerful obstacles to their full development come from the way in which they are joined to this international system and its laws of development.

VI. SOME CONCLUSIONS: DEPENDENT REPRODUCTION

In order to understand the system of dependent reproduction and the socioeconomic institutions created by it, we must see it as part of a system of world economic relations based on monopolistic control of large-scale capital, on control of certain economic and financial centers over others, on a monopoly of a complex technology that leads to unequal and combined development at a national and international level. Attempts to analyze backwardness as a failure to assimilate more advanced models of production or to modernize are nothing more than ideology disguised as science. The same is true of the attempts to analyze this international economy in terms of relations among elements in free competition, such as the theory of comparative costs which seeks to justify the inequalities of the world economic system and to conceal the relations of exploitation on which it is based [14].

In reality we can understand what is happening in the underdeveloped countries only when we see that they develop within the framework of a process of dependent production and reproduction. This system is a dependent one because it reproduces a productive system whose development is limited by those world relations which necessarily lead to the development of only certain economic sectors, to trade under unequal conditions [9], to domestic competition with international capital under unequal conditions, to the imposition of relations of superexploitation of the domestic labor force with a view to dividing the economic surplus thus generated between internal and external forces of domination. (On economic surplus and its utilization in the dependent countries, see [1].)

In reproducing such a productive system and such international relations, the development of dependent capitalism reproduces the factors that prevent it from reaching a nationally and internationally advantageous situation; and it thus reproduces backwardness, misery, and social marginalization within its borders. The development that it produces benefits very narrow sectors, encounters unyielding domestic obstacles to its continued economic growth (with respect to both internal and foreign markets), and leads to the progressive accumulation of balance-of-payments deficits, which in turn generate more dependence and more superexploitation.

The political measures proposed by the develomentalists of ECLA, UNCTAD, BID, etc., do not appear to permit destruction of these terrible chains imposed by dependent development.

We have examined the alternative forms of development presented for Latin America and the dependent countries under such conditions elsewhere [8]. Everything now indicates that what can be expected is a long process of sharp political and military confrontations and of profound social radicalization which will lead these countries to a dilemma: governments of force which open the way to facism, or popular revolutionary governments, which open the way to socialism. Intermediate solutions have proved to be, in such a contradictory reality, empty and utopian.

References

1. Paul Baran, *Political Economy of Growth* (Monthly Review Press, 1967).

2. Thomas Balogh, *Unequal Partners* (Basil Blackwell, 1963).

3. Pablo Gonzalez Casanova, *Sociología de la explotación,* Siglo XXI (México, 1969).

4. Cepal, *La CEPAL y el Análisis del Desarrollo Latinoamericano* (1968, Santiago, Chile).

5. Consejo Interamericano Economico Social (CIES) O.A.S., Interamerican Economic and Social Council, External Financing for Development in L.A. *El Financiamiento Externo para el Desarrollo de América Latina* (Pan-American Union, Washington, 1969).

6. Theotonio Dos Santos, *El nuevo carácter de la dependencia,* CESO (Santiago de Chile, 1968).

7. _____, *La crisis de la teoría del desarrollo y las relaciones de dependencia en América Latina,* Boletín del CESO, 3 (Santiago, Chile, 1968).

8. _____, *La dependencia económica y las alternativas de cambio en América Latina,* Ponencia al IX Congreso Latinoamericano de Sociología (México, Nov., 1969).

9. A. Emmanuel, *L'Echange Inégal* (Maspero, Paris, 1969).

10. Andre G. Frank, *Development and Underdevelopment in Latin America* (Monthly Review Press, 1968).

11. I. V. Levin, *The Export Economies* (Harvard Univ. Press, 1964).

12. Gunnar Myrdal, *Asian Drama* (Pantheon, 1968).

13. K. Nkrumah, *Neocolonialismo, última etapa del imperialismo,* Siglo XXI (México, 1966).

14. Cristian Palloix, *Problemes de la Croissance en Economie Ouverte* (Maspero, Paris, 1969).

READING 16: IMMANUEL WALLERSTEIN

As a graduate student in the 1950s, Immanuel Wallerstein studied politics in Ghana. Like many of the time, Wallerstein was optimistic for the future of African political development. His earliest works demonstrate this fact.[172] Over time, however, as the prospects for development in the southern hemisphere did not improve, Wallerstein developed what he termed "world system theory." In a series of books written in the 1970s Wallerstein traces the historical reasons for the development of mercantilism and capitalism.[173] He argues that, where

---

[172] I am thinking here of *Africa: The Politics of Independence* (New York: Vintage, 1961) and of *Africa: The Politics of Unity* (New York: Vintage, 1967), but Wallerstein has published countless articles and books that express optimism. He continued to express hope in a 1980s book series entitled *The African Liberation Reader.* In his more recent book, *After Liberalism* (New York: New Press, 1995), he expresses the view that, regretfully, his earlier optimism was not warranted.

[173] An ambitious endeavor, to say the least, Wallerstein published three hefty volumes under the title *The Modern World-System* (New York: Academic Press, various dates).

capitalist development occurred, wealth accumulated, largely to the detriment of previously subsistence agriculture economies. That is, the wealth "core" states of the world had created a global capitalist economy that extracted resources from the "periphery" states of the world. Below, Wallerstein expresses his views regarding the future of capitalism.

IMMANUEL WALLERSTEIN,

THE CAPITALIST WORLD-ECONOMY, 1979

THE PRESENT STATE OF THE DEBATE ON WORLD INEQUALITY

It has never been a secret from anyone that some have more than others. And in the modern world at least, it is no secret that some countries have more than other countries. In short, world inequality is a phenomenon about which most men and most groups are quite conscious.

I do not believe that there has ever been a time when these inequalities were unquestioned. That is to say, people or groups who have more have always felt the need to justify this fact, if for no other reason than to try to convince those who have less that they should accept this fact with relative docility. These ideologies of the advantaged have had varying degrees of success over time. The history of the world is one of a constant series of revolts against inequality—whether that of one people or nation *vis-à-vis* another or of one class within a geographical area against another.

This statement is probably true of all of recorded history, indeed of all historical events, at least since the Neolithic Revolution. What has changed with the advent of the modern world in the sixteenth century is neither the existence of inequalities nor of the felt need to justify them by means of ideological constructs. What has changed is that even those who defend the 'inevitability' of inequalities in the present feel the need to argue that eventually, over time, these inequalities will disappear, or at the very least diminish considerably in scope. Another way of saying this is that of the three dominant ideological currents of the modern world—conservatism, liberalism, and Marxism—two at least (liberalism and Marxism) are committed in theory and the abstract to egalitarianism as a principle. The third, conservatism, is not, but conservatism is an ideology that has been very much on the defensive ever since the French Revolution. The proof of this is that most conservatives decline to fly the banner openly but hide their conservative ideas under the mantle of liberalism or occasionally even Marxism.

Surely it is true that in the universities of the world in the twentieth century, and in other expressions of intellectuals, the contending ideologies have been one variant or another of liberalism and Marxism. (Remember at this point we are talking of ideologies and not of political movements. Both 'Liberal' parties and Social-Democratic parties in the twentieth century have drawn on liberal ideologies.)

One of the most powerful thrusts of the eighteenth-century Enlightenment, picked up by most nineteenth and twentieth century thought systems, was the assumption of progress, reformulated later as evolution. In the context of the question of equality, evolution was interpreted as the process of moving from an imperfect, unequal allocation of privileges and resources to some version of equality. There was considerable argument about how to define equality. (Reflect on the different meanings of 'equality of opportunity' and 'to each according to his needs'. There was considerable disagreement about who or what were the obstacles to this desired state of equality. And there was fundamental discord about how to transform the world from its present imperfection to the desired future, primarily between the advocates of gradualism based on education to advocates of revolution based on the use at some point in time of violence.

I review this well-known history of modern ideas simply to underline where I think our current debates are simply the latest variant of now classic debates and where I think some new issues have been raised which make these older formulations outdated.

If one takes the period 1945–60, both politically and intellectually, we have in many ways the apogee of the liberal–Marxist debate. The world was politically polarized in the so-called Cold War. There were two camps. One called itself the 'free world' and argued that it and it alone upheld the first part of the French Revolutions trilogy, that of 'liberty'. It argued that its economic system offered the hope over time of approximating 'equality' through a path which it came to call 'economic development' or sometimes just 'development'. It argued too that it was gradually achieving 'fraternity' by means of education and political reform (such as the 1954 Supreme Court decision in the United States, ending the legality of segregation).

The other camp called itself the 'socialist world' and argued that it and it alone represented the three objectives of the French Revolution and hence the interests of the people of the world. It argued that when movements inspired by these ideas would come to power in all non 'socialist' countries (and however they came to power), each would enact legislation along the same lines and by this process the whole world would become 'socialist' and the objective would be achieved.

These somewhat simplistic ideological statements were of course developed in much more elaborate form by the intellectuals. It has become almost traditional (but I think nonetheless just) to cite W. W. Rostow's *The Stages of Economic Growth* as a succinct, sophisticated, and relatively pure expression of the dominant liberal ideology which informed the thinking of the political leadership of the United States and its western allies. Rostow showed no modesty in his subtitle: which was 'a non-Communist Manifesto'.

His basic thesis is no doubt familiar to most persons interested in these problems. Rostow saw the process of change as a series of stages through which each national unit had to go. They were the stages through which Rostow felt Great Britain had gone, and Great Britain was the crucial example since it was defined as being the first state to embark on the evolutionary path of the modern industrial world. The inference, quite overtly drawn, was that this path was a model, to be copied by other states. One could then analyze what it took to move from one stage to another, why some nations took longer than others, and could prescribe (like a physician) what a nation must do to hurry along its process of 'growth'. I will not review what ideological function such a formulation served. This has been done repeatedly and well. Nonetheless, this viewpoint, somewhat retouched, still informs the developmentalist ideas of the major western governments as well as that of international agencies. I consider Lester Pearson's 'Partners in Progress' report in the direct line of this analytic framework.

In the socialist world in this period there was no book quite the match of Rostow's. What there was instead was an encrusted version of evolutionary Marxism which also saw rigid stages through which every state of geographical entity had to go. The differences were that the stages covered longer historical time and the model country was the USSR. These are the stages known as slavery–feudalism–capitalism–socialism. The absurdities of the rigid formulation which dates from the 1930s and the inappropriateness of applying this on a *national* level have been well argued recently by an Indian Marxist intellectual, Irfan Habib, who argues not only the meaningfulness of the concept of the 'Asiatic mode of production' but also the illogic of insisting that the various historical modes of extracting a surplus must each, necessarily, occur in all countries and follow in a specific order. Habib argues:

> The materialist conception of history need not necessarily prescribe a set universal periodisation, since what it essentially does is to formulate an analytic method for the development of class societies, and any periodisation, theoretically, serves as no more than the illustration of the application of such a method . . . The crucial thing is the definition of principal contradiction (i.e., class-contradictions) in a society, the marking out of factors responsible for intensifying them, and the

delineation of the shaping of the social order, when a particular contradiction is resolved. It is possible that release from the set P–S–F–C-pattern [primitive communism–slavery–feudalism–capitalism] may lead Marxists to apply themselves better to this task, since they would no longer be obliged to look for the same 'fundamental laws of the epoch' (a favourite Soviet term), or 'prime mover', as premised for the supposedly corresponding European epoch.[1]

I give this excerpt from Habib because I very much agree with his fundamental point that this version of Marxist thought, so prevalent between 1945 and 1965, is a sort of 'mechanical copying' of liberal views. Basically, the analysis is the same as that represented by Rostow except that the names of the stages are changed and the model country has shifted from Great Britain to the USSR. I will call this approach the developmentalist perspective, as espoused either by liberals or Marxists.

There is another perspective that has slowly pushed its way into public view during the 1960s. It has no commonly accepted name, in part because the early formulations of this point of view have often been confused, partial, or unclear. It was first widely noticed in the thinking of the Latin American structuralists (such as Prebisch and Furtado) and those allied to them elsewhere (such as Dudley Seers). It later took the form of arguments such as the 'development of underdevelopment' (A. G. Frank, in the heritage of Baran's *The Political Economy of Growth*), the 'structure of dependence' (Theontonio Dos Santos), 'unequal exchange' (Arghiri Emmanuel), 'accumulation of world capital' (Samir Amin), 'subimperialism' (Ruy Mauro Marini). It also surfaced in the Chinese Cultural Revolution as Mao's concept of the continuity of the class struggle under socialist regimes in single countries.[2]

What all these concepts have in common is a critique of the developmentalist perspective. Usually they make it from a Marxist tradition but it should be noted that some of the critics, such as Furtado, come from a liberal heritage. It is no accident that this point of view has been expressed largely by persons from Asia, Africa and Latin America or by those others particularly interested in these regions (such as Umberto Melotti of *Terzo Mondo*).[3]

I would like to designate this point of view the 'world-system perspective'. I mean by that term that it is based on the assumption, explicitly or implicitly, that the modern world comprises a single capitalist world-economy, which has emerged historically since the sixteenth century and which still exists today. It follows from such a premise that national states are *not* societies that have separate, parallel histories, but parts of a whole reflecting that whole. To the extent that stages exist, they exist for the system as a whole. To be sure, since different parts of the world play and have played differing roles in the capitalist world-economy, they have dramatically different internal socio-economic profiles and hence distinctive politics. But to understand the internal class contradictions and political struggles of a particular state, we must first situate it in the world-economy. We can then understand the ways in which various political and cultural thrusts may be efforts to alter or preserve a position within this world-economy which is to the advantage or disadvantage of particular groups located within a particular state.[4]

What thus distinguishes the developmentalist and the world system perspective is not liberalism versus Marxism nor evolutionism versus something else (since both are essentially evolu-

---

[1] Irfan Habib, 'Problems of Marxist Historical Analysis in India', *Enquiry* (Monsoon, 1969). Reprinted in S. A. Shah (ed.), *Towards National Liberation: Essays on the Political Economy of India* (Montreal: n.p., 1973), pp. 8–9.

[2] See my 'Class Struggle in China?' *Monthly Review*, 25: 4 (September 1973), 55–8.

[3] See U. Melotti, 'Marx e il Terzo Mondo', *Terzo Mondo*, 13–14 (September–December 1971). Melitto subtitles the work: 'Towards a Multilinear Schema of the Marxist Conception of Historical Development'.

[4] I have developed this argument at length elsewhere. See *The Modern World-System: Capitalist Agriculture and the Origins of the European World-Economy* (New York and London: Academic Press, 1974) and 'The Rise and Future Demise of the World Capitalist System: Concepts for Comparative Analysis', *Comparative Studies in Society and History* 16: 4 (October 1974), 387–415, and above, ch. 1.

tionary). Rather I would locate the distinction in two places. One is in mode of thought. To put it in Hegelian terms, the developmentalist perspective is mechanical, whereas the world-system perspective is dialectical. I mean by the latter term that at every point in the analysis, one asks not what is the formal structure but what is the consequence for both the whole and the parts of maintaining or changing a certain structure at that particular point in time, given the totality of particular positions of that moment in time. Intelligent analysis demands knowledge of the complex texture of social reality (historical concreteness) within a long-range perspective that observes trends and forces of the world-system, which can explain what underlies and informs the diverse historically concrete phenomena. If synchronic comparisons and abstracted generalizations are utilized, it is only as heuristic devices in search of a truth that is ever contemporary and hence ever changing.

This distinction of scientific methodology is matched by a distinction of praxis, of the politics of the real world. For what comes through as the second great difference between the two perspectives (the developmentalist and the world-system) is the prognosis for action. This is the reason why the latter perspective has emerged primarily from the intellectuals of the Third World. The developmentalist perspective not only insists that the model is to be found in the old developed countries (whether Great Britain–USA or USSR) but also that the fundamental international political issues revolve around the relations among the hegemonic powers of the world. From a world-system perspective, there are no 'models' (a mechanical notion) and the relations of the hegemonic powers are only one of many issues that confront the world-system.

The emergence of the world-system perspective is a consequence of the dramatic challenge to European political domination of the world which has called into question all Europocentric constructions of social reality. But intellectual evolution itself is seldom dramatic. The restructuring of the allocation of power in the world has made itself felt in the realm of ideas, particularly in the hegemonic areas of the world, via a growing malaise that intellectuals in Europe (including of course North America) have increasingly felt about the validity of their answers to a series of 'smaller' questions—smaller, that is, than the nature of the world-system as such.

Let us review successively six knotty questions to which answers from a developmentalist perspective have increasingly seemed inadequate.

Why have certain world-historical events of the last two centuries taken place where and when they have? The most striking 'surprise', at the moment it occurred and ever since, is the Russian Revolution. As we all know, neither Marx nor Lenin nor anyone else thought that a 'socialist revolution' would occur in Russia earlier than anywhere else. Marx had more or less predicted Great Britain as the likely candidate, and after Marx's death, the consensus of expectation in the international socialist movement was that it would occur in Germany. We know that even after 1917 almost all the leading figures of the CPSU expected that the 'revolution' would have to occur quickly in Germany if the Soviet regime was to survive. There was however no socialist revolution in Germany and nonetheless the Soviet regime did survive.

We do not want for explanations of this phenomenon, but we do lack convincing answers. Of course, there exists an explanation that turns Marx on his head and argues that socialist revolutions occur not in the so-called 'advanced capitalist' countries but precisely in 'backward' countries. But this is in such blatant contradiction with other parts of the developmentalist perspective that its proponents are seldom willing to state it baldly, even less defend it openly.

Nor is the Russian Revolution the only anomaly. There is a long-standing debate about the 'exceptionalism' of the United States. How can we explain that the USA replaced Great Britain as the hegemonic industrial power of the world, and in the process managed to avoid giving birth to a serious internal socialist movement? And if the USA could avoid socialism, why could not Brazil or Russia or Canada? Seen from the perspective of 1800, it would have been a bold social scientist who would have predicted the particular success of the USA.

Again there have been many explanations. There is the 'frontier' theory. There is the theory that underlines the absence of a previously entrenched 'feudal' class. There is the theory of the US as Britain's 'junior partner' who overtook the senior. But all of these theories are precisely 'exceptionalist' theories, contradicting the developmentalist paradigm. And furthermore, some of these variables apply to other countries where they did not seem to have the same consequences.

We could go on. I will mention two more briefly. For a long time, Great Britain's primacy (the 'first' industrial power) has been unquestioned. But was Britain the 'first' and if so why was she? This is a question that only recently has been seriously adumbrated. In April 1974 at another international colloquium held here in Montreal on the theme of 'Failed Transitions to Industrialism: The Case of 17th Century Netherlands and Renaissance Italy', one view put forward quite strongly was that neither Italy nor the Netherlands was the locus of the Industrial Revolution precisely because they were too far *advanced* economically. What a striking blow to a developmentalist paradigm.

And lastly one should mention the anomaly of Canada: a country which economically falls into a category below that of the world's leading industrial producers in structural terms, yet nonetheless is near the very top of the list in per capita income. This cannot be plausibly explained from a developmentalist perspective.

If the world has been 'developing' or 'progressing' over the past few centuries, how do we explain the fact that in many areas things seem to have gotten worse, not better? Worse in many ways, ranging from standard of living, to the physical environment, to the quality of life. And more to the point, worse in some places but better in others. I refer not merely to such contemporary phenomena as the so-called 'growing gap' between the industrialized countries and the Third World, but also to such earlier phenomena as the deindustrialization of many areas of the world (starting with the widely known example of the Indian textile industry in the late eighteenth and early nineteenth century).

You may say that this contradicts the liberal version of the developmentalist perspective but not its Marxist version, since 'polarization' was seen as part of the process of change. True enough, except that 'polarization' was presumably within countries and not between them. Furthermore, it is not clear that it is 'polarization' that has occurred. While the rich have gotten richer and the poor have gotten poorer, there is surely a fairly large group of countries now somewhere in between on many economic criteria, to cite such politically diverse examples as Mexico, Italy, Czechoslovakia, Itan, and South Africa.

Furthermore, we witness in the 1970s a dramatic shift in the distribution of the profit and the international terms of trade of oil (and possibly other raw materials). You may say it is because of the increased political sophistication and strength of the Arab world. No doubt this has occurred, but is this an explanation? I remind this group that the last moment of time in which there was a dramatic amelioration of world terms of trade of primary products was in the period 1897–1913, a moment which represented in political terms the apogee of European colonial control of the world.

Once again it is not that there are not a large number of explanations for the rise in oil prices. It is rather that I find these explanations, for what they're worth, in contradiction with a developmentalist perspective.

Why are there 'regressions'? In 1964, S. N. Eisenstadt published an article entitled 'Breakdowns of Modernization', in which he discussed the fact that there seemed to be cases of 'reversal' of regimes to 'a lower, less flexible level of political and social differentiation . . .'[5]

---

[5] S. N. Eisenstadt, 'Breakdowns of Modernization', *Economic Development and Cultural Change* 12: 4 (July 1964), 367.

In seeking to explain the origins of such 'reversals', Eisenstadt restricted himself to hesitant hypotheses:

> The problem of why in Turkey, Japan, Mexico, and Russia there emerge in the initial stages of modernization elites with orientations to change and ability to implement relatively effective policies, while they did not develop in these initial phases in Indonesia, Pakistan, or Burma, or why elites with similar differences tended to develop also in later stages of modernization, is an extremely difficult one and constitutes one of the most baffling problems in comparative sociological analysis. There are but four available indications to deal with this problem. Very tentatively, it may perhaps be suggested that to some extent it has to do with the placement of these elites in the preceding social structure, with the extent of their internal cohesiveness, and of the internal transformation of their own value orientation.[6]

As is clear, Eisenstadt's tentative explanation is to be found in anterior factors operating internally in the state. This calls into question the concept of stages through which all not only must pass but all *can* pass, but it leaves intact the state framework as the focus of analysis and explanation. This of course leads us logically to ask how these anterior factors developed. Are they pure historical accident?

Similarly after the political rebellion of Tito's Yugoslavia against the USSR, the latter began to accuse Yugoslavia of 'revisionism' and of returning to capitalism. Later, China took up the same theme against the USSR.

But how can we explain how this happens? There are really two varieties of explanation from a developmentalist perspective. One is to say that 'regression' seems to have occurred, but that in fact 'progress' had never taken place. The leaders of a movement, whether a nationalist movement or a socialist movement, only pretended to favor change. In fact they were really always 'neocolonialist' stooges or 'revisionists' at heart. Such an explanation has partial truth, but it seems to me to place too much on 'false consciousness' and to fail to analyze movements in their immediate and continuing historical contexts.

The second explanation of 'regression' is a change of heart—'betrayal'. Yes, but once again, how come sometimes, but not always? Are we to explain large-scale social phenomena on the basis of the accident of the biographic histories of the particular leaders involved? I cannot accept this, for leaders remain leaders in the long run only if their personal choices reflect wider social pressures.

If the fundamental paradigm of modern history is a series of parallel national processes, how do we explain the persistence of nationalism, indeed quite often its primacy, as a political force in the modern world? Developmentalists who are liberals deplore nationalism or explain it away as a transitional 'integrating' phenomenon. Marxists who are developmentalists are even more embarrassed. If the class struggle is primary—that is, implicitly the intranational class struggle—how do we explain the fact that the slogan of the Cuban revolution is 'Patria o muerte—venceremos?' And how could we explain this even more astonishing quotation from Kim Il Sung, the leader of the Democratic People's Republic of Korea:

> The homeland is a veritable mother for everyone. We cannot live nor be happy outside of our homeland. Only the flourishing and prosperity of our homeland will permit us to go down the path to happiness. The best sons and daughters of our people, all without exception, were first of all ardent patriots. It was to recover their homeland that Korean Communists struggled, before the Liberation, against Japanese imperialism despite every difficulty and obstacle.[7]

---

[6] *Ibid.,* pp. 365–6.

[7] *Activité Révolutionnaire du Camarade Kim Il Sung* (Pyongyang: Editions en langues étrangères, 1970). Livre illustré, 52nd page (edition unpaginated). Translation mine.

And if internal processes are so fundamental, why has not the reality of international workers' solidarity been greater? Remember the First World War.

As before, there are many explanations for the persistence of nationalism. I merely observe that all these explanations have to *explain away* the primacy of internal national processes. Or to put it another way, for developmentalists nationalism is sometimes good, sometimes bad. But when it is the one or the other, it is ultimately explained by developmentalists in an ad hoc manner, adverting to its meaning for the world-system.

An even more difficult problem for the developmentalists has been the recrudescence of nationalist movements in areas smaller than that of existing states. And it is not Biafra or Bangladesh that is an intellectual problem, because the usual manner of accounting for secessionist movements in Third World countries has been the failure to attain the stage of 'national integration'.

No, the surprise has been in the industrialized world: Blacks in the USA, Québec in Canada, Occitania in France, the Celts in Great Britain, and lurking in the background the nationalities question in the USSR. It is not that any of these 'nationalisms' is new. They are all long-standing themes of political and cultural conflict in all these countries. The surprise has been that, as of say 1945 or even 1960, most persons in these countries, using a developmentalist paradigm, regarded these movements or claims as remnants of a dying past, destined to diminish still further in vitality. And lo, a phoenix reborn.

The explanations are there. Some cry, anachronism—but if so, then the question remains, how come such a flourishing anachronism? Some say, loud shouting but little substance, a last bubble of national integration. Perhaps, but the intellectual and organizational development of these ethno-national movements seem to have moved rapidly and ever more firmly in a direction quite opposite to national integration. In any case, what in the developmentalist paradigm explains this phenomenon?

One last question, which is perhaps only a reformulation of the previous five. How is it that the 'ideal types' of the different versions of the developmentalist perspective all seem so far from empirical reality? Who has not had the experience of not being quite certain which party represents the 'industrial proletariat' or the 'modernizing elite' in Nigeria, or in France of the Second Empire for that matter? Let us be honest. Each of us, to the extent that he has ever used a developmentalist paradigm, has stretched empirical reality to a very Procrustean bed indeed.

Can the world-system perspective answer these questions better? We cannot yet be sure. This point of view has not been fully thought through. But let me indicate some possible lines of argument.

If the world-system is the focus of analysis, and if in particular we are talking of the capitalist world-economy, then divergent historical patterns are precisely to be expected. They are not an anomaly but the essence of the system. If the world-economy is the basic economic entity comprising a single division of labor, then it is natural that different areas perform different economic tasks. Anyway it is natural under capitalism, and we may talk of the core, the periphery and the semiperiphery of the world-economy. Since however political boundaries (states) are smaller than the economic whole, they will each reflect different groupings of economic tasks and strengths in the world market. Over time, some of these differences may be accentuated rather than diminished—the basic inequalities which are our theme of discussion.

It is also clear that over time the loci of economic activities keep changing. This is due to many factors—ecological exhaustion, the impact of new technology, climate changes, and the socioeconomic consequences of these 'natural' phenomena. Hence some areas 'progress' and others 'regress'. But the fact that particular states change their position in the world-economy, from semiperiphery to core say, or vice versa, does not in itself change the nature of the system. These shifts will be registered for individual states as 'development' or 'regression'. The key factor to note is that within a capitalist world-economy, all states cannot 'develop' simultaneously *by definition,* since the system functions by virtue of having unequal core and peripheral regions.[8]

Within a world-economy, the state structures function as ways for particular groups to affect and distort the functioning of the market. The stronger the state machinery, the more its ability to distort the world market in favor of the interests it represents. Core states have stronger state machineries than peripheral states.

This role of the state machineries in a capitalist world-economy explains the persistence of nationalism, since the primary social conflicts are quite often between groups located in different states rather than between groups located within the same state boundaries. Furthermore, this explains the ambiguity of class as a concept, since class refers to the economy which is worldwide, but class consciousness is a political, hence primarily national, phenomenon. Within this context, one can see the recrudescence of ethno-nationalisms in industrialized states as an expression of class consciousness of lower caste-class groups in societies where the class terminology has been preempted by nation-wide middle strata organized around the dominant ethnic group.

If then the world-system is the focus of analysis rather than the individual states, it is the natural history of this system at which we must look. Like all systems, the capitalist world-economy has both cyclical and secular trends, and it is important to distinguish them.

On the one hand, the capitalist world-economy seems to go through long cycles of 'expansion' and 'contraction'. I cannot at this point go into the long discussion this would require. I will limit myself to the very brief suggestion that 'expansion' occurs when the totality of world production is less than world effective demand, as permitted by the existing social distribution of world purchasing power, and the 'contraction' occurs when total world production exceeds world effective demand. These are cycles of 75–100 years in length in my view and the downward cycle is only resolved by a political reallocation of world income that effectively expands world demand. I believe we have just ended an expansionary cycle and we are in the beginning of a contractual one.

These cycles occur within a secular trend that has involved the physical expansion and politico-structural consolidation of the capitalist world-economy as such, but has also given birth to forces and movements which are eating away at these same structural supports of the existing world-system. In particular, these forces which we call revolutionary forces are calling into question the phenomenon of inequality so intrinsic to the existing world-system.

The trend towards structural consolidation of the system over the past four centuries has included three basic developments.

The first has been the capitalization of world agriculture, meaning the ever more efficient use of the world's land and sea resources in large productive units with larger and larger components of fixed capital. Over time, this has encompassed more and more of the earth's surface, and at the present we are probably about to witness the last major physical expansion, the elimination of all remaining plots restricted to small-scale, so-called 'subsistence' production. The counterpart of this process has been the steady concentration of the world's population as salaried workers in small, dense pockets—that is, proletarianization and urbanization. The initial impact of this entire process has been to render large populations more exploitable and controllable.

The second major structural change has been the development of technology that maximizes the ability to transform the resources of the earth into useable commodities at 'reasonable' cost levels. This is what we call industrialization, and the story is far from over. The next cen-

---

[8] As to how particular states can change their position, I have tried to furnish an explanation in 'Dependence in an Interdependent World: The Limited Possibilities of Transformation within the Capitalist World-Economy', *African Studies Review* 17: 1 (April 1974), 1–26, and below, ch. 4.

tury should see the spread of industrial activity from the temperate core areas in which it has hitherto been largely concentrated to the tropical and semitropical peripheral areas. Industrialization too has hitherto tended to consolidate the system in providing a large part of the profit that makes the system worth the while of those who are on top of it, with a large enough surplus to sustain and appease the world's middle strata. Mere extension of industrial activity will not change a peripheral area into a core area, for the core areas will concentrate on ever newer, specialized activities.

The third major development, at once technological and social, has been the strengthening of all organizational structures—the states, the economic corporate structures, and even the cultural institutions—*vis-à-vis* both individuals and groups. This is the process of bureaucratization, and while it has been uneven (the core states are still stronger than the peripheral states, for example), all structures are stronger today than previously. Prime ministers of contemporary states have the power today that Louis XIV sought in vain to achieve. This too has been stabilizing because the ability of these bureaucracies physically to repress opposition is far greater than in the past.

But there is the other side of each of these coins. The displacement of the world's population into urban areas has made it easier ultimately to organize forces against the power structures. This is all the more so since the ever-expanding, market-dependent, propertyless groups are simultaneously more educated, more in communication with each other, and hence *potentially* more politically conscious.

The steady industrialization of the world has eaten away at the political and hence economic justifications for differentials in rewards. The technological advances, while still unevenly distributed, have created a new military equality of destructive potential. It is true that one nation may have a thousand times the fire power of another, but if the weaker one has sufficient to incur grievous damage, of how much good is it for the stronger to have a thousand times as much strength? Consider not merely the power of a weaker state with a few nuclear rockets but the military power of urban guerillas. It is the kind of problem Louis XIV precisely did *not* need to worry about.

Finally, the growth of bureaucracies in the long run has created the weakness of topheaviness. The ability of the presumed decision makers to control not the populace but the bureaucracies has effectively diminished, which again creates a weakness in the ability to enforce politico-economic will.

Where then in this picture do the forces of change, the movements of liberation, come in? They come in precisely as not totally coherent pressures of groups which arise out of the structural contradictions of the capitalist world-economy. These groups seem to take organizational form as movements, as parties, and sometimes as regimes. But when the movements become regimes, they are caught in the dilemma of becoming part of the machinery of the capitalist world-economy they are presuming to change. Hence the so-called 'betrayals'. It is important neither to adulate blindly these regimes, for inevitably they 'betray' in part their stated goals, nor to be cynical and despairing, for the movements which give birth to such regimes represent real forces, and the creation of such regimes is part of a long-run process of social transformation.

What we need to put in the forefront of our consciousness is that both the party of order and the party of movement are currently strong. We have not yet reached the peak of the political consolidation of the capitalist world-economy. We are already in the phase of its political decline. If your outlook is developmentalist and mechanical, this pair of statements is an absurdity. From a world-system perspective, and using a dialectical mode of analysis, it is quite precise and intelligible.

This struggle takes place on all fronts—political, economic, and cultural—and in all arenas of the world, in the core states, in the periphery (largely in the Third World), and in the semiperiphery (many but not all of which stats have collective ownership of basic property and are hence often called 'socialist' states).

Take a struggle like that of Vietnam, of Algeria, or Angola. They were wars of national libera-tion. They united peoples in these areas. Ultimately, the forces of national liberation won or are winning political change. How may we evaluate its effect? On the one hand, these colonial wars fundamentally weakened the internal supports of the regimes of the USA, France and Portugal. They sapped the dominant forces of world capitalism. These wars made many changes possible in the countries of struggle, the metropolises, and in third countries. And yet, and yet—one can ask if the net result has not been in part further to integrate these countries, even their regimes, into the capitalist world-economy. It did both of course. We gain nothing by hiding this from our-selves. On the other hand, we gain nothing by showing Olympian neutrality in the form of equal disdain for unequal combatants.

The process of analysis and the process of social transformation are not separate. They are obverse sides of one coin. Our praxis informs, indeed makes possible, our analytic frameworks. But the work of analysis is itself a central part of the praxis of change. The perspectives for the future of inequality in the world-system are fairly clear in the long run. In the long run the in-equalities will disappear as the result of a fundamental transformation of the world-system. But we all live in the short run, not in the long run. And in the short run, within the constraints of our respective social locations and our social heritages, we labor in the vineyards as we wish, to-wards what ends we choose. We are here today because we want to be. We will make of this colloquium what we want to make of it, and we will draw whatever political conclusions we wish to draw.

■■■■

DEPENDENCE IN AN INTERDEPENDENT WORLD: THE LIMITED POSSIBILITIES OF TRANSFORMATION WITHIN THE CAPITALIST WORLD-ECONOMY

'Dependence' has become the latest euphemism in a long list of such terms. No doubt its orig-inal intent was critical. The term itself emerged out of the 'structuralist' theories of Latin American scholars and was meant as a rebuttal to 'developmentalist' or 'modernization' theories and 'monetarist' policy views.[1] André Gunder Frank has traced its intellectual origins and its limita-tions in a recent combative paper entitled 'Dependence is dead; long live dependence and the class struggle'.[2]

We live in a capitalist world-economy, one that took definitive shape as a European world-economy in the sixteenth century (see Wallerstein 1974a) and came to include the whole world geographically in the nineteenth century. Capitalism as a system of production for sale in a mar-ket for profit and appropriation of this profit on the basis of individual or collective ownership has only existed in, and can be said to require, a world-system in which the political units are not co-extensive with the boundaries of the market economy. This has permitted sellers to profit from strengths in the market whenever they exist but enabled them simultaneously to seek, when-ever needed, the instrusion of political entities to distort the market in their favor. Far from being a system of free competition of all sellers, it is a system in which competition becomes relatively free only when the economic advantage of upper strata is so clear-cut that the unconstrained operation of the market serves effectively to reinforce the existing system of stratification.

This is not to say that there are no changes in position. Quite the contrary. There is constant and patterned movement between groups of economic actors as to who shall occupy various

---

[1] See, as a mere beginning, Bodenheimer 1971, Caputo and Pizarro 1970, Cardoso 1971, Cockcroft *et al.* 1972, *Bulletin of the Institute of Development Studies* 1971.

[2] See Frank 1972a; see also for a similar point of view *Frères du Monde* 1971.

positions in the hierarchy of production, profit, and consumption. And there are secular developments in the structure of the capitalist world-system such that we can envisage that its internal contradictions as a system will bring it to an end in the twenty-first or twenty-second century.

The important thing for living men, and for scholars and scientists as their collective intellectual expression, is to situate the options available in the contemporary situation in terms of the patterns we can discern in the historical past. In this task, conceptual clarification is the most constant need, and as life goes on and new experiences occur, we learn, if we are wise, to reject and reformulate the partial truths of our predecessors, and to unmask the ideological obscurantism of the self-interested upholders of encrusted privilege.

The years 1945–70 were a period of exceptional obscurantism in all fields of study, and African studies has been in the sense typical. *Liberal ideology prevailed in the world of social science reflecting the easy and unquestioned economic hegemony of the United States.* But liberalism has come onto hard days—not least of all in the analysis of 'development'. *If the decline of Cold War polarization in the 1960s effectively reduced the political bargaining power of African states, the beginning of a worldwide economic contraction of effective demand of the 1970s is likely to sweep African aspirations aside as those who are on top of* the world heap struggle with each other to remain there. In the 1960s, African scholars began to worry about 'growth without development'. In the 1970s and 1980s, there is the clear possibility of neither growth nor development.

To understand the issues, we must successively treat the structure of the world-economy, its cyclical patterns including the present conjuncture, and the ways in which the position of particular states may change within this structure. This will, I believe, explain 'the limited possibilities of transformation within the capitalist world-economy'.

The structure of the world-economy as a single system has come increasingly in recent years to be analyzed in terms of a core–periphery image, an image which has been linked with the discussion of 'dependence'. And thus it has been argued, for example, that Third World countries are not 'underdeveloped' nations but 'peripheral capitalist' nations.[3] This is far clearer terminology, but it leads unfortunately to further confusion if the unicity of the world-system is not borne clearly in mind. Ikonicoff argues, for example, that peripheral capitalist economies 'operate by economic laws and growth factors [that] are clearly different from those of the economies one might call the model of classic capitalism' (1972, p. 692). This is only so because our model of 'classic capitalism' is wrong, since both in the sixteenth century and today the core and the periphery of the world-economy were not two separate 'economies' with two separate 'laws' but *one capitalist economic system with different* sectors *performing different functions.*

Once one recognizes the unicity of the system, one is lead to ask if the conception of a bi-modal system is adequate. Clearly, it leaves much unexplained, and thus we have seen the emergence of such terms as 'subimperial' states (see Marini 1969) or 'go-between nations' (see Galtung 1972, pp. 128–9). Both of these terms seem to me unwise as they emphasize only one aspect of their role, each an important one, but not in my opinion the key one. I prefer to call them semiperipheral countries to underline the ways they are at a disadvantage in the existing world-system. More important, however, is the need to explicate the *complexity* of the role which semiperipheral states play within the system as well as the fact that the system could not function without being *tri*-modal.

Before this explication, it is necessary to spell out one more fact. The capitalist system is composed of owners who sell for profit. The fact that an owner is a group of individuals rather than a single person makes no essential difference. This has long been recognized for joint-stock companies. It must now also be recognized for sovereign states. A state which collectively owns

---

[3] See, for example, the whole special issue of *Revue Tiers-Monde* 1972, especially the introduction by Ikonicoff.

all the means of production is merely a collective capitalist firm as long as it remains—as all such states are, in fact, presently compelled to remain—a participant in the market of the capitalist world-economy. No doubt such a 'firm' *may* have different modalities of internal division of profit, but this does not change its essential economic role *vis-à-vis* others operating in the world market.[4]

---

[4] I have argued this at length in my paper, 'The Rise and Future Demise of the World Capitalist System: Concepts for Comparative Analysis' (1974b, and above, ch. 1). Samir Amin makes just about the same point:

The predominance of the capitalist mode of production expresses itself also on another level, that of the *world-system* which constitutes a characteristic of contemporary reality. At this level, the formations (central and peripheral) are organized in a single hierarchical system. The disintegration of this system—with the founding of socialist states, true or self-styled—does not change anything in this hypothesis . . . Socialism cannot be in fact the juxtaposition of national socialisms, regressive with respect to integrated (but not egalitarian) world character of capitalism. Nor can it be a *socialist system* separate from the world-system. It is precisely for this reason that there are not two world markets: the capitalist market and the socialist market; but only *one*—the former—in which eastern Europe participates, albeit marginally. (1972b, p. 13)

CHAPTER SIX

Current Debates

"International politics is a man's world, a world of power and conflict in which warfare is a privileged activity." *J. Ann Tickner (1988)*

"Conflict between civilizations will be the latest phase in the evolution of conflict in the modern world." *Samuel P. Huntington (1993)*

"Culture is not our destiny; democracy is." *Kim Dae Jung (1995)*

"For much of modern history, what characterized governments in Europe and North America, and differentiated them from those around the world, was not democracy but constitutional liberalism." *Fareed Zakaria (1995, 2003)*

Joseph Campbell made a statement that seems particularly appropriate to the conclusion of this text and that is: "You need to learn all the rules, and then forget them." He gives the example of a golfer who knows the rules, how to hold the club, how to swing the club, and yet he is constantly working on improving his game.[174] Campbell did not mean, therefore, that one literally forgets the rules; he meant that the rules simply become part of a foundation from which one may improve a given skill, or thoughts within a chosen discipline. And that, it seems, is what a liberal arts education offers: It is a precious moment in life when one encounters and contemplates the big questions, when one learns the foundation—the *rules*, if you will—of a particular discipline before moving on to any refinement of your chosen craft, or area of study. The purpose of this chapter is simply to whet your appetite; to introduce a few of more recent contributions to the field, with the hope that you, the student, will participate in the debates—at school, at home, with friends, at work—and continue the quest for answers to the big questions of international politics.

---

[174] John M. Maher, et al., eds., *An Open Life: Joseph Campbell in Conversation with Michael Toms* (New York: Harper & Row, 1990).

■▮▯■▯■▮▯■▯▮■▯■ ■▯■▯■▮▯■▯■▮■ ■ ■▯■▯■▮▯■▮

READING 17: SAMUEL P. HUNTINGTON

SAMUEL P. HUNTINGTON,

"THE CLASH OF CIVILIZATIONS," FOREIGN AFFAIRS, 1991

THE NEXT PATTERN OF CONFLICT

World politics is entering a new phase, and intellectuals have not hesitated to proliferate visions of what it will be—the end of history, the return of traditional rivalries between nation states, and the decline of the nation state from the conflicting pulls of tribalism and globalism, among others. Each of these visions catches aspects of the emerging reality. Yet they all miss a crucial, indeed a central, aspect of what global politics is likely to be in the coming years.

It is my hypothesis that the fundamental source of conflict in this new world will not be primarily ideological or primarily economic. The great divisions among humankind and the dominating source of conflict will be cultural. Nation states will remain the most powerful actors in world affairs, but the principal conflicts of global politics will occur between nations and groups of different civilizations. The clash of civilizations will dominate global politics. The fault lines between civilizations will be the battle lines of the future.

Conflict between civilizations will be the latest phase in the evolution of conflict in the modern world. For a century and a half after the emergence of the modern international system with the Peace of Westphalia, the conflicts of the Western world were largely among princes—emperors, absolute monarchs and constitutional monarchs attempting to expand their bureaucracies, their armies, their mercantilist economic strength and, most important, the territory they ruled. In the process they created nation states, and beginning with the French Revolution the principal lines of conflict were between nations rather than princes. In 1793, as R. R. Palmer put it, "The wars of kings were over; the wars of peoples had begun." This nineteenth-century pattern lasted until the end of World War I. Then, as a result of the Russian Revolution and the reaction against it, the conflict of nations yielded to the conflict of ideologies, first among communism, fascism-Nazism and liberal democracy, and then between communism and liberal democracy. During the Cold War, this latter conflict became embodied in the struggle between the two superpowers, neither of which was a nation state in the classical European sense and each of which defined its identity in terms of its ideology.

These conflicts between princes, nation states and ideologies were primarily conflicts within Western civilization, "Western civil wars," as William Lind has labeled them. This was as true of the Cold War as it was of the world wars and the earlier wars of the seventeenth, eighteenth and nineteenth centuries. With the end of the Cold War, international politics moves out of its Western phase, and its centerpiece becomes the interaction between the West and non-Western civilizations and among non-Western civilizations. In the politics of civilizations, the peoples and governments of non-Western civilizations no longer remain the objects of history as targets of Western colonialism but join the West as movers and shapers of history.

THE NATURE OF CIVILIZATIONS

During the cold war the world was divided into the First, Second and Third Worlds. Those divisions are no longer relevant. It is far more meaningful now to group countries not in terms of their political or economic systems or in terms of their level of economic development but rather in terms of their culture and civilization.

What do we mean when we talk of a civilization? A civilization is a cultural entity. Villages, regions, ethnic groups, nationalities, religious groups, all have distinct cultures at different levels of cultural heterogeneity. The culture of a village in southern Italy may be different from that of a village in northern Italy, but both will share in a common Italian culture that distinguishes them from German villages. European communities, in turn, will share cultural features that distinguish them from Arab or Chinese communities. Arabs, Chinese and Westerners, however, are not part of any broader cultural entity. They constitute civilizations. A civilization is thus the highest cultural grouping of people and the broadest level of cultural identity people have short of that which distinguishes humans from other species. It is defined both by common objective elements, such as language, history, religion, customs, institutions, and by the subjective self-identification of people. People have levels of identity: a resident of Rome may define himself with varying degrees of intensity as a Roman, an Italian, a Catholic, a Christian, a European, a Westerner. The civilization to which he belongs is the broadest level of identification with which he intensely identifies. People can and do redefine their identities and, as a result, the composition and boundaries of civilizations change.

Civilizations may involve a large number of people, as with China ("a civilization pretending to be a state," as Lucian Pye put it), or a very small number of people, such as the Anglophone Caribbean. A civilization may include several nation states, as is the case with Western, Latin American and Arab civilizations, or only one, as is the case with Japanese civilization. Civilizations obviously blend and overlap, and may include subcivilizations. Western civilization has two major variants, European and North American, and Islam has its Arab, Turkic and Malay subdivisions. Civilizations are nonetheless meaningful entities, and while the lines between them are seldom sharp, they are real. Civilizations are dynamic; they rise and fall; they divide and merge. And, as any student of history knows, civilizations disappear and are buried in the sands of time.

Westerners tend to think of nation states as the principal actors in global affairs. They have been that, however, for only a few centuries. The broader reaches of human history have been the history of civilizations. In *A Study of History,* Arnold Toynbee identified 21 major civilizations; only six of them exist in the contemporary world.

WHY CIVILIZATIONS WILL CLASH

Civilization identity will be increasingly important in the future, and the world will be shaped in large measure by the interactions among seven or eight major civilizations. These include Western, Confucian, Japanese, Islamic, Hindu, Slavic-Orthodox, Latin American and possibly African civilization. The most important conflicts of the future will occur along the cultural fault lines separating these civilizations from one another.

Why will this be the case?

First, differences among civilizations are not only real; they are basic. Civilizations are differentiated from each other by history, language, culture, tradition and, most important, religion. The people of different civilizations have different views on the relations between God and man, the individual and the group, the citizen and the state, parents and children, husband and wife, as well as differing views of the relative importance of rights and responsibilities, liberty and authority, equality and hierarchy. These differences are the produce of centuries. They will not soon disappear. They are far more fundamental than differences among political ideologies and political regimes. Differences do not necessarily mean conflict, and conflict does not necessarily mean violence. Over the centuries, however, differences among civilizations have generated the most prolonged and the most violent conflicts.

Second, the world is becoming a smaller place. The interactions between peoples of different civilizations are increasing; these increasing interactions intensify civilization consciousness and awareness of differences between civilizations and commonalities within civilizations. North

African immigration to France generates hostility among Frenchmen and at the same time increased receptivity to immigration by "good" European Catholic Poles. Americans react far more negatively to Japanese investment than to larger investments from Canada and European countries. Similarly, as Donald Horowitz has pointed out, "An Ibo may be . . . an Owerri Ibo or an Onitsha Ibo in what was the Eastern region of Nigeria. In Lagos, he is simply an Ibo. In London, he is a Nigerian. In New York, he is an African." The interactions among peoples of different civilizations enhance the civilization-consciousness of people that, in turn, invigorates differences and animosities stretching or thought to stretch back deep into history.

Third, the processes of economic modernization and social change throughout the world are separating people from longstanding local identities. They also weaken the nation state as a source of identity. In much of the world religion has moved in to fill this gap, often in the form of movements that are labeled "fundamentalist." Such movements are found in Western Christianity, Judaism, Buddhism and Hinduism, as well as in Islam. In most countries and most religions the people active in fundamentalist movements are young, college-educated, middle-class technicians, professionals and business persons. The "unsecularization of the world," George Weigel has remarked, "is one of the dominant social facts of life in the late twentieth century." The revival of religion, "la revanche de Dieu," as Gilles Kepel labeled it, provides a basis for identity and commitment that transcends national boundaries and unites civilizations.

Fourth, the growth of civilization-consciousness is enhanced by the dual role of the West. On the one hand, the West is at a peak of power. At the same time, however, and perhaps as a result, a return to the roots phenomenon is occurring among non-Western civilizations. Increasingly one hears references to trends toward a turning inward and "Asianization" in Japan, the end of the Nehru legacy and the "Hinduization" of India, the failure of Western ideas of socialism and nationalism and hence "re-Islamization" of the Middle East, and now a debate over Westernization versus Russianization in Boris Yeltsin's country. A West at the peak of its power confronts non-Wests that increasingly have the desire, the will and the resources to shape the world in non-Western ways.

In the past, the elites of non-Western societies were usually the people who were most involved with the West, had been educated at Oxford, the Sorbonne or Sandhurst, and had absorbed Western attitudes and values. At the same time, the populace in non-Western countries often remained deeply imbued with the indigenous culture. Now, however, these relationships are being reversed. A de-Westernization and indigenization of elites is occurring in many non-Western countries at the same time that Western, usually American, cultures, styles and habits become more popular among the mass of the people.

Fifth, cultural characteristics and differences are less mutable and hence less easily compromised and resolved than political and economic ones. In the former Soviet Union, communists can become democrats, the rich can become poor and the poor rich, but Russians cannot become Estonians and Azeris cannot become Armenians. In class and ideological conflicts, the key question was "Which side are you on?" and people could and did choose sides and change sides. In conflicts between civilizations, the question is "What are you?" That is a given that cannot be changed. And as we know, from Bosnia to the Caucasus to the Sudan, the wrong answer to that question can mean a bullet in the head. Even more than ethnicity, religion discriminates sharply and exclusively among people. A person can be half-French and half-Arab and simultaneously even a citizen of two countries. It is more difficult to be half-Catholic and half-Muslim.

Finally, economic regionalism is increasing. The proportions of total trade that were intraregional rose between 1980 and 1989 from 51 percent to 59 percent in Europe, 33 percent to 37 percent in East Asia, and 32 percent to 36 percent in North America. The importance of regional economic blocs is likely to continue to increase in the future. On the one hand, successful economic regionalism will reinforce civilization-consciousness. On the other hand, economic regionalism may succeed only when it is rooted in a common civilization. The European Community rests on the shared foundation of European culture and Western Christianity. The success of the North American Free Trade Area depends on the convergence now underway of Mexican, Canadian and American cultures. Japan, in contrast, faces difficulties in creating a comparable economic entity in East Asia because Japan is a society and civilization unique to itself. However strong the trade and investment links Japan may develop with other East Asian countries, its cultural differences with those countries inhibit and perhaps preclude its promoting regional economic integration like that in Europe and North America.

Common culture, in contrast, is clearly facilitating the rapid expansion of the economic relations between the People's Republic of China and Hong Kong, Taiwan, Singapore and the overseas Chinese communities in other Asian countries. With the Cold War over, cultural commonalities increasingly overcome ideological differences, and mainland China and Taiwan move closer together. If cultural commonality is a prerequisite for economic integration, the principal East Asian economic bloc of the future is likely to be centered on China. This bloc is, in fact, already coming into existence. As Murray Weidenbaum has observed,

> Despite the current Japanese dominance of the region, the Chinese-based economy of Asia is rapidly emerging as a new epicenter for industry, commerce and finance. This strategic area contains substantial amounts of technology and manufacturing capability (Taiwan), outstanding entrepreneurial, marketing and services acumen (Hong Kong), a fine communications network (Singapore), a tremendous pool of financial capital (all three), and very large endowments of land, resources and labor (mainland China). . . . From Guangzhou to Singapore, from Kuala Lumpur to Manila, this influential network—often based on extensions of the traditional clans—has been described as the backbone of the East Asian economy.[1]

Culture and religion also form the basis of the Economic Cooperation Organization, which brings together ten non-Arab Muslim countries: Iran, Pakistan, Turkey, Azerbaijan, Kazakhstan, Kyrgyzstan, Turkmenistan, Tadjikistan, Uzbekistan and Afghanistan. One impetus to the revival and expansion of this organization, founded originally in the 1960s by Turkey, Pakistan and Iran, is the realization by the leaders of several of these countries that they had no chance of admission to the European Community. Similarly, Caricom, the Central American Common Market and Mercosur rest on common cultural foundations. Efforts to build a broader Caribbean-Central American economic entity bridging the Anglo-Latin divide, however, have to date failed.

As people define their identity in ethnic and religious terms, they are likely to see an "us" versus "them" relation existing between themselves and people of different ethnicity or religion. The end of ideologically defined states in Eastern Europe and the former Soviet Union permits traditional ethnic identities and animosities to come to the fore. Differences in culture and religion create differences over policy issues, ranging from human rights to immigration to trade and commerce to the environment. Geographical propinquity give rise to conflicting territorial claims from Bosnia to Mindanao. Most important, the efforts of the West to promote its values of democracy and liberalism as universal values, to maintain its military predominance and to advance its economic interests engender countering responses from other civilizations. Decreasingly able to mobilize support and form coalitions on the basis of ideology, governments and groups will increasingly attempt to mobilize support by appealing to common religion and civilization identity.

▮▪▮▪

---

[1] Murray Weidenbaum, *Greater China: The Next Economic Superpower?*, St. Louis: Washington University Center for the Study of American Business, Contemporary Issues, Series 57, February 1993, pp. 2–3.

Civilization Rallying: The Kin-Country Syndrome

Groups or states belonging to one civilization that become involved in war with people from a different civilization naturally try to rally support from other members of their own civilization. As the post-Cold War world evolves, civilization commonality, what H.D.S. Greenway has termed the "kin-country" syndrome, is replacing political ideology and traditional balance of power considerations as the principal basis for cooperation and coalitions. It can be seen gradually emerging in the post-Cold War conflicts. The next world war, if there is one, will be a war between civilizations.

■■■■

The West Versus the Rest

The West is now at an extraordinary peak of power in relation to other civilizations. Its superpower opponent has disappeared from the map. Military conflict among Western states is unthinkable, and Western military power is unrivaled. Apart from Japan, the West faces no economic challenge. It dominates international political and security institutions and with Japan international economic institutions. Global political and security issues are effectively settled by a directorate of the United States, Britain and France, world economic issues by a directorate of the United States, Germany and Japan, all of which maintain extraordinarily close relations with each other to the exclusion of lesser and largely non-Western countries. Decisions made at the U.N. Security Council or in the International Monetary Fund that reflect the interests of the West are presented to the world as reflecting the desires of the world community. The very phrase "the world community" has become the euphemistic collective noun (replacing "the Free World") to give global legitimacy to actions reflecting the interests of the United States and other Western powers.[2] Through the IMF and other international economic institutions, the West promotes its economic interests and imposes on other nations the economic policies it thinks appropriate. In any poll of non-Western peoples, the IMF undoubtedly would win the support of finance ministers and a few others, but get an overwhelmingly unfavorable rating from just about everyone else, who would agree with Georgy Arbatov's characterization of IMF officials as "neo-Bolsheviks who love expropriating other people's money, imposing undemocratic and alien rules of economic and political conduct and stifling economic freedom."

Western domination of the U.N. Security Council and its decisions, tempered only by occasional abstention by China, produced U.N. legitimation of the West's use of force to drive Iraq out of Kuwait and its elimination of Iraq's sophisticated weapons and capacity to produce such weapons. It also produced the quite unprecedented action by the United States, Britain and France in getting the Security Council to demand that Libya hand over the Pan Am 103 bombing suspects and then to impose sanctions when Libya refused. After defeating the largest Arab army, the West did not hesitate to throw its weight around in the Arab world. The West in effect is using international institutions, military power and economic resources to run the world in ways that will maintain Western predominance, protect Western interests and promote Western political and economic values.

That at least is the way in which non-Westerners see the new world, and there is a significant element of truth in their view. Differences in power and struggles for military, economic and institutional power are thus one source of conflict between the West and other civilizations. Dif-

---

[2] Almost invariably Western leaders claim they are acting on behalf of "the world community." One minor lapse occurred during the run-up to the Gulf War. In an interview on "Good Morning America," Dec. 21, 1990, British Prime Minister John Major referred to the actions "the West" was taking against Saddam Hussein. He quickly corrected himself and subsequently referred to "the world community." He was, however, right when he erred.

ferences in culture, that is basic values and beliefs, are a second source of conflict. V. S. Naipaul has argued that Western civilization is the "universal civilization" that "fits all men." At a superficial level much of Western culture has indeed permeated the rest of the world. At a more basic level, however, Western concepts differ fundamentally from those prevalent in other civilizations. Western ideas of individualism, liberalism, constitutionalism, human rights, equality, liberty, the rule of law, democracy, free markets, the separation of church and state, often have little resonance in Islamic, Confucian, Japanese, Hindu, Buddhist or Orthodox cultures. Western efforts to propagate such ideas produce instead a reaction against "human rights imperialism" and a reaffirmation of indigenous values, as can be seen in the support for religious fundamentalism by the younger generation in non-Western cultures. The very notion that there could be a "universal civilization" is a Western idea, directly at odds with the particularism of most Asian societies and their emphasis on what distinguishes one people from another. Indeed, the author of a review of 100 comparative studies of values in different societies concluded that "the values that are most important in the West are least important worldwide."[3] In the political realm, of course, these differences are most manifest in the efforts of the United States and other Western powers to induce other peoples to adopt Western ideas concerning democracy and human rights. Modern democratic government originated in the West. When it has developed in non-Western societies it has usually been the product of Western colonialism or imposition.

The central axis of world politics in the future is likely to be, in Kishore Mahbubani's phrase, the conflict between "the West and the Rest" and the responses of non-Western civilizations to Western power and values.[4] Those responses generally take one or a combination of three forms. At one extreme, non-Western states can, like Burma and North Korea, attempt to pursue a course of isolation, to insulate their societies from penetration or "corruption" by the West, and, in effect, to opt out of participation in the Western-dominated global community. The costs of this course, however, are high, and few states have pursued it exclusively. A second alternative, the equivalent of "band-wagoning" in international relations theory, is to attempt to join the West and accept its values and institutions. The third alternative is to attempt to "balance" the West by developing economic and military power and cooperating with other non-Western societies against the West, while preserving indigenous values and institutions; in short, to modernize but not to Westernize.

THE TORN COUNTRIES

In the future, as people differentiate themselves by civilization, countries with large numbers of peoples of different civilizations, such as the Soviet Union and Yugoslavia, are candidates for dismemberment. Some other countries have a fair degree of cultural homogeneity but are divided over whether their society belongs to one civilization or another. These are torn countries. Their leaders typically wish to pursue a bandwagoning strategy and to make their countries members of the West, but the history, culture and traditions of their countries are non-Western. The most obvious and prototypical torn country is Turkey. The late twentieth-century leaders of Turkey have followed in the Attatürk tradition and defined Turkey as a modern, secular, Western nation state. They allied Turkey with the West in NATO and in the Gulf War; they applied for membership in the European Community. At the same time, however, elements in Turkish society have supported an Islamic revival and have argued that Turkey is basically a Middle Eastern Muslim society. In addition, while the elite of Turkey has defined Turkey as a Western society, the elite of the West refuses to accept Turkey as such. Turkey will not become a member of the European Com-

---

[3] Harry C. Triandis, *The New York Times,* Dec. 25, 1990, p. 41, and "Cross-Cultural Studies of Individualism and Collectivism," Nebraska Symposium on Motivation, vol. 37, 1989, pp. 41–133.

[4] Kishore Mahbubani, "The West and the Rest," *The National Interest,* Summer 1992, pp. 3–13.

munity, and the real reason, as President Özal said, "is that we are Muslim and they are Christian and they don't say that." Having rejected Mecca, and then being rejected by Brussels, where does Turkey look? Tashkent may be the answer. The end of the Soviet Union gives Turkey the opportunity to become the leader of a revived Turkic civilization involving seven countries from the borders of Greece to those of China. Encouraged by the West, Turkey is making strenuous efforts to carve out this new identity for itself. . . .

■ ■ ■ ■

THE CONFUCIAN-ISLAMIC CONNECTION

The obstacles to non-Western countries joining the West vary considerably. They are least for Latin American and East European countries. They are greater for the Orthodox countries of the former Soviet Union. They are still greater for Muslim, Confucian, Hindu and Buddhist societies. Japan has established a unique position for itself as an associate member of the West: it is in the West in some respects but clearly not of the West in important dimensions. Those countries that for reason of culture and power do not wish to, or cannot, join the West compete with the West by developing their own economic, military and political power. They do this by promoting their internal development and by cooperating with other non-Western countries. The most prominent form of this cooperation is the Confucian-Islamic connection that has emerged to challenge Western interests, values and power.

Almost without exception, Western countries are reducing their military power; under Yeltsin's leadership so also is Russia. China, North Korea and several Middle Eastern states, however, are significantly expanding their military capabilities. They are doing this by the import of arms from Western and non-Western sources and by the development of indigenous arms industries. One result in the emergence of what Charles Krauthammer has called "Weapon States," and the Weapon States are not Western states. Another result is the redefinition of arms control, which is a Western concept and a Western goal. During the Cold War the primary purpose of arms control was to establish a stable military balance between the United States and its allies and the Soviet Union and its allies. In the post-Cold War world the primary objective of arms control is to prevent the development by non-Western societies of military capabilities that could threaten Western interests. The West attempts to do this through international agreements, economic pressure and controls on the transfer of arms and weapons technologies.

The conflict between the West and the Confucian-Islamic states focuses largely, although not exclusively, on nuclear, chemical and biological weapons, ballistic missiles and other sophisticated means for delivering them, and the guidance, intelligence and other electronic capabilities for achieving that goal. The West promotes nonproliferation as a universal norm and nonproliferation treaties and inspections as means of realizing that norm. It also threatens a variety of sanctions against those who promote the spread of sophisticated weapons and proposes some benefits for those who do not. The attention of the West focuses, naturally, on nations that are actually or potentially hostile to the West.

The non-Western nations, on the other hand, assert their right to acquire and to deploy whatever weapons they think necessary for their security. They also have absorbed, to the full, the truth of the response of the Indian defense minister when asked what lesson he learned from the Gulf War: "Don't fight the United States unless you have nuclear weapons." Nuclear weapons, chemical weapons and missiles are viewed, probably erroneously, as the potential equalizer of superior Western conventional power. China, of course, already has nuclear weapons; Pakistan and India have the capability to deploy them. North Korea, Iran, Iraq, Libya and Algeria appear to be attempting to acquire them. A top Iranian official has declared that all Muslim states should acquire nuclear weapons, and in 1988 the president of Iran reportedly issued a directive calling for development of "offensive and defensive chemical, biological and radiological weapons." . . .

A Confucian-Islamic military connection has thus come into being, designed to promote acquisition by its members of the weapons and weapons technologies needed to counter the military power of the West. It may or may not last. At present, however, it is, as Dave McCurdy has said, "a renegades' mutual support pact, run by the proliferators and their backers." A new form of arms competition is thus occurring between Islamic-Confucian states and the West. In an old-fashioned arms race, each side developed its own arms to balance or to achieve superiority against the other side. In this new form of arms competition, one side is developing its arms and the other side is attempting not to balance but to limit and prevent that arms build-up while at the same time reducing its own military capabilities.

IMPLICATIONS FOR THE WEST

This article does not argue that civilization identities will replace all other identities, that nation states will disappear, that each civilization will become a single coherent political entity, that groups within a civilization will not conflict with and even fight each other. This paper does set forth the hypotheses that differences between civilizations are real and important; civilization-consciousness is increasing; conflict between civilizations will supplant ideological and other forms of conflict as the dominant global form of conflict; international relations, historically a game played out within Western civilization, will increasingly be de-Westernized and become a game in which non-Western civilizations are actors and not simply objects; successful political, security and economic international institutions are more likely to develop within civilizations than across civilizations; conflicts between groups in different civilizations will be more frequent, more sustained and more violent than conflicts between groups in the same civilization; violent conflicts between groups in different civilizations are the most likely and most dangerous source of escalation that could lead to global wars; the paramount axis of world politics will be the relations between "the West and the Rest"; the elites in some torn non-Western countries will try to make their countries part of the West, but in most cases face major obstacles to accomplishing this; a central focus of conflict for the immediate future will be between the West and several Islamic-Confucian states.

This is not to advocate the desirability of conflicts between civilizations. It is to set forth descriptive hypotheses as to what the future may be like. If these are plausible hypotheses, however, it is necessary to consider their implications for Western policy. These implications should be divided between short-term advantage and long-term accommodation. In the short term it is clearly in the interest of the West to promote greater cooperation and unity within its own civilization, particularly between its European and North American components; to incorporate into the West societies in Eastern Europe and Latin America whose cultures are close to those of the West; to promote and maintain cooperative relations with Russia and Japan; to prevent escalation of local inter-civilization conflicts into major inter-civilization wars; to limit the expansion of the military strength of Confucian and Islamic states; to moderate the reduction of Western military capabilities and maintain military superiority in East and Southwest Asia; to exploit differences and conflicts among Confucian and Islamic states; to support in other civilizations groups sympathetic to Western values and interests; to strengthen international institutions that reflect and legitimate Western interests and values and to promote the involvement of non-Western states in those institutions.

In the longer term other measures would be called for. Western civilization is both Western and modern. Non-Western civilizations have attempted to become modern without becoming Western. To date only Japan has fully succeeded in this quest. Non-Western civilizations will continue to attempt to acquire the wealth, technology, skills, machines and weapons that are part of being modern. They will also attempt to reconcile this modernity with their traditional culture and values. Their economic and military strength relative to the West will increase. Hence the West will increasingly have to accommodate these non-Western modern civilizations whose power approaches that of the West but whose values and interests differ significantly from those of the

West. This will require the West to maintain the economic and military power necessary to protect its interests in relation to these civilizations. It will also, however, require the West to develop a more profound understanding of the basic religious and philosophical assumptions underlying other civilizations and the ways in which people in those civilizations see their interests. It will require an effort to identify elements of commonality between Western and other civilizations. For the relevant future, there will be no universal civilization, but instead a world of different civilizations, each of which will have to learn to coexist with the others.

■▮■▮■▮■▮▮▮■▮■▮ ■ ▮■▮■▮■▮▮■▮■ ■ ■ ▮■▮■▮■▮

READING 18: J. ANN TICKNER

J. ANN TICKNER,

"HANS MORGENTHAU'S PRINCIPLES OF POLITICAL REALISM: A FEMINIST REFORMULATION," MILLENNIUM, 1988

It is not in giving life but in risking life that man is raised above the animal: that is why superiority has been accorded in humanity not to the sex that brings forth but to that which kills.

—SIMONE DE BEAUVOIR[1]

International politics is a man's world, a world of power and conflict in which warfare is a privileged activity. Traditionally, diplomacy, military service, and the science of international politics have been largely male domains. In the past, women have rarely been included in the ranks of professional diplomats or the military: of the relatively few women who specialise in the academic discipline of international relations, few are security specialists. Women political scientists who do international relations tend to focus on areas such as international political economy, North-South relations and matters of distributive justice.

Today, in the United States, where women are entering the military and the foreign service in greater numbers than ever before, rarely are they to be found in positions of military leadership or at the top of the foreign policy establishment.[2] One notable exception, Jeane Kirkpatrick, who was US ambassador to the United Nations in the early 1980s, has described herself as 'a mouse in a man's world'. For in spite of her authoritative and forceful public style and strong conservative credentials, Kirkpatrick maintains that she failed to win the respect or attention of her male colleagues on matters of foreign policy.[3]

Millennium: Journal of International Studies. This article first appeared in *Millennium,* (Vol. 17, No. 3, Winter 1988), and is reproduced with the permission of the publisher.

[1] Quoted in Sandra Harding, *The Science Question in Feminism* (Ithaca, NY: Cornell University Press, 1986), p. 148.

[2] In 1987 only 4.8 per cent of the top career Foreign Service employees were women. Statement of Patricia Schroeder before the Committee on Foreign Affairs, US House of Representatives, *Women's Perspectives on US Foreign Policy: A Compilation of Views,* (Washington, DC: US Government Printing Office, 1988), p. 4. For an analysis of women's roles in the American military, see Cynthia Enloe, *Does Khaki Become You? The Militarisation of Women's Lives.* (London: Pluto Press, 1983).

[3] Edward P. Crapol (ed.), *Women and American Foreign Policy* (Westport, CT: Greenwood Press, 1987), p. 167.

Kirkpatrick's story could serve to illustrate the discrimination which women often encounter when they rise to high political office. However, the doubts as to whether a woman would be strong enough to press the nuclear button (an issue raised when a tearful Patricia Schroeder was pictured sobbing on her husband's shoulder as she bowed out of the 1988 US presidential race) suggest that there may be an even more fundamental barrier to women's entry into the highest ranks of the military or of foreign policy-making. Nuclear strategy, with its vocabulary of power, threat, force, and deterrence, has a distinctly masculine ring:[4] moreover, women are stereotypically judged to be lacking in qualities which these terms evoke. It has also been suggested that, although more women are entering the world of public policy, they are more comfortable dealing with domestic issues such as social welfare that are more compatible with their nurturing skills. Yet the large number of women in the ranks of the peace movement suggests that women are not uninterested in issues of war and peace, although their frequent dissent from national security policy has often branded them as naive, uninformed or even unpatriotic.

In this article I propose to explore the question why international politics is perceived as a man's world and why women remain so under-represented in the higher echelons of the foreign policy establishment, the military and the academic discipline of international relations. Since I believe that there is something about this field which renders it particularly inhospitable and unattractive to women, I intend to focus on the nature of the discipline itself rather than on possible strategies to remove barriers to women's access to high policy positions. As I have already suggested, the issues that get prioritised in foreign policy are issues with which men have had a special affinity. Moreover, if it is primarily men who are describing these issues and constructing theories to explain the workings of the international system, might we not expect to find a masculine perspective in the academic discipline also? If this were so, then it could be argued that the exclusion of women has operated not only at the level of discrimination but also through a process of self-selection which begins with the way in which we are taught about international relations.

In order to investigate this claim that the discipline of international relations—traditionally defined by realism—is based on a masculine world view, I propose to examine Hans Morgenthau's six principles of political realism. I shall use some ideas from feminist theory to show that the way in which Morgenthau describes and explains international politics, and the prescriptions that ensue, are embedded in a masculine perspective. Then I shall suggest some ways in which feminist theory might help us begin to conceptualise a world view from a feminine perspective and to formulate a feminist epistemology of international relations. Drawing on these observations, I shall conclude with a reformulation of Morgenthau's six principles. Male critics of contemporary realism have already raised many of the same questions about realism that I shall address. However, in undertaking this exercise, I hope to link the growing critical perspective on international relations theory and feminist writers interested in global issues. Adding a feminist perspective to its discourse could also help to make the field of international relations more accessible to women scholars and practitioners.

Hans Morgenthau's Principles of Political Realism: A Masculine Perspective?

I have chosen to focus on Hans Morgenthau's six principles of political realism because they represent one of the most important statements of contemporary realism from which several generations of scholars and practitioners of international relations have been nourished. Although Morgenthau has frequently been criticised for his lack of scientific rigour and ambiguous use of language, these six principles have significantly framed the way in which the majority of interna-

---

[4] For an analysis of the role of masculine language in shaping strategic thinking see Carol Cohn, "Sex and Death in the Rational World of Defense Intellectuals," *Signs: Journal of Women in Culture and Society* (Vol. 12, No. 4, Summer 1987), pp. 687–718.

tional relations scholars and practitioners in the West have thought about international politics since 1945.[5]

Morgenthau's principles of political realism can be summarised as follows:

1. Politics, like society in general, is governed by objective laws that have their roots in human nature which is unchanging: therefore it is possible to develop a rational theory that reflects these objective laws.

2. The main signpost of political realism is the concept of interest defined in terms of power which infuses rational order into the subject matter of politics, and thus makes the theoretical understanding of politics possible. Political realism stresses the rational, objective and unemotional.

3. Realism assumes that interest defined as power is an objective category which is universally valid but not with a meaning that is fixed once and for all. Power is the control of man over man.

4. Political realism is aware of the moral significance of political action. It is also aware of the tension between the moral command and the requirements of successful political action.

5. Political realism refuses to identify the moral aspirations of a particular nation with the moral laws that govern the universe. It is the concept of interest defined in terms of power that saves us from moral excess and political folly.

6. The political realist maintains the autonomy of the political sphere. He asks "How does this policy affect the power of the nation?" Political realism is based on pluralistic conception of human nature. A man who was nothing but "political man" would be a beast, for he would be completely lacking in moral restraints. But, in order to develop an autonomous theory of political behavior, "political man" must be abstracted from other aspects of human nature.[6]

I am not going to argue that Morgenthau is incorrect in his portrayal of the international system. I do believe, however, that it is a partial description of international politics because it is based on assumptions about human nature that are partial and that privilege masculinity. First, it is necessary to define masculinity and femininity. According to almost all feminist theorists, masculinity and femininity refer to a set of socially constructed categories that vary in time and place rather than to biological determinants. In the West conceptual dichotomies such as objectivity *vs.* subjectivity, reason *vs.* emotion, mind *vs.* body, culture *vs.* nature, self *vs.* other or autonomy *vs.* relatedness, knowing *vs.* being and public *vs.* private have typically been used to describe male/female differences by feminists and non-feminists alike.[7] In the United States, psychological tests conducted across different socio-economic groups confirm that individuals perceive these dichotomies as masculine and feminine and also that the characteristics associated with masculinity are more highly valued by both men and women alike.[8] It is important to

---

[5] The claim for the dominance of the realist paradigm is supported by John A. Vasquez, "Colouring it Morgenthau: New Evidence for an Old Thesis on Quantitative International Studies," *British Journal of International Studies* (Vol. 5. No. 3, Oct. 1979), pp. 210–28. For a critique of Morgenthau's ambiguous use of language, see Inis L. Claude Jr., *Power and International Relations* (New York: Random House, 1962), especially pp. 25–37.

[6] These are drawn from the six principles of political realism in Hans Morgenthau, *Politics Among Nations: The Struggle for Power and Peace,* 5th Revised Ed. (New York: Alfred Knopf, 1973), pp. 4–15. I am aware that these principles embody only a partial statement of Morgenthau's very rich study of international politics, a study which deserves a much more detailed analysis than I can give it here.

[7] This list is a composite of the male/female dichotomies which appear in Evelyn Fox Keller, *Reflections on Gender and Science* (New Haven, CT: Yale University Press, 1985) and Sandra Harding, *op. cit.*

[8] Inge K. Broverman, Susan R. Vogel, Donald M. Broverman, Frank E. Clarkson and Paul S. Rosenkranz, "Sex-Role Stereotypes: A Current Appraisal," *Journal of Social Issues* (Vol. 28, No. 2, 1972), pp. 59–78. Replication of this research in the 1980s confirms that these perceptions still hold.

stress, however, that these characteristics are stereotypical; they do not necessarily describe individual men or women who can exhibit characteristics and modes of thought associated with the opposite sex.

Using a vocabulary which contains many of the words associated with masculinity as I have defined it, Morgenthau asserts that it is possible to develop a rational (and unemotional) theory of international politics based on objective laws that have their roots in human nature. Since Morgenthau wrote the first edition of *Politics Among Nations* in 1948, this search for an objective science of international politics, based on the model of the natural sciences, has been an important part of the realist and neo-realist agenda. In her feminist critique of the natural sciences, Evelyn Fox Keller points out that most scientific communities share the 'assumption that the universe they study is directly accessible, represented by concepts shaped not by language but only by the demands of logic and experiment'.[9] The laws of nature, according to this view of science, are "beyond the relativity of language." Like most feminists, Keller rejects this view of science, which, she asserts, imposes a coercive, hierarchical and conformist pattern on scientific inquiry. Feminists in general are sceptical about the possibility of finding a universal and objective foundation for knowledge that Morgenthau claims is possible. Most share the belief that knowledge is socially constructed: since it is language that transmits knowledge, the use of language and its claims of objectivity must continually be questioned.

Keller argues that objectivity, as it is usually defined in our culture, is associated with masculinity. She identifies it as "a network of interactions between gender development, a belief system that equates objectivity with masculinity, and a set of cultural values that simultaneously (and cojointly) elevates what is defined as scientific and what is defined as masculine."[10] Keller links the separation of self from other, an important stage of masculine gender development, with this notion of objectivity. Translated into scientific inquiry this becomes the striving for the separation of subject and object, an important goal of modern science and one, which Keller asserts, is based on the need for control; hence objectivity becomes associated with power and domination.

The need for control has been an important motivating force for modern realism. To begin his search for an objective, rational theory of international politics, which could impose order on a chaotic and conflictual world, Morgenthau constructs an abstraction which he calls political man, a beast completely lacking in moral restraints. Morgenthau is deeply aware that real man, like real states, is both moral and bestial but, because states do not live up to the universal moral laws that govern the universe, those who behave morally in international politics are doomed to failure because of the immoral actions of others. To solve this tension, Morgenthau postulates a realm of international politics in which the amoral behavior of political man is not only permissible but prudent. It is a Hobbesian world, separate and distinct from the world of domestic order, in which states may act like beasts, for survival depends on a maximisation of power and a willingness to fight.

Having long argued that the personal is political, most feminist theory would reject the validity of constructing an autonomous political sphere around which boundaries of permissible modes of conduct have been drawn. As Keller maintains, "the demarcation between public and private not only defines and defends the boundaries of the political but also helps form its content and style."[11] Morgenthau's political man is a social construct which is based on a partial representation of human nature. One might well ask where the women were in Hobbes' state of nature; presumably they must have been involved in reproduction and childrearing, rather than

[9] Keller, *op. cit.,* p. 130.
[10] *ibid.,* p. 89.
[11] *ibid.,* p. 9.

warfare, if life was to go on for more than one generation.[12] Morgenthau's emphasis on the conflictual aspects of the international system contributes to a tendency, shared by other realists, to deemphasise elements of cooperation and regeneration which are also aspects of international relations.[13]

Morgenthau's construction of an amoral realm of international power politics is an attempt to resolve what he sees as a fundamental tension between the moral laws that govern the universe and the requirements of successful political action in a world where states use morality as a cloak to justify the pursuit of their own national interests. Morgenthau's universalistic morality postulates the highest form of morality as an abstract ideal, similar to the Golden Rule, to which states seldom adhere: the morality of states is an instrumental morality which is guided by self-interest. Morgenthau's hierarchical ordering of morality contains parallels with the work of psychologist Lawrence Kohlberg. Based on a study of the moral development of eighty-four American boys, Kohlberg concludes that the highest stage of human moral development (which he calls stage six) is the ability to recognise abstract universal principles of justice; lower on the scale (stage two) is an instrumental morality concerned with serving one's own interests while recognising that others have interests too. Between these two is an interpersonal morality which is contextual and characterised by sensitivity to the needs of others (stage three).[14]

In her critique of Kohlberg's stages of moral development, Carol Gilligan argues that they are based on a masculine conception of morality. On Kohlberg's scale, women rarely rise above the third or contextual stage but Gilligan claims that this is not a sign of inferiority, but of difference. Since women are socialised into a mode of thinking which is contextual and narrative, rather than formal and abstract, they tend to see issues in contextual rather than in abstract terms.[15] In international relations, the tendency to think about morality either in terms of abstract, universal and unattainable standards or as purely instrumental, as Morgenthau does, detracts from our ability to tolerate cultural differences and to seek potential for building community in spite of these differences.

Using examples from the feminist literature, I have suggested that Morgenthau's attempt to construct an objective, universal theory of international politics is rooted in assumptions about human nature and morality that, in modern Western culture, are associated with masculinity. Further evidence that Morgenthau's principles are not the basis for a universalistic and objective theory is contained in his frequent references to the failure of what he calls the "legalistic-moralistic" or idealist approach to world politics which he claims was largely responsible for both the World Wars. Having laid the blame for the Second World War on the misguided morality of appeasement, Morgenthau's *realpolitik* prescriptions for successful political action appear as prescriptions for avoiding the mistakes of the 1930s rather than as prescriptions with timeless applicability.

If Morgenthau's world view is embedded in the traumas of the Second World War, are his prescriptions still valid as we move further away from this event? I share with other critics of realism the view that, in a rapidly changing world, we must begin to search for modes of behav-

---

[12] Sara Ann Ketchum, "Female Culture, Womanculture and Conceptual Change: Toward a Philosophy of Women's Studies," *Social Theory and Practice* (Vol. 6. No. 2, Summer 1980), pp. 151–62.

[13] Others have questioned whether Hobbes' state of nature provides an accurate description of the international system. See, for example, Charles Beitz, *Political Theory and International Relations* (Princeton, NJ: Princeton University Press, 1979), pp. 35–50, and Stanley Hoffmann, *Duties Beyond Borders* (Syracuse, NY: Syracuse University Press, 1981), ch. 1.

[14] Kohlberg's stages of moral development are described and discussed in Robert Kegan, *The Evolving Self: Problem and Process in Human Development* (Cambridge, MA: Harvard University Press, 1982), ch. 2.

[15] Gilligan's critique of Kohlberg appears in Carol Gilligan, *In a Different Voice: Psychological Theory and Women's Development* (Cambridge, MA: Harvard University Press, 1982), ch. 1.

iour different from those prescribed by Morgenthau. Given that any war between the major powers is likely to be nuclear, increasing security by increasing power could be suicidal.[16] Moreover, the nation-state, the primary constitutive element of the international system for Morgenthau and other realists, is no longer able to deal with an increasingly pluralistic array of problems ranging from economic interdependence to environmental degradation. Could feminist theory make a contribution to international relations theory by constructing an alternative, feminist perspective on international politics that might help us search for more appropriate solutions?

A FEMINIST PERSPECTIVE ON INTERNATIONAL RELATIONS

If the way in which we describe reality has an effect on the ways we perceive and act upon our environment, new perspectives might lead us to consider alternative courses of action. With this in mind, I shall first examine two important concepts in international relations, power and security, from a feminist perspective and then discuss some feminist approaches to conflict resolution.

Morgenthau's definition of power, the control of man over man, is typical of the way power is usually defined in international relations. Nancy Hartsock argues that this type of power as domination has always been associated with masculinity since the exercise of power has generally been a masculine activity; rarely have women exercised legitimised power in the public domain. When women write about power they stress energy, capacity and potential says Hartsock, and she notes that women theorists, even when they have little else in common, offer similar definitions of power which differ substantially from the understanding of power as domination.[17]

Hannah Arendt, frequently cited by feminists writing about power, defines power as the human ability to act in concert, or action which is taken in connection with others who share similar concerns.[18] This definition of power is similar to that of psychologist, David McClelland's portrayal of female power which he describes as shared rather than assertive.[19] Jane Jaquette argues that, since women have had less access to the instruments of coercion, women have been more apt to rely on power as persuasion; she compares women's domestic activities to coalition-building.[20]

All of these writers are portraying power as a relationship of mutual enablement. Tying her definition of female power to international relations, Jaquette sees similarities between female strategies of persuasion and strategies of small states operating from a position of weakness in the international system. There are also examples of states' behaviour which contain elements of the female strategy of coalition-building. One such example is the Southern African Development Co-ordination Conference (SADCC) which is designed to build regional infrastructures based on mutual co-operation and collective self-reliance in order to decrease dependence on the South African economy. Another is the European Community, which has had considerable

---

[16] There is evidence that, toward the end of his life, Morgenthau himself was aware that his own prescriptions were becoming anachronistic. In a seminar presentation in 1978, he suggested that power politics as the guiding principle for the conduct of international relations had become fatally defective. For a description of this seminar presentation, see Francis Anthony Boyle, *World Politics and International Law* (Durham, NC: Duke University Press, 1985), pp. 70–4.

[17] Nancy C. M. Hartsock, *Money, Sex and Power: Toward a Feminist 'Historical' Materialism* (Boston, MA: Northeastern University Press, 1983), p. 210.

[18] Hannah Arendt, *On Violence* (New York: Harcourt, Brace and World, 1969), p. 44. Arendt's definition of power, as it relates to international relations, is discussed more extensively in Jean Bethke Elshtain, "Reflections on War and Political Discourse: Realism, Just War, and Feminism in a Nuclear Age," *Political Theory* (Vol. 13, No. 1, Feb. 1985), pp. 39–57.

[19] David McClelland, "Power and the Feminine Role" in David McClelland, *Power, The Inner Experience* (New York: Wiley, 1975), ch. 3.

[20] Jane S. Jaquette, "Power as Ideology: A Feminist Analysis" in Judith H. Stiehm, *Women's Views of the Political World of Men* (Dobbs Ferry, NY: Transnational Publishers, 1984), ch. 2.

success in building mutual co-operation in an area of the world whose history would not predict such a course of events.[21] It is rare, however, that co-operative outcomes in international relations are described in these terms, though Karl Deutsch's notion of pluralistic security communities might be one such example where power is associated with building community.[22] I am not denying that power as domination is a pervasive reality in international relations, but sometimes there are also elements of co-operation in inter-state relations which tend to be obscured when power is seen solely as domination. Thinking about power is this multidimensional sense may help us to think constructively about the potential for co-operation as well as conflict, an aspect of international relations generally down-played by realism.

Redefining national security is another way in which feminist theory could contribute to new thinking about international relations.[23] Traditionally in the West, the concept of national security has been tied to military strength and its role in the physical protection of the nation-state from external threats. Morgenthau's notion of defending the national interest in terms of power is consistent with this definition. But this traditional definition of national security is partial at best in today's world.[24] When advanced states are highly interdependent, and rely on weapons whose effects would be equally devastating to winners and losers alike, defending national security by relying on war as the last resort no longer appears very useful. Moreover, if one thinks of security in North-South rather than East-West terms, for a large portion of the world's population, security has as much to do with the satisfaction of basic material needs as with military threats. According to Johan Galtung's notion of structural violence, the lowering of life expectancy by virtue of where one happens to be born is a form of violence whose effects can be as devastating as war.[25] Basic needs satisfaction has a great deal to do with women, but only recently have women's roles as providers of basic needs, and in development more generally, become visible as important components in devising development strategies.[26] Traditionally the development literature has focused on aspects of the development process which are in the public sphere, are technologically complex and are usually undertaken by men. Thinking about the role of women in development and the way in which we can define development and basic needs satisfaction to be inclusive of women's roles and needs are topics which deserve higher priority on the international agenda. Typically, however, this is an area about which traditional international relations theory, with its prioritising of order over justice, has had very little to say.

A further threat to national security, more broadly defined, which also has not been on the agenda of traditional international relations, concerns the environment. Carolyn Merchant argues that a mechanistic view of nature, contained in modern science, has helped to guide an

---

[21] These examples are cited in Christine Sylvester, "The Emperor's Theories and Transformations: Looking at the Field Through Feminist Lenses" in Dennis Pirages and Christine Sylvester (eds.), *Transformations in the Global Political Economy* (New York: Macmillan, forthcoming).

[22] Karl W. Deutsch, *Political Community and the North Atlantic Area* (Princeton, NJ: Princeton University Press, 1957).

[23] "New thinking" is a term that is also being used in the Soviet Union to describe foreign policy reformulations under Gorbachev. There are indications that the Soviets are beginning to conceptualise security in the multidimensional terms described here. See Margot Light, *The Soviet Theory of International Relations* (New York: St. Martin's Press, 1988), ch. 10.

[24] This is the argument made in Edward Azar and Chung-in Moon, "Third World National Security: Toward a New Conceptual Framework," *International Interactions* (Vol. 11, No. 2, 1984), pp. 103–35.

[25] Johan Galtung, "Violence, Peace, and Peace Research" in Johan Galtung, *Essays in Peace Research*, Vol. 1 (Copenhagen: Christian Ejlers, 1975), ch. 1.4.

[26] See, for example, Gita Sen and Caren Grown, *Development, Crises and Alternative Visions: Third World Women's Perspectives* (New York: Monthly Review Press, 1987). This is an example of a growing literature on women and development which deserves more attention from the international relations community.

industrial and technological development which has resulted in the environmental damage that is now becoming a matter of global concern. In the introduction to her book, *The Death of Nature*, Merchant suggests that, "Women and nature have an age-old association—an affiliation that has persisted throughout culture, language, and history."[27] Hence she maintains that the ecology movement, which is growing up in response to these environmental threats, and the women's movement are deeply interconnected. Both stress living in equilibrium with nature rather than dominating it; both see nature as a living non-hierarchical entity in which each part is mutually dependent on the whole. Ecologists, as well as many feminists, are now suggesting that only with such a fundamental change in the way we view the world could we devise solutions that would allow the human species to survive the damage which we are inflicting on the environment.

Thinking about military, economic and environmental security in interdependent terms suggests the need for new methods of conflict resolution which seek to achieve mutually beneficial, rather than zero-sum, outcomes. One such method comes from Sara Ruddick's work on "maternal thinking."[28] Ruddick describes "maternal thinking" as focused on the preservation of life and the growth of children; to foster a domestic environment conducive to these goals, tranquillity must be preserved by avoiding conflict where possible, engaging in it non-violently and restoring community when it is over. In such an environment the ends for which disputes are fought are subordinated to the means by which they are resolved. This method of conflict resolution involves making contextual judgements rather than appealing to absolute standards and thus has much in common with Gilligan's definition of female morality.

While non-violent resolution of conflict in the domestic sphere is a widely accepted norm, passive resistance in the public realm is regarded as deviant. But, as Ruddick argues, the peaceful resolution of conflict by mothers does not usually extend to the children of one's enemies, an important reason why women have been ready to support men's wars.[29] The question for Ruddick then becomes how to get "maternal thinking," a mode of thinking which she believes can be found in men as well as women, out into the public realm. Ruddick believes that finding a common humanity among one's opponents has become a condition of survival in the nuclear age when the notion of winners and losers has become questionable.[30] Portraying the adversary as less than human has all too often been a technique of the nation-state to command loyalty and increase its legitimacy in the eyes of its citizens but such behaviour in the nuclear age may eventually be self-defeating.

We might also look to Gilligan's work for a feminist perspective on conflict resolution. Reporting on a study of playground behaviour of American boys and girls, Gilligan argues that girls are less able to tolerate high levels of conflict, more likely than boys to play games which involve taking turns and in which the success of one does not depend on the failure of another.[31] While Gilligan's study does not take into account attitudes toward other groups (racial, ethnic, eco-

[27] Carolyn Merchant, *The Death of Nature: Women, Ecology and the Scientific Revolution* (New York: Harper and Row, 1982), p. xv.

[28] Sara Ruddick, "Maternal Thinking" and Sara Ruddick, "Preservative Love and Military Destruction: Some Reflections on Mothering and Peace" in Joyce Treblicot, *Mothering: Essays in Feminist Theory* (Totowa, NJ: Rowman and Allanheld, 1984), ch. 13–4.

[29] For a more extensive analysis of this issue, see Jean Bethke Elshtain, *Women and War* (New York: Basic Books, 1987).

[30] This type of conflict resolution bears similarities to the problem solving approach of Edward Azar, John Burton and Herbert Kelman. See, for example, Edward E. Azar and John W. Burton, *International Conflict Resolution: Theory and Practice* (Brighton: Wheatsheaf Books, 1986) and Herbert C. Kelman, "Interactive Problem Solving: A Social-Psychological Approach to Conflict Resolution" in W. Klassen (ed.), *Dialogue Toward Inter-Faith Understanding*, (Tantur/Jerusalem: Ecumenical Institute for Theoretical Research, 1986), pp. 293–314.

[31] Gilligan, *op. cit.*, pp. 9–10.

nomic, or national), it does suggest the validity of investigating whether girls are socialised to use different modes of problem-solving when dealing with conflict, and whether such behaviour might be useful to us in thinking about international conflict resolution.

TOWARD A FEMINIST EPISTEMOLOGY OF INTERNATIONAL RELATIONS

I am deeply aware that there is no one feminist approach but many which come out of various disciplines and intellectual traditions. Yet there are common themes in these different feminist literatures that I have reviewed, which could help us to begin to formulate a feminist epistemology of international relations. Morgenthau encourages us to try to stand back from the world and to think about theory-building in terms of constructing a rational outline or map that has universal applications. In contrast, the feminist literature reviewed here emphasises connection and contingency. Keller argues for a form of knowledge, which she calls "dynamic objectivity," "that grants to the world around us its independent integrity, but does so in a way that remains cognizant of, indeed relies on, our connectivity with that world,"[32] Keller illustrates this mode of thinking in her study of Barbara McClintock, whose work on genetic transposition won her a Nobel prize after many years of marginalisation by the scientific community.[33] McClintock, Keller argues, was a scientist with a respect for complexity, diversity and individual difference whose methodology allowed her data to speak rather than imposing explanations on it.

Keller's portrayal of McClintock's science contains parallels with what Sandra Harding calls an African world view.[34] Harding tells us that the Western liberal notion of rational economic man, an individualist and a welfare maximiser, similar to rational political man upon which realism has based its theoretical investigations, does not make any sense in the African world view where the individual is seen as part of the social order acting within that order rather than upon it. Harding believes that this view of human behaviour has much in common with a feminist perspective. If we combine this view of human behaviour with Merchant's holistic perspective, which stresses the interconnectedness of all things including nature, it may help us to begin to think from a more global perspective which appreciates cultural diversity but at the same time recognises a growing interdependence which makes anachronistic the exclusionary thinking fostered by the nation-state system.

Keller's "dynamic objectivity," Harding's African world view and Merchant's ecological thinking all point us in the direction of an appreciation of the "other" as a subject whose views are as legitimate as our own, a way of thinking that has been sadly lacking in the history of international relations. Just as Keller cautions us against the construction of a feminist science, which could perpetuate these same exclusionary attitudes, Harding warns us against schema which contrast people by race, gender or class and which originate within projects of social domination. Feminist thinkers generally dislike dichotomisation and the distancing of subject from object that goes with abstract thinking, both of which, they believe, encourage a we/they attitude so characteristic of international relations. Instead this literature points us toward constructing epistemologies which value ambiguity and difference, qualities that could stand us in good stead as we begin to build a human or ungendered theory of international relations containing elements of both masculine and feminine modes of thought.

MORGENTHAU'S PRINCIPLES OF POLITICAL REALISM: A FEMINIST REFORMULATION

In the first part of this article I used feminist theory to develop a critique of Morgenthau's principles of political realism in order to demonstrate how the theory and practice of international re-

---

[32] Keller, *op. cit.*, p. 117.

[33] Evelyn Fox Keller, *A Feeling for the Organism: The Life and Work of Barbara McClintock,* (New York: Freeman, 1983).

[34] Harding *op. cit.*, ch. 7.

lations may exhibit a masculine bias. I then suggested some contributions which feminist theory might make to reconceptualising some important concepts in international relations and to thinking about a feminist epistemology. Drawing on these observations, I will now conclude with a feminist reformulation of Morgenthau's six principles of political realism, outlined earlier in this paper, which might help us to begin to think differently about international relations. I shall not use the term realism since feminists believe that there are multiple realities: a truly realistic picture of international politics must recognise elements of co-operation as well as conflict, morality as well as *realpolitik,* and the strivings for justice as well as order.[35] This reformulation may help us begin to think in these multidimensional terms:

1. A feminist perspective believes that objectivity, as it is culturally defined, is associated with masculinity. Therefore, supposedly "objective" laws of human nature are based on a partial masculine view of human nature. Human nature is both masculine and feminine: it contains elements of social reproduction and development as well as political domination. Dynamic objectivity offers us a more connected view of objectivity with less potential for domination.

2. A feminist perspective believes that the national interest is multidimensional and contextually contingent. Therefore it cannot be defined solely in terms of power. In the contemporary world the national interest demands co-operative rather than zero-sum solutions to a set of interdependent global problems which include nuclear war, economic well-being and environmental degradation.

3. Power cannot be infused with meaning that is universally valid. Power as domination and control privileges masculinity and ignores the possibility of collective empowerment, another aspect of power often associated with feminity.

4. A feminist perspective rejects the possibility of separating moral command from political action. All political action has moral significance. The realist agenda for maximising order through power and control prioritises the moral command of order over those of justice and the satisfaction of basic needs necessary to ensure social reproduction.

5. While recognising that the moral aspirations of particular nations cannot be equated with universal moral principles, a feminist perspective seeks to find common moral elements in human aspirations which could become the basis for de-escalating international conflict and building international community.

6. A feminist perspective denies the validity of the autonomy of the political. Since autonomy is associated with masculinity in Western culture, disciplinary efforts to construct a world view which does not rest on a pluralistic conception of human nature, are partial and masculine. Building boundaries around a narrowly defined political realm defines political in a way that excludes the concerns and contributions of women.

In constructing this feminist alternative, I am not denying the validity of Morgenthau's work. Adding a feminist perspective to the epistemology of international relations, however, is a stage through which we must pass if we are to begin to think about constructing an ungendered or human science of international politics which is sensitive to, but goes beyond, both masculine and feminine perspectives. Such inclusionary thinking, which, as Simone de Beauvoir tells us, values the bringing forth of life as much as the risking of life, is becoming imperative in a world where the technology of war and a fragile natural environment are threatening human existence. This ungendered or human discourse becomes possible only when women are adequately represented in the discipline and when there is equal respect for the contributions of both women and men alike.

---

[35] "Utopia and reality are . . . the two facets of political science. Sound political thought and sound political life will be found only where both have their place." E. H. Carr, *The Twenty Years Crisis, 1919–1939* (New York: Harper and Row, 1964), p. 10.

Notes

An earlier version of this paper was presented at the symposium on Women and International Relations at the London School of Economics in June 1988. I am grateful to Hayward Alker, Jr. and Susan Okin for their careful reading of the manuscript and helpful suggestions.

■▮▯▮▯▮▯▮▯▮ ■ ▯▮▯▮▯▮▯▮▯ ■ ▯▮▯▮▯▮▯▮▯▮

READING 19: FRANCIS FUKUYAMA

Francis Fukuyama,

"Women and the Evolution of World Politics," Foreign Affairs, 1999

Chimpanzee Politics

In the world's largest captive chimp colony at the Burger's Zoo in Arnhem, Netherlands, a struggle worthy of Machiavelli unfolded during the late 1970s. As described by primatologist Frans de Waal, the aging alpha male of the colony, Yeroen, was gradually unseated from his position of power by a younger male, Luit. Luit could not have done this on the basis of his own physical strength, but had to enter into an alliance with Nikkie, a still younger male. No sooner was Luit on top, however, than Nikkie turned on him and formed a coalition with the deposed leader to achieve dominance himself. Luit remained in the background as a threat to his rule, so one day he was murdered by Nikkie and Yeroen, his toes and testicles littering the floor of the cage.

Jane Goodall became famous studying a group of about 30 chimps at the Gombe National Park in Tanzania in the 1960s, a group she found on the whole to be peaceful. In the 1970s, this group broke up into what could only be described as two rival gangs in the northern and southern parts of the range. The biological anthropologist Richard Wrangham with Dale Peterson in their 1996 book *Demonic Males* describes what happened next. Parties of four or five males from the northern group would go out, not simply defending their range, but often penetrating into the rival group's territory to pick off individuals caught alone or unprepared. The murders were often grisly, and they were celebrated by the attackers with hooting and feverish excitement. All the males and several of the females in the southern group were eventually killed, and the remaining females forced to join the northern group. The northern Gombe chimps had done, in effect, what Rome did to Carthage in 146 B.C.: extinguished its rival without a trace.

There are several notable aspects to these stories of chimp behavior. First, the violence. Violence within the same species is rare in the animal kingdom, usually restricted to infanticide by males who want to get rid of a rival's offspring and mate with the mother. Only chimps and humans seem to have a proclivity for routinely murdering peers. Second is the importance of coalitions and the politics that goes with coalition-building. Chimps, like humans, are intensely social creatures whose lives are preoccupied with achieving and maintaining dominance in status hierarchies. They threaten, plead, cajole, and bribe their fellow chimps to join with them in alliances, and their dominance lasts only as long as they can maintain these social connections.

Finally and most significantly, the violence and the coalition-building is primarily the work of males. Female chimpanzees can be as violent and cruel as the males at times; females compete with one another in hierarchies and form coalitions to do so. But the most murderous violence is the province of males, and the nature of female alliances is different. According to de Waal, female chimps bond with females to whom they feel some emotional attachment; the males are much more likely to make alliances for purely instrumental, calculating reasons. In other words, female chimps have relationships; male chimps practice realpolitik.

Chimpanzees are man's closest evolutionary relative, having descended from a common chimp-like ancestor less than five million years ago. Not only are they very close on a genetic level, they show many behavioral similarities as well. As Wrangham and Peterson note, of the 4,000 mammal and 10 million or more other species, only chimps and humans live in male-bonded, patrilineal communities in which groups of males routinely engage in aggressive, often murderous raiding of their own species. Nearly 30 years ago, the anthropologist Lionel Tiger suggested that men had special psychological resources for bonding with one another, derived from their need to hunt cooperatively, that explained their dominance in group-oriented activities from politics to warfare. Tiger was roundly denounced by feminists at the time for suggesting that there were biologically based psychological differences between the sexes, but more recent research, including evidence from primatology, has confirmed that male bonding is in fact genetic and predates the human species.

THE NOT-SO-NOBLE SAVAGE

It is all too easy to make facile comparisons between animal and human behavior to prove a polemical point, as did the socialists who pointed to bees and ants to prove that nature endorsed collectivism. Skeptics point out that human beings have language, reason, law, culture, and moral values that make them fundamentally different from even their closest animal relative. In fact, for many years anthropologists endorsed what was in effect a modern version of Rousseau's story of the noble savage: people living in hunter-gatherer societies were pacific in nature. If chimps and modern man had a common proclivity for violence, the cause in the latter case had to be found in civilization and not in human nature.

A number of authors have extended the noble savage idea to argue that violence and patriarchy were late inventions, rooted in either the Western Judeo-Christian tradition or the capitalism to which the former gave birth. Friedrich Engels anticipated the work of later feminists by positing the existence of a primordial matriarchy, which was replaced by a violent and repressive patriarchy only with the transition to agricultural societies. The problem with this theory is, as Lawrence Keeley points out in his book *War Before Civilization,* that the most comprehensive recent studies of violence in hunter-gatherer societies suggest that for them war was actually more frequent, and rates of murder higher, than for modern ones.

Surveys of ethnographic data show that only 10–13 percent of primitive societies never or rarely engaged in war or raiding; the others engaged in conflict either continuously or at less than yearly intervals. Closer examination of the peaceful cases shows that they were frequently refugee populations driven into remote locations by prior warfare or groups protected by a more advanced society. Of the Yanomamö tribesmen studied by Napoleon Chagnon in Venezuela, some 30 percent of the men died by violence; the !Kung San of the Kalahari desert, once characterized as the "harmless people," have a higher murder rate than New York or Detroit. The sad archaeological evidence from sites like Jebel Sahaba in Egypt, Talheim in Germany, or Roaix in France indicates that systematic mass killings of men, women, and children occurred in Neolithic times. The Holocaust, Cambodia, and Bosnia have each been described as a unique, and often as a uniquely modern, form of horror. Exceptional and tragic they are indeed, but with precedents stretching back tens if not hundreds of thousands of years.

It is clear that this violence was largely perpetrated by men. While a small minority of human societies have been matrilineal, evidence of a primordial matriarchy in which women dominated men, or were even relatively equal to men, has been hard to find. There was no age of innocence. The line from chimp to modern man is continuous.

It would seem, then, that there is something to the contention of many feminists that phenomena like aggression, violence, war, and intense competition for dominance in a status hierarchy are more closely associated with men than women. Theories of international relations like realism that see international politics as a remorseless struggle for power are in fact what feminists call a gendered perspective, describing the behavior of states controlled by men rather than states per se. A world run by women would follow different rules, it would appear, and it is toward that sort of world that all postindustrial or Western societies are moving. As women gain power in these countries, the latter should become less aggressive, adventurous, competitive, and violent.

The problem with the feminist view is that it sees these attitudes toward violence, power, and status as wholly the products of a patriarchal culture, whereas in fact it appears they are rooted in biology. This makes these attitudes harder to change in men and consequently in societies. Despite the rise of women, men will continue to play a major, if not dominant, part in the governance of postindustrial countries, not to mention less-developed ones. The realms of war and international politics in particular will remain controlled by men for longer than many feminists would like. Most important, the task of resocializing men to be more like women—that is, less violent—will run into limits. What is bred in the bone cannot be altered easily by changes in culture and ideology.

THE RETURN OF BIOLOGY

We are living through a revolutionary period in the life sciences. Hardly a week goes by without the discovery of a gene linked to a disease, condition, or behavior, from cancer to obesity to depression, with the promise of genetic therapies and even the outright manipulation of the human genome just around the corner. But while developments in molecular biology have been receiving the lion's share of the headlines, much progress has been made at the behavioral level as well. The past generation has seen a revival in Darwinian thinking about human psychology, with profound implications for the social sciences.

For much of this century, the social sciences have been premised on Emile Durkheim's dictum that social facts can be explained only by prior social facts and not by biological causes. Revolutions and wars are caused by social facts such as economic change, class inequalities, and shifting alliances. The standard social science model assumes that the human mind is the terrain of ideas, customs, and norms that are the products of man-made culture. Social reality is, in other words, socially constructed: if young boys like to pretend to shoot each other more than young girls, it is only because they have been socialized at an early age to do so.

The social-constructionist view, long dominant in the social sciences, originated as a reaction to the early misuse of Darwinism. Social Darwinists like Herbert Spencer or outright racists like Madsen Grant in the late nineteenth and early twentieth centuries used biology, specifically the analogy of natural selection, to explain and justify everything from class stratification to the domination of much of the world by white Europeans. Then Franz Boas, a Columbia anthropologist, debunked many of these theories of European racial superiority by, among other things, carefully measuring the head sizes of immigrant children and noting that they tended to converge with those of native Americans when fed an American diet. Boas, as well as his well-known students Margaret Mead and Ruth Benedict, argued that apparent differences between human groups could be laid at the doorstep of culture rather than nature. There were, moreover, no cultural universals by which Europeans or Americans could judge other cultures. So-called primitive peoples were not inferior, just different. Hence was born both the social constructivism and the cultural relativism with which the social sciences have been imbued ever since.

But there has been a revolution in modern evolutionary thinking. It has multiple roots; one was ethology, the comparative study of animal behavior. Ethologists like Konrad Lorenz began to notice similarities in behavior across a wide variety of animal species suggesting common evolutionary origins. Contrary to the cultural relativists, they found that not only was it possible to make important generalizations across virtually all human cultures (for example, females are more selective than males in their choice of sexual partners) but even across broad ranges of animal species. Major breakthroughs were made by William Hamilton and Robert Trivers in the 1960s and 1970s in explaining instances of altruism in the animal world not by some sort of instinct towards species survival but rather in terms of "selfish genes" (to use Richard Dawkins' phrase) that made social behavior in an individual animal's interest. Finally, advances in neurophysiology have shown that the brain is not a Lockean tabula rasa waiting to be filled with cultural content, but rather a highly modular organ whose components have been adapted prior to birth to suit the needs of socially oriented primates. Humans are hard-wired to act in certain predictable ways.

The sociobiology that sprang from these theoretical sources tried to provide a deterministic Darwinian explanation for just about everything, so it was perhaps inevitable that a reaction would set in against it as well. But while the term sociobiology has gone into decline, the neo-Darwinian thinking that spawned it has blossomed under the rubric of evolutionary psychology or anthropology and is today an enormous arena of new research and discovery.

Unlike the pseudo-Darwininsts at the turn of the century, most contemporary biologists do not regard race or ethnicity as biologically significant categories. This stands to reason: the different human races have been around only for the past hundred thousand years or so, barely a blink of the eye in evolutionary time. As countless authors have pointed out, race is largely a socially constructed category: since all races can (and do) interbreed, the boundary lines between them are often quite fuzzy.

The same is not true, however, about sex. While some gender roles are indeed socially constructed, virtually all reputable evolutionary biologists today think there are profound differences between the sexes that are genetically rather than culturally rooted, and that these differences extend beyond the body into the realm of the mind. Again, this stands to reason from a Darwinian point of view: sexual reproduction has been going on not for thousands but hundreds of millions of years. Males and females compete not just against their environment but against one another in a process that Darwin labeled "sexual selection," whereby each sex seeks to maximize its own fitness by choosing certain kinds of mates. The psychological strategies that result from this never-ending arms race between men and women are different for each sex.

In no area is sex-related difference clearer than with respect to violence and aggression. A generation ago, two psychologists, Eleanor Maccoby and Carol Jacklin, produced an authoritative volume on what was then empirically known about differences between the sexes. They showed that certain stereotypes about gender, such as the assertion that girls were more suggestible or had lower self-esteem, were just that, while others, like the idea that girls were less competitive, could not be proven one way or another. On one issue, however, there was virtually no disagreement in the hundreds of studies on the subject: namely, that boys were more aggressive, both verbally and physically, in their dreams, words, and actions than girls. One comes to a similar conclusion by looking at crime statistics. In every known culture, and from what we know of virtually all historical time periods, the vast majority of crimes, particularly violent crimes, are committed by men. Here there is also apparently a genetically determined age specificity to violent aggression: crimes are overwhelmingly committed by young men between the ages of 15 and 30. Perhaps young men are everywhere socialized to behave violently, but this evidence, from different cultures and times, suggests that there is some deeper level of causation at work.

At this point in the discussion, many people become uncomfortable and charges of "biological determinism" arise. Don't we know countless women who are stronger, larger, more decisive, more violent, or more competitive than their male counterparts? Isn't the proportion of female criminals rising relative to males? Isn't work becoming less physical, making sexual differences unimportant? The answer to all of these questions is yes: again, no reputable evolutionary biologist would deny that culture also shapes behavior in countless critical ways and can often overwhelm genetic predispositions. To say that there is a genetic basis for sex difference is simply to make a statistical assertion that the bell curve describing the distribution of a certain characteristic is shifted over a little for men as compared with women. The two curves will overlap for the most part, and there will be countless individuals in each population who will have more of any given characteristic than those of the other sex. Biology is not destiny, as tough-minded female leaders like Margaret Thatcher, Indira Gandhi, and Golda Meir have proven. (It is worth pointing out, however, that in male-dominated societies, it is these kinds of unusual women who will rise to the top.) But the statistical assertion also suggests that broad populations of men and women, as opposed to exceptional individuals, will act in certain predictable ways. It also suggests that these populations are not infinitely plastic in the way that their behavior can be shaped by society.

FEMINISTS AND POWER POLITICS

There is by now an extensive literature on gender and international politics and a vigorous feminist subdiscipline within the field of international relations theory based on the work of scholars like Ann Tickner, Sara Ruddick, Jean Bethke Elshtain, Judith Shapiro, and others. This literature is too diverse to describe succinctly, but it is safe to say that much of it was initially concerned with understanding how international politics is "gendered," that is, run by men to serve male interests and interpreted by other men, consciously and unconsciously, according to male perspectives. Thus, when a realist theorist like Hans Morganthau or Kenneth Waltz argues that states seek to maximize power, they think that they are describing a universal human characteristic when, as Tickner points out, they are portraying the behavior of states run by men.

Virtually all feminists who study international politics seek the laudable goal of greater female participation in all aspects of foreign relations, from executive mansions and foreign ministries to militaries and universities. They disagree as to whether women should get ahead in politics by demonstrating traditional masculine virtues of toughness, aggression, competitiveness, and the willingness to use force when necessary, or whether they should move the very agenda of politics away from male preoccupations with hierarchy and domination. This ambivalence was demonstrated in the feminist reaction to Margaret Thatcher, who by any account was far tougher and more determined than any of the male politicians she came up against. Needless to say, Thatcher's conservative politics did not endear her to most feminists, who much prefer a Mary Robinson or Gro Harlem Brundtland as their model of a female leader, despite—or because of—the fact that Thatcher had beaten men at their own game.

Both men and women participate in perpetuating the stereotypical gender identities that associate men with war and competition and women with peace and cooperation. As sophisticated feminists like Jean Bethke Elshtain have pointed out, the traditional dichotomy between the male "just warrior" marching to war and the female "beautiful soul" marching for peace is frequently transcended in practice by women intoxicated by war and by men repulsed by its cruelties. But like many stereotypes, it rests on a truth, amply confirmed by much of the new research in evolutionary biology. Wives and mothers can enthusiastically send their husbands and sons off to war; like Sioux women, they can question their manliness for failing to go into battle or themselves torture prisoners. But statistically speaking it is primarily men who enjoy the experience of aggression and the camaraderie it brings and who revel in the ritualization of war that is, as the anthropologist Robin Fox puts it, another way of understanding diplomacy.

A truly matriarchal world, then, would be less prone to conflict and more conciliatory and co-operative than the one we inhabit now. Where the new biology parts company with feminism is in the causal explanation it gives for this difference in sex roles. The ongoing revolution in the life sciences has almost totally escaped the notice of much of the social sciences and humanities, particularly the parts of the academy concerned with feminism, postmodernism, cultural studies, and the like. While there are some feminists who believe that sex differences have a natural basis, by far the majority are committed to the idea that men and women are psychologically identical, and that any differences in behavior, with regard to violence or any other characteristic, are the result of some prior social construction passed on by the prevailing culture.

THE DEMOCRATIC AND FEMININE PEACE

Once one views international relations through the lens of sex and biology, it never again looks the same. It is very difficult to watch Muslims and Serbs in Bosnia, Hutus and Tutsis in Rwanda, or militias from Liberia and Sierra Leone to Georgia and Afghanistan divide themselves up into what seem like indistinguishable male-bonded groups in order to systematically slaughter one another, and not think of the chimps at Gombe.

The basic social problem that any society faces is to control the aggressive tendencies of its young men. In hunter-gatherer societies, the vast preponderance of violence is over sex, a situation that continues to characterize domestic violent crime in contemporary postindustrial societies. Older men in the community have generally been responsible for socializing younger ones by ritualizing their aggression, often by directing it toward enemies outside the community. Much of that external violence can also be over women. Modern historians assume that the Greeks and Trojans could not possibly have fought a war for ten years over Helen, but many primitive societies like the Yanomamö do exactly that. With the spread of agriculture 10,000 years ago, however, and the accumulation of wealth and land, war turned toward the acquisition of material goods. Channeling aggression outside the community may not lower societies' overall rate of violence, but it at least offers them the possibility of domestic peace between wars.

The core of the feminist agenda for international politics seems fundamentally correct: the violent and aggressive tendencies of men have to be controlled, not simply by redirecting them to external aggression but by constraining those impulses through a web of norms, laws, agreements, contracts, and the like. In addition, more women need to be brought into the domain of international politics as leaders, officials, soldiers, and voters. Only by participating fully in global politics can women both defend their own interests and shift the underlying male agenda.

The feminization of world politics has, of course, been taking place gradually over the past hundred years, with very positive effects. Women have won the right to vote and participate in politics in all developed countries, as well as in many developing countries, and have exercised that right with increasing energy. In the United States and other rich countries, a pronounced gender gap with regard to foreign policy and national security issues endures. American women have always been less supportive than American men of U.S. involvement in war, including World War II, Korea, Vietnam, and the Persian Gulf War, by an average margin of seven to nine percent. They are also consistently less supportive of defense spending and the use of force abroad. In a 1995 Roper survey conducted for the Chicago Council on Foreign Relations, men favored U.S. intervention in Korea in the event of a North Korean attack by a margin of 49 to 40 percent, while women were opposed by a margin of 30 to 54 percent. Similarly, U.S. military action against Iraq in the event it invaded Saudi Arabia was supported by men by a margin of 62 to 31 percent and opposed by women by 43 to 45 percent. While 54 percent of men felt it important to maintain superior world wide military power, only 45 percent of women agreed. Women, moreover, are less likely than men to see force as a legitimate tool for resolving conflicts.

It is difficult to know how to account for this gender gap; certainly, one cannot move from biology to voting behavior in a single step. Observers have suggested various reasons why women are less willing to use military force than men, including their role as mothers, the fact that many women are feminists (that is, committed to a left-of-center agenda that is generally hostile to U.S. intervention), and partisan affiliation (more women vote Democratic than men). It is unnecessary to know the reason for the correlation between gender and antimilitarism, however, to predict that increasing female political participation will probably make the United States and other democracies less inclined to use power around the world as freely as they have in the past.

Will this shift toward a less status- and military-power-oriented world be a good thing? For relations between states in the so-called democratic zone of peace, the answer is yes. Consideration of gender adds a great deal to the vigorous and interesting debate over the correlation between democracy and peace that has taken place in the past decade. The "democratic peace" argument, which underlies the foreign policy of the Clinton administration as well as its predecessors, is that democracies tend not to fight one another. While the empirical claim has been contested, the correlation between the degree of consolidation of liberal democratic institutions and interdemocratic peace would seem to be one of the few nontrivial generalizations one can make about world politics. Democratic peace theorists have been less persuasive about the reasons democracies are pacific toward one another. The reasons usually cited—the rule of law, respect for individual rights, the commercial nature of most democracies, and the like—are undoubtedly correct. But there is another factor that has generally not been taken into account: developed democracies also tend to be more feminized than authoritarian states, in terms of expansion of female franchise and participation in political decision-making. It should therefore surprise no one that the historically unprecedented shift in the sexual basis of politics should lead to a change in international relations.

THE REALITY OF AGGRESSIVE FANTASIES

On the other hand, if gender roles are not simply socially constructed but rooted in genetics, there will be limits to how much international politics can change. In anything but a totally feminized world, feminized policies could be a liability.

Some feminists talk as if gender identities can be discarded like an old sweater, perhaps by putting young men through mandatory gender studies courses when they are college freshmen. Male attitudes on a host of issues, from child-rearing and housework to "getting in touch with your feelings," have changed dramatically in the past couple of generations due to social pressure. But socialization can accomplish only so much, and efforts to fully feminize young men will probably be no more successful than the Soviet Union's efforts to persuade its people to work on Saturdays on behalf of the heroic Cuban and Vietnamese people. Male tendencies to band together for competitive purposes, seek to dominate status hierarchies, and act out aggressive fantasies toward one another can be rechanneled but never eliminated.

Even if we can assume peaceful relations between democracies, the broader world scene will still be populated by states led by the occasional Mobutu, Miloševi´c, or Saddam. Machiavelli's critique of Aristotle was that the latter did not take foreign policy into account in building his model of a just city: in a system of competitive states, the best regimes adopt the practices of the worst in order to survive. So even if the democratic, feminized, postindustrial world has evolved into a zone of peace where struggles are more economic than military, it will still have to deal with those parts of the world run by young, ambitious, unconstrained men. If a future Saddam Hussein is not only sitting on the world's oil supplies but is armed to the hilt with chemical, biological, and nuclear weapons, we might be better off being led by women like Margaret

Thatcher than, say, Gro Harlem Brundtland. Masculine policies will still be required, though not necessarily masculine leaders.

The implications of evolutionary biology for the hot-button issue of women in the military is not as straightforward as one might think. The vast majority of jobs in a modern military organization are in the enormous support tail that trails behind the actual combat units, and there is no reason that women cannot perform them as well if not better than men. While men have clearly evolved as cooperative hunters and fighters, it is not clear that any individual group of women will perform less well than any individual group of men in combat. What is much more problematic is integrating men and women into the same combat units, where they will be in close physical proximity over long periods of time. Unit cohesion, which is the bedrock on which the performance of armies rests, has been traditionally built around male bonding, which can only be jeopardized when men start competing for the attention of women. Commanders who encourage male bonding are building on a powerful natural instinct; those who try to keep sexual activity between healthy 20-year-old men and women in check through "zero tolerance" policies and draconian punishments are, by contrast, seeking to do something very unnatural. Unlike racial segregation, gender segregation in certain parts of the military seems not just appropriate but necessary.

THE MARGARET THATCHERS OF THE FUTURE

The feminization of democratic politics will interact with other demographic trends in the next 50 years to produce important changes. Due to the precipitous fall in fertility rates across the developed world since the 1960s, the age distribution of countries belonging to the Organization of Economic Cooperation and Development will shift dramatically. While the median age for America's population was in the mid-20s during the first few decades of the twentieth century, it will climb toward 40 by 2050. The change will be even more dramatic in Europe and Japan, where rates of immigration and fertility are lower. Under the U.N. Population Division's low-growth projections, the median age in Germany will be 55, in Japan 53, and in Italy 58.

The graying of the population has heretofore been discussed primarily in terms of the social security liability it will engender. But it carries a host of other social consequences as well, among them the emergence of elderly women as one of the most important voting blocs courted by mid-21st century politicians. In Italy and Germany, for example, women over 50, who now constitute 20 percent of the population, will account for 31 percent in 2050. There is no way, of course, of predicting how they will vote, but it seems likely that they will help elect more women leaders and will be less inclined toward military intervention than middle-aged males have traditionally been. Edward Luttwak of the Center for Strategic and International Studies has speculated that the fall in family sizes makes people in advanced countries much more leery of military casualties than people in agricultural societies, with their surpluses of young, hotheaded men. According to demographer Nicholas Eberstadt, three-fifths of Italy's offspring in 2050 will be only children with no cousins, siblings, aunts, or uncles. It is not unreasonable to suppose that in such a world tolerance of casualties will be even lower.

By the middle of the next century, then, Europe will likely consist of rich, powerful, and democratic nations with rapidly shrinking populations of mostly elderly people where women will play important leadership roles. The United States, with its higher rates of immigration and fertility, will also have more women leaders but a substantially younger population. A much larger and poorer part of the world will consist of states in Africa, the Middle East, and South Asia with young, growing populations, led mostly by younger men. As Eberstadt points out, Asia outside of Japan will buck the trend toward feminization because the high rate of abortion of female fetuses has shifted their sex ratios sharply in favor of men. This will be, to say the least, an unfamiliar world.

LIVING LIKE ANIMALS?

In Wrangham and Peterson's *Demonic Males* (said to be a favorite book of Hillary Rodham Clinton, who has had her own to contend with), the authors come to the pessimistic conclusion that nothing much has changed since early hominids branched off from the primordial chimp ancestor five million years ago. Group solidarity is still based on aggression against other communities; social cooperation is undertaken to achieve higher levels of organized violence. Robin Fox has argued that military technology has developed much faster than man's ability to ritualize violence and direct it into safer channels. The Gombe chimps could kill only a handful of others; modern man can vaporize tens of millions.

While the history of the first half of the twentieth century does not give us great grounds for faith in the possibility of human progress, the situation is not nearly as bleak as these authors would have us believe. Biology, to repeat, is not destiny. Rates of violent homicide appear to be lower today than during mankind's long hunter-gatherer period, despite gas ovens and nuclear weapons. Contrary to the thrust of postmodernist thought, people cannot free themselves entirely from biological nature. But by accepting the fact that people have natures that are often evil, political, economic, and social systems can be designed to mitigate the effects of man's baser instincts.

Take the human and particularly male desire to dominate a status hierarchy, which people share with other primates. The advent of liberal democracy and modern capitalism does not eliminate that desire, but it opens up many more peaceful channels for satisfying it. Among the American Plains Indians or the Yanomamö, virtually the only way for a man to achieve social recognition was to be a warrior, which meant, of course, excelling at killing. Other traditional societies might add a few occupations like the priesthood or the bureaucracy in which one could achieve recognition. A modern, technological society, by contrast, offers thousands of arenas in which one can achieve social status, and in most of them the quest for status leads not to violence but to socially productive activity. A professor receiving tenure at a leading university, a politician winning an election, or a CEO increasing market share may satisfy the same underlying drive for status as being the alpha male in a chimp community. But in the process, these individuals have written books, designed public policies, or brought new technologies to market that have improved human welfare.

Of course, not everyone can achieve high rank or dominance in any given status hierarchy, since these are by definition zero-sum games in which every winner produces a loser. But the advantage of a modern, complex, fluid society is, as economist Robert Frank has pointed out, that small frogs in large ponds can move to smaller ponds in which they will loom larger. Seeking status by choosing the right pond will not satisfy the ambitions of the greatest and noblest individuals, but it will bleed off much of the competitive energy that in hunter-gatherer or agricultural societies often has no outlet save war. Liberal democracy and market economies work well because, unlike socialism, radical feminism, and other utopian schemes, they do not try to change human nature. Rather, they accept biologically grounded nature as a given and seek to constrain it through institutions, laws, and norms. It does not always work, but it is better than living like animals.

READING 20: KIM DAE JUNG

KIM DAE JUNG,

"IS CULTURE DESTINY? THE MYTH OF ASIA'S ANTI-DEMOCRATIC VALUES," FOREIGN AFFAIRS, 1995

In his interview with *Foreign Affairs* (March/April 1994), Singapore's former prime minister, Lee Kuan Yew, presents interesting ideas about cultural differences between Western and East Asian societies and the political implications of those differences. Although he does not explicitly say so, his statements throughout the interview and his track record make it obvious that his admonition to Americans "not to foist their system indiscriminately on societies in which it will not work" implies that Western-style democracy is not applicable to East Asia. Considering the esteem in which he is held among world leaders and the prestige of this journal, this kind of argument is likely to have considerable impact and therefore deserves a careful reply.

With the collapse of the Soviet Union in 1991, socialism has been in retreat. Some people conclude that the Soviet demise was the result of the victory of capitalism over socialism. But I believe it represented the triumph of democracy over dictatorship. Without democracy, capitalism in Prussian Germany and Mejia Japan eventually met its tragic end. The many Latin American states that in recent decades embraced capitalism while rejecting democracy failed miserably. On the other hand, countries practicing democratic capitalism or democratic socialism, despite temporary setbacks, have prospered.

In spite of these trends, lingering doubts remain about the applicability of and prospects for democracy in Asia. Such doubts have been raised mainly by Asia's authoritarian leaders, Lee being the most articulate among them. They have long maintained that cultural differences make the "Western concept" of democracy and human rights inapplicable to East Asia. Does Asia have the philosophical and historical underpinnings suitable for democracy? Is democracy achievable there?

SELF-SERVING SELF-RELIANCE

Lee stresses cultural factors throughout his interview. I too believe in the importance of culture, but I do not think it alone determines a society's fate, nor is it immutable. Moreover, Lee's view of Asian cultures is not only unsupportable but self-serving. He argues that Eastern societies, unlike Western ones, "believe that the individual exists in the context of his family" and that the family is "the building brick of society." However, as an inevitable consequence of industrialization, the family-centered East Asian societies are also rapidly moving toward self-centered individualism. Nothing in human history is permanent.

Lee asserts that, in the East, "the ruler or the government does not try to provide for a person what the family best provides." He cites this ostensibly self-reliant, family-oriented culture as the main cause of East Asia's economic successes and ridicules Western governments for allegedly trying to solve all of society's problems, even as he worries about the moral breakdown of Western societies due to too much democracy and too many individual rights. Consequently, according to Lee, the Western political system, with its intrusive government, is not suited to family-oriented East Asia. He rejects Westernization while embracing modernization and its attendant changes in lifestyle—again strongly implying that democracy will not work in Asia.

Family Values (Required Here)

But the facts demonstrate just the opposite. It is not true, as Lee alleges, that Asian governments shy away from intervening in private matters and taking on all of society's problems. Asian governments intrude much more than Western governments into the daily affairs of individuals and families. In Korea, for example, each household is required to attend monthly neighborhood meetings to receive government directives and discuss local affairs. Japan's powerful government constantly intrudes into the business world to protect perceived national interests, to the point of causing disputes with the United States and other trading partners. In Lee's Singapore, the government stringently regulates individuals' actions—such as chewing bubblegum, spitting, smoking, littering, and so on—to an Orwellian extreme of social engineering. Such facts fly in the face of his assertion that East Asia's governments are minimalist. Lee makes these false claims to justify his rejection of Western-style democracy. He even dislikes the one man, one vote principle, so fundamental to modern democracy, saying that he is not "intellectually convinced" it is best.

Opinions like Lee's hold considerable sway not only in Asia but among some Westerners because of the moral breakdown of many advanced democratic societies. Many Americans thought, for example, that the U.S. citizen Michael Fay deserved the caning he received from Singaporean authorities for his act of vandalism. However, moral breakdown is attributable not to inherent shortcomings of Western cultures but to those of industrial societies: a similar phenomenon is now spreading through Asia's newly industrializing societies. The fact that Lee's Singapore, a small city-state, needs a near-totalitarian police state to assert control over its citizens contradicts his assertion that everything would be all right if governments would refrain from interfering in the private affairs of the family. The proper way to cure the ills of industrial societies is not to impose the terror of a police state but to emphasize ethical education, give high regard to spiritual values, and promote high standards in culture and the arts.

Long Before Locke

No one can argue with Lee's objection to "foisting" an alien system "indiscriminately on societies in which it will not work." The question is whether democracy is a system so alien to Asian cultures that it will not work. Moreover, considering Lee's record of absolute intolerance of dissent and the continued crackdown on dissidents in many other Asian countries, one is also compelled to ask whether democracy has been given a chance in places like Singapore.

A thorough analysis makes it clear that Asia has a rich heritage of democracy-oriented philosophies and traditions. Asia has already made great strides toward democratization and possesses the necessary conditions to develop democracy even beyond the level of the West.

Democratic Ideals. It is widely accepted that English political philosopher John Locke laid the foundation for modern democracy. According to Locke, sovereign rights reside with the people and, based on a contract with the people, leaders are given a mandate to govern, which the people can withdraw. But almost two millennia before Locke, Chinese philosopher Meng-tzu preached similar ideas. According to his "politics of Royal Ways," the king is the "Son of Heaven," and heaven bestowed on its son a mandate to provide good government, that is, to provide good for the people. If he did not govern righteously, the people had the right to rise up and overthrow his government in the name of heaven. Meng-tzu even justified regicide, saying that once a king loses the mandate of heaven he is no longer worthy of his subjects' loyalty. The people came first, Meng-tzu said, the country second, and the king third. The ancient Chinese philosophy of Minben Zhengchi, or "people-based politics," teaches that "the will of the people is the will of heaven" and that one should "respect the people as heaven" itself.

A native religion of Korea, Tonghak, went even further, advocating that "man is heaven" and that one must serve man as one does heaven. These ideas inspired and motivated nearly half a million peasants in 1894 to revolt against exploitation by feudalistic government internally and imperialistic forces externally. There are no ideas more fundamental to democracy than the teachings of Confucianism, Buddhism, and Tonghak. Clearly, Asia has democratic philosophies as profound as those of the West.

Democratic Institutions. Asia also has many democratic traditions. When Western societies were still being ruled by a succession of feudal lords, China and Korea had already sustained county prefecture systems for about 2,000 years. The government of the Chin Dynasty, founded by Chin-shih huang-ti (literally, the founder of Chin), practiced the rule of law and saw to it that everyone, regardless of class, was treated fairly. For nearly 1,000 years in China and Korea, even the sons of high-ranking officials were not appointed to important official positions unless they passed civil service examinations. These stringent tests were administered to members of the aristocratic class, who constituted over ten percent of the population, thus guaranteeing equal opportunity and social mobility, which are so central to popular democracy. This practice sharply contrasted with that of European fiefdoms of that time, where pedigree more or less determined one's official position. In China and Korea powerful boards of censors acted as a check against imperial misrule and abuses by government officials. Freedom of speech was highly valued, based on the understanding that the nation's fate depended on it. Confucian scholars were taught that remonstration against an erring monarch was a paramount duty. Many civil servants and promising political elites gave their lives to protect the right to free speech.

The fundamental ideas and traditions necessary for democracy existed in both Europe and Asia. Although Asians developed these ideas long before the Europeans did, Europeans formalized comprehensive and effective electoral democracy first. The invention of the electoral system is Europe's greatest accomplishment. The fact that this system was developed elsewhere does not mean that "it will not work" in Asia. Many Asian countries, including Singapore, have become prosperous after adopting a "Western" free-market economy, which is such an integral part of a democracy. Incidentally, in countries where economic development preceded political advancement—Germany, Italy, Japan, Spain—it was only a matter of time before democracy followed.

The State of Democracy in Asia. The best proof that democracy can work in Asia is the fact that, despite the stubborn resistance of authoritarian rulers like Lee, Asia has made great strides toward democracy. In fact, Asia has achieved the most remarkable record of democratization of any region since 1974. By 1990 a majority of Asian countries were democracies, compared to a 45 percent democratization rate worldwide.ffi This achievement has been overshadowed by Asia's tremendous economic success. I believe democracy will take root throughout Asia around the start of the next century. By the end of its first quarter, Asia will witness an era not only of economic prosperity, but also of flourishing democracy.

I am optimistic for several reasons. The Asian economies are moving from a capital- and labor-intensive industrial phase into an information- and technology-intensive one. Many experts have acknowledged that this new economic world order requires guaranteed freedom of information and creativity. These things are possible only in a democratic society. Thus Asia has no practical alternative to democracy; it is a matter of survival in an age of intensifying global economic competition. The world economy's changes have already meant a greater and easier flow of information, which has helped Asia's democratization process.

Democracy has been consistently practiced in Japan and India since the end of World War II. In Korea, Burma, Taiwan, Thailand, Pakistan, the Philippines, Bangladesh, Sri Lanka, and other countries, democracy has been frustrated at times, even suspended. Nevertheless, most of these countries have democratized, and in all of them, a resilient "people power" has been demonstrated through elections and popular movements. Even in Thailand, after ten military governments, a civilian government has finally emerged. The Mongolian government, after a long period of one-party dictatorship, has also voluntarily accepted democracy. The fundamental reason for my optimism is this increasing awareness of the importance of democracy and human rights among Asians themselves and their willingness to make the necessary efforts to realize these goals. Despite many tribulations, the torch of democracy continues to burn in Asia because of the aspirations of its people.

WE ARE THE WORLD

As Asians increasingly embrace democratic values, they have the opportunity and obligation to learn from older democracies. The West has experienced many problems in realizing its democratic systems. It is instructive, for example, to remember that Europeans practiced democracy within the boundaries of their nation-states but not outside. Until recently, the Western democracies coddled the interests of a small propertied class. The democracies that benefited much broader majorities through socioeconomic investments were mostly established after World War II. Today, we must start with a rebirth of democracy that promotes freedom, prosperity, and justice both within each country and among nations, including the less-developed countries: a global democracy.

Instead of making Western culture the scapegoat for the disruptions of rapid economic change, it is more appropriate to look at how the traditional strengths of Asian society can provide for a better democracy. In Asia, democracy can encourage greater self-reliance while respecting cultural values. Such a democracy is the only true expression of a people, but it requires the full participation of all elements of society. Only then will it have legitimacy and reflect a country's vision.

Asian authoritarians misunderstand the relationship between the rules of effective governance and the concept of legitimacy. Policies that try to protect people from the bad elements of economic and social change will never be effective if imposed without consent; the same policies, arrived at through public debate, will have the strength of Asia's proud and self-reliant people. A global democracy will recognize the connection between how we treat each other and how we treat nature, and it will pursue policies that benefit future generations. Today we are threatening the survival of our environment through wholesale destruction and endangerment of all species. Our democracy must become global in the sense that it extends to the skies, the earth, and all things with brotherly affection.

The Confucian maxim Xiushen qijia zhiguo pingtianxia, which offers counsel toward the ideal of "great peace under heaven," shows an appreciation for judicious government. The ultimate goal in Confucian political philosophy, as stated in this aphorism, is to bring peace under heaven *(pingtianxia)*. To do so, one must first be able to keep one's own household in order *(qijia)*, which in turn requires that one cultivate "self" *(xiushen)*. This teaching is a political philosophy that emphasizes the role of government and stresses the ruling elite's moral obligation to strive to bring about peace under heaven. Public safety, national security, and water and forest management are deemed critical. This concept of peace under heaven should be interpreted to include peaceful living and existence for all things under heaven. Such an understanding can also be derived from Gautama Buddha's teaching that all creatures and things possess a Buddha-like quality.

Since the fifth century B.C., the world has witnessed a series of revolutions in thought. Chinese, Indian, Greek, and Jewish thinkers have led great revolutions in ideas, and we are still living under the influence of their insights. However, for the past several hundred years, the world has been dominated by Greek and Judeo-Christian ideas and traditions. Now it is time for the world to turn to China, India, and the rest of Asia for another revolution in ideas. We need to strive for a new democracy that guarantees the right of personal development for all human beings and the wholesome existence of all living things.

A natural first step toward realizing such a new democracy would be full adherence to the Universal Declaration of Human Rights, adopted by the United Nations in 1948. This international document reflects basic respect for the dignity of people, and Asian nations should take the lead in implementing it. The movement for democracy in Asia has been carried forward mainly by Asia's small but effective army of dedicated people in and out of political parties, encouraged by nongovernmental and quasi-governmental organizations for democratic development from around the world. These are hopeful signs for Asia's democratic future. Such groups are gaining in their ability to force governments to listen to the concerns of their people, and they should be supported.

Asia should lose no time in firmly establishing democracy and strengthening human rights. The biggest obstacle is not its cultural heritage but the resistance of authoritarian rulers and their apologists. Asia has much to offer the rest of the world; its rich heritage of democracy-oriented philosophies and traditions can make a significant contribution to the evolution of global democracy. Culture is not necessarily our destiny. Democracy is.

READING 21: IMMANUEL WALLERSTEIN

IMMANUEL WALLERSTEIN,

"The World-System After the Cold War," Journal of Peace Research, 1993

1. INTRODUCTION

The certainties of the post-1945 era are now over, in particular two. (1) The United States dominated the capitalist world-economy, being the most efficient producer and the most prosperous country. This is no longer true. (2) The USA and the USSR were engaged in an all-encompassing 'Cold War', which shaped all interstate relations. The Cold War is no more. Indeed, the USSR is no more. To understand what this portends, we have three relevant pasts: the past of the US hegemonic era, 1945–90; the past of liberalism as the dominant ideology of the capitalist world-system, 1789–1989; the past of capitalism as an historical system, which started in 1450 and will perhaps be no more by 2050.

2. THE THREE RELEVANT PASTS

The story of the US hegemonic era is the easiest to tell. At the end of World War II, the USA found itself in an exceptional position. Its basic economic forces had been growing steadily stronger in terms of technology, competitiveness, and quantitative share of world production for 100 years. World War II resulted in enormous physical destruction throughout the Eurasian land mass, and thus among all the potential economic rivals of the USA, both those who had been allies and those who had been foes during the war.

The USA was thus able to establish a new world order, a *pax americana,* after the long disorder of 1914–45. The *pax americana* had four pillars. The first was the reconstruction of the major industrial powers, not only its long-time allies in western Europe, but its recent foes, Germany and Japan. The motives were multiple. The world-economy needed the reentry of these countries both as major producers and as major customers for US production. The USA needed a network of associates to maintain the world order. And, ideologically, the USA needed to propagate the idea of a 'free world' that was prosperous as a symbol of hope and therefore of moderation for the world's lower strata.

The second pillar was an arrangement with the only other serious military power in the world, the USSR. The Soviet Union was ostensibly an ideological rival and potentially an expanding power. In fact, it was quite easy to come to an arrangement in which the Soviet Union had its reserved zone (the 'socialist bloc'). There were four conditions to the deal: there would be absolute peace in Europe; the two blocs would be territorially fixed; the two great powers would maintain internal order in their blocs; the socialist bloc would expect no help in reconstruction from the USA. There were, to be sure, many noisy quarrels, but since none of them ended in breaking the arrangement, we may assume that their purpose was largely for show.

The third pillar was US internal unity built around the acceptance of US 'responsibility' in the world-system, anti-Communism at home and abroad, and the end of racial segregation. The fourth pillar was the slow political decolonization of the Third World and modest efforts for its so-called economic development. The emphasis was on the adjectives 'slow' and 'modest'.

If we turn to the second past, that of 1789–1989, we start with the geocultural shock of the French Revolution and its Napoleonic aftermath. The French Revolution changed France less than we believe, but it changed the world-system fundamentally. The French Revolution changed mentalities by imposing the belief that political change was 'normal' and legitimated by 'popular sovereignty'. The attempt to deal with this new reality took the form of the creation of the three ideologies: conservatism, liberalism, and socialism. The ostensible difference was in their attitude towards such normal change: the conservatives dubious and wishing to slow it down maximally, the liberals wishing to manage it rationally, and the socialists wishing to speed it up maximally. In theory, all three ideologies looked with disfavor on the state. But, in practice, all three ideologies found that they had to strengthen the state vis-à-vis society in order to achieve their objectives. In the end, all three ideologies united around the liberal program of orderly 'reform' enacted and administered by 'experts'. The conservatives became liberal conservatives and the socialists became liberal socialists.

In the 19th century, in Europe, liberalism promoted two great reforms: the extension of the suffrage and the creation of the social welfare state. By 1914 both reforms were in place or in process, and widely accepted as legitimate throughout western Europe and North America. The object of the reforms was the integration of the working classes in a way that would tame their anger but not threaten the continuing functioning of the capitalist world-economy. This program was superbly successful, for two reasons. The governments could mobilize their working classes around a double nationalism: an intra-European nationalism and the nationalist superiority of the 'Europeans' to the 'backward' peoples of the world. And, second, the costs of the social welfare state could be borne without too much disruption because of the expanded exploitation of the periphery.

World War I marked the beginning of a long intra-'European' struggle between Germany and the USA as the successor hegemonic power to Great Britain. It would end with US victory and world hegemony in 1945. World War I also marked, however, the moment when the peoples of the periphery began to try to reassert themselves against the European domination of the world-system. The North-South struggle we know today took shape then. The ideological response of the North to this new political reality was Wilsonianism, or the liberal program applied on a world scale. Wilsonianism offered the world equivalent of suffrage, the self-determination of nations. And 25 years later Roosevelt added the world equivalent of the social welfare state, the program of the economic development of the Third World, assisted by Western 'aid'. Leninism, which posed itself as the radical opponent of Wilsonianism, was in fact its avatar. Anti-imperialism was self-determination clothed in moral radical verbiage. The construction of socialism was economic development of the Third World clothed in more radical verbiage. One of the reasons 'Yalta' was possible was that there was less difference in the programs of Wilson and Lenin than official rhetoric maintained.

In the heyday of US hegemony after 1945, this world liberalism also seemed superbly successful. The decolonization of Asia and Africa was rapid and, for the most part, relatively painless. The 'national liberation movements' were full of hope for the future. The United Nations proclaimed the 1970s the 'Development Decade'. But something essential was lacking in the attempt to repeat in the 20th century at the world level what had been the 19th-century success of liberalism within Europe. There was no Third World for the Third World. One could neither mobilize the 'patriotism' of the Third World against a 'Third World' nor count on the income from exploiting a periphery to pay for their social welfare state. The taming of the working classes, so successful within Europe, was a chimera at the world level.

If we now turn to the third past, that between 1450 and today, we see a third 'success story', that of capitalism as an historical system. The raison d'être of capitalism is the endless accumulation of capital. The historical system that has been built, slowly and steadily, has been remarkable in its accomplishments. It has sustained a constant expansion of technology permitting an incredible growth in world production and world population. The capitalist world-economy was able to expand from its initial European base to incorporate the entire world and eliminate all other historical systems from the globe. It has developed a political framework of 'sovereign' nation-states within an ever more codified interstate system which has developed the right proportion of state power vis-à-vis the market so as to permit the maximal accumulation of capital. It has developed a complex system of the remuneration of labor, combining wage and non-wage forms, thereby keeping world labor costs down but offering incentives for efficiency. It has institutionalized both sexism and racism, enabling the construction of a hierarchical labor force which is self-sustaining politically.

Capitalism has been a dynamic system. It has been based not on a stable equilibrium but on a pattern of cyclical swings wherein the 'animal spirits' of the entrepreneurial classes, in pursuing their own interests, regularly and inevitably create mini-crises of overproduction which lead to downturns or stagnations in the world-economy. This is in fact very functional for the system, weeding out the weak producers and creating constraints on the ability of the working classes to pursue their incessant claims for greater reward.

There are, however, some basic contradictions in this historical system, as in all historical systems. The dynamic of the system requires constant spatial expansion; this has reached its limits. The dynamic of the system requires constant externalization of costs by individual producers; this may be coming close to reaching its limits. The dynamic of the system requires the constant, if slow, proletarianization of the working classes of the world; but proletarianization is a negative process from the point of view of the capitalists, in that it increases labor costs and creates political risks. Liberalism as an ideology was a very effective means of containing unrest and 'democratization', but over time it inevitably has put enormous strains on state budgets and created a public debt pyramid which threatens the stable functioning of the system.

3. THE TRANSITIONAL PRESENT

The late 1960s was a turning-point in many ways. It marked the beginning of the downturn ending the incredible post-1945 Kondratieff A-phase expansion. The basic economic reason was obvious. The remarkable economic recovery of western Europe and Japan plus the economic development of the Third World led to such a great increase in the production capacities of the previously most profitable industries (steel, automobiles, electronics, etc.) as to create a profit crunch. We have been living in this Kondratieff B-phase ever since. What has happened is what always happens in B-phases: acute competition among the core powers in a situation of contraction, each trying to maximize its profit margins and minimize its unemployment at the expense of the others; a shift of capital from seeking profits in production to seeking profits in financial manipulations; a squeeze on governmental balance of payments, resulting in debt crises (of the Third World, the ex-socialist bloc, and the United States). There has been a relocation of production at the world level. There has been an intensive search for new product innovations which can be the basis of future quasimonopolies. As in all B-phases, the effects of the downturn have not been felt evenly; some do better than others. In this downturn, the relative success story has been that of Japan and the East Asian 'dragons', which are linked.

At the same time, in 1968, there began a world revolution which, it is now clear, was a revolution against liberalism as the dominant ideology of the world-system. At the time, the social unrest, which occurred throughout the world—France and Germany, the USA and Japan, Czechoslovakia, and China, India and Mexico—seemed to have two common themes everywhere: opposition to US hegemony in the world-system and Soviet collusion; denunciation of the so-called Old Left (Communist and social-democratic parties, national liberation movements) for their complicity with the dominant forces. This revolt of 1968 in fact culminated with the overthrow in 1989–91 of the Communist governments in eastern Europe and the USSR. It is today clearer than it was in 1968 that the two themes—opposition to US hegemony and opposition to the Old Left—are in fact but a single theme, the opposition to reformist liberalism as a justification of the workings of the world-system.

The two principal changes in the geopolitics of the world-system in the 1970s and 1980s have been the decline of the relative power of the USA and the great disillusionment with developmentalism in the Third World. The first is a normal cyclical occurrence. The economic strengths of the European Community and Japan have been steadily rising since the mid-1960s, and the USA has not been able to keep pace. This has of course political and cultural implications. The world policy of the USA has for the past 20 years been centered around ways to slow down this loss of hegemony by exerting pressure on its allies. The second is not a cyclical occurrence at all. It marks the breakdown of the Wilsonian liberal enticement to the working classes of the periphery. The collapse of "statism" in both the Third World and the ex-socialist bloc is the collapse of liberal reformism, and hence the undermining of a crucial pillar in the stability of the capitalist world-economy.

The collapse of the Communist bloc is thus a double setback for the world-system. For the USA, it is a geopolitical catastrophe, as it eliminates the only ideological weapon the USA had to restrain the EC and Japan from pursuing their self-defined objectives. For the capitalist world-economy as an historical system, it marks the onset of an acute crisis, since it lifts the Leninist justification of the status quo without replacing it with any viable substitute.

4. THE UNCERTAIN FUTURE

We have now entered into the post-American era, but also the post-liberal era. This promises to be a time of great world disorder, greater probably than the world disorder between 1914 and 1945, and far more significant in terms of maintaining the world-system as a viable structure. What may we expect?

On the one hand, we may expect the capitalist world-economy to continue to operate in the short run in the way it has been operating for 500 years, but operating in this way will only exacerbate the crisis. Once this current Kondratieff B-phase is finally over (which will only be after one last downward swing), we shall as previously enter into a new A-phase, in which Japan, the USA, and the EC will struggle to obtain quasi-monopolistic control over the new leading industries. Japan stands a good chance of coming out on top, and it is probable that it will make a world economic alliance with the USA as junior partner to ensure this. In this new era of prosperity, the new main areas of economic expansion will be China for the Japan–US grouping and Russia for the EC. The rest of the periphery will be largely excluded from any benefits, and the polarization of world wealth will grow markedly more cute, as will the polarization of population growth.

A further problem is that the collapse of Wilsonian liberalism has led worldwide to a collapse in the faith in the 'state' as the central locus of social change and progress. It has also meant the collapse of long-term optimism, which has long been a key stabilizing political factor in the operation of the system. Polarized wealth without hope leads to generalized fear and the search for structures of security. These are being sought in identity politics, whose meaning is ambiguous but whose force is quite apparent.

There are three obvious sources of major instability in the world-system over the next 50 years. One is the growth of what I shall call the Khomeini option. This is the assertion by states in the periphery of total otherness and rejection of the rules of the interstate system as well as the geocultural norms governing the world-system. This particular option has been largely contained for the moment in Iran, but it is quite likely that other states will resort to it (and not only Islamic states), and it will be much more difficult to contain it if several states try it simultaneously.

The second source of instability is what I shall call the Saddam Hussein option. This is the attempt to challenge militarily the dominance of the North in the world-system. While Saddam Hussein's attempt was stopped cold, it took an extraordinary mobilization by the USA to do it. It is not at all clear that, as the decades go by, this can be repeated, especially if there are several such attempts simultaneously. US military strength will decline because the USA cannot sustain it either financially or politically. The states of the North are looking for a long-term substitute, but there is no clear one in sight. And acute economic and political competition among the core powers during the next upturn of the world-economy may not render such military collaboration too likely.

The third source of instability will be an unstoppable mass movement of people from South to North, including to Japan. The growing polarization of wealth and population makes this an option which no amount of border guards can successfully police. The result will be internal political instability in the North, coming doubly from right-wing anti-immigrant forces and from the immigrants themselves demanding political (and hence economic) rights; and all this in a context where all groups will have lost faith in the state as a means of solving social inequalities.

This is a picture of world turmoil, but it is not necessarily a pessimistic one. Obviously, such world disorder cannot go on indefinitely. New solutions will have to be found. This will undoubtedly mean creating a new historical system to replace the one that has been so efficacious for 500 years, but which is now crumbling because of its very success. We come therefore to the historical choices before us: what kind of new historical system to build, and how? There is no way to predict the outcome. We shall find ourselves in what scientists today are calling a bifurcation far from equilibrium, whose resolution is intrinsically unpredictable, but in which every intervention has great impact. We are thus in a situation of 'free will'. The world of 2050 will be the world we create. We have a considerable say about that creation. The politics of the next 50 years will be the politics of this restructuring of our world-system.

References

My views in this article are stated more elaborately in several places:

Arrighi, Giovanni; Terence K. Hopkins & Immanuel Wallerstein, 1989. *Antisystemic Movements.* London: Verso.

Wallerstein, Immanuel, 1991. *Geopolotics and Geoculture. Essays on the Changing World-System.* Cambridge: Cambridge University Press.

Wallerstein, Immanuel, 1992. 'The Concept of National Development, 1917–1989; Elegy and Requiem', pp. 79–88 in Gary marks and Larry Diamond, eds, *Reexamining Democracy: Essays in Honor of Seymour Martin Lipset.* Newbury Park, CA: Sage.

Wallerstein, Immanuel, 1992. 'The Collapse of Liberalism', pp. 96–110 in Ralph Miliband and Leo Panitch, eds, *Socialist Register 1992: New World Order?* London: Merlin.

READING 22: GEORGE SOROS

George Soros,

"Capitalism's Last Chance?" Foreign Policy, Winter 1998–99

The world is in the grip of an acute financial and political crisis. This crisis, if left unchecked, will lead to the disintegration of the global capitalist system. It is a crisis that will permanently transform the world's attitude toward capitalism and free markets. It has already overturned some of the world's longest established, and seemingly immovable, political regimes. Its effects on the relationships between advanced and developing nations are likely to be permanent and profound.

This situation came about unexpectedly, almost out of a clear blue sky. Even the people who expected an Asian crisis—and my firm, Soros Fund Management, was the first to anticipate the inevitability of the 1997 devaluation of the Thai baht that started the global chain reaction—had no idea of its extent or its destructive power.

What makes this crisis so politically unsettling and so dangerous for the global capitalist system is that the system itself is its main cause. More precisely, the origin of this crisis is to be found in the mechanism that defines the essence of a globalized capitalist system: the free, competitive capital markets that keep private capital moving unceasingly around the globe in a search for the highest profits and, supposedly, the most efficient allocation of the world's investment and savings.

The Asian crisis was originally attributed to various contingent weaknesses in specific countries and markets. Most economists focused initially on policy misjudgments that resulted in overvalued currencies and excessive reliance on foreign-currency borrowing. As the crisis spread, it became clear that such economic misjudgments were symptomatic of deeper sociopolitical problems. Political commentators have put the blame on the nexus of sociopolitical arrangements now described pejoratively as "crony capitalism" but previously extolled as "Confucian capitalism" or "the Asian model." There is some truth to these claims. Most Asian governments did make serious policy misjudgments, in some cases encouraged by international investors and the International Monetary Fund (IMF). They allowed investment and property booms to go unchecked and kept their currencies tied to the dollar for too long. In general, the Asian model was a highly distorted and immature form of the capitalist regime.

However, as the crisis has continued to develop, it has become apparent that its spread cannot be attributed simply to macroeconomic errors or specifically Asian characteristics. Why, after all, is the contagion now striking Eastern Europe, Latin America, and Russia, and even beginning to affect the advanced economies and efficient financial markets of Europe and the United States?

Financial Pendulum or Wrecking Ball?

The inescapable conclusion is that the crisis is a symptom of pathologies inherent in the global system. International financial markets have served as more than just a passive transmission mechanism for the global contagion; they have themselves been the main cause of the economic epidemic.

If it is true that the operation of free financial markets was in and of itself the fundamental cause of the present crisis, then a radical reconsideration of the dominant role that deregulated financial markets play in the world is inevitable. In the absence of urgent reforms, this rethinking could produce a powerful backlash against the global capitalist system, particularly in the developing countries on its periphery.

The essential point is that the global capitalist system is characterized not just by global free trade but more specifically by the free movement of capital. The system can be envisaged as a gigantic circulatory system, sucking capital into the financial markets and institutions at the center and then pumping it out to the periphery, either directly in the form of credits and portfolio investments or indirectly through multinational corporations.

Until the Thai crisis, the center was vigorously sucking in and pumping out money, financial markets were growing in size and importance, and countries on the periphery were obtaining an ample supply of capital from the center by opening up their capital markets. There was a global boom in which the emerging markets fared especially well. At one point in 1994, more than half the total inflow of capital to U.S. mutual funds went into emerging-market funds. The Asian crisis reversed the direction of the flow. Capital started fleeing emerging markets such as Korea and Russia. At first, the reversal benefited the financial markets at the center. But since the Russian meltdown in August 1998, the banking and financial systems at the center have also been adversely affected. As a result, the entire world economy is now under threat.

With the growing realization that the underlying cause of this threat is the inherent instability of deregulated financial markets, the ideology of world capitalism faces a historic challenge. The financial markets are playing a role very different from the one assigned to them by economic theory and the prevailing doctrine of free market capitalism. According to the ideology of free market fundamentalism, which has swept the world since it was pioneered in the early 1980s by Ronald Reagan and Margaret Thatcher, competitive markets are always right—or at least they produce results that cannot be improved on through the intervention of nonmarket institutions and politicians. The financial markets, in particular, are supposed to bring prosperity and stability—the more so, if they are completely free from government interference in their operations and unrestricted in their global reach.

The current crisis has shown this market fundamentalist ideology to be irredeemably flawed. Free market ideology asserts that fluctuations in stock markets and credit flows are transient aberrations that can have no permanent impact on economic fundamentals. If left to their own devices, financial markets are supposed to act in the long run like a pendulum, always swinging back toward equilibrium. Yet it can be demonstrated that the very notion of equilibrium is false. Financial markets are inherently unstable and always will be. They are given to excesses, and when a boom/bust sequence progresses beyond a certain point, it inevitably transforms the economic fundamentals, which in turn can never revert to where they began. Instead of acting like a pendulum, financial markets can act like a wrecking ball, swinging from country to country and destroying everything that stands in their way.

The current crisis presents policymakers with what may be a final opportunity to recognize that financial markets are inherently unstable before the wrecking ball takes aim at the foundations of the global capitalist system itself. What, then, needs to be done?

SAVING CAPITALISM FROM ITSELF

Many of the Widely discussed solutions to today's crisis are designed to improve the efficiency of financial markets and impose more market discipline through such means as deregulation, privatization, transparency, and so on. But imposing market discipline means imposing instability. Financial markets are discounting a future that is contingent on the bias that prevails in markets, and the reflexive interplay between expectations and outcomes yields unstable results. Market discipline is desirable, but it needs to be supplemented by another kind of discipline: Public-policy measures are needed to stabilize the flows of international finance required by the global capitalist system and to keep the inherent instability of financial markets under control.

Within the main capitalist countries, strong frameworks of state intervention already exist to protect against financial instability. The United States has the Federal Reserve Board and other financial authorities whose mandates are to prevent a breakdown in its domestic financial markets and, if necessary, act as lenders of last resort. They have been quite successful. I am confident that they are capable of fulfilling their responsibilities. Indeed, now, in the second phase of the current crisis, as the problems of the periphery have begun to spill over into the center and threaten serious financial instability in U.S. markets, stabilizing mechanisms have been brought powerfully into play. The Federal Reserve has urgently eased monetary policy and made clear that it will continue to print money if that is what financial stability requires. More controversially, the Fed has pressured the private sector into organizing a lifeboat for Long Term Capital management, a hedge fund that the Fed itself declared to be too big to fail.

The trouble is that international mechanisms for crisis management are grossly inadequate. Most policymakers in Europe and the United States worry today whether there countries can be protected from the global financial contagion. But the issue at the global level is much broader and more historically important. Even if the Western economies and banking systems do survive the present crisis without too much harm, those on the periphery have been significantly damaged.

The choice confronting the world today is whether to regulate global financial markets internationally to ensure that they carry out their function as a global circulatory system or leave it to each individual state to protect its own interests. The latter course will surely lead to the eventual breakdown of global capitalism. Sovereign states act as valves within the system. They may not resist the inflow of capital, but they will surely resist the outflow, once they consider it permanent. Malaysia has shown the way. A rapid spread of foreign-exchange controls will inevitably be accompanied by the drying up of international investment and a return to inward-looking economic strategies on the periphery. Economic withdrawal from world markets is likely to be accompanied by political disengagement and domestic repression. (Again, Malaysia stands out as an example.) In short, the global capitalist system will disintegrate.

What can be done to stop this process of disintegration? It is necessary to look beyond transparency, regulation, and other mechanisms that simply improve the efficiency of free markets. The flow of capital—and most importantly of private capital—from the center to the periphery must be revived and stabilized.

In seeking solutions to today's crisis, two common fallacies must be avoided. The first is the mistake of shutting the stable door after the horse has bolted. Reforms designed to improve the global financial architecture in the long term may be desirable, but they will do nothing to help the afflicted economies of today. In fact, the opposite may be true: Greater transparency and tougher prudential requirements are likely to discourage capital flows in the short term, just as the austere financial policies imposed by the IMF to restore the long-term soundness of stricken economies tend to make matters worse in the short term. The second fallacy is to embrace the delusion of market fundamentalism: that if markets can be made more transparent, more competitive, and generally more "perfect," their problems will be automatically solved. Today's crisis cannot be solved by market forces alone.

Emergency efforts to stabilize the world economy must focus on two goals: arresting the reverse flow of capital from the periphery of the global capitalist system to the center and ensuring the political allegiance of the peripheral countries to that system.

President Bill Clinton and Treasury Secretary Robert Rubin spoke in September 1998 about the need to establish a fund that would enable peripheral countries following sound economic policies to regain access to international capital markets. Although the two men did not say so publicly, I believe that they had in mind financing it with a new issue of Special Drawing Rights (SDRs), an international reserve asset created by the IMF to supplement members' existing assets.

Although their proposal did not receive much support at the annual meeting of the IMF in October 1998, I believe that it is exactly what is needed. Loans could be made available to countries such as Brazil, Korea, and Thailand that would have an immediate calming effect on international financial markets. Furthermore, such a mechanism would send a powerful signal because it would reward countries doing their utmost to play by the rules of the global capitalist system rather than succumbing, like Malaysia, to the temptation to cut themselves off. The IMF programs in countries such as Korea and Thailand have failed to produce the desired results because they do not include any scheme for reviving the flow of private capital to these countries or reducing their foreign debt. A debt reduction scheme could clear the decks and allow their domestic economies to recover, but it would force international creditors to accept and write off losses. The problem is that creditors would be unwilling and unable to make new loans, making it impossible to finance recovery in their countries without finding an alternate source of international credit. That is where an international credit guarantee scheme would come into play. It would significantly reduce the cost of borrowing and enable the countries concerned to finance a higher level of domestic activity. By doing so, such a mechanism would help revive not only the countries concerned but also the world economy. It would reward countries for playing by the rules of the global capitalist system and discourage defections along Malaysian lines.

At present, the Clinton proposal is not being seriously pursued because European central banks are adamantly opposed to the issue of SDRs. Their opposition stems from doctrinaire considerations: Any kind of money creation is supposed to fuel inflation. But in using SDRs as guarantees, there would be no new money created; the guarantees would kick in only in case of default.

After the German elections, left-of-center governments are now in power in most of Europe. These governments are likely to prove more amenable to a loan guarantee scheme than their central banks, especially when the recovery of important export markets hinges on it. Japan too is likely to support such a scheme as long as it covers Asia as well as Latin America.

NEEDED: INTERNATIONAL CREDIT INSURANCE

Although I strongly endorse the Clinton proposal, I would go even further. Earlier in 1998, I proposed establishing an International Credit Insurance Corporation. My proposal, however, was premature, as the reverse flow of capital had not yet become a firmly established trend. Moreover, the Korean liquidity crisis in late 1997 was followed by a temporary market recovery that lasted until April 1998. My proposal fell flat then, but its time has now come.

A credit insurance mechanism managed by the IMF could provide the cornerstone for the "new architecture" that policymakers and pundits are talking about these days. The new institution, which could become a permanent part of the IMF, would explicitly guarantee, up to defined limits, the loans that private lenders make to countries. If a country defaults, the IMF would pay the international creditors and then work out a repayment process with the debtor country. The borrowing countries would be obliged to provide data on all borrowings, public or private, insured or not. This information would enable the authority to set a ceiling on the amounts it would be willing to insure. Up to those amounts, the countries concerned would be able to access international capital markets at prime rates plus a modest fee. Beyond these limits, the creditors would be at risk. Ceilings would be set taking into account the macroeconomic policies pursued by individual countries, as well as other overall economic conditions in each country and throughout the world. The new institution would function, in effect, as a kind of international central bank. It would seek to avoid excesses in either direction, and it would have a powerful tool in hand.

The thorniest problem raised by this proposal is how the credit guarantees allocated to an individual country would be distributed among that country's borrowers. To allow the state to make this decision would be an invitation for abuse. Guarantees ought to be channeled through authorized banks that would compete with each other. The banks would have to be closely supervised and prohibited from engaging in other lines of business that could give rise to unsound credits and conflicts of interest. In short, international banks would have to be as closely regulated as U.S. banks were after the breakdown of the American banking system in 1933. It would take time to reorganize the global banking system and introduce the appropriate regulations, but the mere announcement of such a scheme would calm financial markets and allow time for a more thorough elaboration of the details.

The credit insurance plan would obviously help the peripheral countries and the Western banking system to weather the immediate crisis. By providing some inducements for lenders scarred by recent and impending losses, it would help restart the flow of funds from the financial markets toward the peripheral countries. But credit insurance would also strengthen the entire global financial architecture and improve financial stability in the long term. At present, the IMF does not have much influence in the internal affairs of its member countries except in times of crisis when a member country turns to the IMF for assistance. The fund may send its staff to visit and consult with country leaders, but it has neither the mandate nor the tools to shape economic policy in normal times. Its mission is crisis management, not prevention. By giving the new agency a permanent role in the surveillance of participating countries, the credit insurance scheme would help avoid both feast and famine in international capital flows.

Credit insurance would also help counteract the IMF's perverse role in the unsound expansion of international credit. IMF programs have served to bail out lenders, which encourages them to act irresponsibly, thereby creating a major source of instability in the international financial system. This defect of the current architecture is often described as "moral hazard." Moral hazard is caused by the asymmetry in the way that the IMF treats lenders and borrowers. It imposes conditions on borrowers (countries) but not on lenders (financial institutions); the money it lends enables debtor countries to meet their obligations, indirectly assisting the banks to recover their unsound loans. This asymmetry developed during the international crisis of the 1980s and became blatant in the Mexican crisis of 1995. In that case, foreign lenders to Mexico came out whole, even though the interest rates that the Mexican government paid them before the crisis clearly implied a high degree of risk. When Mexico could not pay, the U.S. Treasury and the IMF stepped in and took investors off the hook. The asymmetry and the moral hazard in IMF operations could be corrected by loan guarantees. Instead of bailing out foreign lenders to Mexico in 1995, the IMF would have guaranteed investors up to insured levels and then allowed uninsured debt to be converted into long-term bonds and written off. Had this happened, lenders and investors (myself included) would have been much more cautious about investing in Russia or Ukraine.

THE WILL TO STABILITY?

Some will wonder whether it would be possible for the IMF, let alone any new institution, to carry out the complex tasks I propose. Would it establish the right limits on sound international borrowing and be able to supervise the global circulatory system? A new institution would be bound to make mistakes, but the markets would provide valuable feedback and the mistakes could be corrected. After all, that is how all central banks operate and on the whole they do a pretty good job. It is much more questionable whether such a scheme is politically feasible. There is already a lot of opposition to the IMF from market fundamentalists who are against any kind of market intervention, especially by an international organization. If the banks and financial-market participants that currently benefit from moral hazard and asymmetry cease to support the IMF, it is unlikely to survive even in its present inadequate form.

Constructive reform will require governments, parliaments, and market participants to recognize that they have a stake in the survival of the system—and that this stake is far more valuable than any short-term gains that they may make from exploiting the flaws in the existing deregulated system. The question is whether this change of mentality will occur before or after the global capitalist system has fallen apart.

The Big Fix

The global financial crisis has spawned countless proposals on what to do with the International Monetary Fund (IMF). Herewith some examples:

Tear it down: "Let the IMF be abolished," says economics giant **Milton Friedman** in a November 1998 interview with *Forbes.* "Distribute the assets to each country and let the markets take care of the fallout." His fellow Hoover Institution scholar and former secretary of state **George Shultz** agrees. Instead of throwing money at the IMF, remarks Schultz, Congress should boost the global economy by cutting U.S. taxes by 10 percent across the board.

Clip its wings: The IMF can play a constructive role in crisis management if it avoids finger wagging and excessive interference in a nation's fiscal and monetary policies, says Harvard economics professor and former chairman of the President's Council of economic Advisers **Martin Feldstein.** He urges the fund to focus on coordinating the rescheduling of international obligations for creditors and debtors and to create a collateralized credit facility to lend to governments that are illiquid but able to repay foreign debts through future export surpluses. The Columbia Business School's **Charles Calomiris** say that instead of doling out cash, the IMF should simply offer advice and encouragement and closely monitor government attempts at macroeconomic reform.

Make it bigger and better: Fleshing out proposals made by President Bill Clinton and British prime minister Tony Blair, the **Group of Seven** (G-7) announced in October 1998 a plan for the fund to extend short-term credit lines to any government that implements IMF-approved reforms, drawing from the recently approved $90 billion increase in the IMF's lendable resources. The G-7 ministers also called for increased collaboration between private-sector creditors and national authorities and the adoption by IMF member nations of a code of financial transparency enforced by annual IMF audits.

Create a new institution: Forget the IMF and World Bank, says **Jeffrey Garten,** dean of the Yale School of Management. Instead, create a global central bank that could provide liquidity to ailing nations by purchasing bonds from national central banks; encourage spending and investment by acquiring national debts at discounted prices; and set uniform standards for lending and provide markets with detailed, credible information on the world's banks.

—FP

■■■■■■■■■■■■ ■ ■ ■■■■■■■■ ■ ■ ■■■■■■■■ ■

READING 23: FAREED ZAKARIA

FAREED ZAKARIA,

"THE RISE OF ILLIBERAL DEMOCRACY," FOREIGN AFFAIRS, 1997

THE NEXT WAVE

The American diplomat Richard Holbrooke pondered a problem on the eve of the September 1996 elections in Bosnia, which were meant to restore civic life to that ravaged country. "Suppose the election was declared free and fair," he said, and those elected are "racists, fascists, separatists, who are publicly opposed to [peace and reintegration]. That is the dilemma." Indeed it is, not just in the former Yugoslavia, but increasingly around the world. Democratically elected regimes, often ones that have been reelected or reaffirmed through referenda, are routinely ignoring constitutional limits on their power and depriving their citizens of basic rights and freedoms. From Peru to the Palestinian Authority, from Sierra Leone to Slovakia, from Pakistan to the Phillipines, we see the rise of a disturbing phenomenon in international—life illiberal democracy.

It has been difficult to recognize this problem because for almost a century in the West, democracy has meant *liberal* democracy—a political system marked not only by free and fair elections, but also by the rule of law, a separation of powers, and the protection of basic liberties of speech, assembly, religion, and property. In fact, this latter bundle of freedoms—what might be termed constitutional liberalism—is theoretically different and historically distinct from democracy. As the political scientist Philippe Schmitter has pointed out, "Liberalism, either as a conception of political liberty, or as a doctrine about economic policy, may have coincided with the rise of democracy. But it has never been immutably or unambiguously linked to its practice." Today the two strands of liberal democracy, interwoven in the Western political fabric, are coming apart in the rest of the world. Democracy is flourishing; constitutional liberalism is not.

Today, 118 of the world's 193 countries are democratic, encompassing a majority of its people (54.8 percent, to be exact), a vast increase from even a decade ago. In this season of victory, one might have expected Western statesmen and intellectuals to go one further than E. M. Forster and give a rousing three cheers for democracy. Instead there is a growing unease at the rapid spread of multiparty elections across south-central Europe, Asia, Africa, and Latin America, perhaps because of what happens *after* the elections. Popular leaders like Russia's Boris Yeltsin and Argentina's Carlos Menem bypass their parliaments and rule by presidential decree, eroding basic constitutional practices. The Iranian parliament—elected more freely than most in the Middle East—imposes harsh restrictions on speech, assembly, and even dress, diminishing that country's already meager supply of liberty. Ethiopia's elected government turns its security forces on journalists and political opponents, doing permanent damage to human rights (as well as human beings).

Naturally there is a spectrum of illiberal democracy, ranging from modest offenders like Argentina to near-tyrannies like Kazakstan and Belarus, with countries like Romania and Bangladesh in between. Along much of the spectrum, elections are rarely as free and fair as in the West today, but they do reflect the reality of popular participation in politics and support for those elected. And the examples are not isolated or atypical. Freedom House's 1996–97 survey, *Freedom in the World,* has separate rankings for political liberties and civil liberties, which correspond roughly with democracy and constitutional liberalism, respectively. Of the countries that lie between confirmed dictatorship and consolidated democracy, 50 percent do better on political liberties than on civil ones. In other words, half of the "democratizing" countries in the world today are illiberal democracies.[1]

Illiberal democracy is a growth industry. Seven years ago only 22 percent of democratizing countries could have been so categorized; five years ago that figure had risen to 35 percent.[2]

---

[1] Roger Kaplan, ed., *Freedom Around the World, 1997,* New York: Freedom House, 1997, pp. 21–22. The survey rates countries on two 7-point scales, for political rights and civil liberties (lower is better). I have considered all countries with a combined score of between 5 and 10 to be democratizing. The percentage figures are based on Freedom House's numbers, but in the case of individual countries I have not adhered strictly to its ratings. While the *Survey* is an extraordinary feat—comprehensive and intelligent—its methodology conflates certain constitutional rights with democratic procedures, which confuses matters. In addition, I use as examples (though not as part of the data set) countries like Iran, Kazakstan, and Belarus, which even in procedural terms are semi-democracies at best. But they are worth highlighting as interesting problem cases since most of their leaders were elected, reelected, and remain popular.

[2] *Freedom in the World: The Annual Survey of Political Rights and Civil Liberties, 1992–1993,* pp. 620–26; *Freedom in the World, 1989–1990,* pp. 312–19.

And to date few illiberal democracies have matured into liberal democracies; if anything, they are moving toward heightened illiberalism. Far from being a temporary or transitional stage, it appears that many countries are settling into a form of government that mixes a substantial degree of democracy with a substantial degree of illiberalism. Just as nations across the world have become comfortable with many variations of capitalism, they could well adopt and sustain varied forms of democracy. Western liberal democracy might prove to be not the final destination on the democratic road, but just one of many possible exists.

DEMOCRACY AND LIBERTY

From the time of Herodotus democracy has meant, first and foremost, the rule of the people. This view of democracy as a process of selecting governments, articulated by scholars ranging from Alexis de Tocqueville to Joseph Schumpeter to Robert Dahl, is now widely used by social scientists. In *The Third Wave*, Samuel P. Huntington explains why:

> Elections, open, free and fair, are the essence of democracy, the inescapable sine qua non. Governments produced by elections may be inefficient, corrupt, shortsighted, irresponsible, dominated by special interests, and incapable of adopting policies demanded by the public good. These qualities make such governments undesirable but they do not make them undemocratic. Democracy is one public virtue, not the only one, and the relation of democracy to other public virtues and vices can only be understood if democracy is clearly distinguished from the other characteristics of political systems.

This definition also accords with the commonsense view of the term. If a country holds competitive, multiparty elections, we call it democratic. When public participation in politics is increased, for example through the enfranchisement of women, it is seen as more democratic. Of course elections must be open and fair, and this requires some protections for freedom of speech and assembly. But to go beyond this minimalist definition and label a country democratic only if it guarantees a comprehensive catalog of social, political, economic, and religious rights turns the world democracy into a badge of honor rather than a descriptive category. After all, Sweden has an economic system that may argue curtails individual property rights, France until recently had a state monopoly on television, and England has an established religion. But they are all clearly and identifiably democracies. To have democracy mean, subjectively, "a good government" renders it analytically useless.

Constitutional liberalism, on the other hand, is not about the procedures for selecting government, but rather government's goals. It refers to the tradition, deep in Western history, that seeks to protect an individual's autonomy and dignity against coercion, whatever the source— state, church, or society. The term marries two closely connected ideas. It is *liberal* because it draws on the philosophical strain, beginning with the Greeks, that emphasizes individual liberty.[3] It is *constitutional* because it rests on the tradition, beginning with the Romans, of the rule of law. Constitutional liberalism developed in Western Europe and the United States as a defense of the individual's right to life and property, and freedom of religion and speech. To secure these rights, it emphasized checks on the power of each branch of government, equality under the law, impartial courts and tribunals, and separation of church and state. It canonical figures include the poet John Milton, the jurist William Blackstone, statesmen such as Thomas Jefferson and James Madison, and philosophers such as Thomas Hobbes, John Locke, Adam Smith, Baron de Montesquieu, John Stuart Mill, and Isaiah Berlin. In almost all of its variants,

---

[3] The term "liberal" is used here in its older, European sense, now often called classical liberalism. In America today the word has come to mean something quite different, namely policies upholding the modern welfare state.

constitutional liberalism argues that human beings have certain natural (or "inalienable") rights and that governments must accept a basic law, limiting its own powers that secures them. Thus in 1215 at Runnymede, England's barons forced the king to abide by the settled and customary law of the land. In the American colonies these laws were made explicit, and in 1638 the town of Hartford adopted the first written constitution in modern history. In the 1970s, Western nations codified standards of behavior for regimes across the globe. The Magna Carta, the Fundamental orders of Connecticut, the American Constitution, and the Helsinki Final Act are all expressions of constitutional liberalism.

THE ROAD TO LIBERAL DEMOCRACY

Since 1945 Western governments have, for the most part, embodied both democracy and constitutional liberalism. Thus it is difficult to imagine the two apart, in the form of either illiberal democracy or liberal autocracy. In fact both have existed in the past and persist in the present. Until the twentieth century, most countries in Western Europe were liberal autocracies or, at best, semi-democracies. The franchise was tightly restricted, and elected legislatures had little power. In 1830 Great Britain, in some ways the most democratic European nation, allowed barely 2 percent of its population to vote for one house of Parliament; that figure rose to 7 percent after 1867 and reached around 40 percent in the 1880s. Only in the late 1940s did most Western countries become full-fledged democracies, with universal adult suffrage. But one hundred years earlier, by the late 1840s, most of them had adopted important aspects of constitutional liberalism—the rule of law, private property rights, and increasingly, separated powers and free speech and assembly. For much of modern history, what characterized governments in Europe and North America, and differentiated them from those around the world, was not democracy but constitutional liberalism. The "Western model" is best symbolized not by the mass plebiscite but the impartial judge.

The recent history of East Asia follows the Western itinerary. After brief flirtations with democracy after World War II, most East Asian regimes turned authoritarian. Over time they moved from autocracy to liberalizing autocracy, and, in some cases, toward liberalizing semi-democracy.[4] Most of the regimes in East Asia remain only semi-democratic, with patriarchs or one-party systems that make their elections ratifications of power rather than genuine contests. But these regimes have accorded their citizens a widening sphere of economic civil, religious, and limited political rights. As in the West, liberalization in East Asia has included economic liberalization, which is crucial in promoting both growth and liberal democracy. Historically, the factors most closely associated with full-fledged liberal democracies are capitalism, a bourgeoisie, and a high per capita GNP. Today's East Asian governments are a mix of democracy, liberalism, capitalism, oligarchy, and corruption—much like Western governments circa 1900.

Constitutional liberalism has led to democracy, but democracy does not seem to bring constitutional liberalism. In contrast to the Western and East Asian paths, during the last two decades in Latin America, Africa, and parts of Asia, dictatorships with little background in constitutional liberalism have given way to democracy. The results are not encouraging. In the western hemisphere, with elections having been held in every country except Cuba, a 1993 study by the scholar Larry Diamond determined that 10 of the 22 principal Latin American countries "have levels of human rights abuse that are incompatible with the consolidation of [liberal] democracy."[5] In Africa, democratization has been extraordinarily rapid. Within six months in 1990 much

---

[4] Indonesia, Singapore, and Malaysia are examples of liberalizing autocracies, while South Korea, Taiwan, and Thailand are liberal semi-democracies. Both groups, however, are more liberal than they are democratic, which is also true of the region's only liberal democracy, Japan; Papua New Guinea, and to a lesser extent the Philippines, are the only examples of illiberal democracy in East Asia.

[5] Larry Diamond, "Democracy in Latin America," in Tom Farer, ed., *Beyond Sovereignty: Collectively Defending Democracy in a World of Sovereign States,* Baltimore: Johns Hopkins University Press, 1996, p. 73.

of Francophone Africa lifted its ban on multiparty politics. Yet although elections have been held in most of the 45 sub-Saharan states since 1991 (18 in 1996 alone), there have been setbacks for freedom in many countries. One of Africa's most careful observers, Michael Chege, surveyed the wave of democratization and drew the lesson that the continent had "overemphasized multiparty elections . . . and correspondingly neglected the basic tenets of liberal governance." In Central Asia, elections, even when reasonably free, as Kyrgyzstan and Kazakstan, have resulted in strong executives, weak legislatures and judiciaries, and few civil and economic liberties. In the Islamic world, from the Palestinian Authority to Iran to Pakistan, democratization has led to an increasing role for theocratic politics, eroding long-standing traditions of secularism and tolerance. In many parts of that world, such as Tunisia, Morocco, Egypt, and some of the Gulf States, were elections to be held tomorrow, the resulting regimes would almost certainly be more illiberal than the ones now in place.

Many of the countries of Central Europe, on the other hand, have moved successfully from communism to liberal democracy, having gone through the same phase of liberalization without democracy as other European countries did during the nineteenth century. Indeed, the Austro-Hungarian empire, to which most belonged, was a classic liberal autocracy. Even outside Europe, the political scientist Myron Weiner detected a striking connection between a constitutional past and a liberal democratic present. He pointed out that, as of 1983, "every single country in the Third World that emerged from colonial rule since the Second World War with a population of at least one million (and almost all the smaller colonies as well) with a continuous democratic experience is a former British colony."[6] British rule meant not democracy—colonialism is by definition undemocratic—but constitutional liberalism. Britain's legacy of law and administration has proved more beneficial than France's policy of enfranchising some of its colonial populations.

While liberal autocracies may have existed in the past, can one imagine them today? Until recently, a small but powerful example flourished off the Asian mainland—Hong Kong. For 156 years, until July 1, 1997, Hong Kong was ruled by the British Crown through an appointed governor general. Until 1991 it had never held a meaningful election, but its government epitomized constitutional liberalism, protecting its citizens' basic rights and administering a fair court system and bureaucracy. A September 8, 1997, editorial on the island's future in *The Washington Post* was titled ominously, "Undoing Hong Kong's Democracy." Actually Hong Kong has precious little democracy to undo; what it has is a framework of rights and laws. Small islands may not hold much practical significance in today's world, but they do help one weigh the relative value of democracy and constitutional liberalism. Consider, for example, the question of where you would rather live, Haiti, an illiberal democracy, or Antigua, a liberal semi-democracy. Your choice would probably relate not to the weather, which is pleasant in both, but to the political climate, which is not.

ABSOLUTE SOVEREIGNITY

John Stuart Mill opened his classic *On Liberty* by noting that as countries became democratic, people tended to believe that "too much importance had been attached to the limitation of power itself. That . . . was a response against rulers whose interests were opposed to those of the people." Once the people were themselves in charge, caution was unnecessary. "The nation did not need to be protected against its own will." As if confirming Mill's fears, consider the words of Alexandr Lukashenko after being elected president of Belarus with an overwhelming majority in a free election in 1994, when asked about limiting his powers: "There will be no dictatorship. I am of the people, and I am going to be for the people."

---

[6] Myron Weiner, "Empirical Democratic Theory," in Myron Weiner and Ergun Ozbudun, eds., *Competitive Elections in Developing Countries,* Durham: Duke University Press, 1987, p. 20. Today there are functioning democracies in the Third World that are not former British colonies, but the majority of the former are the latter.

The tension between constitutional liberalism and democracy centers on the scope of governmental authority. Constitutional liberalism is about the limitation of power, democracy about its accumulation and use. For this reason, many eighteenth- and nineteenth-century liberals saw in democracy a force that could undermine liberty. James Madison explained in *The Federalist* that "the danger of oppression" in a democracy came from "the majority of the community." Tocqueville warned of the "tyranny of the majority," writing, "The very essence of democratic government consists in the absolute sovereignty of the majority."

The tendency for a democratic government to believe it has absolute sovereignty (that is, power) can result in the centralization of authority, often by extraconstitutional means and with grim results. Over the last decade, elected governments claiming to represent the people have steadily encroached on the powers and rights of other elements in society, a usurpation that is both horizontal (from other branches of the national government) and vertical (from regional and local authorities as well as private businesses and other nongovernmental groups). Lukashenko and Peru's Alberto Fujimori are only the worst examples of this practice. (While Fujimori's actions—disbanding the legislature and suspending the constitution, among others—make it difficult to call his regime democratic, it is worth noting that he won two elections and was extremely popular until recently.) Even a bona fide reformer like Carlos Menem has passed close to 300 presidential decrees in his eight years in office, about three times as many as all previous Argentinean presidents put together, going back to 1853. Kyrgyzstan's Askar Akayev, elected with 60 percent of the vote, proposed enhancing his powers in a referendum that passed easily in 1996. His new powers include appointing all top officials except the prime minister, although he can dissolve parliament if it turns down three of his nominees for the latter post.

Horizontal usurpation, usually by presidents, is more obvious, but vertical usurpation is more common. Over the last three decades, the Indian government has routinely disbanded state legislatures on flimsy grounds, placing regions under New Delhi's direct rule. In a less dramatic but typical move, the elected government of the Central African Republic recently ended the longstanding independence of its university system, making it part of the central state apparatus.

Usurpation is particularly widespread in Latin America and the states of the former Soviet Union, perhaps because both regions mostly have presidencies. These systems tend to produce strong leaders who believe that they speak for the people—even when they have been elected by no more than a plurality. (As Juan Linz points out, Salvador Allende was elected to the Chilean presidency in 1970 with only 36 percent of the vote. In similar circumstances, a prime minister would have had to share power in a coalition government.) Presidents appoint cabinets of cronies, rather than senior party figures, maintaining few internal checks on their power. And when their views conflict with those of the legislature, or even the courts, presidents tend to "go to the nation," bypassing the dreary tasks of bargaining and coalition-building. While scholars debate the merits of presidential versus parliamentary forms of government, usurpation can occur under either, absent well-developed alternate centers of power such as strong legislatures, courts, political parties, regional governments, and independent universities and media. Latin America actually combines presidential systems with proportional representation, producing populist leaders and multiple parties—an unstable combination.

Many Western governments and scholars have encouraged the creation of strong and centralized states in the Third World. Leaders in these countries have argued that they need the authority to break down feudalism, split entrenched coalitions, override vested interests, and bring order to chaotic societies. But this confuses the need for a legitimate government with that for a powerful one. Governments that are seen as legitimate can usually maintain order and pursue tough policies, albeit slowly, by building coalitions. After all, few claim that governments in developing countries should not have adequate police powers; the trouble comes from all the other political, social and economic powers that they accumulate. In crises like civil wars, constitutional governments might not be able to rule effectively, but the alternative—states with vast security apparatuses that suspend constitutional rights—has usually produced neither order nor good government. More often, such states have become predatory, maintaining some order but also arresting opponents, muzzling dissent, nationalizing industries, and confiscating property. While anarchy has its dangers, the greatest threats to human liberty and happiness in this century have been caused not by disorder but by brutally strong, centralized states, like Nazi Germany, Soviet Russia, and Maoist China. The Third World is littered with the bloody handiwork of strong states.

Historically, unchecked centralization has been the enemy of liberal democracy. As political participation increased in Europe over the nineteenth century, it was accommodated smoothly in countries such as England and Sweden, where medieval assemblies, local governments, and regional councils had remained strong. Countries like France and Prussia, on the other hand, where the monarchy had effectively centralized power (both horizontally and vertically), often ended up illiberal and undemocratic. It is not a coincidence that in twentieth-century Spain, the beachhead of liberalism lay in Catalonia, for centuries a doggedly independent and autonomous region. In America, the presence of a rich variety of institutions—state, local, and private—made it much easier to accommodate the rapid and large extensions in suffrage that took place in the early nineteenth century. Arthur Schlesinger Sr. has documented how, during America's first 50 years, virtually every state, interest group and faction tried to weaken and even break up the federal government.[7] More recently, India's semi-liberal democracy has survived because of, not despite, its strong regions and varied languages, cultures, and even castes. The point is logical, even tautological: pluralism in the past helps ensure political pluralism in the present.

Fifty years ago, politicians in the developing world wanted extraordinary powers to implement then-fashionable economic doctrines, like nationalization of industries. Today their successors want similar powers to privatize those very industries. Menem's justification for his methods is that they are desperately needed to enact tough economic reforms. Similar arguments are made by Abdalá Bucarem of Ecuador and by Fujimori. Lending institutions, such as the International Monetary fund and the World Bank, have been sympathetic to these pleas, and the bond market has been positively exuberant. But except in emergencies like war, illiberal means are in the long run incompatible with liberal ends. Constitutional government is in fact the key to a successful economic reform policy. The experience of East Asia and Central Europe suggests that when regimes—whether authoritarian, as in East Asia, or liberal democratic, as in Poland, Hungary, and the Czech Republic—protect individual rights, including those of property and contract, and create a framework of law and administration, capitalism and growth will follow. In a recent speech at the Woodrow Wilson International Center in Washington, explaining what it takes for capitalism to flourish, Federal Reserve chairman Alan Greenspan concluded that, "The guiding mechanism of a free market economy . . . is a bill of rights, enforced by an impartial judiciary"

Finally, and perhaps more important, power accumulated to do good can be used subsequently to do ill. When Fujimori disbanded parliament, his approval ratings shot up to their highest ever. But recent opinion polls suggest that most of those who once approved of his actions now wish he were more constrained. In 1993 Boris Yeltsin famously (and literally) attacked the Russian parliament, prompted by parliament's own unconstitutional acts. He then suspended the constitutional court, dismantled the system of local governments, and fired several provincial governors. From the war in Chechnya to his economic programs, Yeltsin has displayed a routine lack of concern for constitutional procedures and limits. He may well be a liberal democrat at heart, but Yeltsin's actions have created a Russian super-presidency. We can only hope his successor will not abuse it.

For centuries Western intellectuals have had a tendency to view constitutional liberalism as a quaint exercise in rule-making, mere formalism that should take a back seat to battling larger evils in society. The most eloquent counterpoint to this view remains an exchange in Robert

---

[7] Arthur Schlesinger, Sr., *New Viewpoints in American History,* New York: Macmillan, 1922, pp. 220–40.

Bolt's play *A Man For All Seasons.* The fiery young William Roper, who yearns to battle evil, is exasperated by Sir Thomas More's devotion to the law. More gently defends himself.

> MORE: What would you do? Cut a great road through the law to get after the Devil?
> ROPER: I'd cut every law in England to do that!
> MORE: And when the last law was down, and the Devil turned on you—where would you hide Roper, the laws all being flat?

On December 8, 1996, Jack Lang made a dramatic dash to Belgrade. The French celebrity politician, formerly minister of culture, had been inspired by the student demonstrations involving tens of thousands against Slobodan Miloševi´c, a man Lang and many Western intellectuals held responsible for the war in the Balkans. Lang wanted to lend his moral support to the Yugoslav opposition. The leaders of the movement received him in their offices—the philosophy department—only to boot him out, declare him "an enemy of the Serbs," and order him to leave the country. It turned out that the students opposed Miloševi´c not for starting the war, but for failing to win it.

Lang's embarrassment highlights two common, and often mistaken, assumptions—that the forces of democracy are the forces of ethnic harmony and of peace. Neither is necessarily true. Mature liberal democracies can usually accommodate ethnic divisions without violence or terror and live in peace with other liberal democracies. But without a background in constitutional liberalism, the introduction of democracy in divided societies has actually fomented nationalism, ethnic conflict, and even war. The spate of elections held immediately after the collapse of communism were won in the Soviet Union and Yugoslavia by nationalist separatists and resulted in the breakup of those countries. This was not in and of itself bad, since those countries had been bound together by force. But the rapid secessions, without guarantees, institutions, or political power for the many minorities living within the new countries, have caused spirals of rebellion, repression, and, in places like Bosnia, Azerbaijan, and Georgia, war.

Elections require that politicians compete for peoples' votes. In societies without strong traditions of multiethnic groups or assimilation, it is easiest to organize support along racial, ethnic, or religious lines. Once an ethnic group is in power, it tends to exclude other ethnic groups. Compromise seems impossible; one can bargain on material issues like housing, hospitals, and handouts, but how does one split the difference on a national religion? Political competition that is so divisive can rapidly degenerate into violence. Opposition movements, armed rebellions, and coups in Africa have often been directed against ethnically based regimes, many of which came to power through elections. Surveying the breakdown of African and Asian democracies in the 1960s, two scholars concluded that democracy "is simply not viable in an environment of intense ethnic preferences." Recent studies, particularly of Africa and Central Asia, have confirmed this pessimism. A distinguished expert on ethnic conflict, Donald Horowitz, concluded, "In the face of this rather dismal account . . . of the concrete failures of democracy in divided societies . . . one is tempted to throw up one's hands. What is the point of holding elections if all they do in the end is to substitute a Bemba-dominated regime for a Nyanja regime in Zambia, the two equally narrow, or a southern regime for a northern one in Benin, neither incorporating the other half of the state?"[8]

Over the past decade, one of the most spirited debates among scholars of international relations concerns the "democratic peace"—the assertion that no two modern democracies have

---

[8] Alvin Rabushka and Kenneth Shepsle, *Politics in Plural Societies: A Theory of Democratic Instability,* Columbus: Charles E. Merill, pp. 62–92; Donald Horowitz, "Democracy in Divided Societies," in Larry Diamond and Mark F. Plattner, eds., *Nationalism, Ethnic Conflict and Democracy,* Baltimore: The Johns Hopkins University Press, 1994, pp. 35–55.

gone to war with each other. The debate raises interesting substantive questions (does the American Civil War count? Do nuclear weapons better explain the peace?) and even the statistical findings have raised interesting dissents. (As the scholar David Spiro points out, given the small number of both democracies and wars over the last two hundred years, sheer chance might explain the absence of war between democracies. No member of his family has ever won the lottery, yet few offer explanations for this impressive correlation.) But even if the statistics are correct, what explains them? Kant, the original proponent of the democratic peace, contended that in democracies, those who pay for wars—that is, the public—make the decisions, so they are understandably cautious. But that claim suggests that democracies are more pacific than other states. Actually they are more warlike, going to war more often and with greater intensity than most states. It is only with other democracies that the peace holds.

When divining the cause behind this correlation, one thing becomes clear: the democratic peace is actually the liberal peace. Writing in the eighteenth century, Kant believed that democracies were tyrannical, and he specifically excluded them from his conception of "republican" governments, which lived in a zone of peace. Republicanism, for Kant, meant a separation of powers, checks and balances, the rule of law, protection of individual rights, and some level of representation in government (though nothing close to universal suffrage). Kant's other explanations for the "perpetual peace" between republics are all closely linked to their constitutional and liberal character: a mutual respect for the rights of each other's citizens, a system of checks and balances assuring that no single leader can drag his country into war, and classical liberal economic policies—most importantly, free trade—which create an interdependence that makes war costly and cooperation useful. Michael Doyle, the leading scholar on the subject, confirms in his 1997 book *Ways of War and Peace* that without constitutional liberalism, democracy itself has no peace-inducing qualities:

> Kant distrusted unfettered, democratic majoritarianism, and his argument offers no support for a claim that all participatory polities—democracies—should be peaceful, either in general or between fellow democracies. Many participatory polities have been non-liberal. For two thousand years before the modern age, popular rule was widely associated with aggressiveness (by Thucydides) or imperial success (by Machiavelli) . . . The decisive preference of [the] median voter might well include "ethnic cleansing" against other democratic polities.

The distinction between liberal and illiberal democracies sheds light on another striking statistical correlation. Political scientists Jack Snyder and Edward Mansfield contend, using an impressive data set, that over the last 200 years democratizing states went to war significantly more often than either stable autocracies or liberal democracies. In countries not grounded in constitutional liberalism, the rise of democracy often brings with it hyper-nationalism and war-mongering. When the political system is opened up, diverse groups with incompatible interests gain access to power and press their demands. Political and military leaders, who are often embattled remnants of the old authoritarian order, realize that to succeed that they must rally the masses behind a national cause. The result is invariably aggressive rhetoric and policies, which often drag countries into confrontation and war. Noteworthy examples range from Napoleon III's France, Wilhelmine Germany, and Taisho Japan to those in today's newspapers, like Armenia and Azerbaijan and Milošević's Serbia. The democratic peace, it turns out, has little to do with democracy.

THE AMERICAN PATH
An American scholar recently traveled to Kazakhstan on a U.S. government-sponsored mission to help the new parliament draft its electoral laws. His counterpart, a senior member of the Kazak parliament, brushed aside the many options the American expert was outlining, saying emphatically, "We want our parliament to be just like your Congress." The American was horrified, recalling, "I tried to say something other than the three words that had immediately come

screaming into my mind: 'No you don't!'" This view is not unusual. Americans in the democracy business tend to see their own system as an unwieldy contraption that no other country should put up with. In fact, the adoption of some aspects of the American constitutional framework could ameliorate many of the problems associated with illiberal democracy. The philosophy behind the U.S. Constitution, a fear of accumulated power, is as relevant today as it was in 1789. Kazakstan, as it happens, would be particularly well-served by a strong parliament—like the American Congress—to check the insatiable appetite of its president.

It is odd that the United States is so often the advocate of election and plebiscitary democracy abroad. What is distinctive about the American system is not how democratic it is but rather how undemocratic it is, placing as it does multiple constraints on electoral majorities. Of its three branches of government, one—arguably paramount—is headed by nine unelected men and women with life tenure. Its Senate is the most unrepresentative upper house in the world, with the lone exception of the House of Lords, which is powerless. (Every state sends two senators to Washington regardless of its population—California's 30 million people have as many votes in the Senate as Arizona's 3.7 million—which means that senators representing about 16 percent of the country can block any proposed law.) Similarly, in legislatures all over the United States, what is striking is not the power of majorities but that of minorities. To further check national power, state and local governments are strong and fiercely battle every federal intrusion onto their turf. Private businesses and other nongovernmental groups, what Tocqueville called intermediate associations, make up another stratum within society.

The American system is based on an avowedly pessimistic conception of human nature, assuming that people cannot be trusted with power. "If men were angles," Madison famously wrote, "no government would be necessary." The other model for democratic governance in Western history is based on the French Revolution. The French model places its faith in the goodness of human beings. Once the people are the source of power, it should be unlimited so that they can create a just society. (The French revolution, as Lord Acton observed, is not about the limitation of sovereign power but the abrogation of all intermediate powers that get in its way.) Most non-Western countries have embraced the French model—not least because political elites like the prospect of empowering the state, since that means empowering themselves—and most have descended into bouts of chaos, tyranny, or both. This should have come as no surprise. After all, since its revolution France itself has run through two monarchies, two empires, one proto-fascist dictatorship, and five republics.[9]

Of course cultures vary, and different societies will require different frameworks of government. This is not a plea for the wholesale adoption of the American way but rather for a more variegated conception of liberal democracy, one that emphasizes both parts of that phrase. Before new policies can be adopted, there lies an intellectual task of recovering the constitutional liberal tradition, central to the Western experience and to the development of good government throughout the world. Political progress in Western history has been the result of a growing recognition over the centuries that, as the Declaration of Independence puts it, human beings have "certain inalienable rights" and that "it is to secure these rights that governments are instituted." If a democracy does not preserve liberty and law, that it is a democracy is a small consolation.

LIBERALIZING FOREIGN POLICY

A proper appreciation of constitutional liberalism has a variety of implications for American foreign policy. First, it suggests a certain humility. While it is easy to impose elections on a country,

---

[9] Bernard Lewis, "Why Turkey Is the Only Muslim Democracy," *Middle East Quarterly*, March 1994, pp. 47–48.

it is more difficult to push constitutional liberalism on a society. The process of genuine liberalization and democratization is gradual and long-term in which an election is only one step. Without appropriate preparation, it might even be a false step. Recognizing this, governments and nongovernmental organizations are increasingly promoting a wide array of measures designed to bolster constitutional liberalism in developing countries. The National Endowment for Democracy promotes free markets, independent labor movements, and political parties. The U.S. Agency for International Development funds independent judiciaries. In the end, however, elections trump everything. If a country holds elections, Washington and the world will tolerate a great deal from the resulting government, as they have with Yeltsin, Akayev, and Menem. In an age of images and symbols, elections are easy to capture on film. (How do you televise the rule of law?) But there is life after elections, especially for the people who live there.

Conversely, the absence of free and fair elections should be viewed as one flaw, not the definition of tyranny. Elections are an important virtue of governance, but they are not the only virtue. Governments should be judged by yardsticks related to constitutional liberalism as well. Economic, civil, and religious liberties are at the core of human autonomy and dignity. If a government with limited democracy steadily expands these freedoms, it should not be branded a dictatorship. Despite the limited political choice they offer, countries like Singapore, Malaysia, and Thailand provide a better environment for the life, liberty, and happiness of their citizens than do either dictatorships like Iraq and Libya or illiberal democracies like Slovakia or Ghana. And the pressures of global capitalism can push the process of liberalization forward. Markets and morals can work together. Even China, which remains a deeply repressive regime, has given its citizens more autonomy and economic liberty than they have had for generations. Much more needs to change before China can even be called a liberalizing autocracy, but that should not mask the fact that much has changed.

Finally, we need to revive constitutionalism. One effect of the overemphasis on pure democracy is that little effort is given to creating imaginative constitutions for transitional countries. Constitutionalism, as it was understood by its greatest eighteenth century exponents, such as Montesquieu and Madison, is a complicated system of checks and balances designed to prevent the accumulation of power and the abuse of office. This is done not by simply writing up a list of rights but by constructing a system in which government will not violate those rights. Various groups must be included and empowered because, as Madison explained, "ambition must be made to counteract ambition." Constitutions were also meant to tame the passions of the public, creating not simply democratic but also deliberative government. Unfortunately, the rich variety of unelected bodies, indirect voting, federal arrangements, and checks and balances that characterized so many of the formal and informal constitutions of Europe are now regarded with suspicion. What could be called the Weimar syndrome—named after interwar Germany's beautifully constructed constitution, which failed to avert fascism—has made people regard constitutions as simply paperwork that cannot make much difference. (As if any political system in Germany would have easily weathered military defeat, social revolution, the Great Depression, and hyperinflation.) Procedures that inhibit direct democracy are seen as inauthentic, muzzling the voice of the people. Today around the world we see variations on the same majoritarian theme. But the trouble with these winner-take-all systems is that, in most democratizing countries, the winner really does take all.

DEMOCRACY'S DISCONTENTS

We live in a democratic age. Through much of human history the danger to an individual's life, liberty and happiness came from the absolutism of monarchies, the dogma of churches, the terror of dictatorships, and the iron grip of totalitarianism. Dictators and a few straggling totalitarian regimes still persist, but increasingly they are anachronisms in a world of global markets, information, and media. There are no longer respectable alternatives to democracy; it is part of the fashionable attire of modernity. Thus the problems of governance in the 21st century will likely be problems *within* democracy. This makes them more difficult to handle, wrapped as they are in the mantle of legitimacy.

Illiberal democracies gain legitimacy, and thus strength, from the fact that they are reasonably democratic. Conversely, the greatest danger that illiberal democracy poses—other than to its own people—is that it will discredit liberal democracy itself, casting a shadow on democratic governance. This would not be unprecedented. Every wave of democracy has been followed by setbacks in which the system was seen as inadequate and new alternatives were sought by ambitious leaders and restless masses. The last such period of disenchantment, in Europe during the interwar years, was seized upon by demagogues, many of whom were initially popular and even elected. Today, in the face of a spreading virus of illiberalism, the most useful role that the international community, and most importantly the United States, can play as—instead of searching for new lands to democratize and new places to hold elections—to consolidate democracy where it has taken root and to encourage the gradual development of constitutional liberalism across the globe. Democracy without constitutional liberalism is not simply inadequate, but dangerous, bringing with it the erosion of liberty, the abuse of power, ethnic diversions, and even war. Eighty years ago, Woodrow Wilson took America into the twentieth century with a challenge, to make the world safe for democracy. As we approach the next century, our task is to make democracy safe for the world.

◼▮◼▮◼▮◼▮◼▮◼▮◼ ◼▮◼▮◼▮◼▮◼▮◼▮◼▮◼ ◼▮◼▮◼▮◼▮◼▮◼

READING 24: THEOTONIO DOS SANTOS

THEOTONIO DOS SANTOS,

"THE THEORETICAL FOUNDATIONS OF THE CARDOSO GOVERNMENT: A NEW STAGE OF THE DEPENDENCY-THEORY DEBATE," LATIN AMERICAN PERSPECTIVES, 1998

Brazil's election of Fernando Henrique Cardoso as president of the republic was a very positive step; he was an opponent of the military dictatorship that began in 1964 and also a social scientist, a student of Brazil's economic, social, and political conditions. During his campaign it was alleged that he had recanted his earlier writings, but he has denied this allegation and at the same time published two books of his theoretical writings of the past two decades: *As idéias e o seu lugar: Ensaiao sobre as teorias do desenvolvimento* (1993) and *A construção da democracia: Estudos sobre política* (1993). The works brought together in these collections were originally published mainly in the 1960s, and rereading them confirms the conviction that his current political position is not inconsistent with them but clearly reflects an evolution of his sociological and political ideas. Because many of the recently published works are directed explicitly to a debate with my writings and with those of a group of social scientists of the Centro de Estudos Socio-económicos da Universidade do Chile (CESO) that I directed, I cannot fail to add my testimony to the already ample literature on his thought. I would like to do so with as much calm as possible after the avalanche of political approval that he received in the 1994 elections and continues to enjoy. In such circumstances, it is difficult to maintain objectivity and clarity of intentions.

Theotonio dos Santos, translated by Laura Randall, *Latin Amercian Perspectives*, Issue 98, Vol 25, No. 1. pp 53-70, copyright © 1998 by Latin American Perspectives. Reprinted by permission of Sage Publications, Inc.

OUR AGREEMENTS

Cardoso always presents his criticisms elegantly and respectfully, in the context of the common intellectual adventure, known as dependency theory, in which we participated.[1] He makes it very clear that the development of this movement gave rise to a privileged moment in the history of social ideas in Latin America. The Latin American thought of the time had worldwide repercussions on the social sciences. The work of the UN's Economic Commission for Latin America (ECLA), directed by the Argentine economist Raúl Prebisch, represented a highly advanced stage of reflection about the region's historical evolution, its political experience, and its position in the development of the world economic and political system. In truth, this intense critical intellectual effort, beginning with encounters with various exiles in Chile between 1964 and 1974, was possible only on the basis of the theoretical antecedents that ECLA had synthesized so well. These encounter resulted in the so-called dependency theory or, as Cardoso prefers, dependency studies.

ECLA represented the national-developmentalist ideology in Latin America and in the so-called Third World. The dominant classes in the region declared that they would not accept a return to the condition of simple exporters of agricultural products and raw materials that had characterized the region until the 1920s. They believed that the recent industrialization of various Latin American nations was the basis of their modernization, identifying the process of industrialization with economic, social, and political development. In order to demonstrate the truth of this position, Latin American social thought had to identify the constraints on an economy that relied on primary exports. Assis Chateaubriand, for example, said that Brazil was essentially agricultural in nature, a view shared by a large proportion of the Brazilian and foreign economic and political elite.

Prebisch, using UN data, demonstrated that the exchange between primary products and manufacturers led to a loss in the region's terms of trade: prices of agricultural products and raw materials tended to fall while those of manufactured products tended to remain constant or to rise. The explanation for these declining terms of trade was based on the limits to expansion of food consumption as household income increased. Instead of consuming more food, households increased their consumption of industrial goods and of services. (This phenomenon reflects a law regarding family budgets demonstrated by the German statistician E. Engel.) Raw materials, for their part, were already being replaced by synthetic products. Thus, reliance on primary-product exports was not conducive to economic growth.

---

[1] Only at one point does he abandon his characteristic elegance. Having recognized the existence of a broader intellectual movement in which our theoretical discoveries are situated, he raises the question of the attribution of dependency theory to his sole authorship, citing my work on the new dependency (1968c) as written after his: "Theotônio dos Santos, for example, presents a similar vision in the study which he wrote *after* the discussion, in Santiago, of the essay Faletto and I wrote about Development and Dependency. See dos Santos—*La Nueva Dependéncia,* Santiago, CESO, 1968[c]." Praise of my "simple and clear" exposition of the model of dialectic and unmechanical connection between internal and external interests follows (see Cardoso, 1993b: 147 n. 8). Elsewhere (1993a: 63) he cites the mimeographed version of "La gran empresa y capital estrangero" (dos Santos, 1966a) and tells how I had anticipated the theses of 1968 and he had read a cited them. All this is nonsense. We had various seminars together in Santiago, and in spite of my being younger I believe that we influenced each other. Although many have tried to discover if the creator of dependency theory was myself or Cardoso or André Gunder Frank, I consider this a secondary issue. In Brazil at least Cardoso has already acquired the title of author of the theory, among other reasons because of his electoral performance and has having laid siege to dependency theory in the 1980s when we returned from exile. Internationally, however, this is not the case, and therefore Cardoso counters the view of my protagonist role and that of Frank that is very common in various parts of the world. Criticizing simplistic visions of dependency studies, he says, "Take the most general and formal works of Frank as they express it . . ., add the formal definition of dependency furnished by Theotônio dos Santos, explained at times as subimperialism and marginality, add one or another citation involved in any of my works or those of Sunkel, and take dependency theory as an easily destroyed fantasm" (Cardoso, 1993b: 136).

It is unnecessary here to elaborate on the theoretical significance of these hypotheses. They strike directly at the heart of classical and neoclassical economic theories to the effect that comparative advantage should cause each country to specialize in the products in which it shows the greatest productivity or the best endowment of factors of production. Many concluded from this that the best road to well-being and modernization for a nation was specialization in those products in which it could best compete on world markets. These arguments were used ad nauseam to deny the necessity of industrialization for countries on the periphery in the world economic system.

The developmentalists had too much faith that industrialization would guarantee the modernization of the economy and create national centers of economic decision making or capitalist accumulation. They also identified industrialization with the creation of democratic conditions through the more equal distribution of income and other mechanisms considered intrinsic to industrial capitalism. This was natural in an epoch in which some were speaking of an industrial civilization, identifying the functioning of capitalism in the central countries of the world economy with their material base, modern industry. Dependency theory tried to demonstrate that this industrialization did not have the consequences that were hoped for by this developmentalist and national-democratic vision. It did not bring autonomy of decision making, because industrialization was determined by foreign investment, based on multinational firms whose power continued to be located in the central points of the world economy. It did not bring improved income distribution, because oligopolistic capitalism tended to concentrate power and wealth in large groups of businesses with related interests. At the same time, modern technology raised the incomes of skilled workers, laborers, and managers to the detriment of those of the unskilled, producing great differentiation of income among salaried workers. In addition to this, dependent industrialization was based on an imported labor-saving technology. It did not create sufficient employment to incorporate the laborers who had abandoned the countryside and its self-sufficient subsistence activities. When these subsistence economies were destroyed by the advance of capitalist relations in the countryside, the majority of the workers who went to the cities were unable to transform themselves into urban workers as had happened at the beginning of European industrialization. This was the origin of urban marginalization.

Today marginalization connotes violent social disaggregation as a consequence of the deepening and spread of underemployment and unemployment during the long crisis of the world economy from 1967 to 1994. Cardoso participated in all the discoveries that made us revise our analyses of the nature of our economies. Until then we had thought that their precapitalist nature was the principal obstacle to their development. The new analysis sought to understand the contradictions that appeared within the special or dependent capitalism in which we found ourselves.

Up to this point, we are in agreement. Our analyses extend to other problems of greater theoretical interest, such as the negation of the feudal character of Latin American colonization, the central thesis that these socioeconomic structures are explained far more by the expansion of world capitalism than by the survivals of a supposed feudal economy, the question of the internal character of dependency relations, the difficulties of establishment of a national bourgeoisie, and the importance of a historical-structural dialectic methodology that would solidify our understanding of social processes. These topics are of only momentary interest to a broader public, however, and therefore I will not develop them here. The works cited here deepen the theme.[2]

---

[2] After 1973 I published various works to which Cardoso does not refer: I collected some of my earlier works and revised them in *Imperialismo y dependéncia* in 1978. This book was translated into Japanese and recently into Chinese. From 1974, during my second exile in Mexico, I dedicated myself to the more global question of the scientific-technical revolution, developing along with Immanuel Wallerstein, André Gunder Frank, and Samir Amin, among others, a theory of a world system on which my current research focuses. My last work on this topic was *Economia mundial, integração regional e desenvolvimento sustentável* (1994a).

OUR DIFFERENCES

ARE THERE LAWS OF DEPENDENT DEVELOPMENT?

In the debate over dependency, Cardoso came to insist ever more incisively on the denial of any economic determinism that would claim to identify dependency with the phenomenon set forth above mechanically. Neither overexploitation (such as Ruy Mauro Marini would show to be a mechanism of compensation of international expropriation provoked by the situation of dependency), nor a decline in the terms of trade nor the remittance of surpluses from dependent to dominant regions, nor the consequent regressive distribution of income, nor the growing marginality that it provoked were irreversible tendencies and intrinsic components of the condition of dependency.

Confounding the real issue that divided us, Cardoso asserted (1993a: 143, my emphasis) that there were two polar schools of thought on the process of capitalist development:

> those who believe that "dependent capitalism" is based on the overexploitation of labor and is incapable of broadening the domestic market, continually generates unemployment and marginality, and presents tendencies toward stagnation and is a kind of constant reproduction of underdevelopment (such as Frank, Marini, and *up to a certain point,* dos Santos) and those who think that, at least in some countries of the periphery, the penetration of industrial-financial capital accelerates the production of relative surplus value, intensifies productive forces, generates unemployment during economic recessions, and absorbs labor during expansions, producing, in this respect, *an effect similar to that of capitalism in advanced economies,* where unemployment and absorption, wealth and misery coexist.

"Up to a certain point" is, however, insufficient; I was the Latin American social scientist who most incisively demonstrated that economic growth and especially industrial growth were *essential* characteristics of the new character of Latin American dependent capitalism. In 1964 I opposed all the stagnationist theses of Roberto Campos's monetary stabilization policy that led to the destruction of Brazilian industry. On the contrary, I argued that stabilization policy should lead to a new phase of development based primarily on a higher level of productivity, economic concentration, monopolization, and statization (see dos Santos, 1966b; 1968d). But Marini also could not be included in this stagnationist conception, because his 1967 theses on Brazilian subimperialism were *derived from* the ideal of the growth of financial capital (the union of banking and industrial capital) in Brazil and its strengthening by the military coup. These demonstrated precisely the position of the Brazilian state as the creator of the domestic market in lieu of the structural reforms that the coup had prevented. Frank, who could scarcely be accused of being a stagnationist, was unable to suggest that forms of dependency continued independently of the changes in productive forces, despite his use of structural-functionalist methodology.[3]

Cardoso says that because they have business cycles, dependent capitalist economies may or may not have higher rates of unemployment and underemployment, and I am in complete agreement with him on this. I was one of those who developed the study of long-, medium-, and short-term business cycles in dependent countries and perhaps the first to advance the thesis of *internalization* of industrial cycles in countries such as Brazil. But the question is not whether there is variation in the rates of underemployment and unemployment but whether these rates are higher in dependent countries than in developed ones. Our rates of unemploy-

---

[3] It is a little difficult for the reader to follow in detail the rich debate we began on dependency and how to overcome it. My criticism of Frank was published in the Spanish edition of the *Monthly Review* (1968a). It was later incorporated in my *Dependéncia y cambio social* (1970) and later in *Imperialismo e dependéncia* (1968b).

ment do not tend to be greater, because our population seeks formal employment. Our rates of underemployment tend not only to be many times higher than those of dominant nations but also to be increasing as a result of the destruction of subsistence economies in both rural and domestic urban structures.

We all know that our streets are full of sidewalk peddlers, beggars, and people offering all kinds of services and our homes (including those of the middle class and even skilled workers) are full of servants, and we know how important this unskilled labor force is in the decline of salaries in underdeveloped, dependent capitalist nations. For this reason, the candidate competing with Cardoso, the lathe mechanic Luis Iñacio da Silva or Lula, said that the workers of ABC's greatest fear was of being reduced to indigence as his father had been. This fear affected not only the underemployed and the unskilled but also the bargaining power of skilled workers, who accepted salaries far below the international standard because of it.

Thus the introduction of more sophisticated technologies did not eliminate the overexploitation of our workers. In my studies of the scientific technical revolution[4] and its impact on the international division of labor, I also showed that the industrial expansion of dependent capitalist economies took place at a time when industrial employment was shrinking and that in the service sector was growing. In developed nations this increased employment occurred for workers in services linked to knowledge, culture, and education, communication, leisure, management, and marketing, but these sectors were reserved for the dominant nations in the new international division of labor. There is therefore no indication that our becoming exporters of industrial goods would reverse this tendency toward underemployment, marginality, and social exclusion. The data confirm the deepening of these tendencies. Thus we can conclude that the development of dependent capitalism, especially our conversion into large industrial exporters, will not ensure greater absorption of labor than in the past. On the contrary, everything seems to indicate that the masses of unemployed, underemployed, and marginalized will increase in both absolute and relative terms.

These would be *laws* of the development of dependent capitalism except that it is possible to stop being dependent and invest in the creation of leading technology and high degree of education (as the South Koreans and the Taiwanese, whose dependence on the former Japanese imperialism was profoundly shaken by the latter's defeat during World War II, the agrarian reform imposed by the North American victors, and the economic and political aid of the United States because of the proximity of its ideological enemies China, North Korea, and Vietnam, are desperately trying to do). There is no absolute limit to the full development of productive forces in dependent capitalism; the limits are political. Change in regional and worldwide political and geopolitical conditions could alter national and local political conditions. In 1964, if the confrontation between national-democratic and liberal sectors had been confined to Brazil, the coup d' état of 1964 would clearly have failed as had all earlier coup attempts. Two factors destabilized the balance of power: the conspiratorial action of large international capital investors in Brazil and the direct threat of invasion by North American troops that is today fully recognized since the release of Lyndon Johnson's papers.

NEW INTERNATIONAL POLITICAL CONDITIONS

In the 1960-1975 period, international business cycles determined the fate of dependent nations' actions because these nations lacked the economic and military power to resist the economic interests of international forces. Today the situation is different. North America's dominant classes are divided regarding the international use of force, and their ideological and bureaucratic arrangements are almost entirely in favor of a policy of respect for human rights. For this reason we must separate the analysis of the 1960s from that of the present day.

---

[4] On this topic see, among others, dos Santos (1983; 1987; 1994b).

In 1960-1975 I took a position that Cardoso sharply criticized: the idea of the increasing polarization in the region of fascist and socialist solutions. I said that, on one hand, the urban masses subjected to increasing concentration of power and income and social marginality tended to approve of democratic government, imbuing it with a strong popular content that would give rise to a renewed demand for structural reforms leading to socialism. On the other hand, in response to this tendency toward postcapitalist solutions, the dominant class turned to the use of force whenever their dominance was threatened by the advance of democracy. Socialism or fascism appeared as *political horizons* for the democratic regimes or dictatorships of the region. Cardoso criticized this analysis as mechanical and reflecting an outdated economic determinism. But to say today that I was wrong then is hardly reasonable. Formulated in 1966, these theses were amply demonstrated,[5] and they were followed by the coup of Ongania in Argentina, by Institutional Act no. 5 in Brazil, by the revolutionary regime of the Peruvian military, by the Bolivian Popular Assembly, by the Popular Unity government in Chile, and by the succession of right-wing coups in Bolivia, Uruguay, Chile, and Argentina that, together with the government of Médici in Brazil, formed a para-fascist iron circle in the Southern cone that lasted until 1976–1980. Similar tendencies were indicated in Indonesia, Iran, the Philippines, and elsewhere.

Beginning in 1973, the international attitude toward this topic changed (see dos Santos, 1995). The terror promoted by large international capital that I had identified with fascism had already achieved its principal mission, having overthrown incipient insurrectionist movements, popular governments, and Allende's socialist government. The way had been opened for political accord and the restoration of democracy. The military—which had been the principal instrument of the policy of force and terror—had become a dangerous ally. While in power it had displayed right-wing nationalist aspirations that opposed tendencies toward internationalization under the hegemony of transnational enterprises. It has been out of power for the past 20 years, a process that began with the policy of human rights initiated by the Carter administration, reversing the policy of stimulation and acceptance of military dictatorships adopted by Richard Nixon at the suggestion of Nelson Rockefeller in a 1968 report prepared after his trip to the subcontinent. Samuel P. Huntington—adviser of Golberi do Couto e Silva and a preeminent figure in the Trilateral Commission—had suggested this policy change in a celebrated article in 1973. Recently he has examined the "third democratic wave" that began in 1974 and was still continuing in 1991 when he wrote his book (1994). It should be pointed out that he is not discussing a movement restricted to dependent countries on the periphery; this wave also involves countries that Immanuel Wallerstein calls "semi-peripheral," such as Portugal, Spain, and Greece. Huntington shows that in the past each democratic wave has been followed by a reversal (such as the fascist wave from 1922 to 1942 and the wave of military coups that he places between 1958 and 1975). He next asks if the current situation will not also be followed by a reversal and suggests that this will depend on the confidence in democracy of political leaders. In my opinion it will depend on democracy's ability to withstand the popular pressure for reform of income and wealth that *necessarily* results from the dynamic of democratic regimes (see dos Santos, 1991).

DEPENDENT REFORMISM AND THE END OF DEPENDENCY THEORY

Cardoso's position on dependent reformism and the end of dependency theory is totally divergent from mine. Above all, he tries to demonstrate the possibility that (1) the destructuralizing effects on the world economy of the contradictions created by dependency, the concentration of income and power, and social marginalization can be reduced though social policies and a cer-

---

[5] In addition to my article about the fascist menace (1966b) see my ("Crise econômica e crise política no Brasil," incorporated in large part in *Socialismo o fascismo: Dilema de América Latina* (1968d), and the essay on the economic crisis in dependent nations published in the collection *Capitalism in the 70's*.

tain degree of absorption of labor during phases of economic growth; (2) dependent capitalist accumulation need not be more contradictory than that in central capitalist countries or continue to be based on the overexploitation of labor as Marini et al. (1994–1995) proposes; (3) the development of dependent capitalism—or associated capitalism, as he prefers to call it—can be reconciled with liberal and democratic political regimes; (4) the bureaucratic-authoritarian regimes installed in Latin America from the 1960s to the 1990s were not the product of fascism and were capable of being replaced without violence by viable democratic regimes that could be historically consolidated—the real enemies of development being populism and corporativism, whether of the state or of the institutions of civil society (here we return to the dualist theses—precursors of dependency theory—that made underdevelopment a consequence of the backwardness of our traditional societies rather than of the character of our capitalist development); and (5) as a consequence, the consolidation of democracy in the continent does not depend on breaking dependence, destroying the hegemonic power of monopoly capital, agrarian reform, or any other change in the forms of property.

These are the theses that are fundamental to Cardoso's political action today and clearly exhibited in his government program. They take into account the 20-year-long democratic wave that has stabilized only those democratic regimes implanted during the period. The authoritarian explosions in Peru and in Haiti and the military and popular destabilizations in Venezuela and in Argentina do not represent a new reverse wave as Huntington suggests. The hard battles of the 1960s and 1970s and the neoliberal conservative offensive of the 1980s did not stimulate a greater radicalization of social demands.

Cardoso's electoral victory is therefore no chance occurrence. It is in part a consequence of the political ideas that he has not in any way denied, and it allows the closing of the debate. For some years his followers have spoken of the end of dependency theory in the sense of rejection of the theses it denoted during the 1960s. Every year, however, new books on dependency theory have appeared all over the world—evidence that it is not dead.[6] The main reason for this is the persistence of a world economic system characterized by the difference between central or dominant nations and peripheral or dependent ones, although the North American hegemony that once seemed unassailable has declined steeply since the late 1960s. The recovery of Europe and Japan has accentuated the rivalry between the central powers and resulted in the creation of a hegemonic triad announced by the Trilateral Commission in the 1970s composed of the United States, Europe, and Japan. This relieved the pressure on the Soviet Union, which had been making an intense effort to compete militarily with the United States. The replacement of U.S. domination with shared hegemony gave it sufficient strategic strength to initiate glasnost and perestroika. In an attempt to impede the military polarization imposed by Ronald Reagan's Star Wars, the Soviet Union decided to disarm unilaterally in the 1980s, withdrawing its troops from Eastern Europe, eliminating the Warsaw Pact, and dissolving itself and its Communist party.

This magnificent and courageous action of the Soviet leadership headed by Mikhail Gorbachev has been presented as a defeat for socialism, but it is perhaps the most outstanding step

---

[6] For a theory of dependence considered "buried" it is strange that there is a vast literature produced about it all over the world. In addition to the hundreds of works published on the theme in various years, in the past few years alone the following can be cited: Fukuyama (1992) dedicates his chapter 9 to a critique of dependency theory, according to him "the most recent attempt to keep a form of Marxism alive in the Third World." Marini et al. have published (1994–1995) three volumes of essays on Latin American social thought and three volumes of reference texts that reflect the rebirth of Latin American social thought, somewhat bruised by the neoliberal wave of the 1980s. ECLA is also conducting a review of the thoughts of Prebisch and his various intellectual disciples. Sing C. Chew and Robert C. Denemark (1996) have published a collection of essays in honor of André Gunder Frank that excellently reviews the theme. It falls to me to represent Latin America in the collection, which includes writers from all continents.

in the direction of socialism in history. Marx dissolved the First International, and Lenin decreed the end of the Second. The history of the advance of socialism is one of self-dissolutions that abandoned outworn phases of its development and pointed to new, higher ones and to the employment of a strategic political dialectic. To reach these higher stages it was necessary to eliminate outdated forms such as Soviet Stalinism and the Third International. This does not permit any conclusion in favor of a Fourth International; Trotskyism was a creation of the Stalinist phase and cannot be considered as an alternative to it.

In the new world order a new international division of labor was accentuated that could be anticipated in 1967 (dos Santos, 1967). In this phase there was a great transfer of much of the world's industrial production from the rich nations to countries of intermediate development—Brazil, Mexico, South Korea, Taiwan, and others. Brazil's success during the 1970s was described as a miracle, and the success of the "Asian tigers" during the 1980s created a new propaganda concept. What is important is that these nations, alongside the oil powers and the intermediate economies of southern and eastern Europe, constituted a new area of world power. At the same time, the economic growth of China drastically changed the relative weight of Southeast Asia and of the Pacific in the world economy. In the 1970s the decolonization of Africa was also completed—extinguishing all of the European empires in less than 30 years. If we add to this the industrialization of India, its modernization, and its entrance into the nuclear club, as well as the emergence of oil nations and regional powers in the former empires, such as Turkey, we have a completely new picture of the world.

In this new world, "imperialism" needs a new definition. Since the 1980s the world economic system has been undergoing a change in character. This article is not the place to develop this theme, but I have argued[7] that the next 25 years will be marked by shared hegemony with the United States. This period began in 1993–1994 and ushered in a new phase of long-term economic growth identified as one of the "long waves" of Kondratieff's business cycle. This sustained growth is taking place at the same time as the spread of unemployment, especially in the industrial sector, resulting from automation and robotization. Strong social reform should be undertaken in the central nations based on the drastic shortening of the working day. In the political field, conservatives will give way to a rebirth of the Second International and the ascent to power of green parties.

The crisis of foreign debt of the 1980s reinforced a basic thesis of dependency theory—that the central countries capture economic surpluses from peripheral and dependent nations, a phenomenon which explains a large part of our difficulties. André Gunder Frank, Orlando Caputo, Roberto Pizarro, and others have tried to break the traditional manipulation of statistical concepts of balance of payments, practiced in particular by international organizations, to demonstrate this thesis. The facts have always obscured this negative transfer, which is explained in part by unequal international trade made even more unequal by the payment of interest, "royalties," technical services, and the open or disguised remittance of profits. Cardoso himself has employed the concept of an exportation of surpluses from dependent nations to central nations in various of his works. The foreign debt crisis very clearly demonstrates that we are weak and export our surpluses to the central nations. This fact was recognized in all the international analyses of the debt crisis of the 1980s, and it could not fail to revive the questions raised by dependency theory.

DEBT AND ECONOMIC POLICY
The foreign debt represented an enormous bleeding of our resources and provoked new economic phenomena that are not analyzed in Cardoso's recent books or—apparently—considered

---

[7] I have recently written on the economic and geopolitical changes linked to the neoliberal wave and to the end of the cold war (dos Santos, 1992; 1993a).

in the economic policy that he and his team are implementing. In this period a situation close to hyperinflation was created, and enormous trade surpluses in foreign exchange were generated that were used to pay the interest on the foreign debt. In order to avoid hyperinflation, we paid our exporters in public internal debt certificates, reducing the need to issue more money but generating another bloodletting in the form of interest payments on the internal debt.

Today the foreign debt crisis has been partially overcome because of the political agreements reached in regard to the debt and the dramatic decline in international interest rates. Two factors have generated an enormous improvement in our cash position: the suspension of international interest payments and the drop in state expenditures. The reduction of public spending has created a "surplus" in the national treasury that has permitted more than 50 percent of the state's expenditures to be devoted to the payment of a public debt turned over monthly, bi-weekly, and even daily. The World Bank, the International Monetary Fund, and the dominant classes of this country have never spoken of anything but "fiscal adjustment," but what this meant was not drastically reducing unjustifiable interest payments but further reducing expenditures that should be devoted to meeting the needs of the population. This policy is unsustainable. It goes totally against the laws of the market and the tendencies of the international economy. Brazil today is a country of the highest liquidity. In contrast to firms in the rest of the world, a majority of which have large debts, Brazilian firms operate with enormous cash surpluses and use them in the financial market. Many firms make more from these investments than from their specific activities. Middle- and upper-class families, instead of owing multiples of their income as in the rest of the world, have large financial surpluses, forgoing the purchase of real estate and other investments typical of these social sectors.

This financial surplus should generate a reduction in the interest rate, which would be negative if the financial markets were allowed to function freely. Instead of this, in a case of perverse and self-destructive government intervention, the technocrats who rule the Brazilian state (which has a relatively small debt) have arrived at the absurd practice of issuing government notes based on public debt in order to pay the absurd interest due on an artificially increased public debt—all this in the name of an economic "theory" that a "free" financial market would eliminate savings and generate an "explosion of consumption." What right have they to impose this heavy fiscal burden on the Brazilian people in the name of technocratic guardianship of our economy?

The results of this policy are criminal. It deepens social inequality and strengthens the concentration of national income in the hands of a small group. It privileges a totally useless financial sector. The banks no longer lend for any economic activity in this country; their resources are totally oriented toward speculation in the public debt. At the same time, the high interest rates attract speculative international investment, relieving pressure on the exchange rate but in the medium and long term producing a severe drain of resources.

With all this, the most serious problem is the effect of these very high interest rates (more than 50 percent per year at a time of appreciating real estate and declining inflation) on the average profit rate of the nation. Businessmen cannot be asked to limit their profits when they can obtain more than 50 percent of interest per year without any risk. All this jawboning in favor of the lowering of prices is totally useless. With the average rate of interest that the government ensures, the rate of profit would have to be more than 60 percent—more than six times the world average—and our prices 30-40 percent higher than the international market. If we add to this tendency the appreciation of real estate as domestic inflation continues, it becomes clear how difficult it is to maintain large exports without low salaries, on one hand, and government subsidies to exports (which are also inflationary), on the other. The performance of Brazilian exports was in fact disheartening during the first year of Cardoso's administration. Only public enterprises were able to make the sacrifice (and in fact are making it) in order to guarantee the lowest prices, but it is said that these firms are being sold to capitalists who do not agree to operate with such low profit rates.

Inflationary pressures persist because production costs (which include the average rate of profit that is determined by the average rate of interest) will continue to be extremely high as long as this interest rate policy continues. This perversity allows Brazil to have a financial sector whose participation in national income is at least *five times* greater than in the developed world. It also allows us to receive US$23 billion in 1994 and more than US$70 billion in 1995 to invest in public financial instruments that pay interest rates of 50 percent per year or that could be used for speculation, with little risk, on the stock exchange, yielding more than 100 percent per year. Thus, whether investing in risk-free or speculative operations, in two or three years foreigners investing in Brazil could earn the equivalent of our exchange reserves—obtained at the cost of the misery of the majority of our people. It is necessary to point out that only US$2 billion of the approximately US$70 billion that entered in 1995 were invested in the productive sector. The rest were invested in speculation.

And how could such resources exist for speculation in a country with 32 million people in misery? By means of the *overexploitation* of the working class. The facts demonstrate an enormous increase in the productivity of our firms at least in this decade. The average real salary, however, not to mention the lowest salaries (the minimum wage fell drastically during this decade), did not make up for the losses of 1990 and 1991. As the proportion of the national income represented by the financial sector increased, the proportion represented by the wage sector was dramatically reduced by at least 30 percent of its 1960 figure. This situation is only made worse by the current monetary policy.

What are the consequences of this policy? Unemployment is increasing, despite the immediate relief provoked by the decline in inflation and despite the revival of economic growth that the government is desperately trying to restrain. Violence, marginality, the informal economy, and hunger are increasing, and income is becoming increasingly concentrated.

Cardoso has not been able to convince me that, without more profound structural reforms, countries such as Brazil can stride toward social peace, economic equilibrium, and a peaceful resolution of their contradictions. He himself has said, in a lucid postscript to his book *As idéias e o seu lugar,* that the Asian tigers "that entered the process of internationalization of the economy were more prudent with respect to the capture of foreign financial resources and established more audacious policies for the correction of social inequalities, including in some cases agrarian reform and in all cases the relative increase of salaries" (1993b:236–237). A correction: agrarian reform was applied in *all* cases, since Hong Kong and Singapore are almost entirely urban zones. The Latin American nations pointed to as successful in the internationalization of the 1980s, Mexico and Chile, also carried out agrarian reform. It is therefore lamentable that, knowing this, Cardoso has given a such a low profile to his agrarian colonization policy. Soon after his election he appointed a representative of landlords an official for agrarian reform. Pressured by land seizures led by the landless, he named a more liberal president, who immediately fell from office. He has not displayed the political will to confront this vital question, despite having the approval of the international church itself for a moderate reform.

THE CARDOSO ADMINISTRATION AND THE QUESTION OF DEMOCRACY

Democracy is advancing; this is an unquestionable and positive fact throughout the world. But the people do not have much confidence in this democracy. They protest by abstaining from voting, voting no, and other mechanisms of rejection of a political world that seems strange to them, or they opt for conservative solutions that do not put the democratic advances achieved so painfully at risk. It is only 50 years since the end of World War II, when nazi fascism dominated a large part of the world, and it is only very recently that we have entirely abandoned dictatorship in Brazil and much of the rest of Latin America. The election of Cardoso itself is proof of this. Having first tried to shatter the structures of the nation by electing a playboy president, the Brazilian electorate searched for the conservative formula—conservative in its methods but not necessarily in its objectives—that Cardoso so well embodied.

I do not foresee a social and political crisis or even any revolutionary political commotion in the short term. On the contrary, I am trying to show that there is political space for the reformist conservatism that Cardoso has been able to embody. What I question, however, is that it will produce an attenuation of social and political contradictions in the medium and long term. The enlightened monarchs were unable to substitute for democratic-bourgeois revolutions. The late-19th-century Latin American modernizers were unable to contain the social explosions that began in the 20th century, from the Mexican Revolution through Tenentismo to the populism of the 1930s. The belle époque and the social-democratic reformism of the end of the 19th century were only anticipating the two world wars of the 20th century and the violent social and political radicalization from 1917 to 1945–1949.

I am not predicting cataclysms. I know very well that this would cause me to be disregarded as a "catastrophist." But it is impossible to permit a pragmatism without proposals of right-wing and conservative origin to be imposed at the expense of scientific truth. It is simply insane to deny the gravity of the social problems that have accumulated as a consequence of the achievement of dubious macroeconomic equilibria in the very short run at the cost of other much more serious disequilibria.

Cardoso knows this. His choice makes clear pragmatic sense. Santiago Daunts said at the beginning of the 1960s, in an interview in the journal *O Cruzeiro,* that what Brazil needed was a man from the right speaking the language of the left. This was the solution that he foresaw for a country touched by development but impeded from achieving it by the resistance of the large capitalists—responsible pragmatism on the part of a decadent social class that was trying to prolong its survival in history. The situation is different today. Military dictatorship has been overthrown, and dependent capitalism lacks proposals. Cardoso seems to want to convince us that Brazil today needs a man from the left with the language of the right—responsible pragmatism from a still embryonic worldwide wave of democracy? Daunts failed in his attempt at enlightened reformism. His comrades on the right preferred a coup and confrontation with the left. Will Cardoso be able to guarantee the moderation of the appetite of the enormous masses of dispossessed of Brazil and of the world? Will he also be able to guarantee that the right will not appeal to despair or fascist irrationality?

He will prove his thesis only if he is able to advance social reforms—postponed interminably—in his moderate-conservative government. The Brazilian left should aid him if he chooses this road, but we agree that it should not risk its independence by such a dangerous strategic proposition. In this sense, Cardoso's tendency to talk with the opposition without trying to co-opt it is extremely positive. This is a warning to certain elements of the opposition that wish to change sides. Scientific studies could help to clarify these options, and this is the place for the dependency-theory debate. It has continued to unfold for a long time, despite the attempt of Cardoso and his followers to bury it during the 1970s. The republication of the books discussed here is a proof of this. Dialectic or debate—confrontation of arguments, interests, and strategies and tactics—is the road we take with democracy, and it is in this way that we will encounter our destiny.

References

Apter, David E.

1990 *Rethinking Development: Modernization, Dependency, and Postmodern Politics.* Newbury Park: Sage.

Blomström, Magnus and Björne Hettne

1992 *Las teorías del desarrollo en transición.* Mexico City: Fondo de Cultura Económica.

Cardoso, Fernando Enrique

1993a *A construção democracia: Estudos sobre política.* São Paulo: Siciliano.

1993b *As idéias e o seu lugar: Ensaiao sobre as teorias do desenvolvimento.* Petrópolis: Vozes.

Chew, Sing C. and Robert C. Denemark
1996 *The Underdevelopment of Development.* Newbury Park: Sage.

dos Santos, Theotônio
1966a "La gran empresa y capital estrangero." Mimeo, Santiago.
1966b *Revista Civilização Brasileira* no. 3.
1966c *Crise econômica e crise política no Brasil."* Mimeo, Santiago.
1967 *El nuevo carácter de dependéncia.* Santiago: Centro de Estudios Socio-Económicos.
1968a "El capitalismo colonial según A. G. Frank." *Monthly Review: Selecciones en Castellano* 5 (November).
1968b *Imperialismo e dependéncia.* Mexico City: Era.
1968c *La nueva dependéncia.* Santiago: Centro de Estudios Socio-Económicos.
1968d *Socialismo o fascismo: Dilema de América Latina.* Santiago: Centro de Estudios Socio-Económicos.
1970a *Capitalism in the 70's.*
1970b *Dependéncia y cambio social,* Santiago: Centro de Estudios Socio-Económicos.
1978 *Imperialismo y dependéncia.* Mexico City: Era.
1983 *Revolução científico-técnica e capitalismo contemporâneo.* Petrópolis: Vozes.
1987 *Revolucão científico-técnica e acumulação de capital.* Petrópolis: Vozes.
1991 *Democracia e socialismo no capitalismo dependente.* Petrópolis: Vozes.
1992 "The future of geopolitical alignments." *Ritsumeikan Journal of International Relations,* Kyoto.
1993a *Economia mundial, integração regional e desenvolvimento sustentável.* Petrópolis: Vozes.
1993b "As ilusões do neo-liberalismo." *Carta.*
1994a *Economia mundial, integração regional e desenvolvimento sustentável.* Petrópolis: Vozes.
1994b *Revolução científico-técnica, divisão international do trabalho e sistema económico mundial,* Cadernos ANGE.
1995 *A evolução histórica do Brasil: Da colônia a crise da Nova República.* Petrópolis: Vozes.

Frank, André Gunder
1991 *El desarrollo del subdesarrollo: Un ensayo autobiográfico.* Nueva Sociedad.

Fukuyama, Francis
1992 *O fim da história e o ultimo homem.* São Paulo.

Huntington, Samuel P.
1994 *A terceira onda: A democratização no final do século XX.* São Paulo: Atica.

Marini, Ruy Mauro
1965 Brasilian "Interdependence" and imperialists integration. *Monthly Review* (December).
1974 *Dialéctica de la dependéncia.* Mexico City: Seriz Popular Era.

Marini, Ruy mauro et al.
1994–1995 *La teoría social Latinoamericano.* 4 vols. Mexico City: El Caballito.

Bibliography

Adler, Mortimer J. *How to Think About the Great Ideas: From the Great Books of Western Civilization.* Chicago: Open Court Publishing, 2000.

Ake, Claude. *Social Science as Imperialism: A Theory of Political Development.* Ibadan: Ibadan University Press, 1979.

Allison, Graham, and Phillip Zelikow. *Essence of Decision: Explaining the Cuban Missile Crisis,* 2nd ed. New York: Pearson Longman, 1999.

Amstutz, Mark R. *International Conflict and Cooperation: An Introduction to World Politics.* New York: McGraw-Hill, 1998.

Ashcroft, Bill, et al. *The Empire Writes Back: Theory and Practice in Post-Colonial Literatures.* London: Routledge, 1989.

Beard, Charles Austin. *An Economic Interpretation of the Constitution of the United States.* New York: Macmillan, 1913.

Bhagwati, Jagdish. *Free-Trade Today.* Princeton, NJ: Princeton University Press, 2001.

_____. *World Trade System at Risk.* Princeton, NJ: Princeton University Press, 1991.

Blackburn, Simon. *The Oxford Dictionary of Philosophy.* New York: Oxford University Press, 1996.

Boardman, John, et al., eds. *The Oxford History of the Classical World.* Oxford: Oxford University Press, 1986.

Bronowski, J., and Bruce Mazlish. *The Western Intellectual Tradtion: From Leonardo to Hegel.* New York: Harper & Row, 1960.

Buchanan, Patrick. *A Republic Not an Empire.* Washington, DC: Regenery Publishing, 2002.

Bull, Hedley. *The Anarchical Society.* 3rd ed. New York: Columbia University Press, 1977, 2002.

Bury, J. B. *A History of Greece.* New York: Modern Library, 1913.

Caesar, Julius. *The Conquest of Gaul,* trans. J. A. Hanford. London: Penguin Books, 1983.

Chomsky, Noam. *Deterring Democracy.* New York: Hill and Wang, 1992.

_____. *Rogues States: The Rule of Force in World Affairs.* Cambridge, MA: South End Press, 2000.

_____. *For Reasons of the State.* New York: New Press, 2003.

_____. *The Umbrella of U.S. Power: The Universal Declaration of Human Rights and the Contradictions of U.S. Policy.* New York: Seven Stories Press, 2002.

Chua, Amy. *World on Fire: How Exporting Free-Market Democracy Breeds Ethnic Hatred and Global Instability.* New York: Doubleday, 2002.

Cicero. *The Basic Works of Cicero.* ed. Moses Hadas. New York: The Modern Library, 1951.

Cohn, Theodore. *Global Political Economy.* 2nd ed. New York: Pearson-Longman, 2003.

Collier, Christopher, et al. *Decision in Philadelphia: The Constitutional Convention of 1787.* New York: Ballantine Books, 1986.

Cook, Thomas I. *Two Treatises of Government by John Locke with a supplement Patriarcha by Robert Filmer.* New York: Hafner Press, 1947.

D'Amato, Anthony, et al. *International Law and World Order.* St. Paul, MN: West Publishing Company, 1990.

Denby, David. *Great Books: My Adventures with Homer, Rousseau, Woolf and Other Indestructible Writers of the Western World.* New York: Simon & Schuster, 1997.

Der Derian, James, and Michael J. Shapiro. *International/Intertextual Relations: Postmodern Readings of World Politics.* Lexington, MA: Lexington Books, 1989.

Diamond, Jared. *Guns, Germs and Steel: The Fates of Human Societies.* New York: W. W. Norton & Co., 1999.

Duncan, W. Raymond, et al. *World Politics in the 21st-Century.* 2nd ed. New York: Pearson Longman, 2004.

Durant, Will. *The Life of Greece.* New York: Simon and Schuster, 1939.

Durkheim, Emile. *The Division of Labor in Society.* Glencoe, IL: Free Press, 1947, first published in 1893).

————. *On Morality and Society.* Chicago: University of Chicago Press, 1973.

Falk, Richard. *A Study of Future Worlds.* New York: Free Press, 1975.

Frei, Christoph. *Hans J. Morgenthau: An Intellectual Biography.* Baton Rouge: Louisiana State University Press, 2001.

Friedman, Milton. *Free to Choose.* New York: Harcourt Brace Jovanovich, 1980.

Friere, Paolo. *Pedagogy of the Oppressed.* New York: Herder and Herder, 1970.

Fukuyama, Francis. *The End of History and the Last Man.* New York: Avon, 1993.

Gendzier, Irene L. *Development Against Democracy: Manipulating Political Change in the Third World.* Hampton, CT and Washington, DC: Tyrone Press, 1995.

Genest, Marc. *Conflict and Cooperation: Evolving Theories of International Relations.* New York: Harcourt Brace, 1998.

Goldstein, Joshua S. *International Relations.* 3rd ed. New York: Longman, 1999.

————. *International Relations: Brief Second Edition.* New York: Longman, 2004.

Grant, Michael, ed. *Cicero: Selected Works.* London: Penguin Books, 1971.

————. *The Founders of the Western World: A History of Greece and Rome.* New York: Charles Scribner's Sons, 1991.

Graves, Robert, ed. *Gaius Suetonius Tranquillus: The Twelve Caesars.* London: Penguin Books, 2003.

Hartz, Louis. *The Liberal Tradition in America.* New York: Harcourt Brace Jovanovich, 1955.

Herbst, Jeffrey. *States and Power in Africa: Contemporary Lessons in Authority and Control.* Princeton, NJ: Princeton University Press, 2000.

Herodotus. *The Persian Wars,* trans. George Rawlinson. New York: The Modern Library, 1947.

Hobbes, Thomas. *The Leviathan: Parts I and II,* ed. Herbert W. Schneider. New York: Bobbs-Merrill, 1958.

Hofstadter, Richard. *The American Political Tradition: And the Men Who Made It.* New York: Harcourt Brace Jovanovich, 1955, 1989.

————. *Social Darwinism in American Thought.* New York: Beacon Press, 1992.

Hoogvelt, Ankie. *Globalization and the Postcolonial World.* Baltimore, MD: Johns Hopkins University Press, 1997.

Huntington, Samuel P. *American Politics: The Promise of Disharmony.* Cambridge, MA: Harvard University Press, 1983.

————. *Political Order in Changing Societies.* New Haven, CT: Yale University Press, 1968.

_____, and Lawrence E. Harrison, eds. *Culture Matters.* New York: Basic Books, 2000.

Jackson, Robert H. *The Global Covenant: Human Conduct in a World of States.* New York: Oxford University Press, 2000.

Jefferson, Thomas. *The Life and Selected Writings of Thomas Jefferson.* New York: The Modern Library, 1944.

Johnson, Chalmers. *Blowback: The Costs and Consequences of American Empire.* New York: Owl Books, 2003.

Johnson, Paul. *The Birth of the Modern.* New York: Harper Collins, 1992.

Kagan, Donald. *On the Origins of War and the Preservation of Peace.* New York: Doubleday, 1995.

_____. *Pericles of Athens and the Birth of Democracy.* New York: Free Press, 1991).

King, Gary, et al. *Designing Social Inquiry.* Princeton, NJ: Princeton University Press, 1994.

Kissinger, Henry. *Diplomacy.* New York: Touchstone, 1995.

Kressel, Neil J., ed. *Political Psychology: Classic and Contemporary Readings.* New York: Paragon, 1993.

Krieger, Joel, et al., eds. *The Oxford Companion to Politics of the World.* New York: Oxford University Press, 1993.

Lefebvre, Georges. *The Coming of the French Revolution.* Princeton, NJ: Princeton University Press, 1979.

Lindsay, Jack, trans. *Apuleius: The Golden Ass.* Bloomington: Indiana University Press, 1960.

Lipset, Seymour Martin. *American Exceptionalism.* New York: W. W. Norton & Co., 1997.

Magstadt, Thomas M. *Nations and Governments: Comparative Politics in Regional Perspective.* Belmont, CA: Wadsworth, 2001.

Mahaffy, J. P. *Social Life in Greece.* London: MacMillan, 1894.

Maher, John M., et al., eds. *An Open Life: Joseph Campbell in Conversation with Michael Toms.* New York: Harper & Row, 1990.

Manchester, William. *A World Lit Only by Fire: The Medieval Mind and the Renaissance.* Boston: Little, Brown, 1993.

Mansbach, Richard W. *The Global Puzzle: Issues and Actors in World Politics.* 2nd ed. Boston: Houghton Mifflin, 1997.

McLynn, Frank. *Carly Gustav Jung: A Biography.* New York: St. Martin's Griffin, 1996.

Meier, Christian. *Caesar: A Biography.* New York: MJF Books, 1982.

Mingst, Karen. *Essentials of International Relations.* New York: W. W. Norton & Co., 1999.

Morgenthau, Hans J. *Politics among Nations,* 4th ed. New York: Alfred A. Knopf, 1973, originally published in 1948.

Nelson, Brian R. *Western Political Thought: From Socrates to the Age of Ideology.* Englewood Cliffs, New Jersey: Prentice Hall, 1996.

Oates, Whitney J. *The Stoic and Epicurean Philosophers: The Complete Writings of Epicurus, Epictetus, Lucretius, and Marcus Aurelius.* New York: The Modern Library, 1940.

Penrose, E. F. *The Revolution in International Relations.* London: Frank Cass & Co., Ltd. 1965.

Plekhanov, George. *Essays in Historical Materialism: The Materialist Interpretation of History.* New York: International Publishers, 1940.

Plutarch. *The Lives of the Noble Grecians and Romans.* New York: The Modern Library, n.d.

Radice, Betty, ed. *Livy: The War With Hannibal (Books XXI–XXX of the History of Rome and Its Foundation).* trans. Aubrey de Sélincourt, London: Penguin Books, 1965.

Ravitch, Diane, et al., eds. *The Democracy Reader: Classic and Modern Speeches, Essays, Poems, Declarations and Documents on Freedom and Human Rights Worldwide.* New York: Harper Collins, 1992.

Rawls, John. *Political Liberalism.* New York: Columbia University Press, 1993.

————. *A Theory of Justice.* Cambridge, MA: Harvard University Press, 1971.

Sabine, George H. *A History of Political Theory,* 3rd ed. New York: Henry Holt & Co., 1937, 1966.

Said, Edward W. *Culture and Imperialism.* New York: Vintage, 1993.

Sandbrook, Richard. *The Politics of Africa's Economic Stagnation.* New York: Cambridge University Press, 1985.

Savill, Agnes. *Alexander the Great and His Time.* New York: Barnes & Noble, 1993.

Segal, Robert A. *Joseph Campbell: An Introduction.* New York: Penguin, 1990.

Sélincourt, Aubrey de, trans. *Livy: The Early History of Rome (Books I–V of the Early History of Rome and Its Founations).* London: Penguin Books, 1960, 2002.

Smith, Michael J., *Realist Thought from Weber to Kissinger.* Baton Rouge: Louisiana State University Press, 1986.

Snow, Donald M., and Eugene Brown. *International Relations: Contours of Power.* New York: Pearson, 1999.

Strauss, Leo, and Joseph Cropsey, eds. *History of Political Philosophy,* 3rd ed. Chicago: University of Chicago Press, 1987.

Suetonius, *Gaius Suetonius Tranquillus: The Twelve Caesars.* trans. Robert Graves. London: Penguin Books, 1957, 1979.

Tacitus. *The Complete Works of Tacitus.* New York: The Modern Library, 1942.

Tarnas, Richard. *The Passion of the Western Mind: Understanding the Ideas That Have Shaped Our World View.* New York: Ballantine Books, 1993.

Thucydides. *The Complete Writings of Thucydides.* New York: The Modern Library, 1934.

Wallerstein, Immanuel. *Africa: The Politics of Independence.* New York: Vintage, 1961.

————. *Africa: The Politics of Unity.* New York: Vintage, 1967.

————. *After Liberalism.* New York: New Press, 1995.

Waltz, Kenneth N. *Man, the State and War: A Theoretical Analysis.* New York: Columbia University Press, 1959.

————. *Theory of International Politics.* New York: McGraw-Hill, 1979.

Warburton, Nigel. *Philosophy: The Classics,* 2nd ed. London: Routledge, 2001.

Warrington, John, ed. *Caesar's War Commentaries: De Bello Gallico and De Bello Civili.* London: Everyman's Library, 1915, 1953.

Weston, Burns H., Richard Falk, and Anthony D'Amato. *International Law and World Order.* St. Paul, MN: West Publishing Company, 1990.

Zakaria, Fareed. *The Future of Freedom: Illiberal Democracy at Home and Abroad.* Belmont, CA: Wadsworth, 2003.